BEGINNING LINGUISTICS

Beginning Linguistics

Laurie Bauer

First published 2012 by
PALGRAVE MACMILLAN

Palgrave Macmillan in the UK is an imprint of Macmillan Publishers Limited,
registered in England, company number 785998, of Houndmills, Basingstoke,
Hampshire RG21 6XS.

Palgrave Macmillan in the US is a division of St Martin's Press LLC,
175 Fifth Avenue, New York, NY 10010.

Palgrave Macmillan is the global academic imprint of the above companies
and has companies and representatives throughout the world.

Palgrave® and Macmillan® are registered trademarks in the United States,
the United Kingdom, Europe and other countries.

ISBN 978-0-230-23169-6 hardback
ISBN 978-0-230-23170-2 paperback

This book is printed on paper suitable for recycling and made from fully
managed and sustained forest sources. Logging, pulping and manufacturing
processes are expected to conform to the environmental regulations of the
country of origin.

A catalogue record for this book is available from the British Library.

A catalog record for this book is available from the Library of Congress.

10 9 8 7 6 5 4 3 2 1
21 20 19 18 17 16 15 14 13 12

Printed in China

Contents

List of Illustrative Material

Data-sets

Figures

Tables

A Note for the Teacher

This book is an introduction to core Linguistics, with the 'hyphenated' varieties of Linguistics consigned to the last chapter as ways in which the materials learnt in the core can be used. This is not intended to downplay the importance of these other areas of Linguistics, but is to allow sufficient space to focus on the central parts of Linguistics.

As each teacher, each programme, will have their own preferences about phonological or syntactic theory and this book is intended to deliver on the commonalities that they share, teachers may have to provide their own slant on the material provided here: they may have to select a set of distinctive features or display a commitment (or not) to binarity in syntactic trees. It is my hope that the material here is genuinely introductory enough that it will suit teachers who have very different theoretical presuppositions.

The order of the chapters here is largely traditional, from the smaller units to the larger ones, except that semantics is dealt with first. This is purely to allow the notion of prototype, which is introduced in the semantics chapter, to be used in other chapters. If teachers are willing to introduce that notion as required, the order of the chapters becomes far less significant. Having said that, it does seem to me that there is some pedagogical value in starting with semantics, an area where students already know something but can be challenged, and yet are unlikely to feel that the area is too technical.

Although it would be ideal to presuppose none of the material from any chapter in any other chapter, notions such as noun, verb and adjective are presupposed in almost every chapter (and introduced in detail in Chapter 6), the notion of a morpheme is assumed briefly in Chapter 4. If chapters are read in an order other than the one in which they are presented, such cross-referencing problems are likely to increase, but they are certainly not insuperable.

The advanced material at the end of each chapter is genuinely more difficult than the earlier material. In these sections there is a certain amount of simple extension, but there is also a lot of more typologically-oriented material. The material in these sections can be used to extend the life of the book into other courses, or can be used as material for incentivising students as they work through the chapters.

A Note for the Student

This book allows you to introduce yourself to Linguistics, and check your understanding through answering the frequent questions that appear in the text. At the same time, it is intended for class use, and discussing the material with other students and your teachers is recommended for a deeper understanding. In some places, the text assumes a certain amount of input from your teachers who will, in any case, bring their own set of beliefs and theoretical positions to the material in this book. All of this is to be expected and is no cause for alarm. Your own theoretical position on language is likely to change as you work through your introduction to Linguistics and learn more about the complexities of human language.

The aim of this book is to give you a solid introduction to the core of linguistic study, and to leave the applications of the basic principles developed here until later. The benefit of this standpoint for the book is that it allows more space to be devoted to the fundamentals and more explanation to be given. The disadvantage is that you will not be brought face-to-face with the fascinating questions that the study of language can lead to, as diverse as the teaching of pronunciation to language learners, developing artificial intelligence systems for computers, the way in which languages reflect the structures of communities to the more in-turned consideration of the way in which language develops in history or in the individual's brain and what this tells us about the mind or about being human. Those questions are out there: have patience.

Acknowledgements

I should like to thank the following people for responding to my queries at various points during the development of this project, sometimes providing me with explanations, sometimes providing data or examples, sometimes reading sections or chapters: Sasha Calhoun, Janet Holmes, Barbara Kryk-Kastovsky, Rochelle Lieber, Sharon Marsden, Carolina Miranda, Liz Pearce, Liza Tarasova and Paul Warren.

I should also like to thank the anonymous readers for Palgrave Macmillan, without whose eagle eyes this book would not have been as good as it is. I could not accept all of the advice you offered (sometimes you disagreed), but I appreciated the guidance.

LAURIE BAUER

Symbols and Abbreviations

text in *italics*	words and other forms cited as examples in the text; titles of books, plays, etc.
text in SMALL CAPITALS	lexemes; to mark a consistent word class in a gloss; to mark a grammatical category in a gloss; the name of a lexical set
text in **bold SMALL CAPITALS**	technical terms being introduced; (in the glossary) cross-references to other glossary entries
text in <...>	spellings; numbers of in-text questions
text in [...]	speech sounds, phonetic transcription; syntactic constituents
text in /.../	phonological representations, phonemes
text <u>underlined</u>	a part of the text to which particular attention is drawn, or which is pronounced with greater than average prominence
text in {...}	morphemes; alternatives
text in (...)	optional; parenthetical comments; references; numbers of examples
1, 2, 3	first, second, third person
ABS	absolutive
ACC	accusative
AUX	auxiliary verb
DAT	dative
DU	dual
ERG	ergative
F	feminine
GEN	genitive (case)
INS	instrumental
IPFV	imperfective (aspect)
M	maculine
N	neuter
NOM	nominative
NONFUT	non-future (tense)
OBJ	object(ive)
PART	partitive (case)
PL	plural
PRF	perfective (aspect)

PRS	present (tense)
REDUP	reduplicant
SG	singular
A	subject of a transitive verb
A(P)	adjective (phrase)
Adv(P)	adverb (phrase)
C	consonant
C(P)	complementiser (phrase)
cps	cycles per second
Det	determiner
D(P)	determiner (phrase)
F0	fundamental frequency
F1, F2	formant 1, formant 2
H	high (tone)
I(P)	inflection (phrase)
Hz	Hertz
L	low (tone)
M	mid (tone)
N(P)	noun (phrase)
O	object of a transitive verb
OCP	Obligatory Contour Principle
P(P)	preposition (phrase); postposition (phrase)
S	sentence; subject of an intransitive verb
sp.	species
Su	subject
TBU	tone bearing unit
V	vowel
V2	verb second
V(P)	verb (phrase)
X	a variable over any of the word-classes such as N, V, A, P
Ø	zero
σ	syllable
→	becomes, is rewritten as, can be further expanded as
· [decimal point]	used to divide words into morphs
. [full stop, period]	syllable boundary; used to divide English words in a gloss
*	unacceptable, ungrammatical
?	of dubious acceptability or grammaticality

THE INTERNATIONAL PHONETIC ALPHABET (revised to 2005)

CONSONANTS (PULMONIC)

© 2005 IPA

	Bilabial	Labiodental	Dental	Alveolar	Postalveolar	Retroflex	Palatal	Velar	Uvular	Pharyngeal	Glottal
Plosive	p b			t d		ʈ ɖ	c ɟ	k ɡ	q ɢ		ʔ
Nasal	m	ɱ		n		ɳ	ɲ	ŋ	N		
Trill	ʙ			r					ʀ		
Tap or Flap		ⱱ		ɾ		ɽ					
Fricative	ɸ β	f v	θ ð	s z	ʃ ʒ	ʂ ʐ	ç ʝ	x ɣ	χ ʁ	ħ ʕ	h ɦ
Lateral fricative				ɬ ɮ							
Approximant		ʋ		ɹ		ɻ	j	ɰ			
Lateral approximant				l		ɭ	ʎ	ʟ			

Where symbols appear in pairs, the one to the right represents a voiced consonant. Shaded areas denote articulations judged impossible.

CONSONANTS (NON-PULMONIC)

Clicks		Voiced implosives		Ejectives	
ʘ	Bilabial	ɓ	Bilabial	'	Examples:
ǀ	Dental	ɗ	Dental/alveolar	p'	Bilabial
ǃ	(Post)alveolar	ʄ	Palatal	t'	Dental/alveolar
ǂ	Palatoalveolar	ɠ	Velar	k'	Velar
ǁ	Alveolar lateral	ʛ	Uvular	s'	Alveolar fricative

OTHER SYMBOLS

ʍ Voiceless labial-velar fricative

w Voiced labial-velar approximant

ɥ Voiced labial-palatal approximant

ʜ Voiceless epiglottal fricative

ʢ Voiced epiglottal fricative

ʡ Epiglottal plosive

ɕ ʑ Alveolo-palatal fricatives

ɺ Voiced alveolar lateral flap

ɧ Simultaneous ʃ and x

Affricates and double articulations can be represented by two symbols joined by a tie bar if necessary.

k͡p t͡s

VOWELS

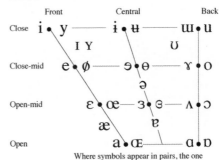

Front   Central   Back

Close i • y ── ɨ • ʉ ── ɯ • u

ɪ ʏ   ʊ

Close-mid e • ø ── ɘ • ɵ ── ɤ • o

ə

Open-mid ɛ • œ ── ɜ • ɞ ── ʌ • ɔ

æ

ɐ

Open a • ɶ ── ɑ • ɒ

Where symbols appear in pairs, the one to the right represents a rounded vowel.

SUPRASEGMENTALS

ˈ	Primary stress	
ˌ	Secondary stress	ˌfoʊnəˈtɪʃən
ː	Long	eː
ˑ	Half-long	eˑ
˘	Extra-short	ĕ
ǀ	Minor (foot) group	
ǁ	Major (intonation) group	
.	Syllable break	ɹi.ækt
‿	Linking (absence of a break)	

DIACRITICS

Diacritics may be placed above a symbol with a descender, e.g. ŋ̊

̥	Voiceless	n̥ d̥	̤	Breathy voiced	b̤ a̤	̪ Dental	t̪ d̪
̬	Voiced	s̬ t̬	̰	Creaky voiced	b̰ a̰	̺ Apical	t̺ d̺
ʰ	Aspirated	tʰ dʰ	̼	Linguolabial	t̼ d̼	̻ Laminal	t̻ d̻
̹	More rounded	ɔ̹	ʷ	Labialized	tʷ dʷ	̃ Nasalized	ẽ
̜	Less rounded	ɔ̜	ʲ	Palatalized	tʲ dʲ	ⁿ Nasal release	dⁿ
̟	Advanced	u̟	ˠ	Velarized	tˠ dˠ	ˡ Lateral release	dˡ
̠	Retracted	e̠	ˤ	Pharyngealized	tˤ dˤ	̚ No audible release	d̚
̈	Centralized	ë	̴	Velarized or pharyngealized	ɫ		
̽	Mid-centralized	e̽	̝	Raised	e̝	(ɹ̝ = voiced alveolar fricative)	
̩	Syllabic	n̩	̞	Lowered	e̞	(β̞ = voiced bilabial approximant)	
̯	Non-syllabic	e̯	̘	Advanced Tongue Root	e̘		
˞	Rhoticity	ɚ a˞	̙	Retracted Tongue Root	e̙		

TONES AND WORD ACCENTS

LEVEL				CONTOUR			
e̋ or	˥	Extra high		ě or	˩˥	Rising	
é	˦	High		ê	˥˩	Falling	
ē	˧	Mid		e᷄	˦˥	High rising	
è	˨	Low		e᷅	˩˨	Low rising	
ȅ	˩	Extra low		e᷈	˧˦˧	Rising-falling	
↓		Downstep		↗		Global rise	
↑		Upstep		↘		Global fall	

1
Introduction

Language is the amber in which a thousand precious and subtle thoughts have been safely embedded and preserved.
(Richard Chenevix Trench 1851)

In this chapter we consider the term *language* and the subject matter of linguistics, show that languages differ from each other, and preview the content of this book.

1.1 A gentle start

A much more famous book than this one is described as having the words

DON'T PANIC

'in large, friendly letters on the cover'. The letters just above might not be large enough or friendly enough, and you have clearly got beyond the cover of this book, but my message here is the same. You are about to begin a new subject. That should be a matter of some excitement. You might not know exactly what linguistics entails, which might lead to a certain amount of trepidation, but it should not be enough to dull the excitement. You may have heard reports from other students that linguistics is very technical or very mathematical. While there is some basis to these comments, it is really rather a small basis. You will not be expected to be able solve differential equations or do long division in order to understand linguistics and enjoy doing it. In fact, what you will mainly need to recall from mathematics is that in a sequence such as $x^2 + y^2$, the x and the y do not represent a single number each, but that values for $x^2 + y^2$ can be found whether x has the value three or the value seven. That's it. You now have the mathematical basis for linguistics.

Your background in language study may not be the same as that of your neighbour. That should not matter, either. If you have learnt French and the person on one side of you has learnt Japanese, and the person on the other has never learnt another language, you should all be able to cope with the subject matter of linguistics. Alternatively, one of you may have learnt German by living in Germany while another has learnt German by being taught it as a subject in school. We will be more concerned with the fact that you know that German and English are not just a single communication system with different words attached than with how you have learnt, or precisely what you have learnt. I'll explain that in a bit more detail in just a moment.

Perhaps you are aware that you have not 'done grammar' in school, while some others appear to have had exposure to this mysterious phenomenon. Don't worry; this book will not assume that you know any of that stuff (and may even contradict some of the things that some people thought they learnt in school, or at least show that it was presented in an overly simplified fashion).

So, given what linguistics is not, what is linguistics? A dictionary definition is something like 'the science of language', but this requires a certain amount of explanation. What does *science* mean in this context? If you have always done 'science' in the form of physics, chemistry or biology, this may not worry you, but if you have not done any of these subjects for a number of years, calling something a 'science' may make it sound terribly technical again. So let's try to explain what we mean by *science*. In a science like biology, the basis of the science is the observation of natural species, their classification, and an explanation of how they function: how respiration works, how a muscle contracts, and so on. In chemistry, the fundamentals of the science are a classification of the fundamental elements, and an understanding of how they combine, all based on observation of the qualities of matter. So in linguistics, the science part is first a matter of observation of language phenomena, but then a classification of the elements of language and an understanding of how they combine and how they work. In all three of these sciences, more complex theory-building derives from this fundamental observation and classification, as we move from the stage of asking, 'what bits are involved?' to asking more complex questions, such as, 'why do the elements have the nature they have?', 'could a complex form have arisen with completely different properties?' But at the moment, all of that is a long way in the future, and observation and classification is what will be involved.

Of course, classification means a certain amount of terminology. Chemists need names for the elements and for their salts, biologists need names for the species and genera, for the bones and the muscles and the parts of a flower, and linguists need names for different classes of word, different kinds of consonant and different relationships between words. The proper use of a particular jargon, in any subject, means that we can communicate precisely what we mean much more efficiently to other interested people. This is just as true in baseball or cricket or knitting as it is in chemistry or physics or linguistics. Sometimes expressions from baseball and cricket leave the specialist domain and become part of everyday language. Yet people from countries where baseball is not played are as bemused by an expression such as *out of left field* as people from countries where cricket is not played are by the expression *on a sticky wicket*. Sometimes the same thing happens with linguistic terms: a technical term like *infinitive* may escape from linguistics, and either cause confusion among people who do not recognise it, or even end up having a slightly different meaning outside linguistics from the meaning it has within linguistics. This does not invalidate the basic point, though: proper use of correct terminology facilitates communication. That is why so much attention will be paid to terminology in this book.

We can begin with two very troublesome terms: *language* and *linguistic*. *Language* has several meanings, even within linguistics. The sense it has in everyday use in phrases like *the Japanese language* or *the German language* is one which linguists accept as a useful shorthand, but which they are rather unhappy with. Linguists do not believe that a language has any reality except in the behaviour of people who speak the language. In other words, what people do is produce bits of language, and claim that they are speaking a particular language like German. But when does German shade off into Dutch? Is Swiss German (which most people from Germany cannot understand) still part of 'the German language' as its name suggests or should it be considered a separate language? Are dialect words part of the German language? (We could rephrase these questions with respect to English: are British and American Englishes the same language or not? Noah Webster wanted to say that they were not, even in the eighteenth century.) The fact that we can ask such questions indicates why it is difficult to determine precisely what should count as a piece of behaviour which instantiates 'the German language'. On the other hand, you may have noticed that I just used the phrase 'bits of language', where *language* had no *a* or *the* preceding it. This is a sense of *language* which many linguists feel far more relaxed about. LANGUAGE, in this sense, is the output of the human faculty, which we all have, for communicating via systems of abstract signs (words and so on). Some linguists would also call the abstract faculty itself *language*. So here we have a case where a term used in linguistics has another use within linguistics, and not just the use it has in everyday speech.

So should we talk about this behaviour as being *language behaviour* or as being *linguistic behaviour*? The two are synonymous; they mean just the same thing. LINGUISTIC is the word meaning 'relating to language' as well as the word meaning 'relating to linguistics'. We might prefer one or the other in individual expressions, but that is a matter of usage, not one of meaning.

TRIVIA: The number of languages

So how many languages are there in the world? You will see estimates varying between about 5,000 and about 7,000. Does that mean that we do not know? That is precisely what it means. One of the reasons that we do not know has already been mentioned: when should we count something as a dialect and when should we count it as a new language? The answer is often a matter of politics as much as – or more than – a question of linguistics. When the former Yugoslavia split up into Serbia and Croatia and the rest, Serbian and Croatian, which had officially been treated as dialects of a single language Serbo-Croat, suddenly became termed separate languages (reflecting the feelings of many of their speakers). So we can gain new languages in this way. But we are losing languages much faster as people stop speaking them – usually because there are no people left alive who speak these languages. Some estimates suggest that the world is losing slightly more than one language every two weeks, and that by the end of the century the number of languages in the world will be closer to 3,000. Of course, this does not mean that individuals have no language to speak; it just means that they speak a different language, typically one with more speakers. These are sometimes rather fancifully called 'killer languages', languages which frequently replace minority languages that disappear.

Similarly, *linguist* is ambiguous. If you are asked by somebody who has never done any linguistics, 'What are you studying?', and you tell them you are doing linguistics, one of the common reactions you will meet is, 'Oh. How many languages do you speak, then?' There is a meaning of *linguist* which is 'person who speaks several languages' (for which we might prefer the term *polyglot*) and another meaning of *linguist* 'person who studies linguistics'. Of course, a single person may be both kinds of linguist – but that does not make the distinction any easier to cope with. No linguist I have met has found a way of warding off this reaction, and my best advice is to get used to it straight away. Some non-linguists try to use the term *linguistician* for the linguistics kind of linguist, but the term comes with such negative overtones because of words like *beautician* and *mortician* that linguists have rejected the term (words like *mathematician*, which are perfectly respectable, have been around a lot longer, and never acquired these pejorative overtones that arose in the twentieth century when words in *-ician* were used to label professions that wanted a better image). So we seem to be stuck with the ambiguous term *linguist*. It is worth making the point that some very successful linguists (linguistics sense) have been monoglots not polyglots.

NOAH WEBSTER

Noah Webster (1758–1843) is known these days primarily as a lexicographer, that is, a dictionary writer. His linguistic endeavours grew out of the fact that he was a political activist who was very anti-British and pro-American. His conviction that he spoke American rather than English, and the subsequent desire to codify the differences between the two 'languages' arose from his political position. He introduced the differences in spelling whereby the word that is spelt as *honour* in Britain is spelt as *honor* in the US, and he advocated removing the <k> which until his time had been found at the end of words like *musick*. The English subsequently adopted this convention themselves. Webster's success can be gauged by the fact that any dictionary was often called a *Webster's* in the United States.

It was noted above that English and German (or any two languages) are not simply the same communication system with different words. This is a very important point when it comes to considering language structures, and it is worth dealing with briefly here. We can also use the opportunity to talk about glosses. If we take an English sentence like

(1)   The hound is dead.

we can translate the sentence fairly easily into German as

(2)   Der Hund ist tot.

To make it clear what the structure of (2) is in German, we can add a GLOSS, that is an element-by-element (here word-by-word) translation of the parts of the sentence, so (2) is better presented as (3).

(3)   Der   Hund   ist   tot
      the   hound   is   dead
      'The hound is dead'

Note that in glossing the German sentence in (3) we have aligned each translation with the word it translates, and given an idiomatic translation at the end. German and English are fairly closely related languages from the same language family, so you can see the resemblance between the words in the two languages. In each instance, one word of German is translated by the corresponding word of English, and it might seem that all we need to do to get from English to German (or vice versa) is change the words: German words give us a German sentence, and English words give us an English sentence. To the extent that seems to be true in (3), (3) is misleading. The first difference is that *Hund* in German and *hound* in English are not actually as equivalent as (3) seems to suggest. *Hund* is the normal word for a canine quadruped in German, including a hunting dog; *hound* is more specialised in English. So a more normal translation of (3) would actually be 'The dog is dead', which misses some of the implications of the first English version. The second difference is hidden in the word *der* 'the'. We can see this if we move on to sentences (4) to (6).

(4)	Der	Hund	biss	den	Kater
	the	dog	bit	the	tom-cat

'The dog bit the tom'

(5)	Der	Kater	biss	den	Hund
	the	tom-cat	bit	the	dog

'The tom bit the dog'

(6)	Den	Hund	biss	der	Kater
	the	dog	bit	the	tom-cat

'The tom bit the dog'

Now we see that there are at least two (in fact, more, if we looked at the whole of the German language) words meaning 'the'. We get *der* when something does the biting, and *den* when something gets bitten. So the difference between *der* and *den* is telling us which animal bit which animal, to such an extent that, as we see in (6), even if we change the order of the cat and the dog, the particular word for 'the' we use determines which animal is understood to do the biting. To clarify this, we should change the glosses for *der* and *den*, to make clear their importance, but the appropriate terms have not yet been introduced, so we will leave (6) as it is for the time being. Note, though, that we now have two ways in which German is completely different from English: (i) it has different words for 'the' depending upon whether the thing the 'the' tells you about is doing something or having something done to it; (ii) English has to use word-order to give you this information (*the dog bit the cat* is different from *the cat bit the dog*), while German can use word-order for other purposes (for instance, to stress something important). So now we can see that German is not just English with different words slotted in, whatever the sentence in (3) might have implied. More generally, we can say that other languages do not work just the way English does. We have to look at each language in its own terms, and see how it works; we cannot make assumptions about how it will work. (More accurately, we have to be very careful about making assumptions about how languages will work: we will see later that there are some recurrent patterns which give us clues.) This does not mean that languages are not built up of the same or similar building blocks: spoken languages all have consonants and vowels, for instance (I say 'spoken languages' because sign languages used by the deaf are real languages but do not have consonants and vowels, for obvious reasons). Rather it means that every language exploits the possibilities provided by the human ability to produce language in a rather different way. This is an important message of linguistics.

---

i

What you must say and what you can say

It is sometimes said that languages differ not in what they can say but in what they must say. In any human language (but not, as Bertrand Russell famously remarked, in any animal communication system) you can say that your parents were poor but they were honest. But as we have just seen with the German examples, in German you have to mark on the word glossed as 'the' whether the thing is performing the action or being affected by it. In English, this is shown by relative position, but not by the words themselves. In English you can say that 'a friend' told you something without having to specify whether the friend was male or female; in some other languages you have to specify that information; in English you might say that Jose played football, without having to specify whether you know that because you saw it happen or whether you simply assume it, or whether someone else told you. In Tariana you would have to specify that information. So even to express a simple idea like *The dog bit the cat* you must specify some information in one language that is not required in another.

1.2 What are the bits?

There are six chapters which make up the core of this book, and their titles probably look unfamiliar to you at the moment. Between them they cover the fundamentals of most linguistics courses, the central ideas of linguistics without which it is hard to move on to larger questions in the study of language. Each chapter introduces you to the basic notions that you need to know about, but then gives you some more advanced material (which is clearly marked as such) to allow you to develop your understanding if you want to (or if your teacher expects it of you!).

SEMANTICS deals with meaning. Of course, the term 'meaning' is not an entirely precise one, and we will need to pin down just which bits of meaning we are dealing with, but that will give you enough of an idea for the moment.

PHONETICS deals with the sounds of speech: the way we make them, the way we classify them, and (although we will spend less time of this aspect) the way we perceive them.

CONTROVERSY: Is phonetics linguistics?

Some linguists take the view that phonetics is not part of linguistics proper. If we are considering how the lungs function to produce a flow of air, what the parts of the mouth are and how the tongue works to make various sounds in that flow, they claim, that is a matter of anatomy and physiology; if we are concerned with the way the speech is transmitted through the air, that is the domain of acoustics (or, more generally, of physics); if we are concerned with the way we hear sounds, that is what perceptual psychology deals with; and if we are concerned with imitating the sounds of speech or transmitting them across space (e.g. by radio or on the telephone), that is a matter of engineering. It is certainly true that phonetics can be a very interdisciplinary subject. Yet there is some of phonetics that we cannot ignore if we want to go on to do phonology or other bits of linguistics: phonology works the way it does because of the way of the constraints imposed by the way we speak; and at the very least, the study of phonetics gives us an alphabet (the International Phonetic Alphabet) for writing down the sounds that occur in the languages of the world, and unless we have some understanding of that, it is hard to understand many other aspects of why languages are the way they are. So phonetics is included here. In the words of one famous linguist, it provides 'the indispensable foundation' for language study.

PHONOLOGY also deals with the sounds of speech, but in a rather different way. While phonetics deals with the individual sounds of any language and the details of their formation, phonology deals with the ways in which the sounds in any given language are related to each other and interact with each other. If we can use an analogy from music, phonetics tells you what it means to play an A, and why A on a flute is different from A on a cello, but phonology tells you how that A can be used to produce harmonies and tunes.

MORPHOLOGY is about the structure of words, how words such as *dislike* are made up of smaller meaningful elements, such as *dis-* and *like*.

SYNTAX is about the ways in which words can be put together to make up larger units, such as sentences. In the German examples dealt with earlier, we saw that word-order in German does not have quite the same function as word-order in English.

PRAGMATICS deals with the way in which we use language to achieve our goals, in ways which might not be obvious from the words we use. To take a simple example, *It's cold in here* might really mean 'Will you please close the window?', but is phrased as a statement which does not overtly require any response.

1.3 What is this book attempting to do?

The obvious answer to the question *What is this book attempting to do?* is *Teach you linguistics*. While that is obviously true, at one level, it is not a complete answer, because there are lots of books that try to teach you linguistics, and they are not all just the same. Some books try to teach you about linguistics, some try to teach you to do linguistics; some books try to teach you a lot about language, but not in any depth, others try to teach you less and in more depth; some books are based on a particular view of how language works (often called a model of language), others are more theoretically eclectic.

Obviously, from what has already been said, this book has a fairly narrow focus in what it attempts to teach, and attempts to deal with those topics in a reasonable amount of detail. Part of this detail means not trying to pull the wool over your eyes. Where things are controversial, you will often be told that they are (as you have already been told about the question of whether phonetics is or is not part of linguistics). We do not always have the answers in linguistics, and it would be misleading to let you believe that everything is well understood and agreed when that is not true. At the same time, this device is used relatively sparingly, or no progress at all could be made. If you go on with your study of linguistics, you will discover places where this introduction has told you something as a fact which is actually rather more complicated than you have been told here. This is not just perverseness; everything is difficult if you look at it in enough detail, and we have to break into the circle somewhere, and show you sufficient for you to be able to understand how the pieces fit together. If you stay with linguistics for long enough, you will have the chance to take some of these fundamentals up for further discussion, and possibly suggest improvements yourself. This is part of the delight of linguistics. Some of the notions are new enough for modifications to them to be accepted regularly.

This book tries to teach you about linguistics, but the exercises are often designed to teach you how to do linguistics. What is the difference? Some people think they have understood an idea if they can cite a definition of the idea. With many of the ideas in linguistics, I do not believe such an approach is sufficient. Unless you can take the idea and apply it to new data yourself, you do not understand the idea fully. So, while the text will provide definitions and explanation of how various notions fit together, a vital part of learning about linguistics is learning to apply the ideas, and very often this will happen through exercises.

Finally, this book takes seriously the idea that linguistics is about languages. It would be perfectly possible to give an introduction to linguistics in which all the examples were taken from a single language. Indeed, such books exist. This has some great advantages: you can assume that the readers understand the language of exemplification as well as the language of exposition, and you can appeal to their intuitions about what is going on in the examples. That approach will be used in some places here, as well, so that the most frequent language of exemplification will be English. Whenever possible, the scope will be widened so that the range of ways in which languages solve a particular problem can be studied. Even when we stick to English, you should be asking yourself whether we might expect to find similar examples in other languages, or how other languages might differ from the kind of thing that is being illustrated for English.

1.4 A user's guide to the book

Much of the text is pure exposition: this is what we need to think about, and a way of thinking about it. This exposition is broken up by short questions so that you can check that you are following the exposition. The answers to most of these questions are provided in Appendix C, but sometimes, when the answer is needed for further exposition, the answer simply follows on in the text.

Some of the exposition, placed at the end of each chapter, is less introductory in nature, and attempts to lead you on to consider wider issues in that particular area of linguistics. Whether you read these will depend on the demands of your course or your own personal curiosity. They are clearly marked (Advanced). These advanced sections introduce new ways of considering data, and in some cases are less conclusive than the earlier sections in the chapter, since they leave you to ask further questions for yourself.

Alongside the text, there are various kinds of interpolation, called *boxes* in publishing. We have already met the first kind of box, the controversy box. You do not have to read the material in controversy boxes, but it is there to indicate points where linguists do not agree, to illustrate that linguistics is business that thrives on dispute, and to indicate that the solution that is presented in the text, while it may be a motivated solution, is not the only possible one.

Other kinds of boxes are the summary information box – designed to give you a quick overview of some point, the trivia box – designed to provide you with some brief bit of information about language or languages, and the person box – designed to introduce you briefly to some great linguist and his or her work.

At the end of each chapter there is:

- a list of the technical terms introduced in the chapter,
- some guidelines for further reading, and
- some comments on sources for various pieces of information or discussions that appeared in the chapter.

At the back of the book, as well as the index, there is a list of languages cited with a small amount of information about each.

 Technical terms introduced in this chapter

Gloss	Phonetics
Killer language	Phonology
Language	Pragmatics
Linguistics	Semantics
Morphology	Syntax

Reading and references

The famous book referred to in the first sentence is Adams (1979). On what you must and can say, see Jakobson (1971: 264) who says 'Languages differ essentially in what they *must* convey and not in what they *can* convey', and makes reference to work by Boas. For Russell on poor but honest parents, see Russell (1948: 74). On the question of endangered and disappearing languages, see Krauss (1992). On linguistics as a science, see Crystal (1985: chapter 3). The term 'the indispensable foundation' is from Sweet (e.g. 1877: v).

Chapter epigraphs in this and other chapters are taken from Crystal and Crystal (2000).
On glossing in general, see the Leipzig Glossing Rules, available from www.eva.mpg.de/lingua/resources/glossing-rules.php.

Data on individual languages comes from the sources identified below.

Tariana   Aikhenvald (2006).

2

Semantics

*'Meaning' is one of the words of which one may
say they have odd jobs in our language*
(Ludwig Wittgenstein 1933–1934)

Semantics is the study of meaning. Here we look at the ways in which words are related to each other in terms of meaning, ways in which words can be said to 'mean' and how we might represent knowledge of meaning that we have about the words of our own language. We look at the way in which meanings deviate from what we might think of as their focal point, and finally, at how the meanings of words go together to make up meanings of sentences.

2.1 The difficulty of meaning

It often looks as though the whole function of language is to construct meaning. We use language to explain things to people: how to get to a place they've never visited before, how to bake a cake, how to programme the DVD player. We use language to tell people things they need to know: that they might trip up, that they should take an umbrella with them when they go out because rain is forecast, why the Crimean War was so important in the development of medical treatment. We use language to tell stories: Rumpelstiltskin and the Iliad. We use language to mislead people: we tell direct lies, or use language which makes bad things sound good or vice versa. In each case we are constructing a message, and we expect our interlocutors to be able to interpret the message in the way in which we intended that they would.

If the message fails to get communicated, we expect to be able to clarify it. 'What does *synaesthesia* mean?' we ask. Or, if the message was ambiguous or unclear, we might say 'I wonder what they meant by that.' For anything to be meaningless is clearly a bad thing, whether we are talking about a sentence or an activity or life itself.

The obvious conclusion is that language is all about meaning; meaning is central to what we do when we use language. Unfortunately that is not all there is to the question. We can use the word *mean* in any of the ways illustrated below, and they all seem to indicate a different idea of meaning:

(1) (a) Clouds mean rain.
    (b) A red light means stop.
    (c) Beanz meanz Heinz.
    (d) *Svelte* means 'slim'.

11

(e) I know the place you mean.

(f) *Je ne sais pas* means 'I don't know'

The sentences in (1) omit uses of *mean* that seem less connected with language: *he didn't mean any harm, that would mean moving to Switzerland, it's meant to be a dog but it looks more like a horse, they were meant for each other, it's meant to be a really good film,* where *mean* variously can be interpreted as 'intend', 'imply' or 'say'.

In (1a) *mean* seems to imply a frequently observed co-occurrence of two natural phenomena, but there is no intention to communicate. (1b), on the other hand, tells us about a situation constructed by humans specifically to communicate a given message. In (1d) one word is said to be equivalent to another, not necessarily in complete detail, but at least to a certain extent. In (1e) it is implied that you have a specific place in mind and that I can identify it. And (1f) could be interpreted in the same way as (1d) (except that this time we are moving between languages), but whereas in (1d) there was equivalence of individual words, in (1f) it is equivalence of the whole structure which is in question, not just of individual elements within the bits which are claimed to be equivalent.

> **<2.1>** In (1c), which is an advertising slogan, there is deliberate play on the use of *mean*. Explain what is going on.

In what follows, we will see that there is a technical vocabulary surrounding much of this, allowing us to be more specific about what we say. We will also see that there are more areas of meaning than have been discussed here. We will begin by looking at meaning as it is portrayed in dictionaries, and then move on to other kinds of meaning.

2.2 Dictionaries and definitions

Consider these definitions extracted from real dictionary entries.

Data-set 2.1		
Some dictionary definitions	glabrous	hairless
	happen	occur
	mere	lake
	slender	slim

Each of these words is defined by providing a word which means (or is intended to mean) just the same thing as the word being defined. To use a technical term which has also become an everyday term, the word and its definition are **SYNONYMS**. *Slender* is **SYNONYMOUS** with *slim*. The two words show a relationship of **SYNONYMY**. In principle, a word may be replaced by its synonym in a sentence without any change in the message conveyed. So (2a) and (2b) should not differ in meaning.

(2)　(a)　She had a slender majority at the election.
　　　(b)　She had a slim majority at the election.

Similarly, you should get the same message from (3a) and (3b).

(3)　(a)　He climbed the hill, and looked down at the mere.
　　　(b)　He climbed the hill, and looked down at the lake.

Here, though, you may feel that there is a difference. Although (3b) would be true on every occasion on which (3a) was true, the word *mere* is much rarer than *lake*, so that you may be totally unfamiliar with it, (3a) may sound more poetic than (3b), or you may only know *mere* as a local dialect word meaning 'lake'. Thus we need to distinguish between the situation in the real world that the word describes, and the emotional overtones that go along with information. We will say that although the word *mere* and the word *lake* can both be used to **DENOTE** the same real-world objects, they have different **CONNOTATIONS**. Alternatively, we might say that *lake* and *mere* have the same **DENOTATION**. The connotations of poeticalness or local homeliness may affect your attitude to what is described, but does not affect the nature of what is named by the word. We find a similar situation in (4).

(4)　(a)　A slender woman in her thirties came into the room.
　　　(b)　A thin woman in her thirties came into the room.

> **<2.2>** How do the two sentences in (4) differ in their meaning?

> **<2.3>** What kinds of difference in connotation might there be between *glabrous* and *hairless*?

With *happen* and *occur* we can find the same kind of thing. In (5), for example, the two words may indicate the same situation, but probably differ in their connotations, with *occur* sounding more formal or official.

(5)　(a)　It happened just as I was leaving home.
　　　(b)　It occurred just as I was leaving home.

However, in (6), we meet a different situation.

(6)　(a)　Did you happen to see who that was?
　　　(b)　*Did you occur to see who that was?

(The asterisk shows that the construction it precedes is in some way impossible.)

Here we see that words which are synonyms in some situations are not necessarily synonyms in all situations. In this case, you might want to say that *happen* has two meanings: 'occur' is one of them, 'chance' is the other. The technical term for this situation is **POLYSEMY**. This assumes that you think there is just one word *happen*. An alternative view might be that there are two words, call them *happen*₁ and *happen*₂, one of them meaning 'occur' and one of them meaning 'chance'. It is not necessarily easy to distinguish between these two cases, but the second case has the technical name of **HOMONYMY**. A clear case of homonymy is provided by *stem*₁ 'part of a plant' and *stem*₂ 'to staunch a flow'.

<2.4> Can you find another instance of two words which are synonyms in one context but not in another?

CONTROVERSY: Polysemy vs homonomy

The difference between polysemy and homonymy seems clear in some instances, but becomes very unclear in others. In many cases, this has very little practical relevance, but some dictionaries distinguish between the two in the way they lay out the entries. You might like to look in some dictionaries and see how they differ in this regard. Consider an example which would probably be considered a clear example of homonymy. *Cricket*₁ 'a sport played by two teams' and *cricket*₂ 'a jumping insect' are so far from each other semantically that we would probably not consider that they might have anything in common. We might say that the name of the sport has the name of the insect as a **HOMONYM**. At the other end of the scale, we would probably agree that *crescent* is a single word with at least two meanings: 'the shape of the moon at certain times in the lunar cycle' and 'a curved street'. The 'street' meaning derives from the 'moon' meaning by a fairly transparent figure of speech. The only real question here is whether we really want to say there are two meanings, or whether we want to say that the meaning of *crescent* is simply a particular shape, and that it can then be used of anything with that shape, whether moon or street or the layout of chairs in an auditorium. Between these two extremes, however, it can be difficult to decide on many occasions. Consider the word *harrier*. It could be said to have a number of meanings, among them 'a dog for hunting' and 'a kind of hawk'. These seem to be related: they both have to do with hunting and preying on animals. But the name of harrier dog (and, following from that, cross-country runners) appears to derive from the word *hare*, while the name of the hawk appears to derive from a word cognate with the German word *Heer* 'army' and basically to mean 'destroyer'. So should we say that there is one polysemous word *harrier* with a number of meanings, or should we set up two homonymous words *harrier*₁ and *harrier*₂ on the basis of what we know about the history of the words? Dictionaries tend to follow the latter course. It is not clear that there are consistently applicable criteria that will allow us to decide in instances where we do not know the history or where we believe that we should judge without reference to the history (after all, most speakers do not know the history of the language they speak).

We have seen that dictionaries can use synonyms as a way of defining words, though they may not be able to pay close attention to connotations, and although words which are synonyms on one occasion may not be synonyms on all occasions. There are also other ways of providing definitions, illustrated below.

Data-set 2.2
Some more
dictionary
definitions

dance	to move rhythmically, esp. to music
doolally	mentally unbalanced
drone	the male of the honey-bee
droshky	a low four-wheeled open carriage used in Russia

In each of these cases, the definition tells you what general kind of thing is being denoted, and then makes it more specific. This is done in grammatically different ways, depending on the kind of word being defined. In the case of *droshky*, for example, you are told that a droshky is a carriage, and then given more details to narrow down the kind of carriage: it is a low carriage, has four wheels, and so on. In the world of lexicographers, this is called a definition *per genus et differentiam* (or, more extensively, *per genus proximum et differentiam specificam*), by type and differentiation. Semanticists call the relationship between, say, *droshky* and *carriage* a relation of HYPONYMY. *Droshky* is a HYPONYM of *carriage*, *carriage* is a HYPERNYM, or HYPERONYM or (more easily distinguishable) SUPERORDINATE TERM for *droshky*.

<2.5> What is the superordinate term given for *dance* in the definition in data-set 2.2?

<2.6> What might some other hyponyms of *honey-bee* be?

Worker and *queen* are other hyponyms of *honey-bee*. *Worker*, *queen* and *drone* are thus COHYPONYMS of the superordinate term *honey-bee* (or, more generally yet, of *bee*).

Each of the words in the list below is defined by what it is not (though the negation is marked in different ways in different examples). Another way of saying this is that these words are defined in terms of their opposites. Unfortunately, the term 'opposite' is an extremely vague one, and we need more specific terms if we wish to be precise in discussing language.

Data-set 2.3
Yet more
dictionary
definitions

gentile	anyone who is not a Jew
ignore	pay no heed or attention to
ill	not well
poorly	unwell

Deep and *shallow* are opposites in the sense that the deeper a lake (for example) gets, the less shallow it is and vice versa. Such 'opposites' are termed GRADABLE ANTONYMS. They are gradable because one lake can be deeper than another: there are degrees of depth. Notice that we tend to prefer one of these terms to the other in normal use. We can ask *How deep is this lake?* even if we suspect that it is shallow, but if we ask *How shallow is this lake?* we imply that we know that it is shallow. Similarly, we can talk about *the depth of the water in the lake*, even if it is not very deep, but to talk about *the shallowness of the water in the lake* implies that it really is shallow. So using *deep* makes fewer assumptions about the state of the world than using *shallow* does, and accordingly *deep* (and *depth*) is commoner than *shallow* (and *shallowness*).

Note also that just because something is not deep, it does not follow that it is shallow. A diver might say that the sea is not deep at a particular point if there is, say, four metres of water, but it would not follow that the sea was shallow there. In fact, the same thing may be deep and shallow at the same time: *I don't know whether this is a deep plate or a shallow bowl*. All of this is typical of gradable antonyms.

The case of *Jew* versus *gentile* is different. Denying that a person is a Jew is, according to the definition provided, equivalent to affirming that he or she is a gentile, and vice versa. While we might argue that it is possible to feel just a little bit Jewish, it would be rather like arguing that someone may not feel very pregnant. We can extend the meaning of these words by playing with the way we express things, but the default reading is that there are not degrees of Jewishness or gentileness. Within the appropriate domain (the domain of people for *Jew* versus *gentile*) you are either one thing or the other, with no grades involved. Words like *Jew* and *gentile* are called **COMPLEMENTARY TERMS**. It is important for complementary terms that there are only two of them in the set. The prefix *non-* is often use to construct complementary terms for existing words, as in *member* and *non-member*, *smoker* and *non-smoker*, and *verbal* and *non-verbal* (communication).

<2.7> What is the relevant domain within which *smoker* and *non-smoker* are complementary terms?

<2.8> Why is the word *pregnant* not a suitable example of a complementary term?

<2.9> Why are the terms called *complementary*?

Yet another kind of opposite is illustrated with pairs of words like *buy* and *sell*, *teach* and *learn*. These can denote the same event, but view it from a different perspective. If X buys Y from Z for £W, then it follows that Z sells Y to X for £W, and if X teaches Y something about Z then it follows (at least in an ideal world) that Y learns something about Z from X. Pairs of opposites like these are called **CONVERSE TERMS**.

<2.10> Can you think of any other kinds of opposite?

In each of the definitions below, the word to be defined is explained as being a part of something else. The semantic relationship here is called **MERONYMY**, so that *ceiling* is a **MERONYM** of *room*, and so on. One of the interesting things about meronymy is that the relations are not always transitive; that is, if A has B as a part, and B has C as a part, it is not always true linguistically that we consider C to be a part of A.

Data-set 2.4
Dictionary definitions

ceiling	the inner roof of a room
deck	the platform of a skateboard
shin	the forepart of the leg below the knee
sole	the bottom of a boot or shoe
spoke	one of the radiating bars of a wheel

Let us contrast this with hyponymy. If *tulip* is a hyponym of *flower* and *flower* is a hyponym of *plant*, it follows that *tulip* is a hyponym of *plant*. We can say *A tulip is a kind of plant*. And if *plant* is a hyponym of *object*, it follows that *tulip* is a hyponym of *object*. We can say *A tulip is a kind of object*. The relation 'is a hyponym of' is passed on from one level to the next; it is **TRANSITIVE**. We would expect the same to be true with meronymy, and sometimes it is. If *shin* is a meronym of *leg* and *leg* is a meronym of *person*, *shin* is a meronym of *person*. Accordingly *a shin is a part of a person* seems like a reasonable statement to make. But if *ceiling* is a meronym of *room*, and *room* is a meronym of *palace* is it true to say that *a ceiling is part of a palace*? You could say *That person's shin [is bruised]*, but could you say *That palace's ceiling [has been painted]*? Your intuitions may not be secure in such instances, but it seems that languages do not treat meronymy as a completely transitive relationship.

 <2.11> Try to find some other examples for yourself where meronymy is or is not transitive.

If you speak other languages, you can see whether the same instances of meronymy are transitive in the other languages.

TRIVIA

A question which has caused discussion since the ancient Greeks (if not longer) is whether a word has its own 'natural' meaning, or whether the link between the sound of a word and its meaning is purely arbitrary. Plato (427–347 BCE) believed there to be an intrinsic link between sound and meaning. Since Saussure (1857–1913), it has generally been accepted by linguists that the link is arbitrary: the word corresponding to English *horse* is *cheval* in French, *hest* in Danish, *Pferd* in German, *loshad'* in Russian, and so on; if the link is natural, how can it be the case that each of these languages functions perfectly well with a very different form–meaning relationship? Thus it makes no sense to argue that they're called *horses* because they look like horses, or *horse* is a very fitting name for that kind of animal (though such arguments can sometimes be heard from children, and occasionally, even from adults).

2.3 Representations and models

2.3.1 Words and the world

You would be justified in asking whether the relationships that have been discussed in the last section are relationships between words or relationships between things. The answer is that they are relationships between words – and we could simply make this true by definition. However, there are reasons for thinking that this really is the case.

The simplest case to argue is the case of synonymy. If *bucket* means the same as *pail*, or *slim* means the same as *slender*, then the obvious conclusion to draw is that we are simply using different words for the same reality, and therefore the relation between such pairs of words hold between the words, as a result of them having the same denotation. We can illustrate the situation with the diagram in Figure 2.1.

Figure 2.1
A simplified
representation
of synonymy

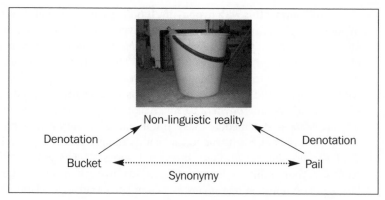

Non-linguistic reality

Denotation   Denotation

Bucket ◄···► Pail
Synonymy

With antonyms and other opposites, the case is less clear. But since, in principle, any member of a set of antonyms could also be a member of a pair of synonyms, the same must hold. So, for example, *small* and *little* could be seen as synonyms, each of which is the antonym of *big* (though with different connotations in this case).

 <2.12> What are the connotations of *little* and *small* that distinguish the usages of the two words?

The case of hyponymy is much easier to argue. In English there is no single word which acts as the superordinate of *chair, table, bed, wardrobe* and so on. We have the word *furniture*, but it denotes a collection of such objects. In French (and a number of other languages), on the other hand, there is such a word: in French it is *meuble*. The objects are the same in English and French, and French has the words *chaise, table, lit, armoire* corresponding to the names of the types of furniture given above. But in French there is word for the superordinate, and so only in French, and not in English, is there hyponymy. In other words, hyponymy depends on the words involved, not the objects. We also have cases where our words class things together that do not, in terms of the extralinguistic reality, belong together. In terms of the real world, blackberries, boysenberries, loganberries, raspberries are aggregate fruits, and different from blackcurrants, gooseberries and grapes, which are berries (defined technically in botany as simple, succulent fruits, enclosed in a skin). Yet most English speakers would feel cheated if they ordered a berry parfait in a restaurant and got no aggregate fruits or strawberries in the dish. *Berry* is a superordinate of *raspberry*, and *gooseberry, raspberry* and *strawberry* are cohyponyms, despite the mismatch with the real world.

 <2.13> Are potatoes and tomatoes vegetables?

Where meronymy is concerned we have already seen that although a nail, by being a part of a toe, must logically be a part of a foot and a limb, *my foot's/limb's nail* or *my limb/leg has a nail* seem odd. So linguistically we are not willing to base ourselves on the part-of relation that exists in the real world. In other words, the relations we use depend upon the words and not upon the state of the world.

Let us then accept that when we build up sentences and use them as utterances we are using words whose representation may not match anything in the real world. If we need any extra proof of this, we can say that we have words like *centaur, mermaid* and *unicorn* whose meanings are familiar to us, but which do not seem to exist in the world we know (except in fictions, including pictures and the like).

Once we accept this fundamental fact, we can ask how the meanings of these words are represented in the brain or modelled by the linguist. This turns out to be an area with no clear answers, but a number of partial suggestions, none of which is entirely satisfactory.

2.3.2 Features

We can start with some things which seem relatively uncontroversial. There are features of words which are referred to by the syntax, and which we thus assume must somehow be part of the specification of the words concerned. An obvious one is gender. In a number of languages, of which German provides a simple example, nouns are divided into classes called 'genders', and articles, adjectives in certain positions, and relative pronouns (as illustrated in Data-set 2.5) must show the appropriate gender when they belong with the noun. Consider the examples from German below:

Data-set 2.5
Gender in German

Das	große	Buch,	das ich	gesehen	habe	'The big book that I saw'
The(N)	big	book	that(N)	I seen	have	
Der	große	Wagen,	den	ich gesehen	habe	'The big car that I saw'
The(M)	big	car	that(M)	I seen	have	
Die	große	Straße,	die	ich gesehen	habe	'The big street that I saw'
The(F)	big	street	that(F)	I seen	have	

The parenthesised F, M, and N indicate feminine, masculine and neuter genders respectively.

Since the relative pronouns (*das, den, die*) require the speaker to have information on the gender of the noun in order to get the correct form, we must assume that the gender is part of the specification of the word.

English might appear to have gender in the same way that German does if we consider sentences like those in (7):

(7) I saw my aunt yesterday and she/*he gave me £10.
I saw my uncle yesterday and he/*she gave me £10.

However, although in (7) the words *aunt* and *uncle* always refer to a female and male respectively, in English we can have words which can refer to either males or females (and so can be referred to as *he* or *she*); the gender is not associated with the particular word, but with some aspect of real life, which makes the situation very different from the German one: in German, the word for girl, *Mädchen*, is neuter gender, not feminine.

<2.14> While in German each word is associated with a particular gender (and that is also true of the English examples in (7)), there are places in English where a given word may be used apparently with different genders. Can you think of any?

Another, more complicated, example is provided by countable and uncountable nouns. **COUNTABLE** nouns are nouns that denote objects that can be counted: *ant, chair, country, leaf, mare, pencil* and so on. **UNCOUNTABLE** (also called non-count or **MASS** nouns) are nouns that denote entities that occur as undifferentiated masses: *ivory, music, porridge, rice, water* and the like. You can ask *how many?* with regard to countable nouns, and give an answer with a number and the plural form of the noun; with uncountable nouns you ask *how much?* and typically cannot have a plural form of the noun. So *How many pencils do you have?* but *How much porridge do you have? I have five pencils*, but not **I have five porridges*. The reason that this particular example is complicated is that speakers of English can exploit this system meaningfully. It is possible to say *How much pencil did you eat while trying to solve this problem?* and thus to treat *pencil* as an uncountable noun; it is equally possible to say *There were five porridges on the supermarket shelves, and I didn't know which one to buy.*

 <2.15> Is *porridge* a countable or an uncountable noun in that last sentence? What is the point of the example?

Despite this, there are still some nouns which it is difficult or very unusual to use as countable nouns: *knowledge* is one celebrated example.

We might consider this simply to be part of the way the world is, a reflection of extra-linguistic reality, if we did not have other languages for comparison. The word meaning 'rice' is countable in some Danish dialects; the word for 'research' is countable in German; the word for 'information' is countable in French; the word *spaghetti* is countable in Italian. And in English, that most countable of all objects, money, is denoted by an uncountable noun: we say *How much money do you have?* not **How many monies do you have?* In other words, the grammatical status of these words is not simply derived from the nature of the world, but is something linguistic.

If this kind of information has to be listed in the dictionary entry for each word, we can ask how we should represent this. Two things need to be made clear about this apparently simple statement. The first is that by 'dictionary entry' we are now talking about the linguist's idea of what the mental dictionary in any speaker's head will look like – we are not talking about a bound volume that sits on your shelf. To make this clear we can talk about the **LEXICON** when we refer to the mental dictionary or our hypothesis about its structure. The second is that our representation of the knowledge in the lexicon is almost certainly different from what is in any speaker's head. It is simply an efficient way of writing the information which we deduce must be present in some form or another.

So how can we represent, for example, that some nouns have one gender, some another and that some nouns are countable, some are uncountable? Since it is not the case that all masculine nouns are countable and all feminine nouns uncountable (or that any other similar simple correlation holds true) we must be able to cross-classify nouns for the two factors independently. One standard way of doing this is by means of a set of **FEATURES**. A feature is a recurrent analysable element of a unit (and here the units are words). We will come back to features on numerous occasions both in this chapter and in later ones, and refine the notion as we go.

We usually give features two values, a plus value and a minus value, so that we might classify *porridge* as [- masculine], [- feminine] and [- countable], while *mare* is classified as [- masculine], [+ feminine] and [+ countable].

> **<2.16>** Why is *porridge* classified as [- masculine] and [- feminine]? Could anything be both [+ masculine] and [+ feminine]?

Note the use of square brackets to enclose the names and values of features. It would also be normal to list a set of features for a single element within a single set of brackets, as illustrated below for the features for *porridge*.

$$\begin{bmatrix} - \text{ masculine} \\ - \text{ feminine} \\ - \text{ countable} \end{bmatrix}$$

Since features we have looked at here mark semantic traits which are used in the syntax we can call them **SEMANTICO-SYNTACTIC FEATURES**. But they raise the question of whether purely semantic traits can also be described by the use of features of this type.

In some cases, they appear to work extremely well. A well-explored example is the case of words for male, female and young animals. Consider the words *man*, *woman* and *child*. All denote humans, but while *man* and *woman* denote adult humans, *child* denotes a non-adult human, and does not specify the gender. This compares well with *stallion*, *mare* and *foal* or *boar*, *sow* and *piglet*, or *ram*, *ewe* and *lamb*. We can imagine a matrix like that shown below. As far as it goes, this seems like a fairly neat solution, though there is one fairly obvious problem with this matrix.

Data-set 2.6
A matrix of features for animal words

	[human]	[equine]	[porcine]	[ovine]	[adult]	[male]	female]
man	+	–	–	–	+	+	–
woman	+	–	–	–	+	–	+
child	+	–	–	–	–		
stallion	–	+	–	–	+	+	–
mare	–	+	–	–	+	–	+
foal	–	+	–	–	–		
boar	–	–	+	–	+	+	–
sow	–	–	+	–	+	–	+
piglet	–	–	+	–	–		
ram	–	–	–	+	+	+	–
ewe	–	–	–	+	+	–	+
lamb	–	–	–	+	–		

> **<2.17>** Can you find at least one problem with the matrix in Data-set 2.6?

The matrix starts to look slightly less neat if we start to add more words. *Boy* and *girl* seem to be easily fitted into the schema, although it may seem odd that we do not have equivalent terms for the other animals mentioned (*heifer* might be taken as an equivalent term for bovine animals), but *teenager* is a problem. Should it be [+ adult] or [- adult] (or both)? Is it equivalent to *colt* for horses? Next, what about *person*, *horse*, *pig* and *sheep*? They are unspecified for adultness and for gender. The number of blank cells (or cells with a ± marking) in the matrix grows considerably when these words are added. Notice, too, that because English has learned words like *porcine* we have been able to use them for the names of the features, but would it change anything if we used the terms *pig* etc. instead? In one sense, it would not, but now it looks as if we are defining the word *pig* by saying that it is [+ pig], which seems less than helpful.

Another problem with the matrix is that it implies that every word that does not denote a human (for example) has a feature [- human]. There must be hundreds of thousands of words in the English language which do not denote humans (everything from *mouse* to *bacterium* to *screwdriver* to *hatred*) so there are a huge number of [- human] markers, some of them redundant (for example, if the word is marked as being [+ porcine]). We can overcome this problem, but only by moving away from the idea of features having two values. If we have a feature [species] with the values [species: human], [species: equine], and so on, we can reduce the number of features considerably, though we still seem to have an implication that every word will have a species, even words like *hatred*, *implication* and *research*.

What would happen if we tried to extend our matrix to encompass canine animals? Dog-breeders have the word *dog* for the adult male (think of *dog-fox*), though many people with no specialist knowledge are unaware of this usage, and simply use *dog* for the general term. Should we have two different words *dog* (say *dog₁* and *dog₂*), should we say we have a singly polysemous word with two definitions in terms of features, or should we try to put all the definitions into the same set of features somehow? Note that although we use *dog*, which is also the term for the male, as the neutral term here, with bovine animals it is the name of the female, *cow*, which is used as the neutral term. There are good cultural reasons for this, no doubt, but in purely linguistic terms it looks odd.

> **<2.18>** Can you find any other examples where we use the word for the female as the general term, or where we use the name for the male as the general term?

Finally consider the words *eunuch, gelding, barrow, wether*. Some of these may not be familiar words to you, but they all denote castrated males of their species: human, equine, porcine and ovine respectively. We could add a new feature [± castrated] to account for the meanings. But note that this meaning applies only if the feature [+ male] already applies.

Controversy: Dependent features

Some scholars assume that the fundamental purpose of features is to cross-classify linguistic units, and that all features thus have equivalent value. In such a view of the function of features, the idea that one feature depends on another does not make sense. Other scholars have no problem with seeing features as structured, so that one feature can apply if and only if a particular value of another feature has been chosen. The latter position implies a rather more complex view of how features operate, but is also more explanatory in cases like the proposed feature [± castrated]. The point to notice here is that the way we use features is determined to some extent by a theoretical framework, and that even apparently simple constructs like features can be subject to differing theoretical interpretations.

This set of words also raises other problems. The first is that although the features that have been suggested here might give an account of the denotation of the words we have considered, they fail to account for the connotations. It is not clear to what extent the word *eunuch* actually means 'a worker in a harem' and to what extent that is simply an association with the word. We might say that *castrato* means the same thing, but has different associations, or we might think that the two words are not synonymous. The word *barrow* is largely obsolete except in some rural dialects. And *wether* is most likely to be familiar in the term *bell-wether*. None of this is captured by our system of features. Note, too, that if *eunuch* does mean 'worker in a harem', it is going to be very difficult to capture this by means of a general feature. Indeed, one of the difficulties with using features to provide an account of the meanings of words is that at some level we either have to give up trying to specify the meaning any more closely or we have to use extremely specific features like [+ harem-worker]. Such specific features are not very useful in allowing us to cross-classify the vocabulary.

<2.19> The real problem with a feature such as [± harem-worker] arises with the negative value of it. Why?

The second problem, albeit a problem of a very different kind, is that once we have introduced the feature [± castrated] we might start asking ourselves what the word corresponding to, say, [+ canine, + adult, + male, + castrated] is. We seem to have a number of LEXICAL GAPS: positions in the matrix for which we have a set of semantic features, but no words. We have already noted the existence of lexical gaps (such as the lack of a superordinate term for *table, chair, wardrobe* in English), but this example points to the fact that such gaps may be numerous in the vocabulary of English, or, indeed, of any language.

2.3.3 Prototypes

We have seen that although semantic features can be used with some success to help model the structure of some parts of the vocabulary, even where they work they bring a number of problems with them. So the question arises as to whether there is any better way of modelling the semantic representation of words. One very important approach (one which will turn out to be of great value in approaching a number of facets of linguistic structure) is the prototype approach. Again we can take a simple example where this approach has been shown to have great value.

> **<2.20>** Provide a definition of the word *bird*.

It will be surprising if your definition does not have a number of criteria attached to it, criteria such as 'has wings', 'lays eggs', 'has feathers'. The psychologist Eleanor Rosch discovered that birds which fit all of these criteria are more central to our notion of bird than birds which do not fit all the criteria, even if those other birds remain birds. Kiwis do not have wings, penguins do not fly, eagles are rather large, ostriches break several of these expectations about birds. They are all birds, but some are better birds than others. It turns out that if you are asked to judge whether a robin is a bird or not (even remembering that a robin is a different bird in North America, in Europe and in Australia), you will decide that it is a bird more quickly than you will decide about a penguin. And that you might take longer to decide that a dragon-fly is not a bird than you would take to decide that a saucepan is not a bird. Rosch said that some birds are closer to the **PROTOTYPE** of what a bird is like than others are. Our concept of *bird* is based on the prototype, so that we respond to prototypical birds as being more bird-like than less prototypical birds are.

This suggests that rather than having a number of necessary and sufficient conditions for something being a bird, we have a mental image of what the prototypical bird is like, and we judge real exemplars by how well they fit the prototype. Real birds diverge from the prototype in various ways. But creatures are likely to be called *birds* as long as they are closer to the prototype for *bird* than to any other prototype. In fact, experiments suggest that even clear-cut categories like *odd number* work in the same way. We tend to think of 7 as being a better odd number than 31 is. In mathematical terms, this is nonsense. In psychological and linguistic terms, it is not.

This view of the way in which semantic categories work might explain some puzzles. The first of these is how we ever learn categories like *bird*. It would be compatible with prototype theory if we retained a trace of everything we had ever seen that was called a *bird*, and our prototype was some kind of average over our entire experience. The second is why we should call an aeroplane a *bird*. A plane has many of the features of a bird, but not all of them: it has no feathers, but it flies, for example. Extension of meaning by metaphor demands that we should be able to see similarities between non-identical things, and attribute them to the nearest proto-type, just as prototype theory does.

There are also benefits for prototype theory over feature theory (usually called **COMPONENTIAL ANALYSIS**) in that some sets of words are resistant to a featural analysis, but seem to work well with a prototype approach. What, for instance, is the difference between a lemon, a lime, an orange, a tangerine, a mandarin, a satsuma and a grape-fruit? You might find difficulty in setting up features to distinguish between the words (especially since oranges and lemons can be green before they are ripe); you might even find that different languages draw different distinctions in this area. Yet you might be able to recognise them all in the fruiterer's. The disadvantage of prototypes for discussing meaning is that they are difficult to formalise in any coherent way, and so difficult to build into a formal theory of grammar. The two ways of approaching meaning are, of course, not necessarily incompatible. We might prefer to use features for things like gender, and prototypes for things like the meaning of the word *bird*.

ELEANOR ROSCH

Eleanor Rosch (1938–) is a cognitive psychologist whose work has been extremely influ- ential in linguistics. Her work on prototypes began when she worked among the Dani people of Papua New Guinea, looking at their perception of colour terms (the Dani language has only two basic colour terms, one for bright and warm colours, one for cool and dark colours). The implications of her work on categorisation was taken up by many linguists, not only because it provided an alternative to the componential approach which had clear problems associated with it, but because of the increasing interest in language as a cognitive phenomenon. Rosch has also contributed studies in other areas such as the psychology of religion.

2.4 Reference

So far, we have discussed words in isolation, and talked about what individual words denote. Figure 2.1 might make it look as though the word *bucket* denotes a particular real-world entity, but to the extent that it does, it is misleading. It should be clear that *bucket* can be used of any of a class of entities, and does not pick out a specific bucket. A noun like *bucket* cannot, by itself, pick out a specific member of the set of things which can be denoted by *bucket*, under normal usage. (Of course, a small child may look at a specific bucket and say 'bucket', and it may not be clear whether the child means, 'this is a member of the set of things called *bucket*' or, 'I want that particular bucket'.) Normally we have to say something like *that bucket, the yellow bucket* or *the bucket in the laundry* if we want to talk about a specific bucket.

Under such circumstances we use a particular grammatical structure, including the word *bucket*, to REFER to a specific entity. It is not the word *bucket* which refers, but the entire REFERRING EXPRESSION *the yellow bucket* (or whatever suffices to pick out an individual on a given occasion).

The implication here is that although a particular grammatical structure may refer to a particular real-world entity on a given occasion, whether REFERENCE succeeds or not depends on the context (and also on such things as the interlocutor's knowl- edge). Where the context is involved we usually talk about pragmatics rather than semantics (see Chapter 7), but the borderline between the two is fuzzy.

CONTROVERSY: Reference

Although the use of the term *refer* that has been introduced here is widespread, it is not universal. Confusingly, some authorities use the term *reference* in much the way in which we have used *denotation*. This can give rise to real misunderstandings, and care needs to be taken with these terms when they are met in the literature.

Although complex expressions like *the yellow bucket in the laundry* can be referring expressions, two kinds of words are typically referring expressions: proper names and pronouns. If we say

(8)   George Washington cut down a cherry tree

the name *George Washington* refers to a particular individual, specifically to a former president of the United States. And if we say

(9)   Basingstoke is north of Winchester

both *Basingstoke* and *Winchester* refer to particular locations in England. Similarly, if I say

(10) I live in New Zealand

not only does *New Zealand* refer to a location, but *I* refers to a particular person.

Note that what is important for successful reference is that it should operate in the context in which it is used. If I happen to say (10) it means something different from what it means if you say it, because the REFERENT of the word *I* (the entity to which *I* refers) changes with the speaker. Similarly, if I say

(11) I saw George last week

I may be referring to a different person from the person of whom you could say the same. What matters is that on any given occasion, the speaker and interlocutor understand the reference. The same is true of complex expressions.

(12) Did you put the car away?

This would be used to refer to one vehicle if spoken in my house but to a different one if spoken in yours, yet the reference may be successful on both occasions.

The form of a referring expression is of some interest. In the examples given above, the referring expressions have been definite noun phrases (a phrase which allows us to pick out a unique entity referred to, in English often being a name or beginning with the word *the*; on nouns and noun phrases, see Chapter 6), but not all definite noun phrases refer, and not all referring expressions are definite. Consider (13) and (14).

(13) Margaret Thatcher was the Prime Minister
(14) Every evening a taxi stops in front of her house

In (13) being the Prime Minister is something that is predicated of Margaret Thatcher, and *the Prime Minister*, though definite, does not refer. The sentence in (14) is ambiguous. It could be the same taxi that stops there every evening (in which case, we might continue with *It is blue, its registration number starts with a 5*), or it could be a different taxi every evening. In the first case we have a non-definite noun phrase referring to an individual.

<2.21> Although *the amphibrach months* is a definite noun phrase, it can fail to refer. Why, and what point does this make?

<2.22> If you quote Oscar Wilde and say, 'I have nothing to declare except my genius', does the pronoun *I* refer, and if so, to whom?

Although reference is clearly part of 'meaning' in the sense that when I use a word like *you*, I 'mean' the person or people I am addressing, there is more to the meaning of referring expressions than simply discovering their referent. The standard example of this phenomenon is provided by expressions used to refer to the planet Venus. When Venus shines brightly early in the morning, it is sometimes called *the morning star*. But Venus can also be seen shining brightly in the evening, usually the first star to appear as the sun sets. Then it is can be called *the evening star*. It is totally appropriate to explain to somebody what the situation is by saying (15), while (16) would be odd.

(15) The morning star is the evening star.
(16) Venus is Venus.

As well as having Venus as its referent, *the morning star* has its own SENSE, and because that sense is different from the sense of *the evening star*, (15) is not tautological in the way that (16) is. There are many similar examples. If a student says to a receptionist *I'd like to speak to the Dean*, the receptionist might say to someone else, *This student would like to speak to Professor Smith*, even if the student is not aware of the name of the Dean. The referent has remained constant, but the sense has changed.

Philosophers have worried about what happens when reference fails. Consider, first, (17) and (18).

(17) The present President of the US is African-American.
(18) The present President of the US is not African-American.

If (17) is true, (18) is false and vice versa. But what happens with (19) and (20)?

(19) The present King of France is bald.
(20) The present King of France is not bald.

We would expect that if (19) is true, then (20) would be false and vice versa. But there is no present King of France. So is it false to say (19)? And if so, is it also false to say (20)? If so, why does negation not change the truth of the sentence? Or is it the case that because *the present King of France* does not refer to a real-world individual, the whole notion of truth and falsehood of the sentences in (19) and (20) becomes moot? And if that is the case, is the same true of (21) and (22), which do seem to contradict each other?

(21) The present phoenix has purple feathers.
(22) The present phoenix does not have purple feathers.

2.5 Words together

We seem to have an in-built prejudice towards assuming that different meanings will be attributed to different words and, correspondingly, that a given word will always mean the same thing. In saying this, we need to look away from homonymy: it might seem odd that we have a form *calf* which sometimes means 'young bovine animal' and sometimes means 'muscular part of the lower leg', or a form *cricket* which sometimes means 'a game' and sometimes means 'an insect', but all languages seem to have such cases, and there does not seem to be much that we can do about them. We might expect that speakers of languages would find homonymy awkward, and try to do away with it, and on some occasions that seems to be true; usually, however, it passes unacknowledged except in jokes.

> **<2.23>** Can you think of a joke that depends upon homonymy?

However, despite this prejudice, we find that dictionaries do not list a single meaning for every word. Rather they give a series of meanings. Some of the meanings seem like rather obvious variations, and in these cases we might ask why two different meanings have been given; others, though, may seem extremely different.

Some of the more obvious differences of meaning depend upon the grammatical patterning of the language we are considering; others may depend on more general cognitive processes. We can look at several types independently.

2.5.1 Grammatically-based variation

We have already seen that a word like *porridge* is, in its basic usage, uncountable. We say *How much porridge would you like?* not *How many porridge would you like?* However, if we go to the supermarket, we may say *There are so many porridges that I don't know which to choose*, where *porridge* has become a countable noun (it has a plural form) meaning, in effect, 'types of porridge'. This variation is well established in English, and is virtually never shown by a difference in form. Even *bread*, which has *loaf* as a countable form, allows *breads* meaning 'types of bread'. There are some nouns in English which resist the two interpretations: abstract nouns are generally harder to use in the plural that concrete nouns. Nevertheless, on the whole, if there is a suitable context, most nouns in English can be used either way. So it is no particular surprise to find a noun like *cheese* given two meanings in a dictionary, one for the uncountable or mass reading, and one for the countable reading.

<2.24> Make up sentences to show countable and uncountable uses of the words *beer*, *cake*, *cloud*, *love*, *thought*.

Something similar is found with verbs (for verbs in general, see Chapter 6). A verb like *walk*, which we probably think of as being fundamentally an intransitive verb (*Penelope walks everywhere*) can easily be used as a transitive verb (*Penelope walks the dog every evening*) (see section 6.5 on intransitive and transitive verbs). In some languages, the second use would be indicated by some kind of affix on the verb (perhaps called a **TRANSITIVISER** or a **CAUSATIVE** marker), but in English the difference is often not marked. Indeed, it may be more surprising to look at some of the cases where the relationship is marked. These days we think of the pairs being made up of independent words, though historically there is clearly a relationship between them (see below).

Data-set 2.7
English causative verbs

Intransitive	Transitive (Causative)
fall	fell
lie	lay
rise	raise
sit	set

There are several related phenomena, which we might mention here briefly. Some otherwise intransitive verbs occur with a cognate object, as in *She smiled a smile, He dreamed a dream*, which is not a causative construction, though it does have the effect of transitivising the verb. Second, some verbs which are basically transitive are sometimes used without any direct object, and thus might look as though they show the same phenomenon in the opposite direction. However, in these cases there is an 'understood' direct object which is tightly constrained. So *She drinks* means not that she drinks tea or milk, but that she consumes alcohol to excess, and *He chews* means (or used to mean, in some circles) that he chews tobacco. Third, there is an apparent parallel with some words which are not formally related in English (though they may be in other languages) such as *die* and *kill*, *learn* and *teach*, *eat* and *feed*. While there is controversy over how, or whether, this is part of the grammar of English, it is clearly part of the semantic structure of English. Again we see that even if *kill* denotes a set of events which could also be expressed as *cause to die*, the senses of the two are not precisely the same.

 <2.25> Why are the senses of *kill* and *cause to die* different? Provide an example where you could not substitute one for the other without changing the interpretation.

Fourth, some verbs in English permit what is called a **MIDDLE VOICE**, in which the agent is not specified. Some examples are given in (23).

(23) This passage reads particularly well
  Soufflés spoil easily
  This car handles like a dream

Just as nouns can be countable or uncountable and verbs can be transitive or intransitive, words can be associated with different kinds of closely related words. These differences are sometimes called differences in **COMPLEMENTATION** patterns, or differences in **VALENCY**. Consider the sentences in (24).

(24) She phoned the fire-brigade
She phoned extension 4592
She phoned the HR manager on extension 4592

The verb *to phone* is transitive in all these examples, but sometimes the person who is phoned is the object, and sometimes the number is the object. In (25) we see various patterns that can occur with a single adjective.

<2.26> The verbs *hire*, *lease* and *rent* show different grammatical patterns, depending on who does the hiring, leasing or renting. Are the patterns the same in all three verbs? Are there any other verbs that work the same way?

(25) That is useful to know
It is useful that you told us what is happening
It will be useful for keeping the rain off
A bicycle will be useful in allowing you to get here on time
This software is useful to businesses throughout the country

The differences in meaning of the word *useful* in these cases are quite subtle, and might be argued to arise through the grammatical structures themselves. Nevertheless, not all adjectives can take the same range of complementation patterns. Note that while *useless* shares many of the patterns that *useful* shows, there is nothing with *useful* that corresponds to (26).

(26) I'm useless at sport.

The nouns *call* and *visit* might seem to be synonyms (at least some of the time), but when we look at the patterns they can occur with, we see that they are really quite different. The judgements below are based on *a call* meaning 'a visit', and not on *a call* meaning 'a telephone call', which would pattern differently again. The table is to be interpreted as follows: if there is a cross in the intersection of *call* and *from a person*, it means we cannot say *[I got/received] a call from a person [or from John/my mother]*

Data-set 2.8
English co-occurrence patterns

	call	visit
a person	✗	✓
a place	✗	✗
from a person	✗	✓
of a period of time	✗	✓
on a person	✓	✗
to a person	✗	✓

in the relevant sense. A tick says this is natural. The patterns would also be different if the verbs were used instead of the nouns.

> **<2.27>** Do you agree with the judgements above? Try to write your own table for the verbs *to call* and *to visit*. Is the relationship between the nouns and the verbs predictable?

All these differences in usage would normally lead to the proliferation of polysemes in a standard dictionary. Some of the differences are predictable, others are not, and clearly belong in a dictionary. However, it is not clear to what extent these differences imply a difference in meaning.

2.5.2 Figures of speech

A clown is a highly skilled performer in, for instance, a circus. But the job of clowns is to make people laugh by making themselves look silly. So it seems natural that we might call anyone who behaves in a self-evidently silly manner a *clown*. This is a **METAPHOR**: calling one thing something else which it resembles in some way. But dictionaries often list metaphorical uses of words as separate meanings of the words. So *clown* might be given two meanings: the circus meaning, and the silly-person meaning.

> **<2.28>** What metaphorical meanings might you find for the words *lion, litany, moan, peach, peacock, scallop*?

Although dictionaries frequently fail to register metaphorical meanings, they are widespread in everyday language usage. For instance, we talk about someone *constructing* a theory, as though a theory were a building. Once this picture is established, then someone else might *demolish* the theory, the theory may *stand* or *fall*, may have *strong foundations*, or may *fall apart* or *collapse*. Another pervasive metaphor is that size is equivalent to importance. We can talk of an important person as being a *big man*, a *big wheel* or a *big noise*. Such a person may be *big in the city*, and make *big money*, even if they make a *big mistake* when they do business *in a big way*. The French have a similar transfer of meaning, but it often goes the other way, so that a large sum of money may be *une somme importante* ('an important sum') and *une importante baisse de prix* is 'a large fall in price'.

Consider the word *rocker* in the sense of 'rocking chair'. Why is it called a *rocker*? It could be because it rocks, or it could be because it is a chair on rockers. We name the whole chair for the relevant part of the chair. Similarly, we might say

(27) I don't want that person under my roof again

where *under my roof* means 'in my house' and we name the house by just part of the house. Or again, we might say that dinner in a particular restaurant is likely to cost £50 a head; *head* here means 'person' – if there was only a head, they would presumably not eat so much!

This figure of speech is called **SYNECDOCHE**, sometimes glossed as *pars pro toto* 'the part for the whole'.

Synecdoche is sometimes not distinguished from **METONYMY**, to which it is very similar. In synecdoche, the whole is named by a part of the whole; in metonymy, the whole is named by something associated with it. When we talk about *the Crown* meaning 'the British government or monarchy', we name the monarchy by reference to an object connected with the monarchy. Similarly, a club is a collection of people, but we can also say to someone that we will meet them *at the club*, meaning at the building where the group usually meets. So the building is named by the group which is associated with the building.

<2.29> Why might there be metonymical readings of the words *chair, head, headache, pot* (think of poker)?

2.5.3 Style

While we are all aware that there are situations in which more formal language is used than is the norm, and others where less formal language is used, specifying which words are restricted to formal or informal registers (or to various specific subtypes of informal usage – conversational, jocular, slang, regional, and so on) is an extremely difficult task. Nonetheless, many dictionaries attempt this, with a greater or lesser degree of success.

For instance, the word *place* can denote any location, but as it is used in

(28) You must all come round to my place

it not only has a specific meaning ('the place where I live') but is rather informal in tone. *Stuff* is a perfectly good verb in something like

(29) I'm going to stuff the turkey with sausage-meat

but when it means 'have sexual intercourse with' it is not only extremely informal but offensive. If someone says

(30) I was proceeding along the high street

they are almost certainly either a member of the police or in a court of law. *Proceed* in the sense of 'go' is very formal, and restricted to legal situations. And whether you eat *chips, crisps* or *chippies* may depend on where you come from, because the same foodstuff can be called any of these things.

<2.30> Why might each of the following words be listed as having a separate 'meaning' based on its style? *divine, frog, gas, grope, sustain*.

2.5.4 Specificity

Some definitions that are listed in dictionaries seem to be specific usages rather than new meanings of the word. Consider the word *root*, for example. Perhaps the first thing that comes to mind when we hear *root* is a plant, perhaps a tree. But we also talk about the roots of teeth and of hair, and these are not necessarily metaphorical uses of the word (unlike, say, *root of the problem*). Or consider the expression *to screw up*. If you screw something up, you make a mess of it. So something which is screwed up, is something which has been made a mess of: perhaps plans for a holiday, for instance. One specific way in which people can be screwed up is if they are mentally and emotionally unstable. Where this is given as a separate meaning of *screw up*, it might seem to be just one specific usage of the expression.

2.5.5 Collocations

It is implicit in some of the examples that have already been given that words take on slightly different meanings in different contexts. In the last section it was suggested that with examples like *root* or *screw up*, it might be excessive to see more than one meaning as being involved. But there are cases where it is extremely difficult to tell how many meanings should be analysed, particularly since there do not seem to be any well-established criteria for determining such a thing.

When we talk of context, we can be extremely vague or very precise. When we are talking about the nearest neighbouring words that go with any given word we speak of **COLLOCATION**. So one of the collocations of *blue* is *sky* and another is *sea*. These are words which are habitually found together.

Consider the case of *soft*. The central meaning of *soft* is probably the one we find in *soft bed*, or perhaps *soft fur*. It has something to do with the sense of touch, and it is a word, in these contexts, with very positive connotations. What then, about *soft furnishings* and *soft palate*? Do they illustrate the same meaning, or a different one? The positive connotations seem to have vanished, but the appeal to the sense of touch is still there. On the other hand, soft furnishings such as drapes may feel a lot harsher than soft fur does. What, then, of *soft cheese* or *soft metal*? These are not *soft* in the same way as soft fur is *soft*, and this is partly because *soft* is being used to classify here, rather than to describe. Cheese may be soft or hard; soft metal refers to a particular type of metal. *Soft pencil* probably fits in here, too, though it is only the lead in the pencil which is soft, and the softness is much more a matter of degree. Now consider *soft heart*, or, perhaps related, *a soft spot* (for someone). These are metaphorical, and there is nothing related to the sense of touch left, although we might be able to see how the expressions arose. *Soft water* may also be related to the sense of touch, at least in origin, if we believe that soft water feels better than hard water. The same cannot be said of *soft drink*, however. *Soft drink* presumably arose as a counterpoint to *hard* (alcoholic) *drink*, but why that should be *hard* is also a mystery. The *soft* in *soft drugs* seems to be parallel. *Soft* here seems to mean something like 'not harmful', which might also explain the uses of *soft* in *soft porn*, and, possibly, *soft job* (though this last case seems a little further removed from the others). None of these uses seems to explain the use in *soft voice*, where, at best, we have a different metaphor, one which retains the positive connotations of the original *soft* but moves it to a different sensory domain. This list of possible collocations with *soft* is not exhaustive. The question is whether there is a different 'meaning' of *soft* in each of these collocations, or whether there is one *Grundbedeutung* 'basic meaning' which applies in all these cases, or whether there is some intermediate position to be taken here. Note that if there is a single *Grundbedeutung*, that meaning must be rather more abstract than the 'meanings' which tend to be given by dictionaries. It seems likely that any *Grundbedeutung* will have, as one of its central parts, the way *soft* acts in the system of English words as an antonym of *hard*.

> **<2.31>** Look at the collocations of *flat* or *rough*, and see how many meanings diction-
> aries provide and how many distinct meanings you believe are involved.

2.5.6 Monosemy versus polysemy

The prejudice we began this section with is a prejudice in favour of a single meaning. We have seen that as words keep different company, they pick up (slightly or grossly) different shades of meaning. At this point we have to ask whether a *Grundbedeutung* persists or not, and if it does, whether it is what is in our brains. The answer to the first part of that seems to be a matter of fundamental philosophy or belief; the answer to the second part is far too complex to try to develop here, even if there were good materials to draw on. Standard dictionaries illustrate the feeling that polysemy is involved; an argument for the contrary notion would be an argument in favour of MONOSEMY.

Examples like *hot* 'of high temperature' or 'spicy' and *funny* 'amusing' or 'strange' seem to show that meanings can drift so far apart that they must be seen as becoming homonyms. The very fact that one could complain that

(31) This curry is hot but is not hot

or that people find it necessary to ask

(32) Do you mean funny 'ha-ha' or funny 'peculiar'?

suggests that, whatever the situation in earlier varieties of English, today these are distinct. So it must be that radical differences in meaning can develop from the slight variations in meaning that come from being used in different contexts, literally or figuratively, more or less specifically, and so on. This is an argument in favour of an analysis in which *hot* and *funny* (and by implication, *soft* and the other words we have considered here) have several distinguishable meanings.

On the other hand, if there is no *Grundbedeutung*, how are we to tell whether a new usage is appropriate or not (or is that not a relevant question)? *Hot* is now used to denote sexually attractive people though this is a relatively new usage that has spread quickly. Is it something in the meaning of *hot* that has allowed this usage, or has the usage caught on despite the meaning of *hot*? *Foxy*, applied to people, used to mean 'cunning' but then moved on to mean 'attractive'. The same question applies here (although it might be more relevant to ask about the word *fox* than the word *foxy*).

2.6 Sentence semantics (Advanced)

So far we have looked at the meanings of individual words, and how those meanings might vary or appear to vary in different contexts. In this section we will consider briefly how the meanings of larger linguistic constructions are built up.

There are various theories and notations concerned with how sentences 'mean'. Here we will consider briefly an approach which comes under the heading of Truth Conditional Semantics, though we will avoid the notation typically associated with this approach. Truth Conditional Semantics is so-called because it assumes that knowing the conditions under which a particular sentence is true is equivalent to knowing what that sentence means. This turns out to be more complex than it appears at first glance.

Consider a very simple sentence like (33).

(33) Indridi laughed.

The first thing that we need to know in order to determine whether (33) is true, is whether there is a person (or some other appropriate entity) called Indridi. If Indridi does not exist (or did not exist at the time to which the sentence refers) then (33) cannot be true. Furthermore, there must be some action which can be suitably described by the word *laugh*. Precisely what that action is belongs to the realm of lexical semantics rather than sentence semantics, and we will not deal with it further here, but merely assume there is such an action. Third, for (33) to be true, Indridi must have carried out this action of laughing at some time in the past. In other words, for (33) to be true, each of the things in (34) must be true.

(34) (a) Indridi exists
(b) Indridi carried out the action of laughing
(c) The action of laughing happened in the past

As we make the sentence we deal with more complex, so the number of conditions increases. Consider (35) and the conditions in (36).

(35) Indridi sat on the chair:
(36) (a) Indridi exists
(b) A chair exists
(c) There is a unique chair which can be determined in the universe of the discourse
(d) Indridi carried out an action of sitting
(e) The action of sitting was carried out in the past
(f) The sitting occurred on the top surface of the chair

<2.32> Given the examples above, what are the conditions required for the following sentence to be true: *The black cat is sitting on the mat?*

We can complicate the sentence again, by introducing a quantifier, like *every*, as in (37).

(37) Every astronomer admires Galileo.

Every astronomer ends up meaning something like 'for all entities, if that entity is a member of the class of astronomers', so we can list the conditions for (37) to be true as in (38).

(38) (a) Galileo exists/existed
    (b) A set of astronomers exists
    (c) For all entities, if that entity is a member of the set of astronomers, then that entity admires something
    (d) What is admired is Galileo
    (e) This action takes place generally in time, including at the present.

Having taken that step, it is interesting to see what happens if we complicate the sentence by one further step.

(39) Every actress loves two roles.

The sentence in (39) is ambiguous. It can either mean that there are two roles such that every actress loves them (the roles might be Lady Macbeth and Hedda Gabler, for instance), while the other means that for every actress it is the case that there are two roles which she loves (so that Judi Dench may love different roles from Maggie Smith, but each will love two). How can we distinguish between these two readings. On solution is given in (40) and (41).

(40) (a) One role exists (namely that of Lady Macbeth)
    (b) One role exists (namely that of Hedda Gabler)
    (c) A set of actresses exists
    (d) For all entities, if that entity is a member of the set of actresses, then that entity loves something.
    (e) What is loved is the roles established in (a) and (b)
    (f) This action takes place generally in time, including at the present.
(41) (a) A set of roles exist
    (b) A set of actresses exists
    (c) For all entities, if that entity is a member of the set of actresses, then that entity loves something.
    (d) What is loved is two members of the set in (a)
    (e) This action takes place generally in time, including at the present.

The interesting thing about a sentence like (39) is that the two readings have to be distinguished in the semantics, because there is only one grammatical structure that can be associated with the sentence. Of course, an approach like this one does not tell us everything we need to know about meaning: it still leaves open the questions of polysemy and monosemy, for instance. If we take a sentence like (42),

(42) I saw the pig

this approach will only tell us that for (42) to be true there has to be some uniquely identifiable thing that can appropriately be called a *pig* which the person referred to by *I* has seen in the past, but it will not clarify whether it is a porcine animal, a lump of lead or iron, a policeman or an unpleasant person, and nor will it elucidate how many different lexical entries should be involved. So a truth conditional approach has to be complemented with an approach to lexical semantics to get a full appreciation of how we extract meaning from utterances.

2.7 Summing up

We have seen that there are various meaning relationships which hold between words, and that there are relationships between words and items in the real world. We have also seen that the meanings of words can be influenced by other words which occur in the discourse, and we have considered one way of looking at the semantics of words occurring in larger units.

 Technical terms introduced in this chapter

Causative
Cohyponym
Collocation
Complementary terms
Complementation
Componential analysis
Connotation
Converse terms
Countable
Denotation
Denote
Feature
Gradable antonym
Grundbedeutung
Homonymy
Hyponym
Hyponymy
Lexical gap

Lexicon
Mass (see uncountable)
Meronym
Meronymy
Metaphor
Metonymy
Middle voice
Monosemy
Polysemy
Prototype
Refer
Reference
Referent
Referring expression
Semantico-syntactic feature
Sense
Superordinate (hypernym, hyperonym)

Synecdoche

Synonym

Synonymous

Synonymy

Transitive (relation)

Transitiviser

Uncountable (non-count, mass)

Valency

Reading and references

The definitions in Tables 2.1 to 2.4 are taken from Brookes (2006), but are not the entire definitions provided in that work. For discussions of synonymy, hyponymy and different kinds of opposite see Lyons (1968) or Cruse (1986). For Eleanor Rosch on birds, see Rosch (1978).

On *the present King of France*, see Russell (1905), Strawson (1950) and Strawson (1964), or the brief summary in Lyons (1977: 182–3).

On the constancy of meanings of words, see Clark (1993).

On causative verbs in English, see Levin & Rappaport Hovav (1994).

While examples of figures of speech and collocations can be found in any dictionary, Sinclair (1987) was used in the development of this section of this work. For the use of metaphor in language viewed from within the cognitive school of linguistics, see the very influential Lakoff & Johnson (1980).

While examples of complementation patterns can be found in any dictionary, Herbst *et al.* (2004) provides a convenient reference work on such matters.

3

Phonetics

*Take care of the sense, and the sounds will take
care of themselves.*

(Lewis Carroll 1865)

In this chapter we learn how the sounds of speech are made and described. Phonetics is
the study of the physical aspects of the sounds of speech. After brief introductions to the
workings of the lungs and the larynx, the focus of the chapter is on how we describe
consonant and vowel sounds, and the terminology we need to do this economically.

3.1 Getting the phonetics right

You probably recognise when people are speaking English with a foreign accent.
Depending on your experience, there are probably some accents that you can recognise quite well. You may, for instance, be able to recognise a French person speaking
English or a Spanish person speaking English or a Japanese person speaking English.
These people will all sound rather different.

<3.1> Why do you suppose that it is possible to recognise people as coming from a
particular language background, and why don't they sound like English speakers?

The obvious answer is that speaking any given language involves a large number
of habits of pronunciation, and that these habits are subtly different from language to
language. Speakers of one language who try to speak a different one take with them
a number of pronunciation habits some of which will be inappropriate for the second
language. But because these are habits, they are difficult to break: after all, we have all
spent a lot of time learning those habits in order to make our first language easy to
speak without conscious effort. Trying to speak one language with the habits of
another leads to a whole set of mispronunciations, some of them extremely subtle,
which together produce a recognisable foreign accent. The same principle works with
different accents of English. You may be able to recognise a Yorkshire accent or a
Glasgow accent or a New York accent, even if you yourself do not speak with one.

<3.2> Can you imitate any accent of English which is not your own successfully?

Consider a specific example. Many Canadian English speakers have a vowel in
words like *out* and *about* which is used by outsiders as a way to tell that they are
dealing with Canadians. But hearing this vowel, British speakers are likely to report

that the Canadians say *oat* and *aboat*, and United States speakers are likely to report that Canadians say *oot* and *aboot*. Both sets of speakers accordingly have difficulty in imitating the vowel correctly.

<3.3> What does this example show about our habits of pronunciation?

Despite what was said in answer to question <3.2>, humans are very good at imitating other humans. Some do this better than others, whether we are talking about copying somebody when they throw a ball or copying the way they talk. So some people are able to learn a new accent or a new language and to sound as if they belong to the relevant community. Most of us never fit in that well – especially not if we start after puberty when we lose some of our ability to hear and imitate sound patterns. That does not mean that we can never be perfectly good foreign language learners, however. If we get the right instruction, we can learn new habits, and even if we never sound just like the natives, we can certainly reach a stage where we are easily comprehensible and where natives do not have to listen hard to understand us. But this implies that our teacher has worked out what we do and what the speakers of the other language do, and how the two differ, and has used this knowledge to teach us to speak more like those whose language it is.

The same kind of knowledge is needed if we want computers to talk to us in a reasonably natural way. We are probably all familiar with things like telephone banking, where the computer has a number of pre-determined messages which are compiled from tapes of a real speaker speaking a couple of hundred distinct phrases, which may then be strung together by the computer to tell you that your balance is two hundred and thirty-one pounds, ninety pence. But what would we need if we wanted computers to discuss a whole range of topics with us, and not just guide us through making a transfer or checking a balance? At that point it might not be reasonable to record the hundreds of thousands of words that make up 'English', and get the computer to string them together. Even if that solution were used, we would need some knowledge of phonetics to tell the computer what to do when the various chunks are put next to each other. But if we wanted the computer to produce the relevant sound sequences by manipulating some analogue of the human organs, we would have to be able to specify, in great detail, how the sounds are put together. Failure to do this gives rise to the very mechanical voices of computer programmes that can read a written text.

In other words, there are practical applications of being able to analyse the sounds of speech, both for the individual and for someone intending to use this knowledge vocationally. This chapter will introduce the necessary framework to allow you to start doing this for yourself.

There are other reasons for linguists to need to think in phonetic terms, as well. One is that in many languages the spelling masks important aspects of the structure of elements. For example, judging by the spelling alone, we could not guess that *deign*, *lane*, *pain* and *Seine* all rhyme in English. To pick out the commonality we have to think in phonetic terms, and transcription of the words – using symbols which represent sounds directly – is a useful tool in this enterprise. When we transcribe, we find that it is clear that [deɪn], [leɪn], [peɪn] and [seɪn] all rhyme. The relationship between the vowels in *tooth* and *teeth* may or may not be the same as that between *foot* and *feet*, depending on our accent of English, but the spelling hides any difference, just as it hides the fact that the relationships between the vowels in *lead* and *led* is precisely the same as that in *meet* and *met*. So phonetics may help provide insights into other aspects of linguistic structure.

3.2 The organs of speech

Every single one of the organs that are used in the production of speech has another function, usually a biologically more important function. For example, the lungs not only allow speech, they are also used to allow oxygen into the blood stream; the tongue is vital in chewing food; and so on. This state of affairs has led many phoneticians to state the paradox that there are no organs of speech, only organs used for speech. However, comparison with other primates shows that this is not quite true. While chimpanzees have lungs, a larynx, a tongue, teeth and lips they are actually incapable of producing the range of sounds that human beings use quite normally in speech. Despite the series of analogues, the human organs have changed considerably in evolutionary time in ways that allow speech to occur. That is, human beings have in evolutionary terms become adapted as speaking animals. The organs used for speech may not have had that original purpose, but they are now formed in such a way as to allow speech. It is thus as misleading to say that there are no organs of speech as it is to claim that birds do not have organs of flight because their wings are adapted from organs which are not used in that way.

In discussing the organs of speech it is helpful to divide them into three systems, the respiratory system made up of the lungs and the trachea, the phonatory system made up of the larynx, and the articulatory system comprised of the mouth and the organs in it (see Figure 3.1). These systems will be dealt with individually below.

3.2.1 The respiratory system

The LUNGS are elastic spongy organs made up of a large number of tubes which branch again and again until they end in small alveoli where oxygen is passed into the blood and carbon dioxide extracted from it. The major tubes emerging from the lungs are the BRONCHI which merge into the TRACHEA or wind pipe.

The amount of air held in the lungs varies considerably depending on the size of the individual and how deeply that individual is breathing. A very large person breathing extremely deeply may hold as much as 6 litres of air in their lungs, but a more normal amount would be about 3 litres. Of this volume between 1 and 1.5 litres is residual air, which is air which cannot be expelled from the lungs, and which remains there even after death. During normal breathing there is a change of volume of air in the lungs of between 500 and 1000 millilitres of air. This is about the amount of air that is available for speech.

The lungs contain almost no muscles, and the analogy with a sponge is quite accurate. When a sponge is compressed, water is forced out of it, and when it is

Figure 3.1

The organs of speech

Source: Adapted from Bauer *et al*. (1980)

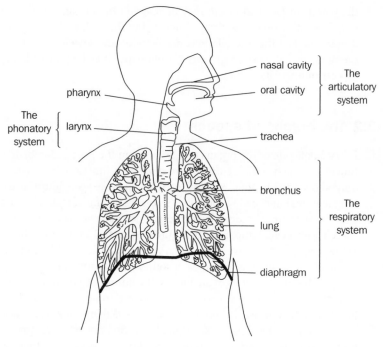

allowed to expand again water from its surroundings is drawn into it. The sponge itself merely holds the water. Similarly, the lungs merely hold the air, which is drawn in and pushed out by the actions of a number of muscles which have the effect of changing the size of the chest cavity. When the chest cavity is enlarged, a partial vacuum is created within it, and so air is sucked in from the surroundings. Then the chest cavity is made smaller, air is forced out of the lungs into the surroundings.

The chest cavity can be enlarged in several ways, the most important of which is by lowering the diaphragm.

The **DIAPHRAGM** is a dome-shaped muscle, which can be imagined as being like an inverted bowl just below the breast-bone. When the diaphragm contracts it pulls downwards, so that it is flatter, and this increases the volume of the chest cavity and so draws air in from the surroundings. As the diaphragm moves downwards it compresses the organs in the abdomen, and this can force the abdomen to bulge outwards. This movement of the abdomen can be felt by placing one's hand on one's abdomen at about waist level.

The diaphragm does actual work only for **INSPIRATION** (breathing in). For **EXPIRATION** (breathing out) the diaphragm merely relaxes, and this is sufficient to force air out of the lungs.

The same is true of the other ways of expanding the chest cavity: work is required only for inspiration, not for expiration.

If a lot of air is needed to say something, then it may be necessary actively to decrease the volume of the chest cavity so as to force more air out of the lungs and through the vocal tract. This can be done, for example, by forcing the diaphragm further up into the chest cavity.

<3.4> So is it true to say that there is no work involved in breathing out?

Finally it must be noted that breathing for speech is not the same as normal quiet breathing. During the latter, inspiration and expiration take approximately equal periods of time, and there are about 12 inspiration-expiration cycles per minute for an adult (but about 43 cycles per minute for a sleeping newborn baby). During speech inspiration is much faster, and expiration lasts up to about nine times as long as inspiration.

<3.5> Why does there need to be such a big difference in the rate of inspiration and expiration in speech?

3.2.2 The phonatory system

The phonatory system is composed of the **LARYNX**, which is also called the voice box or the Adam's apple. Apart from speech, the larynx has non-speech functions. These are:

1. to prevent foreign matter getting into the lungs (or 'going down the wrong way');
2. to eject material which threatens to get into the lungs; and
3. to prevent air escaping from the lungs when a rigid thorax is required, for example, when lifting, pulling, pushing, jumping or defecating.

The larynx is a box of cartilage situated at the top of the trachea. Its cartilageous structure can be seen in Figure 3.2. The top ring of cartilage on the trachea is called the **CRICOID CARTILAGE** ('cricoid' means 'shaped like a signet ring'). Hinged onto that so that it can tilt backwards and forwards is the **THYROID CARTILAGE**, which can be felt in the throat as the knobbly protrusion of the Adam's apple ('thyroid' means 'shaped like a shield'). At the rear of the thyroid cartilage are two small cartilages called the **ARYTENOID CARTILAGES** ('arytenoid' means 'shaped like a ladle'). The arytenoid cartilages are controlled by a complex series of muscles which allow them to move together or apart and to pivot.

The vocal cords or vocal folds are twin muscles which run from the arytenoid cartilages to the thyroid cartilage (see Figure 3.3). In an adult male they are between about 15 mm and 20 mm in length, in an adult female between about 9 mm and 13 mm in length. The term 'vocal cords' is actually misleading since it tends to give the impression that the organs concerned are string like. This is far from the truth. For this reason the term **VOCAL FOLDS** is often preferred. A better analogy might be with the lips. Like the lips, the vocal folds are bands of muscle, though they have relatively hard edges. When they are pulled apart by the arytenoid cartilages, they allow the relatively unimpeded passage of air through the larynx. The word 'relatively' is used here because even when the vocal folds are as wide open as possible, they still leave only about 52% of the cross-section of the trachea free for the passage of air. The vocal folds can be pulled together by the arytenoid cartilages so as to reduce the flow

Figure 3.2

The structure of
the larynx

Source: Adapted from
Thorsen and Thorsen
(1977)

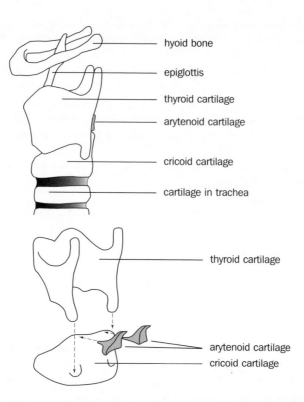

hyoid bone

epiglottis

thyroid cartilage

arytenoid cartilage

cricoid cartilage

cartilage in trachea

thyroid cartilage

arytenoid cartilage
cricoid cartilage

of air from or to the lungs, or to stop it completely. The structure of the larynx as seen from above is shown in Figure 3.3.

The area between the vocal folds is termed the **GLOTTIS**. The glottis is said to be **OPEN** when the vocal folds are apart, or in **VIBRATION** during the production of voice, for instance during the production of a long vowel sound, such as that in *ah!* When the vocal folds are completely closed there is said to be a **GLOTTAL STOP**. A glottal stop is used as a speech sound in many languages of the world including Hawai'ian and Arabic, and can be heard at the beginning and in the middle of the word *uh-oh*, meaning that there is something wrong.

 <3.6> What is the difference between a glottal stop and the onset of a cough?

To produce voice the vocal folds are said to **VIBRATE**. Again the image brought to mind is of a guitar or violin string, and again it is misleading. A better analogy is the way in which the lips vibrate when one says *brrr*, for example when one is feeling cold.

In an adult male the vocal folds tend to vibrate at about 120 times every second or at 120 cps (cycles per second), in the adult female at about 220 cps. Vibrating at this speed they produce a tone, which can be heard when one says *ah*. The vibration can also be felt by placing the fingers lightly on the Adam's apple (thyroid cartilage). Alternatively, one can hear it quite clearly if one puts one's fingers in one's ears and says *ah*. If one says a sound that does not involve voice, for example

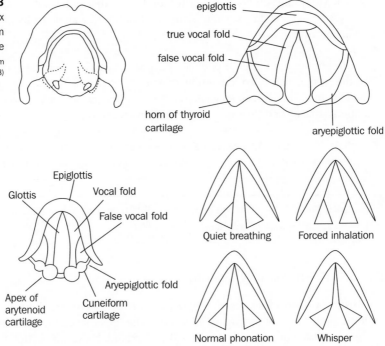

Figure 3.3
The larynx viewed from above

Source: Adapted from Zemlin (1968)

a long hissing sound [sssss], then the glottis is open, and the buzzing tone is absent. The alternation can be felt and heard if one says a long hiss followed by a long buzz, that is, [sssszzzzssss...]. In phonetic terms this brings about a period of voicelessness with the glottis open, followed by a period of voicing with the glottis in vibration.

<3.7> In which of the following sounds can you detect vibration of the vocal folds?
[m] at the beginning of *mother*;
[i:] at the beginning of *eat*;
[v] at the beginning of *very*;
[θ] at the beginning of *thing*;
[l] at the beginning of *leap*.

The precise nature of the mechanism by which the vocal folds produce higher or lower pitch is not fully understood. However, in order to produce higher pitch the following changes may occur:

1. The larynx is raised. This can be felt quite easily with the fingers if they are placed on the Adam's apple while a series of high and low notes are sung.
2. The thyroid cartilage can tilt forwards, thus lengthening the vocal folds and increasing their tension.
3. Extra air can flow through the glottis, causing the vocal folds to vibrate faster.

4. The vocal folds do not necessarily vibrate over their full length. This is equivalent to stopping a guitar or violin string part of the way along its length to provide a higher note.

The important thing for phonetic purposes is that the voice pitch can be changed in the larynx. This is exploited fully in singing, of course, but also in the use of intonation, for example, such as would make the difference between *It's wonderful* spoken enthusiastically and the same phrase spoken sarcastically.

<3.8> Can you detect a difference in larynx height for your pronunciations of the vowels [iː] as in *she* and [ɑː] as in *shah*? Which has the higher larynx? Which has the higher pitch?

<3.9> What is the difference between the [h] at the start of *heart* and the [ɑː] in *art* when the latter word is whispered?

3.2.3 The articulatory system

This section provides a description of the articulatory system. This is done by providing a guided tour of the organs attached to the upper jaw, which we use to name the possible places of articulation. You will understand this section better if you make the sounds referred to and think about the organs you are using.

Starting at the outside, we find the top lip. The adjective relating to lips is *labial*. Accordingly, we will call sounds involving the top lip LABIAL sounds. Sounds like the [p] at the beginning of *pet*, [b] at the beginning of *bet* and [m] at the beginning of *met* are all articulated with the top lip. If you say them, you will discover that they are also articulated with the bottom lip. Correspondingly, these sounds are sometimes referred to as BILABIAL sounds, sounds made with two lips.

Immediately behind the top lip, we find the top teeth, or more accurately, the top incisors. The adjective relating to the teeth is *dental*. If a sound is made by pressing the bottom lip against the top teeth, as in the [f] at the beginning of *fan* or the [v] at the beginning of *van*, we call the sound LABIO-DENTAL (meaning 'articulated with the lip and the teeth'). We use the term DENTAL alone when a sound is articulated with the tongue against the teeth, as in [θ] as at the beginning of *thigh* and [ð] as at the beginning of *thy*.

Immediately behind the front incisors is a hard bony ridge, which you can feel with your tongue or with your finger. This is called the teeth ridge or the ALVEOLAR RIDGE, and sounds articulated using the tongue and the alveolar ridge are called ALVEOLAR sounds. Examples are the [t] at the beginning of *tip*, the [d] at the beginning of *dip* and the [n] at the beginning of *nip*.

Behind the alveolar ridge, there is a steep slope up to the roof of the mouth. Again, this can easily be felt with the tongue or the finger. We call this the post-alveolar area (the area behind the alveolar ridge). Sounds which are articulated with the tongue in this area are called POST-ALVEOLAR sounds. Examples are the [ʧ] at the beginning of *chock* and the [ʤ] at the beginning of *jock*.

Behind the steep slope up, there is a relatively flat area, which still feels hard and bony. This is called the hard palate or just the PALATE, and the corresponding adjective is *palatal*. There is only one PALATAL consonant in English, that is a consonant articulated with the tongue close to the palate, the [j] at the beginning of a word like *yacht*.

Behind the hard palate, the roof of the mouth becomes soft and spongy. You should not try to feel this with your fingers, as this may call forth a gagging reflex, but you can feel it with your tongue. This part of the roof of the mouth is called the soft palate or the VELUM, and the corresponding adjective is *velar*. VELAR sounds, sounds articulated with the tongue against the velum, include the [k] sound at the beginning of *coat* and the [g] sound at the beginning of *goat*.

If you look in a mirror and open your mouth wide, you will see, hanging down at the back of the velum, the UVULA. The adjective corresponding to this is *uvular*. There are no uvular sounds in standard accents of English, but the [ʁ] at the beginning of the French word *rouge* or the German word *rot* (as pronounced with standard French and German accents) is UVULAR, that is, it is pronounced by placing the tongue against the uvula.

Behind the uvula, scarcely visible in the mirror, is the back wall of the throat. The technical name for this part of the vocal tract, between the uvula and the larynx, is the PHARYNX, and the corresponding adjective is *pharyngeal*. Again, English has no pharyngeal sounds, and neither do most of the languages which English speakers are likely to have learnt in school. Maltese, however has a PHARYNGEAL sound in the middle of the word *baħar* 'sea', articulated by drawing the tongue back towards the back wall of the pharynx.

Finally, we come to the larynx, which we have already mentioned in the discussion of voicing. Housed within the larynx are the vocal folds, which produce voicing. They can also, however, be used to articulate some speech sounds themselves. Because the space between the vocal folds is referred to as the GLOTTIS, such sounds are called GLOTTAL sounds. Examples are the [h] at the beginning of *half*, and the glottal stop which is familiar from many British accents of English as a replacement for [t] in words like *bitter*, *better* and *butter*.

<3.10> In the spaces provided in the table, put the labels for the following diagram. Next to each label, list the adjective which is used to refer to the appropriate place of articulation. All this information has been provided in the text above.

Place	Adjective
(1)	
(2)	
(3)	
(4)	
(5)	
(6)	
(7)	
(8)	
(9)	

<3.11> You have not been told the place of articulation of every English sound. See if you can work out the place of articulation of each of the sounds below. It may help to say the sounds on in-drawn breath, because in some cases you will then feel the cold air striking the appropriate place of articulation.

a)   [ʃ], the sound at the beginning of *ship*;
b)   [ŋ], the sound at the end of *sang*;
c)   [s], the sound at the beginning of *sang*;
d)   [ɹ], the sound at the beginning of *rang*.

<3.12> In each of the following sets of sounds, there is one which has a different place of articulation from all the others. All the symbols have been introduced in the text. Find the odd one out in each set of symbols.

a)   ð   d   θ
b)   s   d   n   g
c)   k   ŋ   g   j
d)   ʃ   dʒ   t   ʧ
e)   m   v   b   p
f)   t   s   ʧ   n

Now let us move on to consider the tongue. Unlike the roof of the mouth, the tongue is not neatly divided into anatomical divisions for us, and we have to impose zones on it. This is done by considering what happens to the tongue when it is lying at rest in the mouth. We can define zones of the tongue in terms of which part of the roof of the mouth is above the tongue when it is at rest. The part of the tongue immediately under the alveolar ridge is called the **BLADE** of the tongue, and the adjective used to describe articulations made with the blade of the tongue is **LAMINAL**. The part of the tongue immediately under the hard palate is called (rather infelicitously) the **FRONT** of the tongue. The part of the tongue lying under the velum is called the **BACK** of the tongue. There is no consistent term used to describe articulations using the front of the tongue that does not include other parts, but the adjective **DORSAL** is used to describe articulations made with the back of the tongue. The part of the tongue opposite the pharynx wall is called the **ROOT** of the tongue. Articulations using this part of the tongue may be termed **RADICAL** articulations. We also need to distinguish quite carefully the blade of the tongue from the tip. The **TIP** of the tongue is that part of the tongue which, when the tongue is at rest, lies immediately behind the incisors. If you stick your tongue out, and look at it in the mirror, the tip has a vertical face, while the blade has a horizontal face. Sounds articulated with the tip of the tongue are called **APICAL** sounds.

<3.13> When you say *thin*, do you produce an apico-dental [θ] or a lamino-dental [θ]?

If we wish, we can identify sounds quite precisely as being made, say, between the back of the tongue and the velum or between the blade of the tongue and the alveolar ridge. We would call such sounds dorso-velar and lamino-alveolar respectively. In practice, though, we assume that the part of the tongue used corresponds to the part of the roof of the mouth being named, and we only specify the part of the tongue used when it is out of the ordinary. For instance, many modern Greek speakers have an apico-alveolar [s], while many English speakers have a lamino-alveolar [s] (which we would simply call an alveolar [s]).

<3.14> In the table below, fill in the names for the indicated parts of the tongue in the following diagram, and give the adjective corresponding to each. This information has been given in the text above.

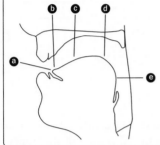

	Part of tongue	Adjective
(a)		
(b)		
(c)		
(d)		
(e)		

<3.15> Describe precisely the place of articulation of the [n] in your pronunciation of the word *tenth*.

Even this degree of detail is not all that could be specified about place of articulation: for example, the velum is quite long, and we could sub-divide it into an arbitrary number of parts. Such distinctions are useful at times, but, for most of the cases we will be interested in, the amount of detail we have now established will be sufficient.

TRIVIA

To speak at a normal rate, you need to send something like 1,400 motor commands to the muscles of your speech organs (the tongue, the larynx, the velum, the lips, etc.) every second. That is more motor commands than a concert pianist would be sending to the playing muscles during a bravura performance. It is scarcely surprising that it takes a lot of practice to pronounce things 'like a native' and that things can go wrong with pronunciation so easily.

3.3 Describing consonants

Most of the time, it will be sufficient for our purposes to give a description of a consonant which contains just three pieces of information: whether the consonant is voiced or voiceless, what the place of articulation of the consonant is, and what the manner of articulation of the consonant is. We shall see later that sometimes some extra information is also necessary, but the simple cases will be dealt with first.

3.3.1 Voicing

We can begin with the question of voicing. We have already dealt with the distinction between sounds like [s] which have no voicing or are **VOICELESS**, and sounds like [z] which have voicing or are **VOICED**. Although there are intermediate possibilities, we do not need to worry about those for the present, and we can make do with this simple distinction between voiced and voiceless.

 <3.16> The sound [ʒ] in the middle of *pleasure* [pleʒə] is voiced. Keep the articulators in the same position, but turn off the voicing. What sound results?

 <3.17> What is the result if you turn the voicing off during the [ɔ:] vowel in the middle of *horse*?

3.3.2 Place

Now we will consider place of articulation. The general rule is that the place of articulation is defined by means of the adjective denoting that part of the upper jaw where the maximum **CONSTRICTION** is made during the articulation of the sound. For example, with an English [t], the blade of the tongue touches the alveolar ridge, and that is the maximum constriction – the vocal tract is completely blocked at that point. Accordingly, [t] is called an alveolar sound. This label tells us about the immobile **PASSIVE ARTICULATOR**. The assumption is that the **ACTIVE ARTICULATOR** in any one of these sounds will be that part of the tongue which lies under the named passive articulator when the tongue is at rest. So the assumption is that an alveolar [t] is made with the blade of the tongue unless otherwise stated. We have already seen that sounds made with both lips are sometimes called 'bilabial' (thus confirming the expected active articulator), and that where we have an unexpected active articulator in sounds like [f], we specify both active and passive articulators, and call these 'labio-dentals'.

 <3.18> What would you expect the passive articulator to be if the active articulator was the front of the tongue? Can you find any English consonant articulated with the front of the tongue? Is your expectation confirmed or not?

There are a few minor complications to this pattern of place of articulation. The first is caused by the retroflex sounds. Retroflex consonants are not common in English, but occur much more frequently in many of the languages of the Indian subcontinent and also in Norwegian and the Australian language Warlpiri. Non-Americans who try to imitate an American *r* usually produce a retroflex sound, though this is not always what Americans do. **RETROFLEX** consonants are produced with the tongue in the post-alveolar region; but unlike [ʃ], which is also produced in the post-alveolar region, retroflex consonants are pronounced with the tongue tip curled up so that the underside of the tongue may be nearest the post-alveolar region.

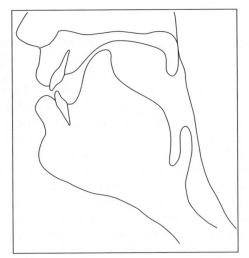

Figure 3.4
The tongue
position in a
strongly
retroflexed [ʂ]

[ʃ] and the other post-alveolar sounds we have discussed so far are produced with the tongue tip pointing downwards, behind the bottom teeth (see Figure 3.4).

The second complication is caused by the fact that some consonants have more than one place of articulation. Such sounds are said to have a **DOUBLE ARTICULATION**. The most familiar example is [w], as at the beginning of the word *win*. If you watch yourself say *win* in a mirror, you will see that your lips are involved in making the sound. What will be less obvious is that the tongue is also involved, and that it moves up towards the velum. If you keep your lips in the correct position for [w] but move your tongue, you can get some very different sounds. Phonetically, the labial articulation and the velar articulation are equally important. In individual languages, one may be more important than the other. Consider what happens in the word *sandwich*. Very few people saying this word fluently actually say a [d], and many do not say an [n] either. Instead, the [n] takes on the place of articulation of the following consonant. This change is a type of **ASSIMILATION**, making sounds more similar so that they are easier to say. The following consonant is [w], so the [n] could take on labial articulation or velar articulation. In fact, both are heard, but not usually in the same dialect. Some people say [sæmwɪtʃ] and others say [sæŋwɪtʃ]. For the first group of people, the labial aspect of the [w] is more important in their variety of language, for the second group of people, the velar aspect of the [w] is more important. Because the [w] remains the same phonetically, we need a label which will capture both of its articulatory features, and we call this sound a **LABIAL-VELAR** sound. The sound [ɥ], which occurs at the beginning of the French word *huit* 'eight' is, in a similar fashion, a **LABIAL-PALATAL** sound. Each of the two places of articulation in a doubly-articulated sound is of equal importance.

<3.19> What are the active and passive articulators for each of the following?
a)   a retroflex [ʈ]
b)   a glottal stop [ʔ]
c)   [w]

3.3.3 Manner

We turn now to consideration of our third way of classifying sounds: manner of articulation.

Let us start with sounds like [p], [b] and [k]. If you say these sounds between
vowel sounds ([æpæ], [æbæ], etc., where [æ] is the vowel sound in the middle of a
word like *cap*) you will discover that to say them you stop the air flowing from the
lungs completely for a brief moment. When you say [æpæ] or [ækæ] there is a brief
period of silence which corresponds to the articulation of the consonant. Consonants
which block the flow of air through the mouth completely in this way and stop it up
are called **STOP** consonants. More specifically, consonants which do this and have a
little explosion on release like [p], [b], [k] are called **PLOSIVES**.

Next consider sounds like [f], [s] and [z]. When you say these sounds between
vowels, the air continues to flow from the lungs all the time. You hear the sounds
because the air is squeezed out between two articulators which are very close
together. As the air flows through the narrow gap, the air flow is made turbulent, and
you hear the friction of the air rubbing on the articulators. These sounds are called
FRICATIVES.

A few sounds have a plosive section immediately followed by a fricative section,
yet they act as though they were a single sound. Such sounds are called **AFFRICATES**. An
example is the [tʃ] at the beginning of the word *cheese*. Most English speakers feel
intuitively that this is a single sound – and it is possible to construct quite an elaborate
argument to support this intuition. Nevertheless, we must recognise two distinct
phases in it phonetically. In affricates the plosive section and the fricative section
always share the same place of articulation, that is they are **HOMORGANIC**. If you think
about what you say when you say [tʃ] you will discover that both the plosive and the
fricative have a post-alveolar place of articulation.

Plosives, fricatives and affricates together form a class of sounds call **OBSTRUENTS**.
All other sounds, the non-obstruents, are **SONORANTS**.

Some sounds are made with a complete blockage of the air flowing from the
lungs, but one which is even briefer than that in a plosive consonant. If there is a
sequence of such blockages in a single sound, we speak of a **TRILL** or a roll (we will
prefer the former term here). An example is the [r] in an Italian word like *rosso*
'red' or a stage Scotsman's pronunciation of *red* (while some real Scotsmen use a
trill in such words, it is by no means universal, and other pronunciations are more
likely to be met). If there is a single, very brief stoppage, we talk of a tap or a flap.
Some, but not all, authorities distinguish between these two labels. For them, a **TAP**
involves a movement of the tongue towards the roof of the mouth and then away
again. An example would be the Maori [ɾ] in a word like *maaori* 'normal', the
Spanish sound in the middle of *pero* 'but', or the colloquial pronunciation of the *tt*
in the middle of *butter* in New Zealand, Australian and American English, a
pronunciation which is sometimes written as *budder* by people who do not have
access to a phonetic alphabet. In all of these cases the tongue moves first in one
direction and then back in the other. A **FLAP**, on the other hand, involves a single
uni-directional movement of the tongue, as in the [ɽ] in Hindi or Urdu [ləɽki]
'girl'.

Sounds like [m] or [n] involve a complete blockage in the mouth of the air flowing from the lungs, but the air keeps flowing through the nose. Such sounds are sometimes called nasal stops, but more usually just NASALS.

Next consider sounds like [j] and [ɹ]. As was true of fricatives, these sounds do not cause a blockage of the air-flow from the lungs. But while, with the fricatives, the air was squeezed between the articulators so that the air-flow became turbulent, with these sounds the articulators are not close enough together to give rise to turbulent air-flow. Such sounds have a variety of names. They are sometimes called frictionless continuants, sometimes semi-vowels, sometimes glides. Here we will prefer the label APPROXIMANTS.

With all the sounds that have been mentioned so far in this section, the air has flowed out from the lungs over the middle of the tongue. If you say [s] or [ɹ] or [k] and breathe in as you say them, you will feel cold air going into the mouth down the centre of the tongue. In contrast, if you say [l] as at the beginning of *light* and breathe in as you say it, you will feel the air going into the mouth over one or both sides of the tongue. Like [ɹ] or [j], [l] does not create a turbulent air-stream, and is an approximant. But unlike [ɹ] or [j], [l] lets the air flow over the sides of the tongue. It is thus a LATERAL approximant, while [ɹ] and [j] are MEDIAN approximants. There are also lateral fricatives, such as [ɬ], the sound at the beginning of the Welsh word *llan* 'church'. Lateral approximants are more common in the world's languages than lateral fricatives, so that if we just say *lateral* we mean 'lateral approximant'.

Some authorities retain the word *consonant* for statements about the use of sounds in individual languages, and use the word CONTOID to denote all those sounds which involve a constriction of the vocal tract greater than that for a vowel. In practice this means that all the sounds we have described here except the median approximants are contoids, while the median approximants (along with all the vowels) are VOCOIDS. While [w], as a median approximant, is a vocoid and not a contoid, in English it functions as a consonant because we say *a witch* and not **an witch*.

There are other types of sound which we could add to these, in particular sounds for which the air does not come from the lungs: sounds which in English are used for imitating horses trotting or for encouraging horses or for making kissing sounds may be consonants in other languages. Symbols for these other types will be found on the chart of the International Phonetic Association's alphabet (reproduced on p. xvii). While such symbols may appear in exercises elsewhere in the book, we will not investigate their articulation any more closely here.

❓ <3.20> Which of the sounds listed in each row below have the manner of articulation given at the start of that row?

a)	plosive	d	l	k	r
b)	nasal	ŋ	ɾ	f	m
c)	trill	r	ɾ	t	v
d)	approximant	j	w	ɹ	v
e)	lateral	l	ɬ	n	f
f)	lateral fricative	l	ɬ	z	ɾ

We are now in a position to give a three-term label for any consonant, and to read the three-term label from the IPA chart. In that chart, each cell contains two columns. Sounds in the first column are voiceless, sounds in the second are voiced. Thus [p], [ʔ] and [ʃ] are voiceless, while [b], [r] and [m] are voiced. Place of articulation can be discovered from the column in which the symbol appears, and manner of articulation from the row in which the symbol appears. So we can see from the IPA chart that [p] is defined as a voiceless bilabial stop, and equally that voiceless bilabial stop uniquely picks out the symbol [p]. Similarly [l] is a voiced alveolar lateral, [ʃ] is a voiceless post-alveolar fricative and [ɬ] is a voiceless alveolar lateral fricative. Note the order of the terms in these three-term labels: voicing + place + manner.

In order to work out phonology problems you will need to be able to assign a three-term label to any symbol from the IPA chart, and assign a symbol to any three-term label. What is more, you will need to be able to do this quickly and accurately. A considerable amount of practice is required to make sure that you can do this. It will also be helpful if you can pronounce the sounds on the IPA chart, although total success in this activity is not a prerequisite for future success in phonology. Use the three-term labels as recipes for building up the sounds. Say them between vowels. Practise saying them in nonsense words.

<3.21> The sounds in each row below share some phonetic feature of voicing, place or manner of articulation. What is it? Is there only one answer?

a)	p	q	g
b)	z	t	l
c)	ɱ	ʋ	f
d)	ʋ	ɹ	j
e)	ɲ	ç	j
f)	q	ɢ	ʁ
g)	ɭ	ʎ	l
h)	r	n	t
i)	j	ʎ	ɻ
j)	d	n	w

<3.22> In each row below, one sound is the odd one out because it does not share a phonetic feature which the others do. Which is the odd one out? What feature do the other sounds share? Is there only one answer?

a)	p	f	ʙ	m
b)	ç	k	ʟ	x
c)	ʀ	ɾ	r	ʐ
d)	l	ɲ	n	z
e)	ʔ	ʕ	ɦ	h
f)	x	ç	ʁ	ɢ
g)	ŋ	d	ç	v
h)	ɖ	q	ʔ	ʕ
i)	ʃ	j	tʃ	dʒ
j)	ɣ	j	ɥ	ɹ

3.4 Describing vowels

When we consider vowels instead of consonants (or, if we wish to use the more precise terminology, vocoids instead of contoids), we find that it is much harder to specify a place of articulation. This is because the tongue does not touch the central part of the roof of the mouth for vowels, and it is hard to classify them in terms of contact. Although the sides of the tongue may touch the molars (side teeth) in slightly different places when we say the [e] in *bet* and the [ʌ] in *butt*, it is very difficult to specify precisely what the difference is. If we watch ourselves in a mirror saying these two vowels, we will see that one of the major differences between the two is that the mouth opens more widely for [ʌ] than for [e]. But it is possible to say both vowels quite distinctly while biting on a pencil, so that the degree of opening of the mouth cannot in itself be distinctive. If, still looking in the mirror, we compare what we can see for the vowel [ɪ] in *bit* and [uː] in *boot*, we can notice a difference in the position of the lips, but specifying what that difference is requires careful observation and a great deal of prose.

A system of vowel description has been developed, associated particularly with the phonetician Daniel Jones, which overcomes all these problems. The quality of a vowel depends basically on two things. The first is the position of the tongue in the mouth, the second is the position of the lips. Let us deal with these two in turn.

HENRY SWEET AND DANIEL JONES

Henry Sweet (1845–1912) and Daniel Jones (1881–1967) were two of the leading British phoneticians of the early twentieth century. Despite undistinguished undergraduate careers, Sweet at Oxford and Jones at Cambridge, they rose to be leaders in their field. Sweet wrote his *Handbook of Phonetics* in 1877, and made phonetics a fashionable science right round Europe. He saw phonetics as 'the indispensible foundation for all study of language'. Despite the recognition of his work, not only in phonetics, but also in descriptive grammar and in the study of the history of English, he never obtained a chair at a University, something which left him feeling bitter. One of his pupils was Jones, who was also a student of the French phonetician Paul Passy. Jones became Professor of Phonetics at the University of London in 1921. He was one of the people involved in setting up the International Phonetic Association and was its president from 1950–1967. He was the person who introduced the term *phoneme* in more or less its current sense (taking into account that there are several slightly different theoretical accounts of the phoneme; see section 4.2). George Bernard Shaw knew both men, and drew upon their expertise (if not their characters) in writing his play *Pygmalion* (which was later made into a musical under the title *My Fair Lady*). Shaw wanted his play to make 'the public aware that there are such people as phoneticians' and how important they are.

3.4.1 The position of the tongue

The major determinant of a vowel's quality is the position in the mouth at which the narrowest constriction between the tongue and the roof of the mouth is situated. This narrowest constriction can be as far forward in the mouth as the hard palate. If it is here, the constriction is between the front of the tongue and the hard palate, and we speak of a **FRONT** vowel. If the narrowest constriction is between the back of the tongue and the velum, we speak of a **BACK** vowel. Since the narrowest constriction can be at any point between the front of the palate and the back of the velum, there is a mid point at the juncture of the hard and soft palates where we talk of a **CENTRAL** vowel. The theory is that the tongue cannot produce a vowel with its highest point in areas further forward than the hard palate or further back than the velum; if the tongue makes a constriction in these areas, it is a consonantal constriction. We will see in section 3.8 that more recent observations suggest that this position needs to be modified.

If the constriction is made slightly wider, different vowel sounds appear. To make the constriction wider, we normally lower the jaw, but a lowering of the tongue is all that is required, which is why we can change the width of the constriction with a pencil clamped between our teeth. There is an infinite number of possible vowels between the one produced with the narrowest possible constriction and the one produced with mouth as wide open (or the tongue as low in the mouth) as possible. To simplify matters, we set up just seven approximately equal steps along this continuum. If the tongue is as close to the roof of the mouth as possible without causing friction, we say that the vowel produced is a **CLOSE** vowel. At the other end of the scale, with the mouth as wide open as possible, we have an **OPEN** vowel. Between these extreme steps we distinguish between **NEAR-CLOSE**, **CLOSE-MID**, **MID**, **OPEN-MID** and **NEAR-OPEN** steps.

CONTROVERSY: Degrees of height

While the International Phonetic Association uses seven steps to indicate vowel height, and labels them as indicated above, some scholars use only four of these labels (close, close-mid, open-mid and open), and other scholars, brought up in a different tradition, use just three labels for vowel height: high, mid and low (occasionally with high-mid and low-mid as extra steps). Clearly these labels cannot match precisely, but the controversy is only about the terminology, not about the facts concerning vowel height.

By specifying one of these degrees of frontness or backness, and one of these steps of height, we can specify the major determinants of a vowel's position. While it would be possible to do this in a simple matrix like that below (Figure 3.5), it is usually done (for reasons which will be explained soon) in terms of a diagram of notional vowel space, as in Figure 3.6.

Figure 3.5
A matrix for vowels

	Front	Central	Back	
close				High
near-close				High
close-mid				Mid
mid				Mid
open-mid				Mid
near-open				Low
open				Low

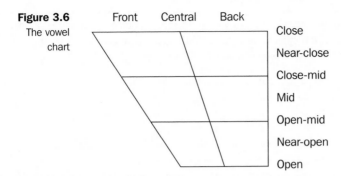

Figure 3.6
The vowel chart

3.4.2 Lip-position

This leaves us with differences of lip-position to account for. Although lip-position, like frontness and backness, varies along a continuum, there are generalisations that can be made. Extreme lip positions occur only with close vowels. These can be pronounced with the lips very spread, in a smile, or with the lips very rounded in a pout. If we try to make these extreme lip positions with the mouth wide open, we discover that it is very difficult. Although it is possible to make differences between open vowels with spread lips and open vowels with rounded lips, the degree of spreading and rounding is not as marked as with close vowels. Generally speaking, the closer the vowel the more extreme the lip-positions that are possible, the opener the vowel, the less extreme the lip-positions that are possible. We can thus leave the precise degree of spreading or rounding to be accounted for by the closeness or openness of the vowel, and simplify this parameter by saying that vowels are either **ROUNDED** or **SPREAD** (sometimes the word 'unrounded' is used in the same meaning, while other authorities have a three-way distinction here).

3.4.3 Putting it together

With these three parameters (spread/rounded, close-open and front/central/back) we can label any vowel sound. The International Phonetic Association provides the symbols below for these vowels (see also the IPA chart). The symbol for the spread vowel appears in the left of each cell in the matrix, the symbol for the rounded vowel on the right. Some cells do not have vowel symbols assigned to them by the IPA.

Figure 3.7
The vowel matrix with symbols

	Front		Central		Back	
close	i	y	ɨ	ʉ	ɯ	u
near-close	ɪ	ʏ				ʊ
close-mid	e	ø	ɘ	ɵ	ɤ	o
mid			ə			
open-mid	ɛ	œ	ɜ	ɞ	ʌ	ɔ
near-open	æ		ɐ			
open	a	ɶ			ɑ	ɒ

<3.23> In each of the following sets of vowels, there is an odd one out, in that it does not share a feature all the other vowels share. Which is the odd sound out? What do the other vowels share? Is there only one answer?

a)	i	Œ	ø	ɯ
b)	ø	ɔ	ʏ	ɜ
c)	a	Œ	ɒ	æ
d)	ə	e	ɘ	æ
e)	ʉ	ɯ	ø	œ

In any particular language, of course, these precise vowels may not occur. But to label a vowel of a particular language phonetically, we use the symbol which is closest to its position on the chart. Vowel sounds can be made corresponding to any position within the chart. This is why we use the chart rather than a simple matrix.

So far we have only described vowels in which the tongue and the lip positions remain constant throughout the articulation. Such vowels are called MONOPHTHONGS. There are also vowels during which the position of the tongue and/or the lips changes in the course of a single syllable (or beat; syllables are discussed further in section 4.5.1), and these are called DIPHTHONGS. Diphthongs can be described in terms of the vowel position from which they start, and the approximate vowel position at which they end. For example, the vowel in the word *boil* starts in approximately the same position as the vowel in *ball*, but changes so that it ends up near the position for the vowel in *bill*. We can thus transcribe diphthongs as being made up of a sequence of two vowels within the same syllable, so that we can transcribe the vowel in *noise* as [ɔɪ].

3.5 Secondary articulations

The three-term labels for consonants explained above describe the PRIMARY ARTICULATION of the consonants. Consonants may also have a SECONDARY ARTICULATION whose description is important. Consider the primary articulation of the [d] at the beginning of *do*. This is a voiced alveolar stop. This description tells us what is happening to the blade of the tongue, and we can assume that because the blade has moved the tip has too. But it does not tell us what is happening to the tongue behind that alveolar articulation. Consider the figures below (see Figure 3.8), where two rather different alternatives are presented.

Figure 3.8
Secondary articulations behind an alveolar contact

 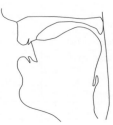

In the first of these figures, the tongue is shown to be raised towards the hard palate, in the second the back of the tongue is raised towards the velum. In neither case is the tongue raised sufficiently to cause friction. In the first case, the tongue is raised as though the vowel [ɪ] were being pronounced at the same time as the consonant, in the second case, it is as though [ʊ] were being simultaneously pronounced. When a consonant is pronounced with a secondary articulation in which the front of the tongue approaches the hard palate, the consonant is said to be PALATALISED. If the back of the tongue approaches the velum, the consonant is said to be VELARISED. These are two of the most important secondary articulations we shall deal with, but many others are possible.

If the lips are rounded during the pronunciation of a consonant we speak of LABIALISATION; if the tongue approaches the back wall of the pharynx, we speak of PHARYNGEALISATION, and if a glottal stop is pronounced simultaneously with the consonant (or even if the glottis is almost closed throughout the utterance of a sound) we speak of GLOTTALISATION (sometimes 'laryngealisation'). Each of these secondary articulations is written down with an appropriate symbol superscripted after the symbol for the primary articulation of the consonant. If air escapes through the nose during the articulation of a non-nasal sound, that sound is said to be nasalised, and a tilde [~] is written over the appropriate symbol to indicate this. Using [z] as the primary articulation, we thus write:

(1) labialised z^w palatalised z^j velarised $z^ɣ$ pharyngealised $z^ʕ$
    glottalised $z^ʔ$ nasalised $z̃$

Note two things about these diacritics. First, note that the diacritic for velarised is a superscripted gamma. Second, note that although we described palatalisation in terms of the adding of an [ɪ] sound, it is transcribed as the adding of a [j] articulation: the two are very similar: if you try to prolong a [j] sound, it will turn into a vowel in the [ɪ] or [i] region. While other secondary articulations would be possible (alveolarised, uvularised and so on) they follow the same basic pattern as the secondary articulations we have seen.

<3.24> Watch yourself closely in a mirror and say the following words: *pip*, *sip*, *tip*, *ship*, *chip*, *kip*, *lip*, *rip*, *hip*. Are any of the initial consonants in these words labialised in the kind of English you speak? If so, which ones, and how would you write them to show this?

Many Slavic languages distinguish between palatalised and velarised consonants. Consider, for instance, the following pairs from Russian:

Data-set 3.1
Russian

pol^jkə	'Polishwoman'
pol^ɣkə	'shelf'
os^j	'axle'
os^ɣ	'of the wasps'
s^jadu	'I shall sit'
s^ɣadu	'garden (dative sg)'

In many varieties of English the two [l]s in a word like *lull* or *little* are phonetically different, the first one being palatalised, the second velarised. These are sometimes referred to as 'clear' and 'dark' [l] respectively. If we wanted to provide more detail in our transcription, we could write *lull* as [lʲʌlˠ], providing what is technically called a '**NARROWER**' transcription. To find out if you make this distinction in your English, say the word *lull* very slowly, stretching out the two [l] sounds. Do they both sound just the same or not? You may not even make an [l] sound, a voiced alveolar lateral, at the end of *lull*, in which case the description given above does not apply to your English.

3.6 Suprasegmentals

3.6.1 Stress

STRESS is what makes the difference between pairs of words such as *insight* and *incite*. The two words contain the same sequence of consonants and vowels, but in *insight* the stress is on the first syllable, and in *incite* the stress is on the second syllable. Marking this distinction according to the conventions of the IPA with a raised stroke immediately before the stressed syllable, we can write *insight* as ['ɪnsaɪt] and *incite* as [ɪn'saɪt]. This distinction is one made in terms of **PRIMARY STRESS**.

<3.25> Mark the primary stress on each of the following words:

a) refer; reference; referee
b) imply; implicate; implication
c) character; characterise; characteristic
d) popular; populous; popularity
e) durable; duration; durability

In some of these longer words, although there is only one place where the primary stress can fall, you may well feel that there is an extra beat, another stress which is not quite so important. This is called the **SECONDARY STRESS**. If you say one of these words as the last word in a sentence, you will discover that the primary stressed syllable remains consistently more prominent than the secondary stressed syllable. If we need to mark secondary stress, we can do so with a lowered stroke, for instance in ˌanti'sep-tic or ˌcolara'tura or 'porcuˌpine. In some varieties of English, there is a vowel which can never appear in a syllable which has primary or secondary stress. This vowel is [ə], called 'schwa', and in these varieties its presence indicates an absence of stress. There is some controversy about the number of levels of stress required to describe English, or even the number of levels that a hearer can consistently distinguish.

<3.26> Mark primary and secondary stress as appropriate on the following words:

a) interpolar; interpolate; interrupt
b) prerogative; preservation; premature
c) universe; university; universal joint
d) subjugate; subcontract (*noun*); sublime
e) disappoint; dishonour; discharge (*noun*)

3.6.2 Tone

In many languages, the variation of pitch in a syllable, or between one syllable and the next, is distinctive and can be used to differentiate words. Such languages are called TONE LANGUAGES, and the various pitch patterns are called TONES. For example, in Igbo, a Nigerian language, the relative pitch of syllables is important.

Data-set 3.2 Igbo			
high-high	ákwá	'crying'
high-low	ákwà	'cloth'
low-high	àkwá	'egg'
low-low	àkwà	'bed'

In a language like Igbo it would be as silly to say [àkwà] when you meant [àkwá] as it would be to say *living* when you meant *loving* in English.

Some tone languages, and Igbo is an example, are best analysed as having a small number of level tones, that is, tones with an invariant pitch. Any phonetic pitch rises or pitch falls that occur in these languages can be attributed to sequences of high and low tones affecting the same syllable. Typically, also, it is the case that such languages have only a small number of different tones. As we saw in the Igbo examples, high tones are usually transcribed by an acute accent over the vowel of the syllable which has high tone, and low tones are transcribed with a grave accent. If a language also has a mid tone, that is usually left unmarked. If the symbol [á] means [a] with a high tone, and [à] means [a] with a low tone, rising tone can be seen as a sequence of low and high, transcribed [ǎ], and falling tone as a sequence of high and low tone, transcribed [â]. In a few cases more complex transcriptions are required, and they follow the same principles.

Other languages have to be analysed as having some moving tones. They may have contrasting falling or rising tones starting from different heights, or contrasts between high level and high rising tones, for example. An example of a language of this type is Cantonese, where six tones can be distinguished (depending on the analysis and the variety). Since accents over the vowel symbols would be too difficult to distinguish, such languages are frequently transcribed with tone letters preceding the syllable, as shown below for Cantonese.

Data-set 3.3 Cantonese			
high, level	˥si:	'silk'
mid, level	˧si:	'to try'
low-mid, level	˨si:	'matter'
low-mid to low, falling	˩si:	'time'
low-mid to high, rising	˦si:	'history'
low-mid to mid, rising	˨si:	'city'

Sometimes tones are described in terms of numbers rather than in terms of tone letters. For example, the Cantonese word meaning 'silk' might be transcribed as [55si:], and the word meaning 'time' as [21si:]. Here, there are five levels of pitch, with '5' marking the highest and '1' marking the lowest. In a language like Cantonese, two numbers are all that is required to show the relevant level and direction of the tone.

<3.27> Which of the following words of Thai contains the highest pitch?

(a)	[21na:]	a nickname
(b)	[32na:]	'field'
(c)	[45na:]	'aunt'
(d)	[24na:]	'thick'

3.6.3 Duration

Some sounds last longer than others. If you were telling someone to be quiet, you would very probably use a longer [ʃ] sound than you would use at the beginning of the word *ship* in a normal sentence. Much of the time, the precise length of the sounds will not be of any great importance. But in some cases it is important to be able to distinguish at least two distinct lengths of sounds. Consider the difference, for instance, between *some others* and *some mothers*. One of the differences is how long the closure for the [m] lasts. We could transcribe this as [sʌm ʌðəz] and [sʌm mʌðəz] just using a double letter for the longer sound, or we could write it as [sʌmʌðəz] and [sʌm:ʌðəz], using the [:] length mark to show the lengthened articulation of the sound. To people who know English, the two are equivalent transcriptions, but that is not necessarily true in other languages. In many languages, such as Finnish, for example, both vowel length and consonant length can be important for meaning. Finnish [kukɑ] means 'who', but [kuk:ɑ] means 'flower' and [uni] means 'sleep' while [u:ni] means 'oven'. The words with long sounds can be transcribed with the length mark (as above) or with **GEMINATE** consonants and vowels as [kukkɑ] and [uuni] (which is the way they are written in normal Finnish spelling). In cases where a sequence of two identical vowels could indicate a sequence of two syllables, the length mark would have to be used to show a long vowel. Thus the Latin distinction between *suus* 'his' [suus] (in two syllables) and *gradūs* 'steps' [gradu:s] would require the use of the length mark rather than a double vowel notation.

<3.28> If you are told that the Even word for *houses* is [dʲuul], can you determine how many syllables the word has?

<3.29> In Italian, the [k] sound in the middle of *ecco* 'here is' [ɛk:o] is not quite twice as long as the [k] sound in the middle of *eco* 'echo' [ɛko]. Does this mean that we cannot transcribe *ecco* with a geminate velar plosive?

3.6.4 Intonation

Intonation is the melody of a language. Every language, whether a language with tones or not, has intonation. While tone operates over individual syllables, intonation operates over longer stretches of language. Imagine someone asks you, *Did you put the car in the garage?* You might answer, *Of course I did.* But there are several ways you might say that: You might be bored, because you've been asked that question every day for the past two years, and you think that people should have realised by now that you do that automatically. You might be indignant, thinking you've been challenged about something when you know you're in the right. You might answer as if it is self-evident that you did this, and any idiot should know it. In each of these cases you would use a different intonation, perhaps as indicated in (2) below.

(2) (a)

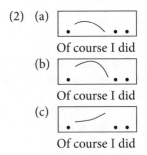

Of course I did

(b)

Of course I did

(c)

Of course I did

The transcription given in (2) has no theoretical status; it simply provides a pre-theoretical way of indicating relative pitch. It uses dots for relatively unstressed syllables and dashes for relatively stressed syllables. Where the stressed syllable also coincides with a change in pitch it is indicated in the transcription. A syllable on which this happens is called the intonational **NUCLEUS**, or the **NUCLEAR SYLLABLE**.

The expected pattern is that the nuclear syllable will fall on the last stressed syllable in the intonational phrase. Putting the nuclear syllable anywhere else gives a reading with some kind of implied contrast. So if we mark the nuclear syllable with underlining, we get the following pattern:

Data-set 3.4
The position of the nuclear syllable in English

	Implication
I saw my aunt last <u>night</u>.	No special implication
I saw my aunt <u>last</u> night.	You seem to be implying it was tonight, but it wasn't.
I saw my <u>aunt</u> last night.	Not my uncle.
I saw <u>my</u> aunt last night.	Not your aunt or anyone else's.
I <u>saw</u> my aunt last night.	That doesn't mean I spoke to her.
<u>I</u> saw my aunt last night.	I don't care whether you did or not.

Where the nuclear syllable falls in an intonational phrase is a matter of **TONICITY**. The different patterns in Data-set 3.4 show different patterns of tonicity in the same intonational phrase.

Sometimes, the nucleus is not on the last stressed syllable of the phrase. When this happens it is usually because the last stressed syllable is in a word which the listener already knows about in context (see section 7.6.3 on given information). So in a sentence like (3), the nucleus is more likely to fall on *Italian* than on the second occurrence of *films*, because *films* is already in the environment.

(3) I enjoy films, and I particularly like Italian films.

Similarly, pronouns rarely make up the nuclear syllable, because by definition a pronoun refers to something we already know about. Consider the examples in (4), where again the nucleus is likely to fall on *Italian* and on *like* rather than on *ones* and *them*.

(4) (a) I like fast cars, and I particularly like Italian ones.
    (b) I know a lot about cars, but I don't particularly like them.

It is also possible to split a given utterance up into more or fewer intonational phrases. This is a matter of **TONALITY**. If we look away from false starts and other disfluencies, a rough approximation to the expected pattern of tonality is for there to be one intonational phrase for every grammatical clause (see section 6.5 on clauses). But if you are very excited, or if you are trying to make a point very forcibly in debate, or even if the clauses are just long, you may use more intonational phrases than that. Consider (5), where you could, under appropriate circumstances, put the nuclear syllables in just one place or in several, as shown.

(5) (a) I hope that a lot of people will come to <u>see</u> the play.
    (b) I <u>hope</u> that a lot of people will come to <u>see</u> the play.
    (c) I <u>hope</u> that a <u>lot</u> of people will come to <u>see</u> the play.
    (d) I <u>hope</u> that a lot of people <u>will</u> come to <u>see</u> the play.

<3.30> Why is *play* not the nuclear syllable in the sentence in (5)?

<3.31> Give situations in which someone might say (5c) rather than (5d) and vice versa.

From what has been said so far, it might seem that intonation is mostly about the attitude that the speaker has to what is being said. It is certainly true that this is an important function of intonation, but not the only one. Intonation also carries out grammatical functions, as is indicated by the examples in (6).

(6) (a) i. The New <u>Zealanders</u>, who are <u>industrious</u>, sell a lot of <u>lamb</u>.
        ii. The New Zealanders who are <u>industrious</u> sell a lot of <u>lamb</u>.
    (b) i. She wore nothing to show her <u>status</u>.
        ii. She wore <u>nothing</u> to show her <u>status</u>.
    (c) i. She had plans to <u>leave</u>.
        ii. She had <u>plans</u> to leave.
    (d) i. The Prime Minister said he really <u>liked</u> students and then the Minister of Education made a <u>joke</u>.
        ii. The Prime Minister said he really <u>liked</u> students and then the Minister of <u>Education</u> made a joke.

In (6ai) all New Zealanders are industrious and sell a lot of lamb, while in (6aii) only those who are industrious sell the lamb. In (6bi) she did not wear a sash or a badge of office, while in (6bii) she was naked. In (6ci) she was planning to depart, while in (6cii) she was depositing architectural drawings. In (6di) what the Prime Minister said has nothing to do with the joke, while in (6dii) that the Prime Minister really liked students is the first joke of two. In examples like these, intonation gives the listener clues to the grammatical (and semantic) structure of the sentences. Intonation can do a lot more than express the speaker's feelings about what is being said.

In some languages, the difference between statements and questions can be carried by intonation alone. Italian is such a language. In Italian (7a) is a statement, and (7b) is a question, and the difference is shown by the question mark in writing, but by intonation in speech, with rising intonation on (7b). While similar phenomena can be observed in English, they are less frequent.

(7) (a) È finito.
         is finished
         'It is finished.'
     (b) È finito?
         is finished
         'Is it finished?'

Since questions are incomplete, in that they require an answer, while a statement is presented as something complete, it is sometimes said that a fall indicates completeness and a rise incompleteness in any language. Thus, in French, for example, intonation phrases which do not end sentences are generally said to rise, while those that finish sentences (those that are statements at least) fall, as in (8).

(8) (a)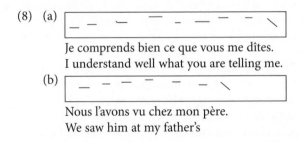

Je comprends bien ce que vous me dîtes.
I understand well what you are telling me.

     (b)

Nous l'avons vu chez mon père.
We saw him at my father's

While there is sufficient truth in this to form a very rough starting position, there are innumerable cases where it does not hold. These include questions starting with the words *where, when, who, what, why, how* in English (often called **WH-QUESTIONS**) which, despite the fact that they are questions and require an answer, are frequently said on falling intonation patterns, as in (9).

(9)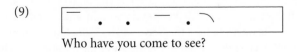

Who have you come to see?

<3.32> With a partner (or in your mind) play out a question and answer session between a lawyer in a courtroom and a witness, in which the lawyer wants to establish for the record the identity of the witness and why the witness is there. What kind of intonation is used on questions? How are questions marked?

3.7 Acoustics (Advanced)

3.7.1 Sound waves

Sounds travel in waves. If you drop a pebble in a puddle, the water waves travel outwards from the point of impact. Those waves are caused by the compression of the water at the point of impact by the pebble. The water is compressed as the pebble moves molecules of water sideways, and then rarefied, as the water moves back to its original position. A cork placed on the surface of the puddle will move up and down as the wave passes under it, but will not move outwards: the pattern of compression and rarefaction moves outwards, but the individual molecules of water stay basically in the same position.

The same is true for sound waves, though they move outwards from the source of the disturbance in three dimensions. They correspond to patterns of compression and rarefaction of the air at the source. That source can be anything that starts the air moving in a suitable way: vibration of the vocal folds, or pushing air through a narrow gap when we are dealing with speech sounds, a pin dropping or a bomb exploding when it comes to non-speech sounds.

There are two fundamentally different kinds of sounds: tones and noise. A TONE is a sound made by a periodic wave – a sound wave with a regular structure. NOISE has no such regular structure. A stereotypical example of a tone is the sound made by a tuning fork. A tuning fork is manufactured so as to always provide the same tone. It does this because the tines of the fork always vibrate at the same speed. That speed is counted in cycles per second (cps) or Hertz (Hz) (the two mean the same thing). For example, the sound that makes the A that an oboe produces at the beginning of a symphony concert vibrates 440 times each second, so its frequency is 440Hz or 440cps. If a pencil lead were attached to one of the tines of such a tuning fork, and it was dragged along a sheet of paper while vibrating, the pencil lead would produce a trace like that in Figure 3.9. If Figure 3.9 were extended to show the vibrations from a whole second, there would be 440 cycles (like the difference between A and B or C and D in the figure) in that one second. The distance the trace of the wave is from the base-line is referred to as the AMPLITUDE of the wave. In simple terms, greater amplitude leads to greater perceived loudness (though loudness is also affected by other factors, so that INTENSITY, which makes reference to these other factors is a better measure of loudness than amplitude alone). The distance between comparable points on adjacent cycles of the wave is called the WAVELENGTH of the wave. If this wave recurs 440 times every second, and sound travels at 340m per second in air, then the wavelength of this wave will be 340/440m or approximately 0.77m. The longer the wavelength of a sound (or the lower the number of cycles per second in the tone) the lower the perceived pitch will be. A wave with a frequency of 880Hz will be an A but an octave higher than the A at 440Hz.

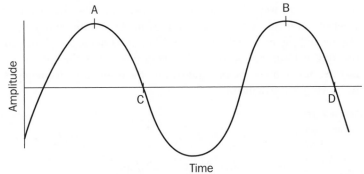

Figure 3.9
A sine wave

The wave illustrated in Figure 3.9 shows the simplest form of tone. This is called a **SINE WAVE**, or a simple tone. Speech sounds such as vowel sounds are much more complex tones, made up of a number of different sine waves superimposed on each other to make **COMPLEX WAVES**.

The wave form in Figure 3.9 is clearly periodic: it repeats the same pattern again and again on a regular basis. Noise has no such periodicity, but is aperiodic. Noise is characterised by a lot of sounds at different frequencies in an unpatterned structure. In speech, the sounds connected with fricatives such as [f] or [s] are made up of noise. Non-speech sounds with similar characteristics are fat spitting in a frying pan or rain falling.

3.7.2 Resonance

It is quite difficult to hear the sound made by a tuning fork if it is just held in the air. If you want to hear the note made by a tuning fork, you can hold it close to your ear, or you can put the base of the fork on, for example, a table, and the sound will be amplified. You can put any tuning fork on a table, and it will amplify the sound, because the table is not particularly fussy about what notes it amplifies. But other things amplify quite specific sounds.

You will be familiar with the idea of a bottle partly filled with water making different notes depending on how much water there is in the bottle. As the bottle is filled with water, the column of air at the top of the bottle gets smaller, and it responds to a higher note. The air in the bottle **RESONATES** at a higher frequency the smaller the body of air becomes. The sound the bottle makes when it is hit is at the frequency at which the body of air in the bottle resonates.

The cliché of a soprano breaking a wine glass by singing the appropriate note is another illustration of the same principle. The wine glass resonates at a very specific pitch: if the soprano hits that note, the wine glass vibrates at that pitch, and amplifies the note, to the extent that the vibrations can shatter the glass. The glass amplifies only the small range of frequencies at which it resonates, and ignores other frequencies. Our voices, produced by our vocal folds, produce quite a broad range of frequencies, and the glass responds to a particular sound in that range.

While we have neither bottles filled with water nor wine glasses in our articulatory mechanisms, the vocal tract does provide two linked tubes, which function in much the same way. The first of these is made up of the pharynx up as far as the point where the tongue is closest to the roof of the mouth, and second is between the tongue and the lips. Each of these tubes can be made longer or shorter (by moving the tongue, lowering/raising the larynx or protruding the lips, for example), and also broader or narrower. We can thus control the resonating frequency of these two tubes by moving our articulators.

Figure 3.10
Vocal tract
as dual
resonator

Tube 2

Tube 1

Position of
vocal folds

3.7.3 The spectrogram

One of the main tools of the acoustic phonetician is the SPECTROGRAM. This is a display from a machine which analyses sounds into their component parts. The display on the spectrogram shows the intensity of the sound present at different frequencies in time. Although the original spectrograms were obtained by passing an electrical charge through specially treated paper, these days everything is done much more quickly and cleanly by a computer. You can download a program called Praat from www.praat.org and carry out your own acoustic analysis of speech on your own computer. A spectrogram produced by this program is presented in Figure 3.11.

Figure 3.11
A spectrogram

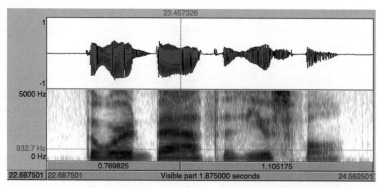

The top part of the figure presents the wave form from an utterance. In this case, the utterance is a young American woman saying 'The word *bath* is useful'. The bottom part of the figure is the spectrogram. You can see the frequency of the sound present at each point marked on the scale at the left-hand margin: the spectrogram shows frequencies from 0Hz to 5000Hz. On the other axis, you can see how the energy present at different frequencies changes as she says the different words, and you can see the computer giving the number of seconds since the beginning of the utterance. If you look a bit to the left of the vertical grey line (which is simply a marker) you will see a white vertical stripe. This corresponds to the /b/ at the beginning of *bath*. There is virtually no acoustic energy present here.

<3.33> Why is there so little acoustic energy present at this point?

Near the end of the spectrogram in Figure 3.11, you will see a black patch at the top of the picture. This is noise (in the technical sense used above), and its frequency shows that it corresponds to an alveolar fricative rather than to any other fricative of English, so this is the /s/ in *useful*. You can see that the noise for the adjacent /f/ is far less strong than the noise for the /s/.

TRIVIA

Spectrograms are sometimes called Voice Prints, the idea being that they are like fingerprints and allow individuals to be recognised by the acoustic patterns produced by the resonant system of their vocal tracts. If this were true, we would be able to identify people by the way they speak in the same way that we can identify people by, say, a retinal scan. However, it is well-known that security systems that try to work from spectrographic evidence give many false results: perhaps because the speaker has a cold, is chewing, is slightly hoarse, speaks more loudly than usual, and so on. There is little evidence to support the notion that a voice print is really accurate, though it may be sufficient to be sure that two utterances are not from the same speaker.

Note the horizontal bands of energy at various points throughout the utterance. These are called **FORMANTS**, and they are numbered from the bottom up, Formant 1, Formant 2, Formant 3, and so on (often abbreviated as F1, F2, F3, etc.). The **FUNDAMENTAL FREQUENCY** (often labelled F0), is the frequency at which the vocal folds vibrate, and that can be seen as a bar along the base-line on the spectrogram, because the scale is not enough to let us pick the small variations in that frequency. The grey lines cross in the middle of the vowel in *bath*, and the grey figures on the left-hand side of the spectrogram show the frequency of the formant (F1) at that point.

The values of F1 and F2 correspond to the frequencies with which the tubes in the vocal tract resonate. The values of F1 and F2 are sufficient to allow us to identify the vowel concerned. Below you can find some average figures for F1 and F2 for some of the vowels of New Zealand English, spoken by young males. Even a cursory glance at the figures shows that the different vowels have different acoustic make-up.

Data-set 3.5
Formant values in Hz of some New Zealand English vowels

Vowel	F1	F2
i	315	2336
æ	536	1890
ɒ	630	999
ɔː	382	955
uː	434	1369

Value of Formant 1 in Herz ------>

		300	350	400	450	500	550	600	650
<------ Value of Formant 2 in Herz	900								
	1000								
	1100								
	1200								
	1300								
	1400								
	1500								
	1600								
	1700								
	1800								
	1900								
	2000								
	2100								
	2200								
	2300								

Figure 3.12
A grid for plotting vowel qualities from formant frequencies

The values given in Table 3.5 are for New Zealand English and do not match those for British or American English – this is part of what lets us hear the differences between varieties of English. The symbols used, though, are those for English RP, the standard accent of English in England. Correspondingly, the values for the vowels may not always match the value expected from the symbol. To turn these values into something more familiar, we can plot the values for the vowels on a graph, such as the one in Figure 3.12.

The position for /uː/ will probably be rather surprising, but you should be able to see that this corresponds relatively well to the kind of description that we gave in terms of the vowel chart earlier in the chapter (see Figure 3.5). That is, we can use the acoustic structure of vowels as a proxy for the articulatory/auditory analysis that was provided earlier.

<3.34> Why is the position for /uː/ on this graph surprising?

<3.35> Given the figures provided above, what can you deduce about the vowel /æ/ as pronounced with an American accent as opposed to when it is pronounced with a New Zealand accent? Remember that the American speaker will have the vowel /æ/ in the word *bath*.

3.8 The sounds of languages (Advanced)

Why does any particular language have the sounds that it does? Clearly, a large part of the reason that English, say, has /p/ is that there was such a sound in Old English and in Common Germanic. Modern English simply inherits the sound. Yet there are some things which do not seem to occur in natural languages. We do not seem to find a language which has only three vowels and they are /u/, /o/ and /ɯ/, for instance. We could say that this is because no language has ever inherited just this set of vowels, but there seems to be some more fundamental principle underlying this failure: possibly a principle which determines what possible systems can arise, at least within certain limits.

In exploring these matters, this section is avowedly speculative. At the same time, by thinking about such matters, we think not only about the nature of the sounds of languages, but also about the notion of a possible language.

To discuss such matters, though, we need to think what it might mean for language L to 'have' sound S. As a concrete example, take the much cited statement that any language which has a fricative consonant has an [s]. As it stands, this is just plain wrong. There are several languages which have no [s], including Maori and Tiwi. Maori has a glottal fricative [h] and another fricative which in the variety of Maori used in second-language teaching today is [f], but which historically was probably [ʍ] or [ɸ] (with some dialectal variation). When English words containing English [s] were borrowed into Maori, they were generally represented as [h], as in *Hātarei* 'Saturday' and *hiraka* 'silk'. The value of this example is that it suggests that there are limits to what might count as [s]: [f] and [h] are outside the limit. On the other hand, there is quite a wide variety of sounds that falls within the limit. Castilian Spanish is described as having an apical alveolar [s] sound. About half of English speakers apparently have an apical alveolar [s], while the others have a laminal alveolar [s]. Yet the Spanish [s] sounds different from all English [s] sounds, probably because the tongue is more hollowed behind the tongue tip. French is variously described as having a laminal alveolar and a laminal dental [s]. Modern Greek is said to have a much deeper pitched [s] sound, more [ʃ]-like in quality from some speakers. The moral is that the rough and ready descriptions of the sounds of a language gained from many elementary works may easily be misleading, and may mask a great deal of variation. We must be on our guard, and be willing to go beyond simple commentaries if we wish to discover phonetic truth.

3.8.1 Vowels

We can begin this speculative survey by considering the kinds of vowel systems that languages have. First let us make some assumptions. The main assumption that we need to make is that part of the value of having a set of vowels is that it allows a range of different words to be distinguished: we can tell the difference between *bid*, *bed* and *bad* because we happen to have in English the three different vowels that are required to do so (see section 4.2 for the value of this and a terminology to discuss it). If we have a lot of words like *bid*, *bed* and *bad*, it would seem that the more clearly we can distinguish between these vowels, the more efficient our communication will be. We do not have unlimited freedom to distinguish between such sets of vowels, though, because English also has words like *bud*, *bawd*, *bard*, *bird*, *booed* and so on, into whose territory we must not intrude for fear of failing to make the distinction between other word pairs clear to our listeners. Nevertheless, within the limits imposed by the vowels in the system, spreading vowels out fairly evenly seems like a sound principle.

So imagine that the vowel chart set out in Figure 3.6 is a box: that chart has two dimensions, but the dimension of lip-rounding adds a third dimension. And imagine, further, that for the vowels we 'have' in a given language, we have a set of identical under-inflated balloons. If we put the balloons into the box, and put a lid on, the balloons will be free to move around to a certain extent, but the most efficient way for them to fill the box will be for them to be fairly equally spaced within the confines of the box. This will not give us identical sets of phonetic vowels for every language which has a given number of vowels, but does give us an expectation of the types of patterns of vowels we are likely to find. We might expect to find patterns like (a) in Figure 3.13, but not patterns like (b).

Before we push this squishy-balloon-in-a-box idea any further, let us revise the nature of vowel sounds.

We have seen that as well as giving an articulatory description of a vowel sound, it is possible to give an acoustic description, in terms of the formants involved. If we plot the values of the first and second formants against each other, we get a close replica of the vowel chart that we saw earlier. This is done below with the vowels of Spanish. You will see that the value of the first formant increases as the vowel

Figure 3.13 (a)   (b)

Possible
distributions of
3 vowels in
vowel space

becomes more open, and that the value of the second formant increases as the vowel becomes more front.

The formants are taken from a single female speaker's pronunciation of the words *piso*, *peso*, *paso*, *pozo*, *puso*, illustrated in the figures below, where the Praat formant tracker marks the formants in the first vowel of each item (see Figures 3.14 and 3.15).

The benefit of the acoustic analysis for present purposes is that it provides a description of vowel space which exists in only two dimensions instead of three. We can thus simplify our squishy-balloon-in-a-box model by having only two-dimensional equivalents of balloons in a box: outline shapes in a two-dimensional vowel chart. However this two-dimensional picture should do everything our three-dimensional notion did and more. For example, consider the fact that most languages which have five vowels have the vowels [i], [e], [a], [o], [u] (perhaps in strict IPA chart terms: [i], [ɛ], [ɐ], [ɔ], [u]).

 <3.36> Why should these languages have rounded back vowels but spread front and central vowels?

So the obvious question is whether the vowel systems of real languages appear to adhere to the principles implicit in this theory. There is a large amount of evidence that they do, and a certain amount of evidence that they do not. While there seem to be more languages that follow the predictions of the theory than do not, the cases which do not match what is predicted may be more enlightening, because they force us to evaluate the theory more carefully and may suggest ways of improving the theory.

Data-set 3.6
The formant
frequencies of
Spanish

Vowel	Formant 1	Formant 2
i	361	2723
e	679	2496
a	1065	1497
o	679	1156
u	361	769

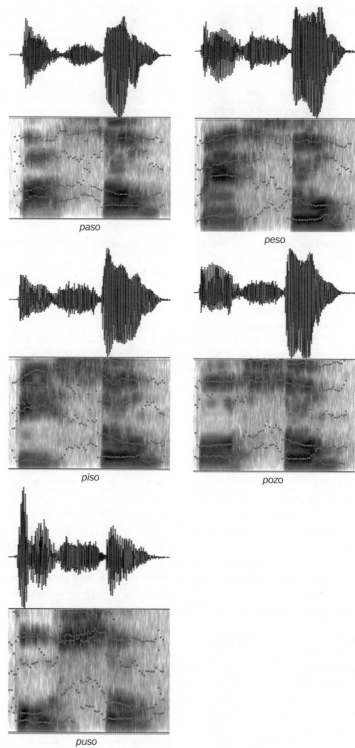

Figure 3.14
Spectrographs of Spanish words with the formants marked by Praat

paso

peso

piso

pozo

puso

Figure 3.15
A graphic representation of the vowel space of Spanish

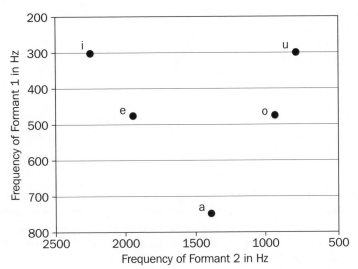

So what kinds of vowel systems do we find in languages? First let us make it clear that this theory only makes predictions about monophthongs, and so we should ignore diphthongs in attempting to evaluate the theory. Many languages with large numbers of vowels (such as Dutch and Cantonese) have large numbers of diphthongs, and these permit more auditorily distinct sounds to fit into the vowel space than would be true if only monophthongs were allowed. However useful diphthongs may be in this regard, we need a different theory to account for their patterning. Second, there are many languages which differentiate between long and short vowels: Latin was one such language, Finnish is another, Samoan yet another. Some examples from Pukapukan are given below. The predictions of the theory we are discussing do not impinge on vowels of different lengths: rather long vowels and short vowels have to be treated as separate systems, and dealt with independently. Thus we can talk of languages having a particular number of distinct vowel qualities, ignoring length (and also, in other languages, factors such as breathy voice, nasalisation or glottalisation).

Data-set 3.7
Vowel length in Pukapukan

papa	'rock bottom'	tutu	'burn'
papaː	'European'	tutuː	'lower a bunch of coconuts'
paːpaː	'father'	tuːtuː	'picture'
paːpa	'short, square haircut'	tuːtu	'suit of clothes'

About 5 per cent of the world's languages have just three distinct vowel qualities. In the vast majority of cases, these vowels are reported as being [i], [a] and [u]. We must realise that the symbol [a], in the lack of any conflicting vowel, probably means a central open vowel rather than the front open vowel that its position on the IPA chart would suggest. The vowels [i], [a] and [u], therefore, represent a maximally dispersed system, which we might draw as in Figure 3.16 rather than in the standard vowel quadrilateral.

Vowel systems such as this are reported from languages as diverse as Aranda (Arrente), Cree, Greenlandic, Lak.

Figure 3.16

A maximally
dispersed three
vowel system

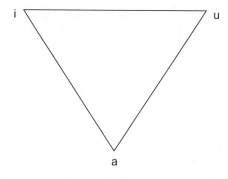

<3.37> How far is the partly-inflated-balloon image appropriate in cases like these?

Where languages have four distinct vowel qualities, we also find balanced patterns, like those in (10).

(10)   i   u   i   u   i   u   i   ɨ   u
      ɛ   ə   ɔ
          ɒ   a   a   a
   Wichita   Pashto   Bardi   Rukai

Any of the patterns in (10) might be considered to be more or less within the spirit of the theory of dispersion, particularly given that there is often a large amount of uncertainty as to just what the various symbols indicate.

Various counts have been carried out, and they agree that somewhere between 20 per cent and 30 per cent of languages are said to have five-vowel systems. The typical five-vowel system is illustrated in (11), and is found, with minor deviations only, in languages such as Armenian, Beembe, Irish, Maung, Spanish, Tigre, Tucano, Zulu, and so on. Standard Japanese replaces [u] with [ɯ].

(11)   i   u
      ɛ   ɔ
        a

Similarly, seven-vowel systems are frequently of the form illustrated in (12), found in Ewe, standard Italian, Kpelle, Nengone, and so on.

(12)   i   u
      e   o
      ɛ   ɔ
        a

All of this seems very hopeful: with some minor variation the vowels are well distributed, just as the theory predicts. Unfortunately, if we look a little further, things seem less well in line with the distribution theory.

First, consider some of the three-vowel systems that we have not yet mentioned. Some are listed in (13).

(13)

	i			ɪ	ʊ	ɪ	u	
e		o			o			
				ə				
	a			a			a	
Amuesha			Mura		Tagalog		Nunggubuyu	
Alabama								

<3.38> How far do you think these vowel systems fit the expectations of dispersal theory?

Although the Mura system might be said to have found another kind of method of dispersing the vowels in vowel space, the others seem to be failing to exploit the space that is available to them. The vowels are clearly far enough apart for them to be kept distinctive in everyday usage in the languages concerned, but the dispersion theory would predict that they would be further apart.

If we look at other kinds of four-vowel systems, they often appear to be five-vowel systems with missing values. Some examples are given in (14).

14)

ɪ		i	u	i		ɪ	ɯ	i	ʊ
ɛ	ɔ	ɛ		e	o		o	e
a		a		a		a		ɑ
Navajo		Moxos		Campa		Amahuaca		Cayapa
		Bandjalang				Tiwi*		

* But with [u] rather than [ɯ].

It appears that the most frequently 'missing' vowel in such cases is [u], but that may be because [e] and [ɛ] (and also [o] and [ɔ]) are counted separately. Note that the system for Moxos is very similar to that given for Wichita in (10). There it was suggested that the system might be balanced. The same might be concluded for Moxos, though it looks as though the case might be harder to make. Cayapa, however, could fit into the same pattern.

There is an alternative theory of vowels which might help explain some of this. According to this theory, the notion that there are just two places of articulation for vowels (front and back) is mistaken. Rather there are four: palatal, velar, upper pharyngeal and lower pharyngeal. The evidence for this comes from X-ray photographs of vowel articulations. While the standard notation which deals just with front vowels and back vowels implies that the narrowest constriction for any vowel will be in one of two positions, the X-ray photographs show constrictions in the pharynx as well. Palatal vowels are said to be vowels like [i], [ɪ] and [ɛ] and their rounded equivalents, velar vowels are ones like [u], [ʊ] and [ɨ], upper pharyngeal vowels are in the area of [o], [ɤ] and [ɔ], and lower pharyngeal vowels include [æ], [a] and [ɑ].

<3.39> How would a three-vowel system fit with this approach to description?

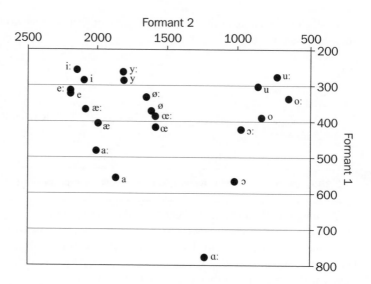

Figure 3.17 A graphic representation of the vowel space of Danish

If we apply this theory, then we would expect a four-vowel system to take one vowel from each of these four focal areas as a way of maximising articulatory difference between them. That is true of the system shown in (14) for Tiwi, but not of the others, which have two vowels from the palatal area. The theory works well in predicting any of the three-vowel systems that have been discussed, with the possible exception of Tagalog.

This theory, though, seems not to predict the general preference for five-vowel systems. The most basic five-vowel system, shown in (11) contains two palatal vowels and one from each of the other areas. We need an explanation of why the palatal vowels should be so widely preferred, rather than any of the other three areas.

A hint at a possible solution comes from four relatively closely related languages: Danish, Dutch, North Frisian and the New Zealand variety of English. In all of these languages, a relatively recent development is that the vowels tend to cluster in the palatal region of the chart. These are all languages which have relatively large numbers of vowels, but the palatal region is nevertheless overly crowded. An example of the vowels in Danish is given in Figure 3.17 to illustrate this overcrowding. Although there are languages like Dan and Punjabi with three low vowel qualities, it does not appear to be the case that quite the same degree of overcrowding is found in any other part of the vowel chart.

These two observations lead to the suggestion that the perceptual correlate of the palatal vowel space is larger than palatal vowel region of our charts. Older versions of the vowel chart show more space between [i] and [e] than the modern charts show, and the acoustic structure of vowels in this area is such that the formants are relatively distant from each other, which may allow the ear greater discriminatory powers for vowels in this particular area of the chart. This is no more than speculation, but it would explain some of our recurrent findings.

In this section we have seen how theories of vowel perception and production may influence one's expectations about the patterns of vowel systems which are likely to be recurrent across languages, and how vowel systems, despite being inherited and liable to change in the qualities of individual vowels, nonetheless may retain patterns which are relatable to universal phonetic tendencies.

3.8.2 Consonants

We can consider consonants and consonant systems in the same way. We can begin with plosives.

In the production of a plosive, air flows from the lungs into the oral cavity, where it meets a complete blockage of the cavity caused by the active articulator being in contact with the passive articulator. As air flows from the lungs, the pressure inside the oral cavity behind the point of closure increases. This is eventually released when the plosive is released, and can be heard in the explosive burst which gives plosives their name. However, the oral cavity is not particularly large, and though it may be expanded (e.g. by expanding the cheeks), the air flowing from the lungs is likely to raise the pressure in the oral cavity rapidly to such an extent that air can no longer flow from the lungs. This means that because of the physiology of the articulatory system, it is difficult to make the closure part of the stop very long.

If the plosive is voiced, matters are even more difficult. For there to be voicing, there must be airflow through the glottis, causing the glottis to vibrate. For there to be airflow through the glottis, the air pressure below the glottis must be higher than the pressure above the glottis. An oral closure which is held for too long will make this physiologically impossible.

Thus we might make two predictions. The first is that voiceless plosives will be easier to make than voiced ones, especially where the plosive does not occur between voiced sounds (e.g. intervocalically). The second is that voiced geminate stops or long stops will be extremely rare. Furthermore, if it is difficult to maintain voicing in voiced plosives, this must be even more difficult with velar plosives than with labial ones, because the size of the cavity behind a velar stop is much smaller than behind a bilabial stop, and so the pressure within it will rise more quickly than the pressure behind a bilabial stop. A third prediction will therefore be that if a language is missing one of a series of voiced plosives, it is more likely to be the voiced velar plosive that is missing than the voiced bilabial plosive.

The first of these predictions is extremely successful. There are many languages in the world which have voiceless plosives without having any distinct voiced plosives, and very few where there is a voiced plosive without any corresponding voiceless plosive.

The second of these predictions is more difficult to evaluate, partly because there are relatively few relevant languages. One count over more than 900 languages gives only seven with [pː], but only five with [bː], nine with [kː] but only four with [gː]. The higher number of long velar plosives than of long bilabial plosives seems to contradict the third prediction. On the other hand, we do find languages with stops as illustrated in (15).

(15)

(a)	Kurdish	p	t		k	q	?
		b	d		g		
(b)	Yurak	p	t		k	?	
		b					
(c)	Efik		t		k		
		b	d				
(d)	Khasi	p	t		k	?	
		pʰ	tʰ		kʰ		
		b	d				
(e)	Dutch	p	t		k		
		b	d				

All of the languages illustrated in (15) are clearly in the spirit of the third prediction made above.

Another result of the difficulty in maintaining the voicing of voiced plosives is that occasionally voiced plosives are replaced by implosives (which arise because the larynx drops to keep the voicing going, and this causes a decrease in the pressure of air in the vocal tract), by pre-nasalised stops (where the voicing is continued backwards into a short segment before the plosive) and into voiced fricatives, where it is easier to maintain the vibration of the vocal folds. Thus we find systems like those in (16), though these types of systems are not in themselves particularly frequent.

(16)

(a)	Hakka	p	t	k			
		pʰ	tʰ	kʰ			
		ᵐb	ⁿd	ⁿg			
(b)	Vietnamese		t	c	k	?	
			tʰ				
		ɓ	ɗ				
(c)	Kunjen	p	ʈ	t	c	k	
		pʰ	ʈʰ	tʰ	cʰ	kʰ	
			ð			ɣ	

Like plosives, fricatives cause an obstruction in the vocal tract, but this time only a partial one. This nevertheless has the effect of slowing down the flow of air, so that air pressure in the vocal tract can build up during the pronunciation of a fricative. Just as for plosives, this means that it can be difficult to maintain voicing through a fricative, with the result that, despite languages like Kunjen, most languages – if they have any fricatives at all – have at least as many voiceless fricatives as voiced ones, and many have only voiceless fricatives. In some cases, as we have seen, voiced fricatives may arise from voiced plosives, which may explain some of the exceptions to the general rule. The reason that [s] is the most frequent fricative (as mentioned earlier) is probably that because the position of the tongue directs a jet of air onto the edge of the lower teeth, the turbulence is greater for [s] than for most other fricatives, with the result that it is easier to hear [s] than nearly any other fricative. On the other hand, [ɸ] and [h] are the least clearly audible fricatives, and Maori, which has no [s], may have had both of these fricatives at an earlier stage (it now has [f] rather than [ɸ] or [ʍ]).

It seems that for fricatives, as indeed for plosives, there are some places of articulation that regularly recur across languages, and places of articulation which are more likely to belong to fricatives in languages which have only a small number of fricatives. In general, this is linked to the notion that gradual articulatory changes do not always lead to equally gradual auditory effects: there are places where small articulatory changes have no auditory effect. The result is that these places of articulation are easier to hit, since less accuracy of tongue-movement is required to produce the right auditory effect. The relevant places of articulation for fricatives are not necessarily the same as the places of articulation for plosives. Thus about one in nine languages has an [ʃ] fricative, but fewer than one in a hundred languages has a voiceless laminal post-alveolar plosive (that is, one at the same place of articulation as [ʃ]). The theory that there are such stable points for articulation is referred to as the 'quantal' theory of articulation, and it works for positions of vowels as well as for consonants, and also for features such as voicing and voicelessness.

Clearly, we can continue to talk about other patterns of consonants in similar terms. All sonorant consonants allow the free flow of air through the vocal tract, and so voicing is not an issue for them. Accordingly, we expect voiceless sonorants to be rare and voiced sonorants to be frequent, and this is what we find. The places of articulation for nasals appear to be closely related to the places of articulations for plosives. The preference for [j] and [w] as approximant consonants, we would hypothesise, may have something to do with quantal positions for such sounds.

There are two general messages to take from all of this. The first is that a better understanding of how sounds are produced can help us understand the way in which systems of sounds are built up, and why some systems are more stable than others. The second is that we have various theories to explain certain facts about the way in which the sounds of languages are distributed, but that these theories still need further development. Moreover, there are some things that these theories still do not seem to explain very well. Accordingly, more work is needed on the theoretical underpinnings of work of this nature, and that in turn demands a better understanding of the ways in which sounds are produced and transmitted.

3.9 Summing up

In this chapter we have seen how to describe consonant and vowel sounds, looked briefly at some of the other aspects of phonetic structure such as stress, tone and intonation, seen how the articulatory descriptions are reflected in acoustic facts and seen how languages exploit the phonetic possibilities available to them. In the next chapter, we move on to considering how the phonetic facts are exploited within individual languages.

Technical terms introduced in this chapter

Active articulator
Affricate
Alveolar
Alveolar ridge (teeth ridge)
Amplitude
Apical
Approximant (frictionless continuant, semivowel, glide)
Arytenoid cartilage
Assimilation
Back
Back (vowel)
Bilabial
Blade
Bronchus (pl. bronchi)
Central
Close
Close-mid
Complex wave
Constriction
Contoid
Cricoid cartilage
Dental
Diaphragm
Diphthong
Dorsal
Double articulation
Expiration
Flap
Formant
Fricative
Front
Front (vowel)
Fundamental frequency
Geminate
Glottal stop
Glottalisation
Glottis
Homorganic
Inspiration
Intensity
Labial
Labial-palatal

Labial-velar
Labialisation
Labio-dental
Laminal
Larynx (Adam's apple, voice box)
Lateral
Lung
Median
Mid
Monophthong
Nasal
Near-close
Near-open
Noise
Nucleus
Nuclear syllable
Obstruent
Open
Open-mid
Palatal
Palatalised
Palate (hard palate)
Passive articulator
Pharyngeal
Pharyngealisation
Pharynx
Plosive
Post-alveolar
Primary articulation
Primary stress
Radical
Resonance
Retroflex
Root
Rounded
Secondary articulation
Secondary stress
Sine wave
Sonorant
Spectrogram
Spread
Stop
Stress

Tap	Uvular
Thyroid cartilage	Velar
Tip	Velarised
Tonality	Velum
Tone (1)	Vibrate/ vibration
Tone (2)	Vocal folds (vocal cords)
Tone language	Vocoid
Tonicity	Voiced
Trachea (windpipe)	Voiceless
Trill (roll)	Wavelength
Uvula	WH-question

References and further reading

Any Linguistics textbook will give a brief introduction to articulatory phonetics, but for greater detail read Abercrombie (1967) or Ladefoged (1975). For more advanced coverage of some of the matters dealt with in this chapter, Catford (1977) and Laver (1994) are recommended. On acoustic phonetics read Fry (1979) or Johnson (1997). A major source for this chapter is Zemlin (1968). On the number of motor commands per second it takes to speak, see Laver (1994: 1), who cites Lenneberg (1967).

On the X-ray analysis of vowel articulation, see Wood (1979); on the dispersion theory of vowels, see Liljencrants & Lindblom (1972); for counts of long consonants, and [ʃ] fricatives see Maddieson (1984); on quantal theory, see Stevens (1989) and Johnson (1997). See also Johnson (1997) for the acoustics and auditory features of plosives and fricatives.

For a lot of material on language typology, including the distribution of vowel sounds, see Haspelmath *et al.* (2005), also available online at http://wals.info/

Information on the various languages mentioned has been taken from the sources mentioned below:

Alabama	Maddieson (1984)	Cantonese	Zee (1999);
Amahuaca	Maddieson (1984)		Yip (2002)
Amuesha	Lass (1984);	Cree	Lass (1984)
	Maddieson (1984)	Dan	Maddieson (1984)
Aranda	Maddieson (1984)	Danish vowels	Steinlen (2005)
Armenian	Maddieson (1984)	Dutch	Booij (1995)
Bandjalang	Maddieson (1984)	Efik	Maddieson (1984)
Bardi	Maddieson (1984)	English [s]	Ladefoged &
Beembe	Lass (1984);		Maddieson (1996)
	Maddieson (1984)	Even	Malchukov (1995)
Campa	Maddieson (1984)	Ewe	Maddieson (1984)

83

Finnish	Aaltio (1964)	New Zealand	Bauer and Warren
French	Armstrong (1964)	English	(2004); Easton and
French [s]	Armstrong (1964);		Bauer (2000)
	Malécot (1977)	North Frisian	Bohn (2004)
Greek	Mackridge (1985)	Nunggubuyu	Maddieson (1984)
Greenlandic	Maddieson (1984)	Pashto	Maddieson (1984)
Hakka	Maddieson (1984)	Pukapukan	Salisbury (2002)
Igbo	Hyman (1975: 213)	Punjabi	Maddieson (1984)
Irish	Maddieson (1984)	Rukai	Maddieson (1984)
Italian	Chapallaz (1979)	Spanish /s/	Navarro Tomás
Khasi	Maddieson (1984)		(1926)
Khmer	Maddieson (1984)	Tagalog	Maddieson (1984)
Kpelle	Lass (1984)	Thai	Laver (1994: 469)
Kunjen	Maddieson (1984)	Tigre	Maddieson (1984)
Kurdish	Maddieson (1984)	Tiwi	Maddieson (1984)
Lak	Maddieson (1984)	Tucano	Maddieson (1984)
Maung	Maddieson (1984)	Vietnamese	Maddieson (1984)
Moxos	Maddieson (1984)	Wichita	Maddieson (1984)
Mura	Maddieson (1984)	Yurak	Maddieson (1984)
Navajo	Lass (1984)	Zulu	Maddieson (1984)
Nengone	Lass (1984)		

4

Phonology

Syllables govern the World.
(John Selden 1689)

Phonology is about the ways sounds pattern in languages. The most important theoretical notion here is the phoneme, and that is introduced, as well as notions required to discuss the syllable. Distinctive features are introduced, and a notation for writing rules.

4.1 Learners' problems and related matters

Some of the difficulties we have in learning to pronounce a foreign language as adults are phonetic: German and French speakers learning English typically have problems pronouncing [θ] and [ð], for example, and English speakers learning French or German have difficulty in pronouncing [ʁ]. But in other cases, a foreign accent can arise despite the fact that the phonetic properties of the new language do not in themselves provide difficulties. For instance, Germans learning English have no difficulty in pronouncing the [d] in a word like *credit*, but seem to be unable to pronounce it in a word like *fade* (which invariably sounds like *fate*). English speakers learning French might be able to pronounce the words *fête* 'feast' and *fée* 'fairy', but may nevertheless have difficulty in distinguishing between the words *donnait* 'was giving' and *donné* 'given' where the vowels in those words occur in final position. Speakers of many varieties of Chinese may be able to say the English word *tea* with no problem, but find difficulty in pronouncing *eat* comprehensibly.

These problems arise because of the difference in the phonologies of the languages involved. Phonology as an area of study deals with the ways in which the sounds of individual languages are used and how they are concatenated to make larger structures (syllables, words, and so on). Phonology is concerned with how sounds can be arranged, and what changes occur to the sounds to make particular arrangements possible.

For example, we all know that when a word is borrowed (or stolen) from one language into another, it is not pronounced in precisely the same way it was pronounced in the original language. We can find many examples in the languages we know. Some of the differences are phonetic, as when we hear French speakers talking about *un parking* [œ̃ paʁkiŋ] 'a parking lot or parking building' using the [ʁ] of French and the French vowel sound in the last syllable. Or the German word *Handy* [hɛndiː] 'mobile telephone', although apparently borrowed from English, may be incomprehensible to English speakers, not only because of its meaning, but because the quality of the first vowel is so far from the English original. Equally,

Germans may have difficulty in understanding the English pronunciation of the names of German composers such as Bach, Beethoven and Handel. But in other cases, the problems seem to be more than just phonetic. Consider for example, the Japanese word *tsunami*, which is usually pronounced with an initial [s] in English. Why, then, should it be written with an initial <ts>? The obvious answer is that it is pronounced with [ts] in Japanese. English speakers are happy to say [ts] in *cats*, but not in *tsunami*. Similar problems can be seen in the words *Sri Lanka* and *mnemonic*. These are usually pronounced with an initial [ʃ] and [n] respectively in English, but not in the languages they come from. The Maori word *ngaio*, the name of a tree, but also used as a personal name, is pronounced with an initial [ŋ] in Maori, but with an initial [n] in English. The Czech composer Dvorak's name is pronounced in Czech with an initial [dv], but English speakers usually insert a vowel between the consonants.

Advertisers who make up names for new products are usually very careful to make up names which fit the permitted patterns for the appropriate languages. *Kodak* starts like *code* and finishes like *lack*, and fits easily into the range of English words. Similar comments could be made about *Exxon, frug, scag, Yaris*. The situation of the French record shop called *fnac* (with no capital), pronounced [fnak] despite the fact that no native French word begins with a voiceless fricative followed by an [n] is very much the exception rather than the rule.

 <4.1> Show how *Exxon, frug, scag* and *Yaris* fit the patterns of English.

In summary, the patterns in which we allow sounds to occur in our languages are an important part of the way in which we use sound, and an important part of the way in which languages can differ from each other. That is the focus of this chapter.

4.2 Same but different: the importance of contrast

Think about how you say the word *rue* in English. In particular, consider the first consonant in this word. The discussion below assumes that you speak with an English accent, but you may find that what is said is true even if you have an Australian, New Zealand or other accent.

 <4.2> What is the three-term label for this consonant?

We can transcribe this sound as [ɹ]. Next consider the consonant represented by <r> in the word *drew*.

 <4.3> What is the three-term label for this consonant?

We can transcribe this sound as [ɻ]. The important thing to notice is that it is phonetically distinguishable from the sound at the beginning of *rue*.

Next consider the consonant written with <r> in the word *true*.

<4.4> What is the three-term label for this consonant?

We can transcribe this sound as [ɹ̥]. Finally, consider the consonant written with an <r> in *through*.

<4.5> What is the three-term label for this consonant?

In phonetic terms, therefore, we can distinguish, for some accents of English, four different r-sounds here. But the fact that we can call them all 'r-sounds' is significant. Until you started reading this chapter, you probably thought that they were all the same. And the truth is that they all function as though they were the same. What does it mean in this context to say that they have the same function?

It means two things. The first is that you can never distinguish between two different words of English by replacing one of them with another of them. Although the voiceless alveolar fricative in *sue* can be replaced by its equivalent voiced alveolar fricative to give *zoo*, which means something different, we can never replace the voiceless alveolar fricative in *true* with its voiced equivalent to give a new word, nor can we replace the voiced alveolar fricative in *drew* with its voiceless equivalent to give a new word. A pair of words like *sue* and *zoo* which mean something different and differ in only one segment is called a MINIMAL PAIR.

<4.6> Find some more minimal pairs in which the difference between [s] and [z] leads to a difference in meaning.

The second point is the reason why we can never find minimal pairs. We can predict in advance where the various r-sounds will occur. We always find [ɹ] at the beginning of a word, we always find [ɹ̯] immediately following a [d], we always find [ɹ̥] following a [t], and if we find a [ɾ], it will be immediately following a [θ]. In other words, all these various types of r-sound occur in different places in the word, and that is why there can never be a minimal pair between them. Elements which are distributed this way are said to be COMPLEMENTARY DISTRIBUTION. Note the spelling of *complementary* in this phrase. The various r-sounds complement each other in that between them they form the complete set of positions in which an r-sound can occur in (the relevant varieties of) English.

We need some technical vocabulary to discuss all of this. Let us call each of the consonants and vowels we actually utter SPEECH SOUNDS or PHONES. So in the example above, [ɹ] and [ɾ] and so on are different phones. However, there is another sense in which these are all variants of a single unit. We will call that unit the PHONEME. We will say that the various phones we discussed are BOUND VARIANTS (because they are tied or linked to specific positions) or ALLOPHONES of the phoneme /r/. And notationally we enclose the r-symbol between slashes to say that we are considering the phoneme as an abstract unit which is made up of the very specific phones which realise it. Now we can transcribe the word *true* as /tru:/ (when we are not worried about the minute phonetic detail, but only about which phonemes are involved) or as [tɹ̥u:] (when we are thinking about the phonetic

87

detail of at least some element in the string). The first transcription is called a **PHONEMIC TRANSCRIPTION** or sometimes (not quite equivalently) a **BROAD TRANSCRIPTION;** the second transcription is called a **PHONETIC TRANSCRIPTION,** but because that label is ambiguous, also being used for a phonemic transcription, it is more frequently called a **NARROW TRANSCRIPTION.**

<4.7> Provide a broad and a narrow transcription of the words *drew* and *through*, as described earlier.

A phoneme, then, is a set of phones, each of which is phonetically similar to the others, which are in complementary distribution and which together function as a single unit in the sound system of a particular language. It is typically the case that native speakers of a language feel themselves to be speaking in phonemes in that they hear differences between phonemes, but fail to hear differences between sounds which belong to the same phoneme.

One of the points to note in this definition is the notion of phonetic similarity. We can define phonetic similarity in terms of the three-term labels which were introduced in Chapter 3. But phonetic similarity is not a matter of similar and not similar; it is a matter of more similar and less similar. And the phones which belong together in the same phoneme are the most similar sounds possible, other things being equal.

<4.8> The [n] we find in *ten* is alveolar, that in *tenth* is dental; the [l] we find in *foul* is alveolar, that in *filth* is dental (as long as you speak a variety of English in which there is an [l] consonant in these words at all – some speakers of southern English varieties or New Zealand varieties have a vowel here instead). Dental [l] is in complementary distribution with both alveolar [n] and with alveolar [l]; dental [n] is in complementary distribution with both alveolar [n] and alveolar [l]. Which phones are allophones of the same phoneme, and why?

In one of his celebrated dictums, the Swiss linguist Ferdinand de Saussure said that 'in language only the differences count'. In the present context, what that means is that what is important about /r/ is not so much that it is an /r/ but that it is something distinct from /l/, /d/, and so on. We can show this by providing minimal pairs such as *rate* and *late*, *rate* and *date*, where we can see that /r/ and /l/ and /d/ **CONTRAST,** that is, they allow us to change from one word to another. The point about the differences being important can be seen when English speakers listen to Japanese speakers saying words with /r/ and /l/. A Japanese speaker saying *plurality*, sounds to an English speaker as though they are saying /pruːlærɪti/. This seems to imply that they say /r/ for /l/ and /l/ for /r/, but that is not true. They produce the same sound where English speakers have both /r/ and /l/, but this sound is neither an English /r/ nor an English /l/. When English speakers expect /r/ they hear something which does not sound like /r/ and so they interpret it as /l/ and vice versa. In other words, we hear the differences, the contrasts.

FERDINAND DE SAUSSURE

Ferdinand de Saussure (1857–1913) is sometimes called 'the father of modern linguistics'. He himself never published on his theory of linguistics; rather his ideas were put together posthumously by his students on the basis of lecture notes. The book, *Cours de linguistique générale* ['Course in general linguistics'], published in Paris in 1916, set the foundations for subsequent linguistic studies. In particular, Saussure argued that you could undertake a scientific study of a language as it is at a particular time, and not just of the way in which language changed over time. Many of the fundamental ideas and analogies now used in the study of languages were first introduced by Saussure. Saussure's work is the basis on which all structuralist work developed, not only in linguistics, but also in other areas such as anthropology, philosophy and semiotics.

CONTROVERSY: The phoneme

The phoneme as it has been described here is theoretically an extremely controversial entity. Despite that fact, it is one of the most enduring and practical concepts that linguists have developed, and despite its theoretical problems it continues to be used even by those linguists who find it obscure. There are many problems with the phoneme, some of which would take a long time to explain. The result is that the term 'phoneme' might be used in different ways by different theoreticians, and you have to be aware of this. Let us consider just one of the problems.

The notion of the phoneme demands a huge amount of idealisation of data. We have to assume a consistent accent, one that is not changing, and which is also used in the same way all the time. We have to assume a maximally clear pronunciation of words. We have to assume that we know what words are. All of this provides difficulties. Nobody speaks an entirely consistent variety of any language. You do not speak the same way to a new-born baby that you speak to your parents; you do not speak to your parents the same way that you speak to a judge in court; you do not speak in precisely the same way when you are talking very slowly as you do when you are talking fast. And all language is constantly in a state of change (albeit not usually dramatic change). We rarely speak in the maximally clear form. Many English speakers will pronounce *support* as [spʰɔːt] (see below, section 4.3.1 for more on aspiration), and yet it will be different from *sport* which will not have an aspirated [pʰ] and will be pronounced [spɔːt]. This might look like a minimal pair between aspirated and non-aspirated bilabial plosives, but that does not seem to correspond to the way in which speakers of English perceive their language. Last, but not least, the notion of word is less obvious than might be supposed: is *alright* one word or is it two words *all right*?

Moreover, we tend to talk about phonemes as though they are the fundamental units of sound-structure, but children acquiring their first language must hear the phones rather than the phonemes, and deduce the phonemes on the basis of the phones. In principle, therefore, it ought to be possible to speak a language without any knowledge of the phonemes, as long as you had sufficient knowledge of the phones. Yet speakers behave as if they know about the phonemes: they typically fail to hear differences between allophones, for example.

Whatever the reality underlying speakers' and hearers' behaviour, the central notion of contrast must surely play a role. The difference between *I want this horse shod* and *I want this horse shot* is important. Language works because we can make such distinctions (despite the possibility of homophones).

To illustrate how this works, we will consider some data from some unfamiliar languages.

Consider the distribution of [t] and [tʲ] below, and then consider whether these sounds are allophones of a single phoneme or whether they belong to separate phonemes.

Data-set 4.1
Moseten

taraʔtaraʔ	'big rat'
tərərətʲi	'throat'
hiritʲ	'one (masc.)'
tʲabitʲiʔ	'fisherman'
tʲabaʔ	'sponge'
hirhaijiti	'swallow the wrong way'
taiʔji	'slip'
sanakitʲ	'pencil'
hekte	'bring him'
jahkite	'someone has left him there'
tʲapʰjeti	'someone grabs him'
mintʲiʔ	'man'
tʲeje	'I give you'
tʲak	'ten'
mitiʔ	'she fries it'
mitʲiʔ	'your thing'

<4.9> Are [t] and [tʲ] in Table 4.1 allophones of a single phoneme, or do they belong to separate phonemes?

<4.10> What does this imply about speakers' perception of Moseten?

<4.11> If you were trying to devise a writing system for Moseten, how many symbols would you need to represent [t] and [tʲ]?

Now consider a different problem. Consider the sounds [b] and [β] in Data-set 4.2.

<4.12> Are [b] and [β] in Daur allophones of the same phoneme or do they belong to separate phonemes?

<4.13> What does this imply about speakers' perception of Daur?

Data-set 4.2
Daur

aβtaːl	'front of the saddle'
kaβis	'slice'
dəβəɣ	'improve'
xəβ	'gentle'
xarəβ	'ten'
akənbu	'accomplish'
bonbur	'ball'
bələn	'ready'
bal	'berry'
aβil	'lack'
bɔdʲ	'prairie'
barʲ	'catch'
ambən	'official'
bunʲ	'tomorrow'
gʷarbə	'three'

 <4.14> If you were trying to devise a writing system for Daur, how many symbols would you need to represent [b] and [β]?

 <4.15> Assuming that the transcription above is in other respects phonemic, write a phonemic transcription of the words meaning 'berry' and 'gentle'.

The question of **PHONETIC SIMILARITY** is often misunderstood, so it is worth being explicit about it here. In Mandarin, there is a phoneme /ŋ/ which never appears at the beginning of a syllable, only at the end. There is also a phoneme /s/, which only appears at the beginning of a syllable, never at the end. These two are in complementary distribution, but could not be allophones of the same phoneme because they have nothing in common phonetically.

 <4.16> What are the phonetic features of [ŋ] and what are those of [s]?

They share no phonetic feature (contrast the case of [b] and [β] in Daur, which shared two of the three labels in the three-term label). It is in this sense that they are said to have nothing in common phonetically (even though both are pronounced of air flowing out of the lungs, for instance). In fact, there are a host of consonants in Mandarin which are in complementary distribution with [ŋ], since only [n], [ŋ] and, in some varieties, [r] can occur at the end of syllables. Most analyses do not pair [ŋ] with any of them, and a large part of the reason is the problem of phonetic similarity.

If we return to Moseten, we find a similar, although much more restricted, example there. In Moseten, [ʔ] only occurs syllable finally, while [ʧʰ] occurs only syllable initially. They are in complementary distribution, and this time they are both voiceless and both stops. But there is another voiceless stop [k] in Moseten which can occur in either position. If we stop just counting labels and think in terms of articulatory distance, [k] is closer to [ʔ] than [ʧʰ] is. That is, there is another sound in the

Figure 4.1
How to determine whether two phones belong to the same phoneme or to different phonemes

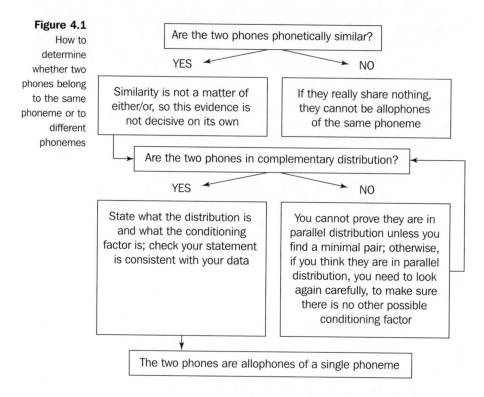

language which is phonetically closer to either [ʧʰ] or to [ʔ] than they are to each other, and which is in parallel distribution with both. So we cannot take [ʧʰ] and [ʔ] to be phonetically close enough to be allophones without some overwhelming evidence to the contrary (evidence which appears to be lacking in Moseten).

TRIVIA

If two words are made up of the same set of phonemes, we would normally conclude that they are **HOMOPHONES**, that is, the two words sound identical. So that if you say *write, right, rite* (all transcribed /raɪt/), a listener should not be able to tell which of the words you have said (did you repeat one of the words, for example, or what order did you say them in?). Yet it appears that once words are used in context and not cited in isolation, this homophony no longer holds. The word *time*, for example is measurably shorter than the word *thyme*, even though both are /taɪm/. It appears that this is mainly related to the frequency of the two words. The more frequent a word is, the more likely it is to be shorter, the less frequent, the longer it is. You may not be able to hear the difference, but it is measurable. Interestingly, it is not the number of times that precise phonological copies recur that makes the difference, but the number of times that any form of the relevant words occur. So *know* also has *knows, knew, knowing* and together these are more frequent than *no*. So you don't just get practice in saying the sequence /taɪm/ and get faster at saying that sequence, you get faster at saying that sequence when it means 'time'.

Data-set 4.3
Passamaquoddy

apʧ	'again, next'
babɛhʧimawa	'they asked them'
bɛdʒijɛ	's/he arrives'
bihʧɛ	'far away'
deppu	's/he sits in something'
ɛhpid	'woman'
gapskʷ	'waterfall'
kpilaskumək	'on your paper'
kpidin	'your hand'
nidab	'my friend'
npizun	'medicine'
psidɛwɛn	'everyone'
pʧihtɛhmən	'if I hit it accidentally'
skidab	'man'

Consider the distribution of [b] and [p] above.

<4.17> Are [b] and [p] phonetically similar? Are they in complementary distribution in the data shown in Table 4.3? Are they allophones of the same phoneme in Passamaquoddy, or do they belong to separate phonemes?

<4.18> What does this imply about speakers' perception of Passamaquoddy?

<4.19> If you were trying to devise a writing system for Passamaquoddy, how many symbols would you need to represent [b] and [p]?

<4.20> Provide a phonemic transcription of the words meaning 'your hand' and 'my friend'. Note, however, that in this case the rest of the transcription is definitely not phonemic, because all obstruents work the same way in Passamaquoddy.

<4.21> The name of the language suggests that something else has been done. What is the problem?

Now consider a point about English. For some speakers of British English, the sound [θ] is articulated with the tip of the tongue behind the upper incisors. For some speakers of American English, and for some speakers of New Zealand English, [θ] is pronounced with the blade of the tongue making contact with the upper incisors, and the tongue tip protruding slightly between the teeth. We could transcribe this variant as [θ̪]. Some speakers may even vary, but it is not a matter of variation being bound to a particular environment. It is not predictable from the phonetic environment which sound will occur. This situation is called **FREE VARIATION**. The occurrence of the two variants may be (partly or wholly) determined by factors such as the regional origin, sex and age of the speaker, but in terms of the phonological system there is a free choice between them.

The same thing is true for variation between phonemes in words like *economics*, pronounced either with an initial /iː/ or with an initial /e/. In such cases, phonemes (which by definition contrast with each other) fail to contrast in particular words. While /siːt/ and /set/ are sufficient to prove that /iː/ and /e/ contrast, /iːkənɒmɪks/ and /ekənɒmɪks/ are not different words. We can speak here of lexically conditioned suspension of contrast.

> **<4.22>** Can you find any other words in which /iː/ and /e/ are in free variation?

> **<4.23>** Can you find any words with consonant phonemes in free variation?

Although the main job of phonemes is to contrast (i.e. to provide differences in meaning), the example of *economics* shows that there are some places where phonemes fail to contrast. We can distinguish between three situations in which there is a lack of contrast between phonemes, though not all linguists have made as many distinctions as this.

1. There is the situation illustrated above with *economics*, where the lack of contrast is lexically determined. It is a fact about the word *economic(s)* that it allows either pronunciation, not a fact about the position in the word ([iːtʃ] and [etʃ] are different words of English) or about the following consonant ([ɹiːk] and [ɹek] are different words of English), etc. We can call this lexically conditioned suspension of contrast.

2. There is the situation in which two phonemes (sometimes more) which have phonetically similar allophones fail to contrast in a particular phonological environment. A simple example is provided by words such as *spill, still, skill* in English. Although *pill* and *bill, till* and *dill, kill* and *gill* (as of a fish) are different words, showing that /p/ and /b/, /t/ and /d/, /k/ and /g/ contrast, it is impossible to distinguish words by replacing a /p/ with a /b/ immediately following a word-initial /s/: [spɪl] and [sbɪl], if you can say them at all, are simply variant pronunciations of the same word. We can call this phonologically conditioned suspension of contrast between similar phonemes, but the common label is **NEUTRALISATION**. We say that /p/ and /b/ are **NEUTRALISED** following an /s/.

3. There is the situation where a particular phoneme fails to occur in a particular environment, even though this is not a matter of a small number of phonemes with phonetically similar allophones failing to contrast. For example, for speakers of many varieties of English, a very limited set of consonants can occur after /aʊ/. The phonemes /t/ and /d/ are permitted but /p/ and /b/, /k/ and /g/ are not, for example. There is no obvious reason why [laʊb] should not be a possible word of English, but it isn't. Here we would normally say that the labial and velar stops have a **DEFECTIVE DISTRIBUTION**, and do not occur after this particular diphthong.

The distinction between defective distribution and neutralisation is not always clear, and some scholars fail to draw it, even though there are different implications for the two. In the case of neutralisation, but not in the case of defective distribution, for instance, it may be the case that the speech sound actually produced is not a typical member of either of the phonemes involved, but a compromise. In the case of /p/ and /b/ following /s/, cited above, this is true. In the word *pill* the [p] is voiceless and aspirated (that is, there is short [h]-like puff of air following the [p]); in the word *bill* the [b] is (partly) voiced and unaspirated (that is, the voicing for the vowel starts as soon as the lips open after the [b]); in the word *spill* the labial plosive is voiceless and unaspirated. That is, the plosive in *spill* is neither like a typical /p/ nor like a typical /b/, it is a compromise. While this is not a necessary result of neutralisation, it is one common one. Talking in terms of neutralisation helps to explain why we should find a phonetic compromise in such positions.

> **<4.24>** There are no monosyllabic words of English (Southern Standard British English, anyway) that end [ʊɡ], though there are some like *look* that end [ʊk]. Is this neutralisation, lexically conditioned suspension of contrast or defective distribution? How can you tell?

4.3 Transcribing English

Making a transcription of any language involves making decisions about the phonological structure of the language, or the variety of the language, to be transcribed. In this section we will look at the way in which we establish a set of phonemes for English, and the way in which we choose how to transcribe those phonemes. We will begin with the consonants, since those are less controversial, and then move on to look at the vowels. With the vowels in particular we will also have to consider what happens in a range of varieties of English, since not all varieties of English have the same number of contrasts.

4.3.1 Consonants

In Data-set 4.4, a set of minimal pairs is set up which establishes a number of different consonant phonemes in English. There are a few extra consonants which are not found in all varieties, and they will be discussed later. There are also a few places where there are other points to be made.

> **<4.25>** Some of the columns in Data-set 4.4 show multiple spellings of the same vowel sound. What does this say about the English spelling system?

Given the analysis here, /ŋ/ does not occur initially, /ʒ/ may not occur initially, but does for some speakers in borrowed words like *jabot*, *genre* and *Zhivago*, /j/ and /w/ do not occur finally (we will come back to this in the next section). Data-set 4.4

Data-set 4.4

Consonantal minimal pairs in English

p	pat	pie	poo		copper	leap	sheep	sup	cap
b	bat	buy	boo		cobber				cab
t	tat	tie	two	sitter	matter	leat	sheet		cat
d		die	do		madder	lead	she'd	sud	cad
k	cat	kye	coo	sicker	lacking	leak	suck		
g	gat	guy	goo		lagging	league			
ʧ	chat	chai	chew		catcher	leech		such	catch
ʤ		Jew			catcher				cadge
m	mat	my	moo	simmer	coming			sum	cam
n	gnat	nigh		sinner	cunning	lean	sheen	sun	can
ŋ				singer				sung	
f	fat	fie			luffing	leaf	sheaf		
v	vat	vie			loving	leave	sheave		
θ		thigh			ether	Leith	sheath		Cath
ð	that	thy		cither	either[c]		sheathe		
s	sat	sigh	sue		fussy	lease		suss	
z			zoo	scissor	fuzzy	lees	she's		
ʃ		shy	shoe		Aleutian	leash	sheesh	cash	
ʒ					allusion	liege			cas[b]
h	hat	hi	who		ahead				
r	rat	rye	rue	sirrah[d]	arrive		sheer[a]		
l		lie	loo		alive		she'll		
j			you		beyond				
w		Y	woo		bewail				

Notes:

[a] For some speakers; others have no consonant at the end of this word.

[b] As an abbreviation of *casual*.

[c] For some speakers; see comments on variation in *economics* above.

[d] For those speakers who have an /r/ in *sheer*, this is not a proper minimal pair with others in the column.

allows minimal pairs for most of the sounds listed to be found, but there is one notable exception: there is no reliable minimal pair for /j/ versus /ʒ/. Here we have to rely on the intuition of speakers that these are, indeed, separate phonemes.

<4.26> Do your intuitions agree with this comment? Can you find anything close to a minimal pair for [ʒ] and [j]?

<4.27> Table 4.4 does not provide a minimal pair between [ð] and [ʒ]. Can you find one? Is there any other reason to believe that they belong to separate phonemes?

Some varieties of English in England have no /h/. Many Scottish and South African varieties of English have an extra phoneme /x/ in words like *loch* (/lɒx/, in contrast to *lock* which is /lɒk/) or *gogga* /xɔ:xɑ:/ 'creepy-crawlie'. Some speakers from both North America and England, and many from Scotland and Ireland have a distinction between *watt* and *what*, *Wales* and *whales*, where the second member of each pair could be transcribed with /ʍ/ or as a sequence of /hw/.

The phoneme /r/ has a number of different phonetic realisations including [ʁ] for speakers of traditional Durham (England) dialect, to [r] for some Scottish speakers, to [ɻ] for some Americans and some speakers from the English south-west. Very few people these days actually use a trill [r], but that symbol is used as being the most neutral symbol. Most speakers in England and Australasia use [ɹ]. An increasing number, but still a minority in these areas, use [ʋ].

The symbols used in this data-set would suffice for a phonemic transcription system – one which transcribes nothing which is not predictable. However, there are various places in the consonant system where there are some major allophones of these phonemes. We will mention just a few.

The variation in /r/ has already been discussed in section 4.2. While not all speakers of English have all these variants, all have some variation. There are also differences in where /r/ is found. In British RP /r/ cannot occur at the end of a word spoken in isolation or immediately before another consonant, while in North American broadcast standards, /r/ is the norm in these environments. So for many Britons, Australians and New Zealanders *tuba* and *tuber* sound alike, while for many North Americans, Scots and Irish they sound different.

The phoneme /l/ also has a number of allophones. All speakers have a voiceless version of /l/, which could be transcribed [l̥] or [ɬ], in words like *please* and *clot*. This is different from the fully voiced [l] in *lees* and *lot*. This will be discussed below from a different point of view. Speakers of RP have a difference in quality between a **PREVOCALIC** (i.e. found before a vowel) /l/ in *leaf* and a **POSTVOCALIC** /l/ in *feel*: the former is palatalised [lʲ], the latter is velarised [lˠ]. Speakers of Welsh English may have a palatalised [lʲ] in both these positions, while speakers of Glasgow English, or some US varieties, may have velarised [lˠ] in both positions. Speakers of Australian or New Zealand Englishes may have a similar distinction to that in RP, but the prevocalic /l/ will be velarised, and the postvocalic one uvularised or pharyngealised. Other speakers of Australian, New Zealand or South-East English varieties may not have a phonetic [l] at all in some or all post-vocalic positions, and will have a vowel instead. The precise vowel varies from place to place, but *feel* may be pronounced as [fiːo], [fiːʊ] or [fiːɤ].

> **<4.28>** The version of /l/ found in *play* has been said to be devoiced. Is that all there is to say about the allophone found in that word?

Most speakers of English will have variation between aspirated allophones of voiceless plosives and unaspirated ones. We can mark aspiration as in [pʰ], and unaspirated ones as in [p˭] where specific marking is required. As the transcription implies, the aspirated plosive is followed by a brief [h]-like sound, a puff of air following the release of the plosive. There are many languages that have phonemic distinctions between aspirated and unaspirated plosives. An example is given in the next data-set.

In English the presence of aspiration is not contrastive, but predictable. However, the same sets of predictions are not valid for all varieties of English. Typically, though, a voiceless plosive occurring without any other consonants at the beginning of a

Data-set 4.5
Swahili
aspiration

tembo	'palm wine'	tʰembo	'elephant'
kata	'ladle'	kʰata	'head pad'

stressed syllable will be aspirated, so in words like *pill, till* and *kill,* but a voiceless plosive occurring immediately after an /s/ will be unaspirated (and may sound rather [b]-like) in words like *spill, still* and *skill.* Between vowels, voiceless plosives are unaspirated in British RP but aspirated in New Zealand English; in many varieties of North American and Australasian English, /t/ is pronounced as [ɾ] when it occurs between vowels as in *betting, mutter* and, for many, *get eggs.* For some speakers there may not be any difference between /t/ and /d/ when they occur intervocalically, so that the distinction is neutralised, and *latter* and *ladder* may sound the same. For some British speakers /t/ is replaced by [ʔ] in the same environment, so that *bitter* is [bɪʔə] (or [bɪʔər]) and *bidder* is [bɪdə] (or [bɪdər]). The phoneme /t/ may also be realised as [ʔ] before an /n/ or an /l/ (where the /l/ is not **VOCALISED** (or pronounced as a vowel)). We find this in some British, North American and Australasian accents in words like *Britain* [bɹɪʔn], *button* [bʌʔn], *cattle* [kʰæʔl], *metal* [meʔl].

<4.29> Final plosives have not been mentioned here. How do you pronounce the plosives at the ends of the words *flap, flat* and *flack* said in isolation? Is that the same as you say in more frequent words like *stop, what* and *back?* What happens if these words are not final, but are in phrases such as *stop it, what if, back up?*

Aspiration is perhaps better seen as a subtype of delayed **VOICE ONSET TIME.** After the plosive, the voicing does not start immediately, but is delayed slightly so that the first part of the next segment is voiceless. When we have a voiceless vowel, it is perceived as an [h] (see section 3.3.1). But in words like *pewter* [pjuːtə(r)], *trip* [tɹɪp], *queen* [kwiːn], *plate* [pleɪt] and the like, the next segment is a sonorant consonant, and that is devoiced, just as the vowel is in *pill, till* and *kill.* The degree of devoicing of the consonant may differ from individual to individual or from one accent to another, but some devoicing is general.

Where the delayed voice onset time affects a vowel, at least with /t/ and /k/, the aspiration is variably replaced with affrication – the plosive is released through a homorganic fricative – so that we find realisations such as *table* [tˢeɪbl], *cow* [kˣaʊ]. This friction can be seen on spectrograms.

4.3.2 Vowels

When we come to transcribing the English vowels, we have many factors to take into consideration. One obvious one is the variety of English we are transcribing: typically Scottish varieties of English have fewer vowel phonemes than English ones, with American ones somewhere in between. Another is which symbols to use: English has rather a lot of vowels (see section 3.8), and sometimes two of them have similar qualities, so that thought has to be given to the symbols which will be used for the individual vowels. As well as questions of phonetic accuracy, there are factors such as which symbols are easiest to read and write and general traditions of transcribing English. A third question is the matter of how to transcribe diphthongs. Most British transcriptions use vowel symbols for the second element of a diphthong, but there is a strong American tradition of using consonant symbols for this purpose.

A major question to be considered here is the question of vowel length. Middle English had a series of long vowels and a series of short vowels, and the length values of these vowels have, on the whole, been inherited in modern English. But very often the vowel qualities have changed in the meantime. So while Middle English had a long and a short version of /i/, probably with much the same quality, as is the case in modern Finnish, Japanese and Maori for example, the short version has shifted to become modern [ɪ]. We now have a distinction between a long vowel which we might transcribe [i:] and a short vowel which we might transcribe [ɪ]. Since these differ in both length and quality, we do not strictly need to mark both these qualities in our transcription system, since one can always be predicted from the other. So we could choose to distinguish *bead* from *bid* as [bid], [bɪd] or as [bi:d], [bid]. Given that [bid] can thus mean *bead* or *bid* depending on the system of transcription used, a single word transcribed in isolation may be ambiguous, and so many linguists prefer to use the redundant transcription of [bi:d] versus [bɪd], but this is less economical than might be considered ideal.

<4.30> There is an appeal to economy here. Why should economy matter? Are there advantages to lack of economy?

In the next data-set a number of different ways of transcribing the vowels of British RP (the accent that has been transcribed in this book where there is no particular point being made) are provided, which illustrate some of the different ways of visualising the phonological system of English in terms of the vowels. System 1 is the one which is used in this book; system 2 marks length and makes the reader imply the quality differences, while system 3 marks quality and leaves the reader to deduce the length differences. System 4 uses consonants rather than vowels at the end of diphthongs (and some long monophthongs). System 5 uses a double spelling to show length, and correspondingly uses fewest symbols, which makes it the most economical system. The cue words are the names of lexical sets for English devised to allow comparison between accents of English.

<4.31> Consider the claim that the system with the fewest symbols is the most economical one. Do you find this claim convincing?

System 4 is interesting because, as we saw in section 4.3.1, /j/ and /w/ do not otherwise occur postvocalically in English; this transcription system fills in that gap in their distribution. The system works better for North American varieties of English which have a postvocalic /r/, so that the START, NURSE, NEAR, SQUARE and CURE vowels have a following /r/, and all of the long vowels can be transcribed with a final consonant symbol. When applied to RP, the neatness of this system is less obvious.

Data-set 4.6

Alternative transcriptions systems for RP vowels

Cue word	1	2	3	4	5
KIT	ɪ	i	ɪ	ɪ	i
DRESS	e	e	ɛ	ɛ	e
TRAP	æ	a	a	a	a
STRUT	ʌ	ə	ʌ	ʌ	ʌ
LOT	ɒ	ɔ	ɒ	ɒ	ɔ
FOOT	ʊ	u	ʊ	ʊ	u
FLEECE	iː	iː	i	ij	ii
START	ɑː	aː	ɑ	ɑ	aa
NURSE	ɜː	əː	ɜ	ɜ	əə
THOUGHT	ɔː	ɔː	ɔ	ɔ	ɔɔ
GOOSE	uː	uː	u	uw	əu
FACE	eɪ	ei	eɪ	ej	ei
PRICE	aɪ	ai	aɪ	aj	ai
CHOICE	ɔɪ	ɔi	ɔɪ	ɔj	ɔi
MOUTH	aʊ	au	aʊ	aw	au
GOAT	əʊ	əu	əʊ	ow	əu
NEAR	ɪə	iə	ɪə	iə	iə
SQUARE	eə	eə	ɛə	ɛə	eə
CURE	ʊə	uə	ʊə	ʉə	uə
commA	ə	ə	ə	ə	ə
happY	i	i	ɪ	ɪ	i

The data-set opposite provides some transcription systems for different varieties of English where there are different numbers of phonemes and here the phonetics of the vowels found in the various lexical sets can be markedly different.

<4.32> Transcribe each of the following quotations. Makes sure that all the vowel symbols you use come from the same system set out in the tables: do not mix and match.

- I go to the opera whether I need the sleep or not.
- Madam, don't you have any unexpressed thoughts?
- Why is 'abbreviated' such a long word?
- Many thanks for your book. I shall waste no time in reading it.
- A professor is someone who talks in someone else's sleep.
- If men liked shopping, they'd call it research.
- If you think squash is a competitive activity, try flower arrangement.
- My hamster died yesterday. Fell asleep at the wheel.
- What's another word for thesaurus?
- The early bird may catch the worm, but it's the second mouse that gets the cheese.
- I'm on two diets at the moment, because you simply don't get enough to eat on one.
- An idea isn't responsible for the people who believe in it.
- Literature is mostly about having sex and not much about having children. Life is the other way round.
- Why is the alphabet in that order? Is it because of the song?
- When I get a lot of tension and headaches, I do what it says on the aspirin bottle: take two and keep away from children.
- Some people come by the name of genius in the same way as an insect comes by the name of centipede – not because it has a hundred feet but because most people can't count above fourteen.

Data-set 4.7
Vowel transcriptions for various varieties of English

Cue word	RP	North American	Standard Scottish	Northern English	Australian
KIT	ɪ	ɪ	ɪ	ɪ	ɪ
DRESS	e	ɛ	ɛ	ɛ	e
NEVER	e	ɛ	ë	ɛ	e
TRAP	æ	æ	a	a	a
STRUT	ʌ	ə, ʌ	ʌ	ʊ	ʌ
LOT	ɒ	ɑ[a]	ɔ	ɒ	ɒ
FOOT	ʊ	ʊ	ʉ	ʊ	ʊ
FLEECE	iː	i	i	iː	əi
START	ɑː	ɑr	ar	ɑː	aː
BATH	ɑː	æ	a	a	aː
NURSE	ɜː	ɝ	ʌr	ɜː	øː
THOUGHT	ɔː	ɔ	ɔ	ɔː	oː
NORTH	ɔː	ɔr	ɔr	ɔː	oː
FORCE	ɔː	oʊr	ɔr	ɔː	oː
GOOSE	uː	u	ʉ	uː	əʉ
FACE	eɪ	eɪ	e	eː	ai
PRICE	aɪ	aɪ	ʌe[b]	aɪ	ɑi
CHOICE	ɔɪ	ɔɪ	ɔe	ɔɪ	oi
MOUTH	aʊ	aʊ	ʌʉ	aʊ	ɛʊ
GOAT	əʊ	oʊ	o	oː	ʌʊ
GOLD	əʊ	oʊ	o	oː	ɒʊ
NEAR	ɪə	ɪr	ɪr	iə	iə
SQUARE	eə	ɛr	ɛr	ɛə	eː
CURE	uə	ʊr	ʉr	uə	uə
happY	ə	ə	ə	ə	ə
lettER	ə	ɚ	ər	ə	ə
commA	i	i	i	ɪ	əi

Notes:
[a] May not be distinct from the THOUGHT vowel, in which case, use the symbol for THOUGHT.
[b] The vowel in *tide* [tʌed] is distinct from that in *tied* [taed], but the distinction is predictable, being related to general principles of Scottish English.

4.4 The elements of sounds

When we discussed the description of consonants and vowels, we used three-term labels to describe each segment. Each of the terms in these labels is more usually called a FEATURE, and that term has already been used in this chapter and in Chapter 2. More specifically, they are called DISTINCTIVE FEATURES, because if you think about what distinguishes between *pat* and *bat*, you will see it is not so much the entire first consonant as the feature of voicing which is distinctive. The set of labels from these three-term labels can thus be seen as providing a system of distinctive features.

The benefits of dealing with distinctive features rather than phonemes are at least two-fold. First, using features allows you be more precise in locating the distinctiveness of particular phonemes or, in other instances, of saying precisely what has changed in phonological change, what has assimilated in instances of assimilation, and so on. Using distinctive features thus allows you to be more precise. Second, using distinctive features allows you to see sounds not simply as isolated units, but as belonging to classes. If we think of a [p], for example, it is simply a consonantal sound; but if we think of it by its features, we can see it as a member of a class of voiceless sounds, a class of bilabial sounds, and a class of plosive sounds. This becomes very important when we want to talk about phonological processes, since the same phonological process very often affects all members of a particular class. If you read more widely, you will find these classes referred to as **NATURAL CLASSES**. The idea behind the word 'natural' is that any collection of sounds might be a class. For instance, it is conceivable that the sounds [p], [n], [ɾ] and [v] should be grouped together as a class for some purposes. But this would not be a natural class because it would not be based on the phonetics of the sound, and accordingly we would not expect it to be influenced by any phonetic or phonological change or process. So we can summarise by saying that distinctive features allow us to specify natural classes of sounds, and that ideally these classes act together in undergoing some phonological process or change.

> **<4.33>** What natural class might the sounds [p], [t], [k], [ʔ] belong to?

Unfortunately, although the traditional three-term labels define many of the natural classes we wish to talk about in phonology, they do not do a good enough job.

Consider a class of English phonemes made up of /s, z, ʃ, ʒ, tʃ, dʒ/. According to the features you know this cannot be defined as a natural class. Yet it acts as one: it is precisely this set of consonants of English which demands that an immediately following plural should be realised as /ɪz/ rather than /s/ or /z/. If we want to say what class causes this using the three-term labels you have learnt, we cannot do it; we need some more or some different distinctive features if we are to do that.

> **<4.34>** Prove to yourself that the claim made above is correct. What are the plurals of each of the following words (transcribe them): *lip*, *fib*, *kit*, *lid*, *bitch*, *ridge*, *pick*, *pig*, *riff*, *sieve*, *kiss*, *quiz*, *dish*, *rim*, *sin*, *thing*, *pill*? If you can think of nouns which end in /ð/ or /ʒ/ add them to the list.

Second, consider [i] and [j]. We have already seen that these two sounds are phonetically very similar to each other. Yet we would term [i] a front close unrounded vowel and [j] a voiced palatal approximant, which gives no clue to their phonetic (and sometimes phonological) similarity. If we want to show similarities between consonants and vowels, we need different features.

CONTROVERSY: The nature of features

Although everybody agrees on the need for distinctive features, virtually everything else about them is controversial. Should they be based on the way the sounds are articulated (as the phonetic features we have already used are), or should they be based on the acoustic structure of the sounds or the way in which that acoustic structure is perceived? Should they all be formally alike, or are there grounds for having several types of feature? Should a single set of features apply to all human languages, or should we set up a different set for each language? Should we think of features as having two values: being either present (a plus value) or absent (a minus value)? One alternative is simply to think of features being there or not being mentioned at all. Another alternative is to think of some features as having a number of different values, not just plus or minus. For example, it might be possible to have a feature for vowel height with different values for different heights. Despite the huge amount of discussion there has been about distinctive features, there is no generally agreed answer to any of these questions, and it is therefore impossible to provide a set of distinctive features which everyone will agree about. Virtually every book you consult will have its own set of distinctive features, though this may not be made clear.

Because it is not possible to give a definitive set of features, the best that can be done is to provide a list of some typical features. These will be dealt with in groups, depending on the way the features might be assumed to operate (though, as noted in the box, any assumptions here are controversial). Examples of their value in specifying natural classes are also provided. A table of the distinctive features discussed here is presented in the data-set overleaf and Figure 4.2.

Figure 4.2 Distinctive features for English

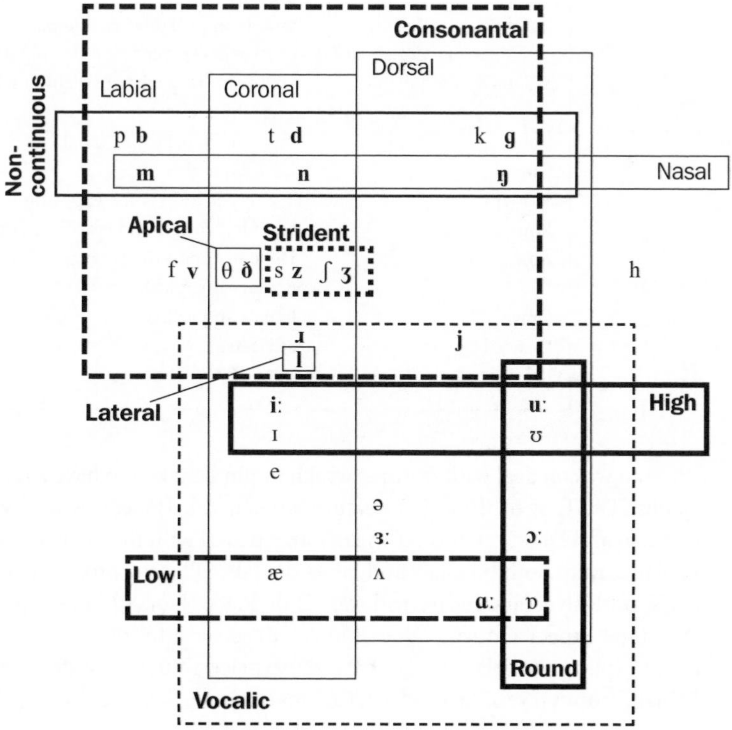

Note: **bold** font voiced in consonants, tense/[+ATR] in vowels.

Data-set 4.8

The distinctive features discussed in this chapter

Feature	Value	Relevant segments
Place	Labial	p, b, m, ɱ, ɸ, β, f, v, ʋ; rounded vowels; labialised consonants
	Coronal	t, d, ʈ, ɖ, n, ɳ, θ, ð, s, z, ʃ, ʒ, ʂ, ʐ, r, l, ɭ, ɽ, ɬ; front vowels
	Dorsal	c, ɟ, ɲ, ç, j, ʎ, j, k, g, ŋ, x, ɣ, ʟ, q, ɢ, χ, ʁ, ɴ, ʀ; back vowels
	Radical	ħ, ʕ, ʔ
Height	High	i, ɪ, ɨ, ʉ, ʊ, u
	Mid (if used)	e, ø, ɘ, ɵ, ɤ, o; ɛ, ə, ɜ, ɞ, ʌ, ɔ
	Low	æ, a, Œ, ɐ, ɑ, ɒ
Voice	Voiced	b, β, v, d, ð, z, ʒ, ɖ, ʐ, ɟ, j, g, ɣ, ɢ, ʁ, ʕ, ɦ; all sonorant consonants unless specifically stated to be unvoiced; all vowels unless specifically stated to be unvoiced
	Voiceless	p, ɸ, f, t, θ, s, ʃ, ʈ, ʂ, c, ç, k, χ, q, χ, ħ, ʔ, h; other segments specifically identified as voiceless
Sonorant	Sonorant	all nasals, taps, trills, approximants and vowels
	Obstruent	stops, fricatives and affricates
Continuant	Continuant	all fricatives, liquids, approximants and vowels
	Stop	all stops, affricates and nasal consonants
ATR	Tense	i, u; in some expositions e, o; others depending on the language
	Lax	ɪ, ʊ; in some expositions ɛ, ɔ; others depending on the language
Vocalic	Vocalic	vowels, approximants, liquids
	Consonantal	obstruents (except glottals), nasals, liquids
Syllabic	Syllabic	vowels in the peaks of syllables; syllabic consonants
	Non-syllabic	everything else
Nasal		m, ɯ, m, n, ɲ, ɳ, ŋ, ɴ; nasal vowels
Lateral		l, ɬ, ɮ, ʎ, ʟ
Strident		s, z, ʃ, ʒ, ʂ, ʐ; in some expositions f, v
Round		rounded vowels and labialised consonants
Apical		Depends upon the language; in British English dentals are apical.
Grave		labials and velars
Delayed Release		affricates

First we can deal with features which might be taken to have a number of different values. The first of these is a feature we can call [Place], whose values are Labial, Coronal and Dorsal. 'Coronal' means 'articulated with the blade of the tongue'. [Place: Labial] covers both bilabials and labio-dentals, [Place: Coronal] covers dentals, alveolars, post-alveolars and retroflexes, and [Place: Dorsal] covers palatals and velars. We might expect a fourth value, Radical, to account for pharyngeals, but this is rarely made explicit. Vowels can also have these place values: rounded vowels have [Place: Labial], front vowels have [Place: Coronal] and back vowels have [Place: Dorsal].

In Maori, most consonants can occur before most vowels, but the [Place: Labial] consonants /w/ and /f/ (which was almost certainly [ʍ] in earlier Maori) do not occur before the rounded vowels [u] and [ɔ] in native words (borrowings from English such as /furutu/ 'fruit' do occur). The plosive /p/ is found in this position in words like /pu:/ 'flute'. This seems to have been in origin a constraint against sequences of consonant and vowel both pronounced with rounded lips, but with the loss of rounding in /f/ has become a constraint against non-stop [Place: Labial] consonants with [Place: Labial] vowels.

In standard varieties of English from America and England, only consonants with the feature [Place: Coronal] are found after the diphthong /aʊ/ in monosyllabic words. Relevant words are *mouth, mouth* (verb); *out, loud; house, house* (verb); *howl; town; tower* (in varieties with postvocalic /r/); *couch, gouge*. There are no monosyllabic words ending /aʊʃ/ or /aʊʒ/, though Australian and New Zealand English have a word *stoush* /staʊʃ/ 'fight, dispute'. There is nothing obviously difficult with forms such as /taʊv/ or /maʊg/, but they do not occur.

> **<4.35>** Can you find any counter-examples to this claim in your variety of English?

There are surprisingly few exceptions. The few that do exist suggest, though, that the constraint is a fairly weak one in English, one which can be over-ridden.

> **<4.36>** If retroflex consonants have [Place: Coronal], why were none of them illustrated in the list above?

The other feature which seems to have a range of values is the feature for vowel height. The difficulty here is that it is not clear what the values should be. Typically, phonologists have made do with [Height: High] and [Height: Low], leaving as a third value something which is neither high nor low. This has the disadvantage that when a language has four distinct vowel heights, as conservative French does, for instance, with *si* /si/ 'if', *ces* /se/ 'these', *c'est* /sɛ/ 'it is', *sa* /sa/ 'his/her (FEM)', the open-mid and the close-mid vowels have to be said to be distinguished by some feature other than height. We could solve this easily by adding a third value, [Height: Mid], but this has been resisted over the years, probably on the grounds that mid vowels seldom seem to act as a natural class.

CONTROVERSY: Consonant height?

If there is a feature [Height] with a number of values, we might argue that that there are two heights with the active articulator closer to the passive articulator than for vowels, namely the position for fricatives and the position for stops. Such a claim would allow a relatively simple description of changes such as that whereby an earlier [g] in Danish has become [ɯ] and then [ʊ], for example, in the word *sagfører* 'lawyer', now pronounced ['saʊføːɐ]. While this seems a perfectly reasonable analysis, it is one which is rarely made in the discussion of distinctive features, and consonant manner of articulation and vowel height are instead defined by separate features.

Close and near-close vowels both count as having [Height: High] under this system, and open and near-open vowels are both [Height: Low]. Thus in conservative RP English, where the vowel /ɪ/ can occur word finally in a word like *pity* /pɪtɪ/, we can find a weak palatal link between either that or /iː/ and a following word initial vowel.

<4.37> Do you pronounce the word *pity* in the way transcribed above? If not how do you pronounce it? If you do not pronounce this word as transcribed above, does that invalidate the argument?

The 'weak palatal link' referred to above sounds as though it might be a [j], but *say 'S'* /seɪ es/ is not the same as *say 'yes'* /seɪ jes/ where there is a real /j/ phoneme. The IPA does not give us a really good way of transcribing this phenomenon, but we could perhaps write [pɪtɪ ʲ ɪt] and [siː ʲ ɪt], for example. This palatal glide arises only after vowels which are front and [Height: High].

Next, we can consider features which are typically treated as binary: that is, having both a plus and a minus value. Typically such features are needed where both the plus value and the minus value can delimit natural classes. An alternative approach to such features is to name both of the poles independently, and both approaches will be sketched below.

The obvious feature of this type is [±Voice] (or equivalently [Voiced] and [Voiceless]). Variants of the English plural, possessive and third person singular present tense markers are distributed according to voicing, with the /s/ variant following [Voiceless] or [-Voice] sounds, and the /z/ variant following [Voiced] or [+Voice] sounds (this is an oversimplification, because we have already seen that there is a third variant, but true as far as it goes). Thus we find *cats* /kæts/, *cuffs* /kʌfs/, *walks* /wɔːks/, *stops* /stɒps/ as opposed to *dogs* /dɒgz/, *hills* /hɪlz/, *things* /θɪŋz/, *shoes* /ʃuːz/ and so on.

<4.38> Find five English nouns that have regular plurals, and check that they take the predicted form for the plural marker.

Another feature that works this way is [±Sonorant] (or equivalently [Obstruent] versus [Sonorant]). Universally, [Sonorant] sounds tend to be [Voiced], while [Obstruent] sounds tend to be [Voiceless], though there are clear counter-examples in both directions – which explains why we need both features/feature-pairs. English has voiced obstruents such as /v/, /z/ and so on, and Burmese has voiceless sonorants such as /m̥/: /m̥jín/ 'be high' contrasts with /mjín/ 'raise, make higher'.

If stops are not marked as such by virtue of the [Height] feature, they need to be marked in some other way. This is often done with a feature [±Continuant] (or equivalently [Stop] and [Continuant]). Stops include affricates and nasals, and we will see features which can distinguish these from other stops below. Trills are usually included as [Continuant] because they can be extended in articulation. Less clear is what should happen to taps and flaps. They are neither clearly stops, nor clearly continuants. They are usually classified as [Continuant], although this may seem odd, and may not be appropriate in some languages (e.g. where [ɾ] is an allophone of /d/).

In Wari', only [Stop] consonants can occur word-finally, so that we find words like /pakun/ 'mountain', /miʃem/ 'be dirty', /kep/ 'hold', /ʧek/ 'day', /konoʔ/ 'die' but no words like */pakuh/, */miʃeɾ/, */kew/ although all these phonemes occur in the language.

A distinction which applies only to vowels is captured by the feature [±ATR], where 'ATR' stands for 'Advanced Tongue Root'. This feature has had many names in its chequered history, so that the equivalent polar terms may be [Tense] and [Lax] or, in the case of English, [Long] and [Short]. Vowels which are [+ATR] ([Tense]) are produced with the root of the tongue further forward in the pharynx, and so with an expanded pharyngeal chamber. Vowels which are [-ATR] ([Lax]) have a narrowed pharynx. In English it is generally assumed that the long vowels are [+ATR], though this is a slightly dubious assumption. There are probably better ways of representing the differences between long and short vowels in English, ways which depend on the different patterns in which these vowels can occur. We will not go into this here.

One feature which may or may not belong in this category is what I shall term [±Vocalic]. It is usually broken down into two distinct features [Consonantal] and [Vocalic], each of which may be viewed as binary. In such a view, obstruents and nasals are [+Consonantal, -Vocalic], vowels are [+Vocalic, -Consonantal], sonorant consonants such as approximants and [r]- and [l]-sounds (often grouped as LIQUIDS) are [+Consonantal, +Vocalic], and [h] is [-Consonantal, -Vocalic]. It is not clear that we need all of this, however, since we can already distinguish obstruents from sonorants, and we will see below we have ways of distinguishing nasals and laterals. There are two things that this use of features might give us. The first is that it allows us to group /j, w, r, l/ together if we need to, and we do need to. In English initial consonant clusters where there are three consonants, as in words like *spray* and *stupid* (for RP English at least; for some speakers *stupid* is not a relevant example), the first is always /s/, the second is a stop, and the third is precisely a member of the group under consideration.

 <4.39> Provide some English words to illustrate the patterns which occur here.

 <4.40> Why isn't *stupid* relevant for some speakers?

The other thing that having [±Consonantal] and [±Vocalic] might be useful for is if [h] does not act like other fricatives. This depends on the language. In Japanese, the usual analysis is that /h/ has [h], [ɸ] and [ç] as allophones ([ç] occurs before /i/ as in /hito/ 'person' pronounced [çito], and [ɸ] occurs before /ɯ/ so that /hɯne/ 'ship' is pronounced [ɸɯne]) so that treating all the allophones as fricatives has some value. There are languages which behave differently, though. In Kiowa, for instance, the sequence /jh/ is pronounced [jhj], but the same spread of the palatal consonant is not found with any other fricatives.

We will discuss syllables in more detail later (sections 4.5.1, 4.7). In the meantime, we can use a lay notion of a syllable, and say that anything which forms a syllable by itself is syllabic. The feature [±Syllabic] (or [Syllabic] versus [Non-Syllabic]) is used to distinguish vowels from glides like [j] and [w] and also to distinguish syllabic consonants from non-syllabic ones. The vowel [i] is [+Syllabic], while [j] is [-Syllabic], and the [n] at the end of the word *button* if it is pronounced [bʌtn] with no vowel between the [t] and the [n] is [+Syllabic].

Last, there are a number of features which are either present or not. Many of these are applicable only if some other feature is already chosen.

[Nasal] is one of these. Either consonants or vowels can be [Nasal]. It is superimposed on another articulation by the action of velic opening.

Similarly [Lateral], which usually applies to sounds which are [Place: Coronal] can be used to distinguish between, for example, [l] and [ɾ].

[Strident] is one whose precise application is controversial. Everyone agrees that fricatives and affricates involving a groove in the tongue are [Strident]. This includes [s, z, ʃ, ʒ, ʂ, ʐ] and excludes [θ, ð, ɕ, ʑ, ç, j] and the corresponding affricates. All of these have the feature [Place: Coronal]. Some authorities see [f] and [v] as strident in relation to [ɸ] and [β] as well. In English, the regular plural is realised as /ɪz/ following the [Place: Coronal, Strident] sounds, as illustrated by /pɑːsɪz/, /pʊʃɪz/, /wɒtʃɪz/, /dʒʌdʒɪz/ and so on.

The feature [Round] can be seen as a more specific marking which applies to some [Place: Labial] sounds. Labial vowels are often round, rather than merely made with the involvement of the lips. There are also a number of languages which have contrastively labialised consonants. Lezgian has contrastively labialised versions of all dental, velar and uvular obstruents. Note that this implies that sounds may have two places of articulation simultaneously. This might be seen as an argument for separating these places of articulation out into distinct features rather than treating them as values of a single feature.

The feature [Apical] is needed in a language like Basque to distinguish between two different strident fricatives. So the word /s̺agu/ 'mouse' has an apico-alveolar fricative, while /s̻akur/ 'dog' has a lamino-alveolar fricative. The same feature can also be used to distinguish retroflexes from post-alveolars and, in many languages, dentals from alveolars. In some Australian languages, apical alveolars and apical retroflexes behave in different ways from laminal dentals and post-alveolars/palatals. For example, in Pitta-Pitta apical but not laminal consonants may occur as the first consonant in CC clusters.

The feature [Grave] is used by some scholars as a way of grouping labials and velars together. For example, in Pitta-Pitta, the second consonant in a CC cluster must be either labial or velar, and in Danish /a/ is realised as [ɑ] before labials and velars, but not before coronals.

Some authorities have a feature [Delayed Release] which can apply only to stops, marking them as being affricated. In German, for instance, /pf/ and /ts/ would be marked as [Delayed Release], in contrast with /p/ and /t/.

Not all groups of sounds that act as a class can be defined by a single feature. The set of fricatives, for example, would be defined as [Obstruent, Continuant] (or [-Sonorant, +Continuant]). The set of front rounded vowels (in a language like French) would be defined by the features [Vowel, Place: Coronal, Round]. Note that, while sets of features have been presented here with commas between them as a space-saving device, they are frequently displayed set above each other, especially in the formulation of rules. In this layout, the set of features for front rounded vowels would look like this:

$$\begin{bmatrix} \text{Vowel} \\ \text{Place: Coronal} \\ \text{Round} \end{bmatrix}$$

4.5 Sonority

Not all sounds carry equally well. If you imagine yourself listening to a conversation from a distance of 3 metres, 10 metres and 20 metres, you will realise that the further away you are from the speakers the less you are likely to hear of the conversation. Nevertheless, it might still be possible to hear some sounds at 20 metres. On the whole, the sounds you would be most likely to hear at that distance would be the vowels, and those you would be least likely to hear would be the obstruents. Let us say that this carrying power or relative loudness in comparison with other sounds produced with the same length, stress and pitch, is SONORITY. We can also note that on the whole greater sonority correlates with greater openness of the vocal tract.

The result is that we can set up a hierarchy of sonority. The sounds produced with the most open vocal tract and the sounds that carry best are the vowels (we could make subdivisions with vowels if we wanted to, but it would not be helpful at this stage). The next most open sounds are the approximants, but specifically the non-lateral approximants (i.e. the vocoids). The next stage down is usually labelled the 'LIQUIDS', but this term is very poorly defined in phonetic terms; it may be considered a poetic term referring to r-sounds and l-sounds, sounds which are considered appropriate for describing, in an onomatopoetical manner, flowing things such as streams (although the *Oxford English Dictionary* suggests alternative reasons for the label, and gives something of its mixed history). We can define the term rather more specifically in phonetic terms as follows: a liquid is a non-nasal sonorant which is a contoid. An alternative approach is to say that liquids are laterals, taps and trills. Nasals are less sonorant than liquids, and obstruents are the least sonorous of all sounds (again we could subdivide obstruents, but it would not be helpful). That is, we have a hierarchy of sonority as shown in Figure 4.3.

 <4.41> Put the following set of sounds in order of decreasing sonority: [l, t, n, u].

Figure 4.3
A sonority
hierarchy

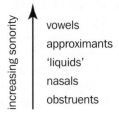

vowels
approximants
'liquids'
nasals
obstruents

increasing sonority

4.5.1 Using sonority 1: Syllable peaks

How many syllables are there in the words *causing, pretty* or *spasm*? You will probably say that each of these words contains two syllables, and that the line *To be or not to be, that is the question* contains eleven syllables. The question we need to ask is what it means to say that a word or a line contains that many syllables. At first glance it may seem that it has something to do with the number of vowels in a word or a line, and certainly there is a high correlation; but the correlation is not always perfect. While some speakers may have two (phonetic) vowels in *spasm*, others only have one, yet would probably agree that the word contained two syllables. Some speakers pronounced words like *hidden* or *little* with only one vowel sound (the stressed [ɪ] in both cases), but still say that these words contain two syllables.

But if the correlation with vowels is not perfect, there seems to be a much better correlation with sonority. To see this, consider graphs of the three words in Figure 4.4 in which the segments are plotted against their degree of sonority as given in the sonority hierarchy in Figure 4.3. In each case, the number of syllables corresponds to the number of peaks of sonority. We can then define the number of syllables in a word as the number of peaks of sonority in the word.

One of the benefits of this approach is that it explains why the words *lilt* [lɪlt] and *little* [lɪtl], even if they contain the same segments, should have different numbers of syllables: because the [l] in *little* comes after an obstruent, it forms a new peak of sonority, while in *lilt* there is only one peak of sonority, and so only one syllable.

This approach to finding the number of syllables is not without its problems, although the problems appear to be superable. Two such problems will be mentioned here, although this is not an exhaustive list.

The first can be illustrated with the pair of phrases *hidden aims* and *hid names*. Each of these can have the transcription [hɪdneɪmz], yet the first has three syllables and the second has two. Clearly, if the same transcription is used in each case, there cannot be differences in peaks of sonority. The solution here seems to be that the units with which syllable numbers are associated are words, not phrases. *Hidden aims* has three syllables because the word *hidden* has two, and *hid names* has two because each of the words that make up the phrase has one syllable.

The second can be illustrated with the word *seeing* [siːɪŋ]. We would probably agree that this has two syllables, but it has only one peak of sonority, which just lasts for a long time. We can contrast this with what happens in words like *loud* [laʊd] where there is also one peak of sonority, again lasting for a long time, but only one syllable. There are at least two possible solutions to this problem. The first depends upon transcription. If we adopt a transcription system in which diphthongs and long vowels are represented as sequences of short vowel plus glide, so that *see* is transcribed [sij] and *how* is transcribed [haw] (see section 4.3.2, Table 4.6), we will obtain the transcriptions [sijiŋ] and [lawd], which will give *seeing* two syllables and *loud* just one. (Alternatively, if we use the type of transcription given just under <4.37>, we would get a similar result.) There is something unsatisfactory, though, about having the number of syllables we recognise in a word being dependent upon the particular transcription system we happen to choose, so that an alternative approach would clearly be preferable. We can speculatively suggest that this preferable approach

Figure 4.4
Sonority graphs
for three words

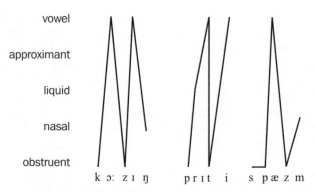

might be to extend the kind of explanation we used to distinguish *hid names* from *hidden aims*. There we said that syllables were associated with particular words. If we consider *seeing*, we find that it contains the word *see* and then has the affix *-ing*. It might be the case that certain affixes (like *-ing*) behave phonologically as though they are separate words, and that *seeing* contains two syllables because *see* contains one and *-ing* contains one. If this were the case it would also allow us to draw the distinction between *lightning* [laɪtnɪŋ] 'flash of light causing thunder' and *lightening* [laɪtn̩ɪŋ] 'getting lighter' which, for some speakers at least, are distinguished not by the segments involved but by the number of syllables in the words. If we treat *-ing* as a separate phonological word, then *lighten* has two syllables, *-ing* has one so *lightening* has three, whereas *lightning*, which is a single phonological word, contains only two syllables because it contains only two peaks of sonority. There are other reasons for believing that affixes like *-ing* require particular phonological treatment, but we will not discuss those here.

4.5.2 Using sonority 2: A first approach to phonotactics

It follows from this way of counting syllables that any word which has a single syllable peak must have consonants before that peak ordered according to increasing sonority, and consonants after that peak ordered in terms of decreasing sonority. Thus, while [kjuːt], [blʌnt], [smæk] and [kɪlnz] are all monosyllabic English words which fit the general pattern, [jkuːt], [lbʌtn], [msæk] and [kɪnlz] are either completely impossible or would involve more than one syllable if they were found.

In English, this general pattern of fitting words to the sonority hierarchy is adhered to very firmly. There are no examples of words which break this pattern for most speakers (some speakers think that *prism* is a monosyllabic word, but very few). In other languages the adherence to the general rule is not so firm, although most words seem to fit the overall pattern even in these languages. For example, Russian has words such as [rdetʲ] 'to blush', [lgatʲ] 'to tell lies', [mgla] 'fog' which are viewed by speakers of the language as being monosyllabic. Speakers of French generally feel that *prisme* [pʁism] 'prism' is a monosyllabic word. And in Bella Coola, [qʼ.ps.tÿ.tx] is a four-syllable word (with the syllable boundaries marked by the full stops) meaning 'I taste it'. In such languages we might have to redefine the hierarchy in order to come up with a version which would tell us what counted as a syllable for that language, either merging adjacent steps or subdividing the steps given in Figure 4.3. Alternatively or additionally, we might have to say that to form a new syllabic peak, the graph had to show an increase of at least two steps (or some other suitable number), or that there could be no new syllable unless the sonority graph passed a certain threshold. In the Bella Coola example it might be that stops count as separate syllables when they are adjacent to other stops – we would need more data to be sure. As a final resort, it might be necessary to look beyond sonority for an explanation of what a syllable is, though this approach is not currently favoured.

<4.42> A narrower transcription of the French word *prisme* would be [pʁism̥], with a voiceless nasal. That being the case, is it a good example of a breach of the sonority hierarchy? Why (not)?

4.6 More phonotactics

The sequences of sounds that are allowed in, say, monosyllabic words are constrained far more tightly than the sonority hierarchy alone would suggest. We will look at just a few constraints here, going from the most general to the most specific, and focussing on English.

First, languages have individual permissible syllable structures. Many languages, of which Maori is one, permit only OPEN syllables (that is syllables which end in a vowel), while others permit both open and CLOSED syllables (ones that end in a vowel or ones that end in a consonant). Mandarin permits closed syllables, but restricts the consonants that can occur in the final position to two: [n] and [ŋ] (and, at least in Beijing, [r]). English is far more liberal, allowing up to three initial consonants (in words like *splay* /spleɪ/, *strike* /straɪk/, *square* /skweə/) and – at least in maximally clear speech – four final consonants (in words like *sixths* /sɪksθs/, *twelfths* /twelfθs/).

<4.43> In colloquial speech would you have four consonants at the ends of these words? Are there implications for the statements of phonotactic patterns? Is there any reason to base such statements on maximally clear speech?

To discuss such matters we need some terminology. Words such as *mat* and *fat* rhyme, so let us call the bit of the syllable that is used in rhyming the RHYME of the syllable, and the initial consonant the ONSET (if there is one). We can then divide the rhyme into the PEAK (sometimes called the nucleus) and the consonantal CODA (if there is one). Each of the onset, the peak and the coda can be made up of more than one element, as illustrated in Figure 4.5.

Using such terminology we can define an open syllable as one that has no coda, and a closed syllable as one that has a coda.

Now consider onsets in English which are made up of three consonants. Some examples of relevant words have already been given, and we can add *spew*, *spray*, *stew*, *scream*, *skew*, *sclerosis*. In every single one of these words, the first consonant is an /s/.

Figure 4.5
Syllable
structures

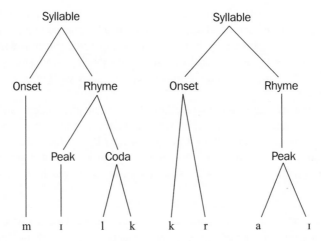

There are no English words such as **fklerosis*, **thpew* and so on. Second, in each of these words, the second position is filled by a stop consonant. And in third position there is always a (median or lateral) approximant: /l/, /r/, /j/ or /w/.

> **<4.44>** Ornithologists might be familiar with the word *smew* /smjuː/ 'a small merganser'. What modification does this word imply for the formulation of the constraint on word-initial three-consonant clusters? Why? Are there any other possible three-conso-nant clusters not already illustrated?

Second, consider clusters of obstruents in the same syllable. Such clusters always agree in voicing. Some examples are marked in the words below, and are either all voiceless or all voiced.

Data-set 4.9
English

glɪm<u>ps</u>t	æ<u>dz</u>
twel<u>fθs</u>	hɑː<u>vd</u>
<u>sp</u>leɪ	bʌl<u>dʒd</u>
eɪt<u>θ</u>	kɑː<u>vz</u>
kɪɒ<u>sks</u>	bʌl<u>bz</u>

There are very few possible counter-examples to this generalisation. The first is that some people pronounce <sv> in words like *svelte* as /sv/; others regularise this to /sf/. The second is that in the words *breadth* and *width*, some speakers have the cluster /dθ/; others regularise these either to /dð/ or to /tθ/. It must be recalled that this constraint was phrased as holding within the syllable: over syllable boundaries in words like *obstruent*, *absurd*, *subtend*, *adhere* obstruents that disagree in voicing are permitted (although even then some speakers say /əbzɜːd/ or /əpsɜːd/, etc.).

Next consider morphemes that end in a nasal and a plosive. The following are single-morpheme words of English: *limp*, *lint*, *link*, *wind* (that blows), but there are no single-morpheme words such as **[lɪŋp]*, **[wɪmk]* (on morphemes, meaningful units, see section 5.4). That is, all the single-morpheme words that end in a nasal and a plosive have both nasal and stop articulated at the same place of articulation: the nasal and the plosive are homorganic. A word like [hɑːmd] which has a non-homorganic nasal plus plosive cluster thus indicates by its very form that it must be made up of more than one morpheme, in this case *harm* + the past tense morpheme.

Note that the question of whether the unit of phonotactic statements is the morpheme or the word is an important one. All three- and four-consonant clusters at the ends of words in English end in /s/, /z/, /t/, /d/ or /θ/, and in almost every case this consonant represents a morpheme (a few words like *mulct* are the exceptions). The phonotactic possibilities in morphemes are thus much more restricted than those in words.

<4.45> Make a list of ten words that begin with consonant clusters which do not involve approximants (including lateral approximants). Can you find any patterns in such clusters?

4.7 Syllabification

Although a sonority-based system as illustrated in section 4.5 can tell us how many syllables there are in a given word, it does not tell us where the syllables begin and end. We can assume that the boundary will fall near the points of minimum sonority, but does the /t/ in *pretty* belong to the first or the second syllable, for instance? In some languages questions of this type are very easy to answer. In Maori, any intervocalic consonant (and there can only ever be one) belongs to the following syllable. Some linguists suggest that this strategy should be elevated to the status of a language universal, although we will see shortly that there are reasons why it might not be appropriate in all cases for English. Similarly, in many languages, any intervocalic sequence of two consonants is divided so that the first belongs to the preceding syllable and the second to the following syllable. Thus the French words *absent* [ap.sã] 'absent', *franchement* [fʁɑ̃ʃ.mã] 'frankly', *parti* [paʁ.ti] 'departed', the division into syllables between the adjacent consonants as shown seems to match speaker's intuitions and their performance when they slow the pronunciation of the words down, for example under emphasis.

Although some authorities try to use similarly simple rules in English, they nearly always end up giving nonsensical results in some places. There is one rule, though, that most people seem to agree upon. It is that only the clusters that are allowed in monosyllabic words should be allowed in syllables. If we consider a word like *athlete* /æθliːt/, we find that no monosyllabic word could end in /θl/ (because it would become disyllabic due to its sonority profile), and no monosyllabic word begins /θl/, so the syllable boundary must come between the two consonants: [æθ.liːt]. When we move on to other rules, though, things become less clear.

Consider, for example, a suggestion based on the notion that onset consonants are to be preferred to coda consonants, namely that all consonants should belong to the following syllable where this is allowed by the general rules of English phonotactics. This would suggest that *display* and *displease* should both be divided into syllables with the [dɪ] in the first syllable and the [spl] beginning the second. But the pronunciation of [spl] is not the same in the two instances. In *display* (which does not contain the word *play*) the [l] is fully voiced, while in *displease* (which does contain the word *please*) the [l] is devoiced just as it would be at the beginning of *please*. This devoicing, as a realisation of aspiration (see section 4.3.1), would follow automatically from having the /s/ in the same syllable as the /pl/ in *display* but not in *displease*, since a /p/ is not aspirated following an /s/ in the same syllable. In other words, we have here evidence that the pronunciation of these words is influenced by the morphological structure – here by the fact that the <dis> in the first word is not a prefix, while in the second it is.

The phonotactics of English also seem to force different syllabifications on very similar words. The short vowels of English, when stressed, must be followed by a consonant. We can have words like /bɪt/, /pen/, /kæt/, /rʌt/, /pʊt/, but we cannot have words like */bɪ/, */pe/, */kæ/, */rʌ/, */pʊ/. The word *sitting*, therefore, must be /sɪt.ɪŋ/ to allow a consonant after the stressed /ɪ/ vowel. The word *seating*, on the other hand, has no need for a consonant following its stressed vowel (since /si:/ *see/sea* is not only a possible, but an actual word of English), so we can allow the generalisation to apply about consonants being initial when possible, and syllabify the word as /si:.tɪŋ/. However, in this case, the syllabification disagrees with the allophonic information, since in those varieties of English which allow glottal stop to accompany or replace a /t/ in some positions we can find both [sɪʔɪŋ] and [si:ʔɪŋ]. This glottal allophone of /t/ is generally taken to occur only in syllable codas; it is mostly found at the ends of words and the place where it is most often found is in complex codas like *sent* [senʔ], *salt* [sɔ:lʔ]. The phonotactic analysis, by contrast, would put this [ʔ] in different places in the syllable.

If we move on from there to *testing* (contrasted in this instance with *tasting*), the short /e/ means that we must have at least one consonant in the same syllable as the vowel. The allophones suggest that the /s/ and the /t/ belong together in the same syllable (whichever it is), because the /t/ is not aspirated. The morphological analysis would suggest [test.ɪŋ]. That would be possible under the allophonic analysis, as would [te.stɪŋ]. Under the rule of putting the maximum possible consonants into the onset, we would get [tes.tɪŋ]. However we deal with this, something seems to be wrong.

<4.46> What would your analysis of *tasting* be under the three ways of considering the syllabification? Do you have the same problem?

<4.47> How can we see that the Hanks (1979) syllabification in the controversy box is not entirely 'phonetic'?

> **CONTROVERSY: Syllabification**
>
> Most discussions of syllabification in English consider only the rule of putting consonants into onsets wherever possible (often sloganised as 'maximise onsets') or the allophonics; very few consider the morphological aspect. It is, of course, possible to accept only one kind of evidence, but the result is often something which does not fit with native speaker's intuitions about the syllabic structure of words. One potential source about speakers' intuitions might be normal print dictionaries, except that they are more concerned with the orthographic correlate of syllabification than with anything phonological. Hanks (1979) gives the syllabification below for orthography but puts the /sp/ of *display* in the same syllable in his transcription.
>
> >   dis.play
> >   dis.please
> >   seat.ing
> >   sit.ting
> >   test.ing
>
> Ironically, Hanks (1979: x) says that the principles used for syllabification are 'phonetic rather than etymological', yet gives [test.ə] for 'one who tests' and [tes.tə] for 'canopy over a four-poster bed'.
>
> Another option is that intervocalic consonants are **AMBISYLLABIC**, that is, they belong to both syllables, wherever the phonotactic possibilities of English permit such an analysis. This possibility solves some of the problems we had above, but is equally unpopular with some theorists. It does not solve the *display/displease* problem discussed earlier, for example. It also leads to unusual tree structures.
>
> The result of all this is that there is a great deal of disagreement about principles for syllabification in English, and a great deal of disagreement about where syllable boundaries go. Fortunately, not all languages are as recalcitrant as English to general principles in this area

4.8 More or less than a syllable

Some languages, whether or not they have linguistic processes which depend on the recognition of syllables, also make use of a unit intermediate between the phoneme and the syllable. That unit is called the **MORA**. Consider the data-set opposite.

Here there are three constructions. The data is presented in Maori orthography, where a macron over a letter shows vowel length. No lexical word in Maori can be made up of a consonant (or no initial consonant) and a short vowel: the minimum length for a lexical word involves two distinct vowels or one long vowel. In the imperatives, if there is one long vowel or two short vowels (independent of the number of consonants), an extra vowel is added before the verb to make it imperative. Where the verb has three or more vowels, no extra vowel is needed. Similarly with vocatives. To call someone whose name contains only a long vowel or two short ones, you need the extra vowel, but with longer names, there is no need. With reduplication, if the base word consists of two vowels, both of them are copied, while if it consists of more than two, just the last two are copied. A better way to look at this is to say that there is, in

Data-set 4.10
Maori

Imperatives:			
E tū!	'stand!'	Haere!	'go!'
E noho!	'sit!'	Whakarongo!	'listen!'
Vocatives:			
E Mere!	'Mary!'	Hōne!	'John!'
E Wī!	'Wi!'	Wiremu!	'William!'
Reduplication:			
haere	'go'	hāerēre	'stroll about, meander'
ako	'learn'	akoako	'consult'

Maori, a unit made up of (C)V (that is, an optional consonant and a vowel). This unit is the mora. A long vowel is made up of VV; it is the equivalent of two vowels and so is two moras long (or *morae*, either plural is used). Where a word has just two moras the extra element is needed for the imperative or the vocative to ensure that the phrase is at least three moras long. In the reduplication pattern illustrated, the last two moras are copied.

<4.48> So what would you expect the reduplicated form of Maori *paru* 'dirt' to be?

Japanese is another language that uses moras. We are familiar with the Japanese Haiku in English, but we report it as being made up of 17 syllables, in three lines of five, seven and five syllables. This is not right. The poem is made up of 17 moras; Japanese counts moras not syllables. Consider the examples below:

Data-set 4.11
Japanese
Haiku

Ran no ka ya	/ra.n. no. ka. ja.	The fragrant orchid
Chō no tsubasa ni	tɕo.o. no.tsu.ba.sa. ni.	Into a butterfly's wing
Takimono su	ta.ki.mo.no. su./	It breathes the incense.
Goroppon	/go.ro.p.po.n	Five or six pieces
Namaki tsuketaru	na.ma.ki tsu.ke.ta.ru.	Of freshly cut timber
Mizutamari	mi.zu.ta.ma.ri./	Over a muddy pool.

In the first haiku, the /n/ at the end of the first word counts as a mora by itself, even though /ran/ is only one syllable; the first word of the second line also counts as two moras, but a single syllable, because a long vowel counts as two moras, as in Maori. In the first line of the second haiku, we also see that a double consonant counts as being in two moras.

English does not count moras the way Maori and Japanese do. Nevertheless, we can say that a short vowel (and any syllable onset) counts as a single mora; a long vowel or a diphthong counts as two; an extra consonant following the vowel counts as another mora. In other words, *above* counts as being two syllables, the first of which has a single mora in it (/ə/), the second of which contains two moras (/bʌ/ and /v/), while *about* counts as two syllables, the first of which contains a single mora, and the second of which contains three: /ba/, /ʊ/ and /t/. A distinction is sometimes made in English between

LIGHT syllables (which contain a single mora) and a HEAVY syllable (which contains two or more moras). These behave differently in terms of attracting stress in English.

> **<4.49>** Consider two sets of words: on the one hand we have *arena, collector, semolina* [ə.riː.nə, kə.lekt.ə, se.mə.liː.nə] which are stressed on the penultimate syllable (the second from the end); on the other we have *anthropology, harmony, lexicon* [æn.θrə.pɒl.ə.dʒi, hɑː.mə.ni, lek.sɪ.kɒn] which are stressed on the antepenultimate syllable (the third from the end). Why should we find this difference?

Just as there are units smaller than the syllable, so there are larger ones. The next one is the FOOT. In English the foot always begins with a stressed syllable and includes all the immediately following unstressed ones. In other languages the stress may come at the beginning of the foot or at the end, but is generally expected to behave regularly. So English words like *tablet* or *fortunate* are made up of single feet, the first made up of two syllables, the second made up of three syllables. In *amphibrach* and *oxymoron* there are two feet: in *amphibrach* the second foot contains only a stressed syllable, in *oxymoron* it contains two. Note that secondary stress (see section 3.6.1) counts as stress for these purposes. Words like *prefer* and *industrial* have an unstressed syllable which is not attached to any foot at the beginning.

For some varieties of English it makes sense to say that voiceless plosives are aspirated only when they occur as the first sound in a foot. Thus feet can be useful in determining the domain of particular allophonic changes. The foot also seems to be what is counted in English verse, with a great deal of English verse being based on a line containing four feet, as illustrated below, where the vertical line is used to show the start of a foot (and hence the beginning of a stressed syllable).

|Rings on her |fingers and |bells on her |toes
And |she shall have |music wher|ever she |goes.

|Send for the |doctor, |send for the |nurse,
|Send for the |lady with the |alligator |purse.

4.9 Rules

The everyday meaning of the term RULE is that it is some kind of constraint imposed by some person or people in a position of power, and that breaking the rule will lead to some penalty on the person who breaks the rule. This is the meaning we find in expressions like *school rules, rules and regulations, rules of the road,* and so on. The term in linguistics is used very differently. In linguistics, a rule is a statement of observed regularity of behaviour. So if you always switch off your alarm clock in the morning and then go back to sleep for five minutes, a linguist might describe this as a rule of your behaviour, even though there is no penalty if you break this rule and even if it is not a rule which has been imposed on you by anyone else.

Although rules could be expressed in ordinary language, as was done just above, rules in linguistics are usually expressed using a notational shorthand which allows

Data-set 4.12
Koiari

koiɐri	language name
reketoɾe	'evening star'
olo	'come'
eɾe	'see'
lɐimɐ	'I stand'
ɐlɐi	'bamboo'
emoɾiɐ	'python sp.'
toviɾiviɾi	'motor vehicle'
elume	'and'
bulu	'garden'
gologoteki	'sicken'
mɐlu	'cook'

for a concise, precise and unambiguous statement of what it is that the rule says. In this section, some of that notation will be introduced, and its use will be illustrated.

We can begin with this data-set illustrating allophones of a single phoneme in Koiari.

<4.50> In the data-set, [ɾ] and [l] are allophones of the same phoneme. Describe the complementary distribution of the two sounds.

We could state the distribution of the allophones as is done in the answer to <4.50> where it is simply stated where each allophone occurs, but rule notation prefers an alternative way of writing such things. It is usually phrased as though one thing turns into another in a specific environment. So here we might say that the phoneme turns into a particular allophone in a given environment. This implies that we know which of the symbols [ɾ] and [l] to use for the label for the phoneme (alternatively, how to choose a label for the phoneme if it is not going to be one of these). This in turn implies that we have some sort of guidelines to help us make a decision. Some guidelines were given earlier in the answer to <4.20>, and a fuller set are given in the information box ('What do we call the phoneme?'). In the case in point we can see that [ɾ] appears before two vowels, [l] before three, so [l] is the allophone with the widest distribution (the elsewhere variant), and is also the symbol which it is easiest to type. We will choose to call the phoneme /l/.

Having made that decision, we want to say that /l/ is realised as (or becomes) [ɾ] when it occurs before certain vowels. We can write that as in (1):

$$(1) \quad l \rightarrow ɾ \ / \ \underline{\quad} \left\{ \begin{array}{c} i \\ e \end{array} \right\}$$

So we have the /l/ (which we write without any enclosing brackets when it is in the rule format) and the arrow says that it becomes something. The [ɾ] (again no brackets in the rule) is what it turns into. The single slash is to be read as 'in the following environment'. The underscore or **ENVIRONMENT BAR** shows where the change occurs in relation to other segments. Here the change takes place before /i/ or /e/, so the environment bar is found immediately before /i/ and /e/, with the braces (or curly brackets) having their usual meaning of free choice between the two options enclosed. In other words, 'l is realised as ɾ when it occurs immediately before one of i or e'.

---

i

What do we call the phoneme?

1. We look for the allophone with the widest distribution, and use the symbol for that.
2. We use the symbol which will make it easiest to write the rules. Very often, if all the allophones are transcribed using diacritics, the symbol used for the phoneme will omit all diacritics.
3. We use the symbol that allows us to make the phoneme part of a series of phonemes in the language: e.g. if we have a lot of velars and no other palatals, a phoneme with allophones [ç] and [x] will be called /x/.
4. We use the phonetically simplest allophone as the label for the phoneme (the voiceless member of a voiceless/voiced pair of allophones, the non-nasal member of a nasal/non-nasal pair of allophones).
5. We use a symbol which is a letter of the Roman alphabet. This may not be very scientific, but is extremely helpful in devising writing systems for unwritten languages.

We can improve upon (1) because it seems likely that this process occurs because of the features which /i/ and /e/ share: they are the only front vowels in this language. It is standard to use V to mean 'vowel' and C to mean 'consonant', a notation which was used earlier. Using this shorthand, we can provide a better statement as in (2).

(2) $l \rightarrow \mathfrak{r} / \underline{\quad} \begin{bmatrix} V \\ \text{Place: Coronal} \end{bmatrix}$

Note the use of square brackets to enclose all the features for a single segment, a convention that has already been introduced.

Consider another example. In the word [ten] the [n] is pronounced with the blade of the tongue in contact with the alveolar ridge. In [tenθ] on the other hand, the [n̪] is pronounced with the tip of the tongue in contact with the upper incisors.

Using the same notation as before, we can write

(3) $n \rightarrow n̪ / \underline{\quad} θ$

which is read as 'alveolar [n] is replaced by dental [n̪] in the environment immediately preceding a [θ].'

<4.51> In Japanese /t/ becomes [ts] before /ɯ/, so that /tetɯ/ 'iron' is pronounced [tetsɯ]. Write a rule for this process in rule notation.

Now return to the question of dental [n̪] in English. We have seen that [n̪] is found before [θ]. If we compare the articulations of the /n/s in *in* and *in the*, we find that we can also write a rule

(4) $n \rightarrow n̪ / \underline{\quad} ð$

Rules (3) and (4) can be conflated as

$$(5) \quad n \rightarrow \eta / \underline{\quad} \left\{ \begin{array}{c} \theta \\ \eth \end{array} \right\}$$

Rule (5) is read as 'alveolar [n] is replaced by dental [ṇ] in the environment immediately preceding either a [θ] or a [ð].' If we add more data, we can extend this rule still further, so as to make a more general statement. Consider the following data from RP (but note that some speakers of other varieties will not have an [l] at all in (c), and also that [wɪtθ] is an alternative pronunciation to [wɪd̪θ]) (see below).

Data-set 4.13				
English dentals	(a)	eɪt	eɪt̪θ	eɪt̪ ð̪ə fuːd
	(b)	waɪd	wɪd̪θ	hɪd̪ ð̪ə tɹeʒə
	(c)	hiːl	hel̪θ	hil̪ ð̪ə sɪk

In the light of such data we might want to make rule (5) more general, so as to cover more cases. The best way to do that is to use features instead of segmental transcriptions, because we can generalise the data as saying that alveolars except [s] and [z] become dental before dentals, which in rule notation is

$$(6) \quad \left[\begin{array}{l} \text{Consonantal} \\ \text{Place: Coronal} \\ -\text{Strident} \end{array} \right] \rightarrow [\text{Apical}] \; / \; \underline{\quad} \; [\text{Apical}]$$

The advantage of (6) over (5) is that it gives a more accurate picture of the phonological process by saying precisely what class of sounds it applies to, and it explains why the change should take place by marking which feature is assimilated, that is modified to be more similar to something in the environment.

If the words *had* and *ham* are compared, it will be discovered that for most speakers the vowel in *ham* is considerably more nasalised than that in *had* (which may not be nasalised at all). If we use 'V' as a cover symbol to mean 'any vowel' and 'C' to stand for any consonant, we can write a rule to show this process, using the notation already discussed.

$$(7) \quad V \rightarrow [\text{Nasal}] \; / \; \underline{\quad} \left[\begin{array}{c} C \\ \text{Nasal} \end{array} \right]$$

'any vowel becomes nasalised in the environment preceding a nasal consonant'.

Consider now the pair *hem/helm*. The nasalisation of the vowel can still be heard in *helm*, even if there is a lateral consonant before the nasal. We can write a rule (8) to account for such pairs:

$$(8) \quad V \rightarrow [\text{Nasal}] \; / \; \underline{\quad} \; [\text{Lateral}] \left[\begin{array}{c} C \\ \text{Nasal} \end{array} \right]$$

'any vowel becomes nasal before a sequence of a lateral (i.e. [l]) and a nasal consonant'. Note that for people who have this nasalisation, the /l/ will be nasalised too.
However, this complicating factor will be ignored here for present purposes. Rules (7)
and (8) have a lot in common, and illustrate what is basically the same process. This
can be captured by conflating the two rules in the following way.

(9)   V → [Nasal] / ___ ([Lateral]) $\begin{bmatrix} C \\ Nasal \end{bmatrix}$

where the parentheses show that the rule applies either with (as in rule (8)) or without
(as in rule (7)) the lateral. In other words, the lateral segment is optional in the application of the rule. Rule (9) is thus read as 'A vowel becomes nasalised before a nasal
consonant, which may optionally be preceded by a lateral' or 'even when a lateral
intervenes between the vowel and the nasal'.

A similar modification could be made to rule (6). As the data on which that rule
was based shows, the process described by (6) applies both within the word and over
word-boundaries. The symbol '#' is used to indicate a word-boundary. Every word
has a boundary at each end, so that we could write *hippopotamus* as #hippopotamus#.
If we want to put these boundaries into a phrase like *bold hippopotamus*, we must
remember that each word carries its own boundaries, so that we get #bold#
#hippopotamus#. In other words, where two words are adjacent, we need two '#'-
signs. That being the case, we can rewrite (6) as (10).

(10) $\begin{bmatrix} Consonantal \\ Place: Coronal \\ -Strident \end{bmatrix}$ → [Apical] / ___ (##) [Apical]

<4.52> In French, when a word is pronounced in isolation, the stress falls on the last
non-schwa vowel in the word. If the last vowel of the word is [ə], there may be up to
three consonants between the previous vowel (which will never be [ə]) and the [ə]. There
is never a final consonant after the [ə]. The possibilities are illustrated below. Write a rule
which will provide the correct stress. Your rule should begin

$$V \rightarrow [+ \text{stress}] /$$

ˈde	'dice'
iˈde	'idea'
ideˈɛl	'ideal'
maˈʁi	'husband'
maˈʁiə	a name
maˈʁin	'marine'
pəˈtitə	'small (fem)'
ˈɛtʁə	'to be'
deˈzastʁə	'disaster'

The same kind of rule can also be used to insert or delete segments. Consider the case of three obstruents occurring together in English: where the middle one is a stop, it is frequently deleted, so that [left tɜn] becomes [lef tɜn], [kept kwaɪət] becomes [kep kwaɪət] and so on. This can be written in a rule as

(14) $\begin{bmatrix} -\text{Continuant} \\ +\text{Obstruent} \end{bmatrix} \rightarrow \emptyset \, / \, [+\text{Obstruent}] \, \_\_\_ \, \#\# \, [+\text{Obstruent}]$

that is, 'a stop becomes zero (i.e. is deleted) when it occurs word-finally between two other obstruents'.

Some speakers of English do not distinguish between *mince* /mɪns/ and *mints* /mɪnts/, but pronounce both of them as /mɪnts/. Other parallel examples are *chance* (pronounced like *chants*), *consonance* (pronounced like *consonants*), *dance*, *incidence* (pronounced like *incidents*), *once*, *prince* (pronounced like *prints*), and so on. We can write the rule as

(15) $\emptyset \rightarrow \begin{bmatrix} -\text{Continuant} \\ \text{Place: Coronal} \\ -\text{Voice} \end{bmatrix} \, / \, \begin{bmatrix} \text{Nasal} \\ \text{Place: Coronal} \end{bmatrix} \, \_\_\_ \, \begin{bmatrix} +\text{Obstruent} \\ -\text{Voice} \end{bmatrix}$

Here the zero symbol (∅) has been placed to become something else; in other words, something is inserted.

So far in writing rules we have always written them in terms of the linear sequence of segments and boundaries to which they apply. However, there are alternatives. In many cases the environment is better specified in terms of the structure in which the rule occurs.

There is a rule of German (a similar rule is found in Vietnamese and in some varieties of Arabic), that no word begins with a vowel; all apparently vowel-initial words actually begin with a glottal stop. We can rephrase this rule as 'an empty onset is replaced by a glottal stop'. While it would be possible to write rules of this type using the notation introduced above by using labelled brackets for onsets, syllables and so on, it would be very complex. It is now more normal to write such rules by drawing a partial tree, as follows:

(16) Onset
        |
        ∅ → ʔ

The labels for the tree are frequently abbreviated. In particular, the syllable is frequently written with the Greek letter σ.

A comment was made earlier that in some varieties of English, voiceless plosives are aspirated only when they occur at the beginning of a foot. This could be dealt with in a similar manner.

 <4.53> Write a rule to show this process.

4.10 Tone (Advanced)

In this section we will consider some of the peculiarities of the phonology of tone, and some of the ways in which phonologists have dealt with such matters.

The first point to note about tone is that, in many ways, the behaviour of the tone seems to be independent of the behaviour of the segments that carry the tone. Some simple examples will serve to make this point.

Consider what happens in language games. LANGUAGE GAMES are linguistic utterances in which speakers deliberately manipulate the normal structure of words, often in order to mask the meaning from the outsider who does not play the game. A language game in English is Pig Latin, in which the onset of the first syllable of every word is moved to the end, and then the vowel /eɪ/ is added to the end of every word. *Pig Latin*, by this process, becomes *igpay atinlay*, which is hard to understand for outsiders to the game. There is a French criminal slang called Verlan where the order of syllables in the word is changed according to quite complex rules: *Verlan* comes from the standard French *à l'envers* 'inside out'. These are language games.

In the African language games illustrated below, syllables are reordered, as in the French Verlan, but, crucially, the tones are not reordered. The relevant examples are presented below:

Data-set 4.14			
Language games from two African tonal languages	(a)	Bakwiri	
		mɔ̀kɔ̀ > kɔ̀mɔ̀	'plantain'
		kwélí > líkwé	'death'
		mɔ̀kɔ́ > kɔ̀mɔ́	'one person'
		kwéli̱ > líkwè	'falling'
	(b)	Kisi	
		tùŋndó > ndòtúŋ	'dog'
		ɲààjó > jòŋáá	'cat'
		súúkúúnɔ́ɔ̀ > kúúnɔ́ɔ̀sùù	'student'

What we see in Table 4.14 is that the tonal pattern is maintained independently of the segmental pattern of consonants and vowels. Independence is the key: the two do not function together as if the tone was attached to a particular segment or sequence of segments.

This is usually dealt with by phonologists by putting the tone on a different TIER from the segmental MELODY. At some stage the tones have to be associated with TONE BEARING UNITS (TBUs) in the segmental or melodic tier, but it is possible for some phonological rules to apply to the tone without affecting the segments, while other rules apply to the segments without affecting the tone. The TBUs are usually annotated as if they are vowels, though properly they should be moras or syllables (depending on the language concerned). This follows on from the tradition of marking tone symbols over vowels, as we have been doing here. The association of tones with TBUs is shown schematically by means of ASSOCIATION LINES linking the two. The tones are indicated by L (for low) and H (for high) – and where necessary, M for mid – on the tonal tier. So the word for 'falling' in Bakwiri can be represented as in (17).

(17   H L   H L
      | | | |
    kweli likwe

There are cases where the tones seem to stay the same, the segments seem to stay the same, but the association lines get moved. An example comes from Lango, and is shown in (18), where (a) represents the tones as they would be pronounced on each word in isolation, and (b) represents the situation when the whole sentence is pronounced.

(18)   (a)   L H   L
              \/   /\
             nɛn   ogwaŋ

            'see-IMPER meerkat'

            'Look at the meerkat!'

       (b)   L   H L
              /\   \/
             nɛn   ogwaŋ

As with the representation of the tones illustrated in section 3.6.2, when a high and a low both fall on the same TBU, the phonetic result is a fall if the order is HL, but a rise if it is LH.

Another phenomenon which indicates the separation of the tonal tier and the melodic tier is called **SPREADING**. In spreading, tones whose origin is on one TBU expand their domain to cover more TBUs. One place where this is very visible is with forms which have varying numbers of syllables, but the same overall tonal pattern. Consider the example from Kisi overleaf.

Here we have a set of verbs in the perfective aspective which take a low-high pattern. Where there is just one mora to carry the tone, the low and the high coalesce as a rise on that mora; where there are two, the low and the high occur on adjacent moras, whether or not the second mora has an initial consonant; where there are more than two moras, the high tone spreads to the other moras in the word.

Note how this spreading is annotated, with dotted association lines showing the spreading. Spreading can be from left to right, as illustrated overleaf, or from right to left. In Caddo a high tone spreads left over a sonorant consonant, so that *naná* 'that, that one' is pronounced [náná]. The extent of the spreading can also be variable. Consider the example in Data-set 4.16.

In this example, spreading goes from left to right, but always stops at the end of penultimate syllable of the prosodic word.

There is yet another phenomenon which indicates the independence of tonal phonology from segmental phonology, and that is what happens when TBUs are elided. Sometimes, when a syllable is elided, the tone that goes with it is also omitted; but very often what happens is that the tone which originally belonged

Data-set 4.15

Spreading
in Kisi

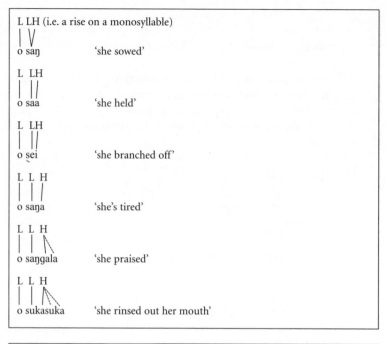

L LH (i.e. a rise on a monosyllable)

o saŋ   'she sowed'

L LH

o saa   'she held'

L LH

o sei   'she branched off'

L L H

o saŋa   'she's tired'

L L H

o saŋgala   'she praised'

L L H

o sukasuka   'she rinsed out her mouth'

Data-set 4.16

Shambaa
high tone
spreading

mawe magana mana na miloŋgo mine '440 stones'
mawe = 'stones', *mana* = '4'
magí mágána matátú ná mílóŋgo mine '340 eggs'
magí = 'eggs' *matátú* = '3'

<4.54> What must the various elements in these two expressions mean? Draw a tree to show the spreading. How many prosodic words must there be in each example?

with the TBU is not deleted but remains in the tonal sequence, and is transferred to an adjacent syllable. Consider the following simple example from Efik. In (19) we see that a vowel can be deleted when two vowels become adjacent at word boundaries.

(19)   ké étó 'on the tree' > kétó

In (20) we see that when a high and a low tone are involved, they merge in a fall, rather than one just being deleted.

(20)   ké ùbōm 'in the canoe' > kûbōm (macron = mid tone)

<4.55> In (19), rather than saying that the first high tone is deleted with the TBU that carries it, we might prefer to say that a sequence of two highs merges as a single tone. Why?

4.56 How might you account for the difference between tones that are elided along with the TBUs with which they are associated and those which are retained?

A final phenomenon is worth consideration here. It is called a **FLOATING TONE**. A floating tone is one whose position in relation to a particular word or element can be deduced by the behaviour of surrounding tones, even though the floating tone itself is not pronounced in isolation. A simple example comes from Ngiti, where the vocative of a noun is formed by the addition of a floating high tone at the end of the word. This floating high tone does not affect a final high tone at all, so that the vocative case of the word for 'grasshopper' is the same as the nominative, *kamàlí*. However, when a word ends in a low or a mid tone, that tone is changed into a rise by the presence of the floating high tone. Thus we get the forms shown in (21), where an unmarked tone is a mid tone.

(21)   àbamà 'my father' L.M.L > L.M.LM in the vocative
        aguna 'father-in-law' M.M.M > M.M.MH in the vocative

If tones can spread to adjacent syllables, the question naturally arises: if we have a sequence of high or low tones on the surface, do they arise from spreading or not? One hypothesis about this is named the **OBLIGATORY CONTOUR PRINCIPLE** (OCP). According to the OCP it is not possible to have sequences of the same item on any tier: where these occur on the surface, they must arise from some spreading mechanism.

<4.57> If the OCP applies to all tiers, including the segmental tier, what are the implications for geminates and for long vowels (i.e. bimoraic vowels)?

Evidence comes from a language like Shona. In this language, we find the data shown in below:

Data-set 4.17
Shona

mbwá 'dog'
hóvé 'fish'
mbúndúdzí 'army worms'
né-mbwà 'with a dog'
né-hòvè 'with a fish'
né-mbùndùdzì 'with army worms'

<4.58> What is the generalisation as to what happens after the prefix glossed as 'with'?

If we are to explain the change that takes place in this dataset, it will be much easier if each of the words illustrated has a single High, which spreads to all the syllables. While it would no doubt be possible to write a rule or series of rules which lowered one or two or three high tones, a single lowering process is clearly more economical.

Despite cases such as the one illustrated from Shona, there are other places where the OCP does not appear to function as predicted, which is why it was introduced as a hypothesis. Where it does work, the OCP does not always work in the same way: sometimes it works only in elements of words, sometimes in whole words, sometimes in longer stretches, for instance. Nevertheless, it is a very influential hypothesis, and reference is often made to it in the literature.

To deal with the phonology of tone, therefore, we need to be able to show how the tone may act independently of the segments on which the tone is realised. To do this, we analyse the tone as being on a separate tier from the segments, and deal with the phonology of each relatively separately. At some point, though, we have to link the two again, since on the surface the tone and the segments are pronounced simultaneously, and we need to know which segments are pronounced with which tones. We keep track of this with association lines, and can use the manipulation of association lines as part of the statements of rules about tone.

4.11 Summing up

In this chapter we have introduced the notion of the phoneme, and we have applied that to providing a transcription system for English. We have seen that we can interpret the data that English provides in different ways to give different phonemic solutions: this is typical. There is rarely only one possible phonemic analysis for a given set of data.

We have also looked at some larger phonological structures: moras, syllables and feet, and shown that some languages pay more attention to some of these structures than to others for some purposes (e.g. in their poetic traditions).

We have looked at the notion of linguistic rules, and some ways of writing them. Finally, we have also looked at some of the facets of the phonology of tone.

The notion of complementary distribution, which we appealed to in discussing the phoneme, will recur in other chapters, and the notion of a rule is fundamental in linguistics, and will also recur.

 Technical terms introduced in this chapter

Allophone	Defective distribution
Ambisyllabic	Distinctive feature
Association lines	Elsewhere
Bound variant	Elsewhere variant
Broad transcription	Environment bar
Closed	Floating tone
Cluster	Foot
Coda	Free variation
Contrast	Grapheme
Complementary distribution	Homophone
Convention (in transcription)	Homorganic

Language game
Liquid
Melody
Minimal pair
Narrow transcription
Natural class
Neutralisation
Obligatory Contour Principle (OCP)
Onset
Open
Parallel distribution
Peak
Phone
Phoneme

Phonemic transcription
Phonetic similarity
Phonetic transcription
Postvocalic
Prevocalic
Rhyme
Rule
Sonority
Speech sound
Spreading
Tier
Tone bearing unit (TBU)
Voice Onset Time

Reading and references

The phoneme is introduced in all linguistics textbooks. Sommerstein (1977) and Lass (1984) are still worth reading on this topic. Most recent phonetics or phonology textbooks discuss sonority and syllable structure (see e.g. Gussenhoven & Jacobs 1998, Spencer 1996), although most of them give a rather more detailed hierarchy of sonority and then have to cope with more apparent breaches. Similarly, most authorities prefer a different set of principles or strategies for assigning syllable boundaries. Wells (1990) discusses allophony and the assignment of syllable boundaries. On *time* and *thyme*, see Gahl (2008). On lexical sets see Wells (1982).

Information on the various languages mentioned has been taken from the sources mentioned below:

Bakwiri	Childs (2003: 79)	Koiari	Dutton (1996)
Basque	Hualde & Ortiz de Urbina (2003)	Lango	Noonan (1992: 49)
		Lezgian	Haspelmath (1993)
Burmese	Wheatley (1987)	Maori	Bauer (1993)
Caddo	Melnar (2004)	Moseten	Sakel (2004)
Danish	Basbøll (2005)	Ngiti	Lojenga (1994: 166)
Daur	Wu (1996)	Passamaquoddy	Leavitt (1996)
Efik	Westermann & Ward (1933: 149)	Pitta-Pitta	Dixon (1980)
		Shambaa	Childs (2003: 89)
German	Kenstowicz (1994: 282)	Shona	Gussenhoven & Jacobs (1998: 143)
Japanese	Hinds (1986)		
Kiowa	Watkins (1984: 54)	Wari'	Everett & Kern (1997)
Kisi	Childs (1995: 56; 2003: 79)		

129

5

Morphology

With words you can build a system.
(Goethe 1808)

Morphology is the study of the relationship between form and meaning within the word. Prefixes and suffixes, for example, are added to bases to change the meaning of the base in a number of ways. Various other processes can influence the ways in which words are made up, and there are generalisations about where the morphological markers (the prefixes and suffixes) will occur, as well as about how the bits of words interact with each other semantically.

5.1 The legal importance of analysing words

In 1996 a linguistically interesting court case was heard in the US District Court for the District of Columbia. The defendant, a Texan, had, on a visit to New Orleans, bought a packet of joke certificates which were headed 'Temporary Coon Ass Certificate' and instructed the recipient of the certificate to behave in a number of generally positive ways. For people from outside Louisiana or the immediate surroundings (including parts of Texas), the term *Coon Ass* will require quite a lot of explanation. First it must be remembered that a variety of French is spoken in Louisiana. *Coon ass* (also written as *coonass*) is derived from the French word *con(n)asse*, which is in standard French a rude word of disapprobation, but which in Louisiana has become a term denoting a person of Cajun background. The certificate was thus jokingly welcoming the recipient as an honorary local of Louisiana. However, the defendant, who was a white male, had given one of these certificates to a female African-American employee. She complained that it was racially offensive and created a hostile environment in the workplace because *coon* is an extremely offensive term for an African-American (and *ass* is scarcely complimentary and could be interpreted as being a term of harassment). Although the defendant professed himself to be bemused by this interpretation of the word, the court found against him.

This case illustrates two important linguistic principles for us. The first is that we do not have to know the origins of a word or how it is made up in order to use it appropriately. This makes good sense. Once we know what a word means and how to use it, it is more economical to get on with using it than to worry about how it gained its particular meaning. You will know from your own experience of learning a foreign language that you do not have to understand why French *s'il vous plaît* means 'please' in order to use it properly or why German *auf Wiedersehen* means 'goodbye' to use that. One linguist tells the story of his small daughter's delight when she discovered that orange juice had something to do with oranges.

<5.1> Why do you think the following English words have their current meaning? If necessary, consult a dictionary which gives etymologies to discover. Have you ever considered this point before? Can you use these words properly?

carriage, floodlight, health, hedgehog, sensual

The second important linguistic principle illustrated by the coonass story is that when we do not know a word we meet, we try to analyse its elements to understand it, or at least make it more memorable. One place where this becomes particularly obvious is in the way in which we occasionally treat foreign words. If we do not know the language concerned we may try to interpret the sounds we hear in terms that are meaningful for us. Eventually, of course, once the word becomes familiar, we stop worrying about such matters again. This phenomenon is so common that it has gained a special name: **FOLK ETYMOLOGY** or **POPULAR ETYMOLOGY**. As a simple example, consider the word *cockroach*. This has nothing to do with cocks, in any of the possible meanings of that word. It is borrowed from Spanish *cucaracha*, and someone obviously thought that the beginning sounded like *cock*. Perhaps more interestingly, our word *female* is borrowed from French *femelle* in which there is no reference to male at all. *Female* was linked to *male*, and its form followed.

<5.2> You may be familiar with the tongue-twister: *How much wood would a woodchuck chuck if a woodchuck could chuck wood?* If a woodchuck cannot chuck wood, why is it called a *woodchuck*? You should be able to guess the answer. A polecat does have something to do with one of poles and cats, but which? It takes an etymologist to know.

5.2 The bits of words

Why would we expect words to be analysable into meaningful bits? The simple answer is because so many of them are. A warthog is a pig-like creature with things like warts on its skin. A muskrat is a rodent (not, it is true, strictly a rat) which smells musky. Someone who looks to be thirtyish is probably around thirty, and if someone is hospitalised they are admitted to a hospital. So in *warthog* we can recognise meaningful bits *wart* and *hog*, in *muskrat* we can recognise *musk* and *rat*, in *thirtyish* we can recognise at least *thirty*, and we may also recognise the *-ish* which shows up in a number of parallel words like *fortyish, greenish, slimmish*.

<5.3> Can you recognise the bits in *hospitalise*, and find words which seem to provide parallels for it, in the same way as the words given above are parallel to *thirtyish*?

While ordinary speakers are pleased to recognise any part of an unfamiliar word to which they think they can assign a meaning, linguists are fussier. Ordinary people were obviously quite content to see *male* in *female*, and did not worry about what the *fe-* part of the word might mean. Linguists are happy to recognise such meaningful parts only if they can analyse the whole word with no residue. So linguists want to treat *female* as an unanalysable whole just like *book* or *elephant*. On the other hand, they are happy to split *hedgehog* or *thirtyish* up into smaller units because *hedge* and *hog* between them explain the entire form of *hedgehog*, and because *thirty* (meaning '30') and *-ish* (meaning 'approximately') explain why *thirtyish* means what it does. When they do split words in this way, they call each of the meaningful bits a **MORPH**. So *hedge* and *hog* in *hedgehog* and *thirty* and *-ish* in *thirtyish* are morphs. In this book, the decimal point will be used to separate morphs from each other when it is useful for the exposition, so we can write *hedge·hog* and *thirty·ish*.

<5.4> Some words, like *book* and *elephant*, contain only one morph, others like *hedgehog* and *thirtyish* contain two, some like *unfriendliness* contain several. How many morphs do each of the English words listed below contain, and what are the morphs? How can you tell?

carpet, decentralise, distressing, sensitivity, tarragon

Words like *book* and *elephant* and *hedge* are said to be **MORPHOLOGICALLY SIMPLE**, or **MONOMORPHEMIC** (made up of just one morphological element). Words like *hedgehog* and *thirtyish* are **MORPHOLOGICALLY COMPLEX**. A word like *hedgehog* may be said to be **BIMORPHEMIC** (made up of just two morphological elements). Although words with more morphological elements are found (like *unfriendliness*) we do not usually use a special term for them on the basis of the number of morphs they contain.

You will have noticed that when we divide *hedgehog* into its constituent morphs, each morph is itself a word which could stand alone. Such morphs are often termed **POTENTIALLY FREE MORPHS**: they have the potential to occur independently of any other morphs. However, while *hospital* in *hospitalise* is a potentially free morph, *-ise* is not. It is an **OBLIGATORILY BOUND MORPH**. It can only occur bound to or attached to some other morph. There are several types of obligatorily bound morph, which can be distinguished by their position in the word, as we shall see below.

We will begin with a simple set of data from English:

Data-set 5.1
English

bird	birdcage
cage	cagebird
song	birdsong
	songbird

In the first column in we have some morphs which actually do form words by themselves, and so whose potential to be free morphs is illustrated in the data. In the second column we have words which contain two morphs.

<5.5> Divide the words in the second column of into morphs. What kinds of morph do you find there?

When we find words made up of two (or more) potentially free morphs we call the words **COMPOUND WORDS** or **COMPOUNDS**. The process of forming such words is called **COMPOUNDING** or **COMPOSITION**. This definition is not general enough to cover all languages, but will suffice for our purposes here.

Notice that the data-set is inevitably selective. Enough examples are presented to make the point that is to be illustrated, but no more. You might wonder why *cagesong* and *songcage* are not listed, for instance. One answer is that they are not listed in the dictionary I happened to consult when I was looking for the data. Because the language here is English and I might be expected to know more about English than simply what is listed in a particular reference book, a slightly fuller answer might be that there is nothing for these words to denote. This leaves open the question of whether these are **POSSIBLE** words of English or not, but certainly suggests that they are not **ESTABLISHED** words, words accepted as normal words in the community which speaks the relevant language. The word *songbird-cage* could possibly have been listed, to illustrate the point that compounds can have more than two elements in them. If this is established, it is rare enough not to be listed in dictionaries. In most cases when foreign language examples are provided, it is only possible to list established words, because reference books tend not to give information about what might be possible but is not attested. If you did not speak any English, you might not be able to tell whether a Table like 5.1 indicated that there are only four compound words in the whole of English, or whether these words illustrate a larger pattern. In most cases we will not be concerned with such questions. All that will matter is that the pattern illustrated in the data-set exists and has to be described.

Following that digression, consider the data-set which lists a number of words of Finnish and their translation:

Data-set 5.2
Finnish

talo	'house'	talossa	'in the house'
puu	'tree'	puussa	'in the tree'
maa	'country'	maassa	'in the country'
auto	'car'	autossa	'in the car'
pullo	'bottle'	pullossa	'in the bottle'

In the first column we see some free morphs, which are repeated in the third column, but in the third column there is an obligatorily bound morph attached to each of the potentially free morphs.

 <5.6> What is the obligatorily bound morph illustrated in Data-set 5.2? What does it mean?

Note that we cannot tell from Data-set 5.2 that the second morph of each of the words in the third column is obligatorily bound. That piece of information was extra information, although if you accept that the data you are presented with is typical, you might also have deduced it. An obligatorily bound morph which is attached following another morph is called a **SUFFIX**. It will be useful to have a term for the morph to which a suffix (or some other obligatorily bound morph) is attached, and we will use the term **BASE** for this. So in *auto·ssa*, *auto* is the base and *-ssa* is a suffix. The fact that *-ssa* is obligatorily bound is shown by writing it with a hyphen when we cite it in isolation.

It is important to note that suffixes do not all look alike. Above, the suffix added a whole syllable to the base (*talo* is two syllables long, *taalossa* is three, and so on), but that is not always the case, as illustrated in the following data-set:

Data-set 5.3
Finnish

auto	'car'	autot	'cars'
maa	'country'	maat	'countries'
talo	'house'	talot	'houses'
hylly	'shelf'	hyllyt	'shelves'
pullo	'bottle'	pullot	'bottles'

<5.7> Assuming that only the morphs which are shown to occur as words in their own right are potentially free, what are the morphs in word *pullot*, and what kinds of morph are they? What does each morph mean?

It should not be surprising that we find a suffix which is made up of just a consonant is Finnish since precisely the same is true in some of the English translations: *bottle·s* is also made up of a base and a suffix where the suffix is made up of a single consonant.

Now move on to the next data-set, this time from an African language. Again we find a base and another morph, and again that second morph is obligatorily bound. But there is a subtle difference here:

Data-set 5.4
Swahili

ɓawa	'wing'	maɓawa	'wings'
ɓega	'shoulder'	maɓega	'shoulders'
tofali	'brick'	matofali	'bricks'
elezo	'explanation'	maelezo	'explanations'
ɗuka	'shop'	maɗuka	'shops'

<5.8> What morphs are illustrated in the Swahili word meaning 'explanations'? What is the form of the obligatorily bound morph? Is there a base in this word, and if so what is it? What does each morph mean?

Here the obligatorily bound morph is attached in front of its base, and is correspondingly called a **PREFIX**. So *matofali* is made up of the prefix *ma-* and the base *tofali*. Like suffixes, prefixes are not always a syllable long.

Because it is sometimes useful to be able to discuss obligatorily bound morphs of various kinds as a group, we have the word **AFFIX**. Prefixes and suffixes are both kinds of affix, and we will see some other types immediately below:

Data-set 5.5
Khmer

tbaːɲ	'weave'	tɔmbaːɲ	'loom'
khos	'be wrong'	kɔmhos	'a wrong'
khɨŋ	'be angry'	kɔmhɨŋ	'anger'
sdɤy	'speak'	sɔmdɤy	'speech'

135

A third kind of affix is illustrated in Data-set 5.9 from an Asian language:

<5.9> What is the base in the word meaning 'speech'? What is the form of the affix – that is, what set of phonemes or letters makes up this particular affix? What does the affix mean?

The Khmer data-set introduces an infix. An **INFIX** is an affix which interrupts the morph to which it is added. The form of the infix in this data-set is /ɔm/. Because an infix is not placed randomly within its base, we have to be able to state where it is inserted in the base morph. In the data just provided we do not have enough data to be sure what the rules are, but one possibility is that the infix is inserted immediately after the initial consonant of the base. That is certainly consistent with the data to hand.

The meanings of morphs are often quite difficult to determine or to specify. In this particular case, the infix appears to turn a verb into the noun with which you carry out the action. Technically we would probably call it an **INSTRUMENT** noun.

There is one other kind of affix we need to consider here, and it is of a rather different kind. In all the examples we have seen so far, the affix has had a constant form. Sometimes, though, the affix takes its form or part of its form from the base to which it is attached. Consider the following, where a durative gives the meaning of 'keeping on **VERB**ing':

Data-set 5.6
Tümpisa
Shoshone

English gloss	Basic form	Durative form
'lie (down)'	hapi	happi
'sit'	katuɪ	kattuɪ
'think'	mukuatu	mukuattu
'stand'	wuɪnuɪ	wuɪnnuɪ
'cry'	jake	jakke

<5.10> What is the affix in the form *happi*? What kind of affix is it? How is the form of the affix determined?

In this particular case the form of the infix is determined by the final consonant in the base. That consonant is doubled or geminated. In effect we get a second copy of that consonant. The process of creating an affix by copying phonological material in the base is called **REDUPLICATION**. Reduplication can be used to form suffixes or prefixes as well as infixes, and can copy different amounts of the base. Consider the following data, where rather more is copied.

<5.11> Precisely what is reduplicated in the data shown in Data-set 5.7?

This is a particularly complicated case of reduplication, and shows that the material copied may be quite difficult to specify. We will come back to reduplication in section 5.8.

Data-set 5.7
Comox

English gloss	singular	plural
'bear'	mɪχaɬ	məχmɪχaɬ
'land otter'	q'a:tl'	q'ətl'q'a:tl'
'horn'	sapaχos	səpsapaχos
'man'	tumɪʃ	təmtumɪʃ
'box'	χəsəm	χəsχəsəm
'house'	tl'əms	tl'əmtl'əms
'index finger'	ts'əma:lah	ts'əmts'əma:lah

Sometimes we find patterns in languages where what is often done by adding an affix in the same language or in other languages is done instead by changing the segmental make-up of the base or its make-up in terms of stress, tone, and so on, that is, suprasegmentals. A simple example, and one which will feel familiar to people who know English, is provided by Icelandic, a language which is related to English and in which we can see many of the same patterns operating.

In Dataset 5.8 the words in the first column all carry a suffix with the form -*a* which marks them as being infinitives. Icelandic, like English, has a whole set of verbs where the grammatical relationship illustrated in this data-set is marked by the use of affixes rather than as here. You should be able to state the relationship between the words in columns 1 and 3 in terms of a process by which one is produced from the other.

Data-set 5.8
Icelandic

bera	'to carry'	bar	'I carried'
detta	'to fall'	datt	'I fell'
drekka	'to drink'	drakk	'I drank'
drepa	'to kill'	drap	'I killed'
éta	'to eat'	át	'I ate'
fela	'to entrust'	fal	'I entrusted'
gefa	'to give'	gaf	'I gave'
geta	'to be able to'	gat	'I could'
hverfa	'to disappear'	hvarf	'I disappeared'
kveða	'to say'	kvað	'I said'

<5.12> What is the process by which the past tense is derived from the infinitive? You should be able to recognise some (but not all) of the words in this data-set as having cognates in English. [Cognate words in two languages are words which have both been inherited from the parent language, in this case common Germanic. Cognates differ predictably in form from language to language, but not necessarily in terms of meaning.] What do you think the cognate of the Icelandic word for 'I said' might be?

You might have been tempted to call these vowels 'infixes' but that is not really true. There is no feeling in languages like Icelandic that there is a morph -*a*- and a separate morph *g_f*, for example: the *a* does not exist independently of the *g_f*. Rather we want to say that a phonological change in the make-up of the word has had an effect comparable to the effect of affixation. We say that these words are related by a process of **INTERNAL MODIFICATION**. There are special names for various kinds of internal modification, and the example here illustrates **ABLAUT** or **APOPHONY**.

All the examples so far have, with the exception of the Comox, been fairly simple ones. We now need to consider some slightly more complicated examples. We can begin by having another look at Data-set 5.8. As was stated above, the words in the first column contain a suffix. What is that suffix added to? We have already seen that affixes are added to bases, so presumably we can see *ber*, *dett*, *drep*, and so on. as the bases in these instances. However, we have a problem here, because **ber*, **dett* and **drep* do not occur by themselves. They are not potentially free morphs, they are obligatorily bound. In other words, it is not only affixes which are obligatorily bound, some bases are as well. This raises the question of how we can differentiate between bases and affixes when both are obligatorily bound. The answer is not difficult, but it has more to do with semantics than with morphology as such. The affixes provide grammatical information (like 'infinitive' in the example we have here) while the bases provide detailed semantic information about the cognitive content of the words (like 'carry', 'fall' and 'kill' in these examples).

> **<5.13>** Go back and look at the data in 5.1–5.8 again. Does the affix always provide grammatical information in all those examples? Does the base always provide at least some lexical information? Note that in Data-set 5.1 we do not have any affixes, we have two bases coming together. Also note that in examples like those in Data-set 5.2, we may write *in* as a separate word in English, but that does not prove it gives lexical information: prepositions, articles and auxiliaries are often said to provide grammatical information even in languages (like English) where they are treated as separate words.

A more complex set of data is provided below, at least as far as the number of words being illustrated is concerned. Since this data-set is taken from English, there is no need to provide glosses. The data-set is presented in transcription to make you think about the sounds rather than the spellings.

Data-set 5.9
English

dɪvəʊt	dɪvəʊʃən	dɪvəʊʃənəl	dɪvəʊʃənəlɪst
edjʊkeɪt	edjʊkeɪʃən	edjʊkeɪʃənəl	edjʊkeɪʃənəlɪst
ɪntjuːɪt	ɪntjuːɪʃən	ɪntjuːɪʃənəl	ɪntjuːɪʃənəlɪst
kɒnstɪtjuːt	kɒnstɪtjuːʃən	kɒnstɪtjuːʃənəl	kɒnstɪtjuːʃənəlɪst

There are not many cases in English where all four of these possible forms are established words, and some of these words are accordingly rare. This does not affect the general points to be made.

Notice that deciding on the form of the suffix illustrated in the second column is not simple. If you did not know this language, you would probably conclude that one sound was deleted and then another added; because you know English, you may not be satisfied with that analysis. What is illustrated here is an instance where putting two morphs together causes changes in the phonemic make-up of one (or both) of them. This comes under the heading of **MORPHOPHONEMICS**, something to which we will return later in section 5.5.

<5.14> What affixes are illustrated in the above date-set. Are there any infixes illustrated? If so, what are they, and if not, why not? What is the meaning of each morph?

One of the things worth noting about this data-set is the way the meaning of the whole becomes specialised as the word becomes longer. For example, *devote* could just mean 'spend' of time as in *He devoted the whole afternoon to painting the skirting board*. But in *devotion* that meaning is no longer possible, and in *devotional* and *devotionalist* it is quite clear that the meaning relates to devoting oneself to God, perhaps specifically through prayer. This process, whereby, as a result of its specific historical development, the longer word comes to have a meaning which is more specific than or different from the meaning you would expect it to have, is called **LEXICALISATION**. Lexicalisation can lead to the semantic relationship between a word and its base being quite obscure. We have already seen this with the examples *carriage* and *health*, cited at the start of this chapter.

<5.15> What is the base of the word /edjʊkeɪʃənəlɪst/?

If we keep taking affixes away from words, we eventually come to a base which is made up of just one morph. This monomorphemic form, the form which is left when all affixes are removed, is called a **ROOT**. A root is thus a special kind of base.

Now consider the next data-set, from a language we have already considered.

Data-set 5.10
Tümpisa
Shoshone

gloss	singular	plural
'son'	tua	tuttuammɯ
'daughter'	petɯ	peppetɯmmɯ
'man'	tangu	tattangummɯ
'older sister'	patsi	pappatsiammɯ
'aunt'	tokkapɯ	tottokkapɯammɯ

<5.16> What is the base in the word meaning 'older sisters'? How do you go about creating the plural form from the singular?

The important thing about the examples above is that, as far as we can tell, we must have both the prefix and the suffix together to change these words to mean 'plural'. This phenomenon is relatively rare, but not exceptional. It has a number of names. When the two affixes which have to co-occur to give the appropriate meaning surround the base, as in this case, it is normal to talk of a **CIRCUMFIX**. More generally where we require two or more bits of form or change of form simultaneously we can talk about a **SYNAFFIX** or of **PARASYNTHESIS**.

A rather different example of parasynthesis is presented in the next data-set from a Semitic language. This data, in Data-set 5.11, is presented in the ordinary Maltese spelling: <q> is pronounced /ʔ/ and <j> is pronounced /j/.

<5.17> What kinds of affix are involved in the parasynthesis?

Data-set 5.11
Maltese

English gloss	3sg perfect	3sg imperfect (present)
'strike'	ħabat	jaħbat
'oppress'	ħaqar	jaħqar
'create'	ħalaq	jaħlaq
'snatch'	ħataf	jaħtaf
'divide'	qasam	jaqsam

It would take a lot more data to show it conclusively, but the roots in these words are actually just made up of the three consonants shown in the middle column. All the vowels appear and vanish by multiple Ablaut (there are, of course, more different vowels than happen to be illustrated in this particular example). Languages that work in this way are said to show ROOT-AND-PATTERN morphology. The three consonants are the root, and the vowels form patterns with those three consonants (and with prefixes and suffixes as well). The Arabic loan words in English *Muslim* and *Islam* are both based on the root *slm* which indicates submission. The word /matˤbax/ 'kitchen' is related to /tˤabax/ 'he cooked' just as /madxal/ 'entrance' is related to /daxal/ 'he entered' and /maktab/ 'office' is related to /katab/ 'he wrote'.

Yet another example is provided in the next data-set which illustrates a Ugandan language. The accents over the vowels indicate tones; an acute is a high tone, a circumflex is a falling tone and a grave indicates a low tone.

Data-set 5.12
Lango

intransitive verb	gloss	transitive verb	gloss
ódô	'pound'	òddò	'pound'
ɔ́lɔ̂	cough'	ɔ́llɔ̀	'cause to cough'
ɔ́mô	'yawn'	ɔ̀mmò	'cause to yawn'
kɔ̀bɔ̀	'migrate'	kɔ̀bbɔ̀	'transfer'
kódô	'blow'	kòddò	'blow'
lélô	'rejoice'	lɛ̀llò	'rejoice over'
lwòŋò	'call'	lwòŋŋò	'call'
ɲìkò	'move away slightly'	ɲìkkò	'move away slightly'
régô	'grind'	règgò	'grind'
tèdò	'cook'	tèddò	'cook'
wálô	'boil'	wàllò	'boil'

<5.18> Why do we have to analyse this particular case as an instance of parasynthesis? What is the form of each part of the parasynthetic set of changes that show the change from intransitive to transitive verb?

<5.19> How does English show transitivisation of the type shown by this parasynthesis in Lango?

5.20 If this is a morphological process in Lango, should the same process be viewed as morphological in English or should it simply be viewed as a case of polysemy in English?

However you answer <5.20>, there is a general feeling that there are instances where lack of change of form may nevertheless function in precisely the same way as change of morphological form. Some instances are given in Data-set 5.13 where lack of change of form seems to parallel change of form in other words of the same language.

Data-set 5.13
English

Adjective	Verb	Meaning of verb
tender	tenderise	'to make tender'
humid	humidify	'to make humid'
weak	weaken	'to make weak'
empty	empty	'to make empty'

Verb	Noun	Meaning of noun
expose	exposure	'act of exposing'; 'result of exposing'
digress	digression	'act of digressing'; 'something which digresses'
adjust	adjustment	'act of adjusting'
stow	stowage	'act or manner of stowing'; 'place for stowing'
attempt	attempt	'act of attempting'
guess	guess	'result of guessing'

CONTROVERSY: Zeros in morphology

While most morphologists agree that it is occasionally useful to be able to resort to the notion of a zero morph, some are more profligate with their zeros than others. Very few would now be happy with the idea that a meaning which is never shown by an affix could be said to have a zero realisation. Thus English has suffixes to show that nouns are plural (and some cases of internal modification as well), but we would not put a zero on the end of *cat* in the singular to contrast with the -s on the end of the plural, because there is never any morphological marker of the singular. Rather we would say that the singular of English nouns is **UNMARKED** (in one sense of this rather overused term). The difficulty with the overuse of zeros can be illustrated with the example of *empty*. Not only do we have a verb *empty* as illustrated in Data-set 5.13, we also have a noun, as in *She put all the empties in the rubbish*. Now, if the verb *empty* is *empty·Ø*, presumably the noun is *empty·Ø*, but with the distinction that the two zeros are not identical, since they have different effects, one creating a verb and the other creating a noun. So we have a number of zeros, none of which we can see or hear, which contrast with each other. Moreover, the adjective *empty*, under this analysis, is presumably *empty*, with no final zero. So we have a zero contrasting with a lack of zero, that is, with nothing at all. While there is not necessarily any contradiction here, it seems to be a rather complex system for real speakers to have in their heads; it is not clear how the learner could discover what the system is in the absence of morphological evidence.

Precisely how to express the meanings of the nouns in the last part of the data-set is something that could be discussed at greater length. What is important here is that the same kind of gloss is valid for the instances where there is no change of form between the verb and the noun as for the instances where there is a change of form.

Some scholars wish to stress the parallelism between these various examples, and talk of a zero affix or ZERO MORPH in cases like the verb *empty*, which they then write as *empty*·Ø, with the zero-symbol as a place-holder. Others are far less happy with the notion of a zero (i.e. no form) morph (i.e. form), and prefer to see examples like the verb *empty* as being the output of an identity operation. Such examples are then termed instances of CONVERSION.

5.3 Two types of affix and their implications

Two rather different types of affix have been illustrated in the data presented in this chapter. One kind is relatively syntactic in nature (that is, it provides words with different shapes to show their different functions in sentences) and tends to be relatively regular. The other kind is relatively lexical in nature (that is, it provides new words to name new things, whatever their function might be) and tends to be much less regular in its application. The difference between these two types of affix (and the corresponding difference in the ways of building words) has an important effect on the use of morphological terminology, because it is seen as being a fundamental difference in the tasks that are performed by morphological processes. First a typical example of each type will be discussed, then the terminology associated with each will be introduced, and finally we will consider how to distinguish between these two types.

The first example (see below) comes from Italian, and illustrates just one of the patterns that are found with verbs in that language.

Data-set 5.14
Italian

cantare 'to sing'	present indicative
1 SG	canto
2 SG	canti
3 SG	canta
1 PL	cantiamo
2 PL	cantate
3 PL	cantano

The present indicative means that these forms translate as 'I sing', 'you sing', 'he/she/it sings' and so on. We can see from the presentation that there is a PARADIGM here, a set of words in which one part in the complex form is substituted with each change of meaning. Given that we find different words like these, we can see that, even if they are not always formed the same way, we are going to need a corresponding set for virtually every verb in the language, and that which of these forms is required is going to be determined by the syntactic and semantic environment. Where we find all the choirboys singing, we are going to need the word *cantano*, and where just the singular addressee is singing, we will need *canti*, and so on. We would thus be surprised if it were not the case that we would be able to predict the form that would be required for a verb that we have never used before. Not only will we be able to predict the relevant form – even for a verb which we have just invented – we will know what a particular form means very precisely. We would not expect a third singular form for one specific verb to mean 'someone in high authority does this' unless the verb is, by its meaning, something that is only done by people who exercise high authority, such as pronouncing judgement or opening parliament. Affixes which fit this general picture are often called INFLECTIONAL affixes, and we speak correspondingly, in more general terms, of this being an example of INFLECTIONAL MORPHOLOGY.

In contrast, consider the example below from English. English is used as the language of exemplification here to allow you think about the data more closely than might be possible with a language you do not know so well.

Data-set 5.15
English

cool	coolant	cooler
defend	defendant	defender
descend	descendant	descender
enter	entrant	
inform	informant	informer
propel	propellant	propeller
protest	Protestant	protester
relax	relaxant	
serve	servant	server
sleep		sleeper
walk		walker

<5.21> Do you agree that there is no established word which fits in the empty slots here? In which of these cases is the word in the middle column a synonym of the word in the right-hand column? Are any differences in meaning predictable from the form of the word? Do all the words here have the same relationship to the word in the left-hand column or not? For example, if a *protester* is 'a person who protests', will the same form of gloss fit *server* and *sleeper* and so on? Do any of these words have more than one meaning? You may need to check some of these words in a dictionary to support your own intuitions.

Although it might be the case that most verbs do have a corresponding noun meaning 'the person who carries out the action specified in VERB', it is clearly not the case that the form of that noun is predictable. Neither is it the case that the noun will simply mean 'one that VERBS', although that might be at the core of the meaning: very often there is some further specific meaning. Moreover, that specific meaning is not predictable for either of the suffixes illustrated. Sometimes the word created denotes a person, sometimes an instrument, sometimes it is ambiguous between those two readings, and in the case of *sleeper* there is even a third reading whereby a *sleeper* can be 'a carriage or a compartment in a carriage on a train in which one can sleep'. Finally, neither the *-er* suffix nor the *-ant* suffix illustrated here is ever demanded for the syntactic structure of any sentence to be complete. We never have a situation where we call someone an *informant* if the word happens to be in the subject of the sentence or the addressee, but an *informer* under other circumstances (or equivalently for the other pairs illustrated). Where we have a word ending in this *-er*, we can equally well have a different word with no *-er*.

(1)   The $\left\{ \begin{array}{l} \text{sleeper} \\ \text{woman} \end{array} \right\}$ snored loudly.

All of this contrasts with the situation illustrated in Data-set 5.14. The affixes illustrated in Data-set 5.15 are called DERIVATIONAL affixes, and more generally we talk about affixation of this kind as being DERIVATIONAL MORPHOLOGY. Words created using derivational morphology can be termed DERIVATIVES.

This distinction between inflectional and derivational morphology is reflected in the terminology connected with the two types. For example, the base used in inflectional morphology, though not usually in derivational morphology, may be termed a STEM. (There are other uses of this term as well, so care must be taken in interpreting it.) And the words produced by the two types of morphology are also given different names. Words produced by derivational morphology are termed LEXEMES, while those produced by inflectional morphology are termed WORD-FORMS. This reflects the fundamental difference between inflection and derivation. Derivation produces new words in the sense that it produces new items which are new dictionary entries in our idealised mental dictionaries or lexica. Both *propellant* and *propeller* are new names for things connected with being propelled. On the other hand, the word-forms illustrated in Data-set 5.14 might all be said to be forms of the same word, namely *cantare* 'to sing'. So *cantare* is the name for the lexeme, the so-called CITATION FORM, and the words in the paradigm are the word-forms of that lexeme. When it is useful to distinguish between the two, we can do so by writing, for instance, '*canto* is the first person singular present indicative of CANTARE'. This is a notational shorthand for 'the word-form *canto* is the first person singular present indicative form of the lexeme CANTARE'.

Notice that one of the results of this difference in function is that we need to have a lexeme in order to determine what its word-from in a particular sentence will be. This means that derivational affixes generally occur closer to the root than inflectional affixes when both are present and both are on the same side of the root. For instance, if we accept that *broadens* contains the root *broad*, the derivational affix *-en* and the inflectional affix *-s*, then the order of the affixes in *broadens* is not haphazard, but due to a general principle. While there are some well-known exceptions to this general principle, it remains a relatively robust generalisation.

The terminological distinctions are summarised in Table 5.1.

	base	output word-type
inflection	stem	word-form
derivation		lexeme

Table 5.1 Summary of terminology associated with inflection and derivation

<5.22> Consider the word *rejections*. What is the root? What affix is added to that root? Does the root act as a stem in this word or not? Why (not)? What kind of word is produced by this process of affixation? If there are any other affixes in the word, repeat the question.

The categories of inflection and derivation are prototypical categories, which means that actual instances of these categories may resemble the prototype to a greater or lesser degree. Nevertheless, some clues have been given as to how to distinguish the two: inflection is strongly syntactically influenced, tends to be formally and semantically regular and predictable, tends to affect all or most of the lexemes in a particular word-class, and its affixes tend to be found peripherally in word-forms; derivation is fundamentally lexical in motivation, is frequently semantically and/or formally irregular or unpredictable, often affects only a few bases in the relevant word-class, and its affixes tend to occur closer to the root than those marking inflections. Because of their regularity, inflectional affixes tend to mark categories which have very wide application to whole sets of bases, like tense and person in verbs, case and number in nouns. However, while much inflection marks such categories, it does not follow that any morphology marking these categories is necessarily inflectional.

CONTROVERSY: Degrees of inflection

There is quite a lot of disagreement in the literature about precisely what is an example of inflection and what is an example of derivation. As might be expected, these disagreements do not affect those instances which are close to the prototypes, but the middle fuzzy ground. In English, the plural of nouns, the comparative of adjectives and the *-ly* which creates adverbs (e.g. *happily*, *superbly*) have all been claimed to be inflectional by some scholars and derivational by others. The reasons for the disagreement differ from author to author. If there are enough of these cases, the question inevitably has to be answered as to whether the categories of inflection and derivation are linguistically important, or whether they represent distinctions which may be important in one language and lacking in another, or possibly simply the result of the frequency with which different forms are met. This question has not been satisfactorily answered as yet. What we can say is that inflection and derivation are categories which are widely used and understood in linguistics, and that it is not necessarily easy to draw a firm line between the two in any given language. One attempt to solve this dilemma suggests that the difficulty arises because the class of inflectional morphology is not homogeneous, and it should be divided between CONTEXTUAL INFLECTION – determined entirely by the syntax, like agreement for gender and number between adjectives and their nouns in many Indo-European languages – and INHERENT INFLECTION – obligatorily marked in the syntax, but allowing free choice on the part of the speaker, like tense on verbs. Although this distinction is clearly useful, it does not provide all the answers.

Inflectional or derivational?

A summary of the difference between inflection and derivation is presented in the table below. Other sources will give slightly different versions of this material: for instance, some authorities claim that only derivation can change word-class, while others allow word-class changing inflection, too. It needs to be recalled that the two categories should be seen as prototypes, not as neat categories which can be defined by necessary and sufficient conditions.

Inflection	Derivation
Is syntactic (it shows function in a sentence)	Is lexical (it creates new lexemes)
Regular in form	Less regular in form
Applies widely (is productive); affects (nearly) all the words in a class	Applies less widely (is less productive)
Has regular and predictable meaning	Has less regular meaning, not always totally predictable
Is needed by the syntax (a sentence will become ungrammatical without it)	Is not needed by the syntax
Is marked peripherally in the word-form	Where both inflection and derivation are marked in the word-form, the derivational affix is closer to the root
Marks semantic or grammatical categories which affect a large number of words	May mark more specific semantic categories

5.4 The same but different revisited

Consider the data below and the questions which follow:

Data-set 5.16
Malayalam

Citation	Past	Present	Future	Gloss
ceyyuka	ceytu	ceyyunnu	ceyyum	'do'
kaaṇuka	kaṇṭu	kaaṇunnu	kaaṇum	'see'
viṭuka	viṭṭu	viṭunnu	viṭum	'leave'
peruka	perru	perunnu	perum	'give birth to'

 <5.23> Consider first the present and future forms of these verbs. What is the affix meaning 'present' and what is the affix meaning 'future'? What is the base for each of the four verbs illustrated? Is the same base found in the past? What is the affix meaning 'past'?

Let us make a suggestion that bases (stems) for past-tense suffixation may not contain a long or geminate segment at all, but that any long segments are shortened. That would account for the forms we see in Data-set 5.16. As far as the suffix is concerned, it seems that its default value is -*tu*, but that it starts with a retroflex consonant when the last consonant of the stem is retroflex, and with an <r> when the last consonant of the stem is <r>. This seems like a fairly simple case of assimilation. But the result is that we now have some verbs which have two bases and that we have three past tense suffixes: -*tu*, -*ʈu* and -*ru*. Despite having two different bases for the verb meaning 'see', we do not want to say that there are two verbs 'see' in Malayalam. We are told that there is only one citation form for this lexeme. Rather we want to say that in one set of circumstances (in the citation form, in the present and in the future) we get a long-vowel variant, and in another set of circumstances (in the past) we get the other variant. So we have two different morphs, but they can both, under appropriate circumstances, do the same job or serve the same function, namely act as the base of the verb meaning 'see'. Similarly, we have three different morphs meaning 'past tense', but they all have the same function (to mark the past tense), and we can always predict which one we will get in a given word, by looking at the last consonant of the stem. They are in complementary distribution. In both of these cases we want to say the same thing: that there is a family of morphs each of which has the same function but can appear only in its appropriate environment. To talk about this more abstract level, rather than talking about morphs, we will say that we have a **MORPHEME**. And each of the morphs belonging to the morpheme that is linked to its own specific environment, we will term an **ALLOMORPH**. So -*tu*, -*ʈu* and -*ru* are allomorphs of the morpheme {-tu} (or equivalently of the morpheme {past tense}) which are in complementary distribution. The **CONDITIONING FACTOR**, which determines which of these allomorphs occurs in any particular word, is the last consonant of the stem.

CONTROVERSY: Allomorphs or synonymous morphemes?

There is no agreement about how to recognise allomorphs of the same morpheme. As an example, consider ways of making nouns plural in English. In the words *cats*, *dogs* and *horses* we find three different allomorphs of the morpheme {plural}, namely /s/, /z/ and /ɪz/. So much is not controversial, though we might want to argue that this is a matter of phonology rather than of morphology, since the reason we do not find /*kætz/ or /*dɒɡs/ is to do with the phonotactic impossibility of these strings. However, consider the plurals in *oxen* and *children*. Are the -*en* in *oxen* and the rather complex modification in *children* further allomorphs of the same morpheme {plural}, or do they realise synonymous morphemes (call them {plural$_2$} and {plural$_3$} or alternatively {-en}, {-ren})? Some scholars class all these things together as allomorphs of the same morpheme on the basis that meaning is what determines the outcome. Others, who believe that the morpheme is at the intersection of form and meaning, prefer the solution with synonymous morphemes. It should be noted that most of those who adopt the single-morpheme solution here are less happy to adopt it when they consider *bewitch*, *encage*, *hospitalise* and *personify* which have non-homophonous but arguably synonymous affixes. It seems that somewhere there is a boundary between what are acceptable as allomorphs of the same morpheme and what are not, but the boundary is not in the same place for everyone. One of the factors in determining how much variation will be accepted may be whether we are dealing with inflectional or derivational morphology.

Some morphemes have a large set of allomorphs, some do not. Consider, for example, the English morph *dog*. This form is the form in which the base of this lexeme always appears in all of the words *dog, dogs, doggy, dog collar, dog-trot* and so on. There is only one morph which represents this lexeme. Nevertheless, by a parallel with those cases where there are several allomorphs, we can still talk of the morpheme {dog}. Note the convention of putting morphemes in braces as a piece of notation for making it clear what we mean.

> **<5.24>** What are the affixes in *bewitch, encage, hospitalise* and *personify* and why might we be able to argue about whether they are or are not synonymous and whether or not they should be seen as allomorphs of the same morpheme?

5.5 Phonological effects in morphology

It has already been shown that phonological differences within a word can have morphological effects. These were the instances of internal modification illustrated, for instance, in Data-sets 5.8 and 5.11. There is another way in which phonology affects morphology, and that is in the way in which morphs change their phonological shape when they are juxtaposed.

A simple example is given from English below. In this data-set, only a subset of verbs is considered, namely those whose phonological form ends with a voiceless obstruent. The forms are transcribed so that you can consider their form. You may add other verbs which fit the phonological criterion to the list if you wish, as long as they are not irregular verbs, since it is regular morphology which is the focus in this particular case.

Data-set 5.17
English

bake	beɪk	cite	saɪt
collapse	kəlæps	dart	dɑːt
sniff	snɪf	hate	heɪt
trap	træp	want	wɒnt

Add your own examples below

> **<5.25>** The exercise here is to make each of these verbs into a past tense form (so, if the verb were *incarcerate*, you would come up with *incarcerated*). Think about the phonological form of the past tense form. In particular, does it have the same number of syllables as the base you were given above, or does it have a different number?

If you have worked out the answer to this exercise, you should be able to follow the conclusion which follows from it. We have two allomorphs of the morpheme {past tense} in English (more if we look beyond the examples in Table 5.18). That is, the same morpheme has two different phonological forms. English spelling does not recognise this variation, but writes <(e)d> in both instances. English spelling, that is, acknowledges the unity of the morpheme rather than the variation of the allomorphs. We can say that in this instance, English spelling is morphophonemic, ignoring the alternation between phonemes in the representation of the morpheme. This alternation is termed morphophonemic alternation or morphophonemic variation.

The next data-set takes up material that has already been displayed in Data-set 5.2, and adds some more. There we saw that we had a suffix -ssa meaning 'in'.

Data-set 5.18 Finnish	talo·ssa	'in the house'	læævæ·ssæ	'in the cow-shed'
	puu·ssa	'in the tree'	lœyly·ssæ	'in the steam
	maa·ssa	'in the country'	tœnœ·ssæ	'in the cabin'
	auto·ssa	'in the car'	tœrky·ssæ	'in the rubbish'
	pullo·ssa	'in the bottle'	væylæ·ssæ	'in the channel'

Here we see that sometimes the form of the suffix meaning 'in' is -ssæ.

<5.26> What is the conditioning factor which tells us which of the allomorphs of this particular suffix will be found?

If we concentrate on this particular suffix only, we could write a simple rule like that in (2), though we would have to make this rule considerably more complex if we wanted to account for the whole of Finnish.

(2) $\begin{bmatrix} V \\ \text{Coronal} \end{bmatrix}$ CC   V
                                    ↓
                              [Coronal]

The conditioning factor is expressed in (2) as being the quality of the final vowel in the stem, though we might also reformulate (2) to make the conditioning factor the quality of the vowels in the base in general. What is important is that the same morpheme has two different phonological forms on different occasions, and that the distribution of those forms is predictable on phonological grounds. There are many ways of viewing this in the literature, one simple one being to write the affix as -ssA in the abstract, where the capital A is taken to stand for a vowel which alternates between /æ/ and /ɑ/ or is specified as being a low unrounded vowel, but is not specified as being either front or back.

<5.27> If you were to extend this notational system to the English past tense examples, what might you write for the past tense morpheme?

Thus far there is no problem. We are not in any doubt as to the desirability of stating some general rule to give accounts for such instances of allomorphy. Speakers clearly can extend past tenses and 'in' marking to words they have not heard before, and must subconsciously be applying some such rule. The only question might be whether these rules are simply phonological rules (as is implied by (2)) or whether they are in some way morphological rules – and even that may simply be a matter of convenience or preference.

In contrast consider the next data-set, again from English, and again transcribed because the sounds are important:

Data-set 5.19
English

deride	dɪraɪd	derision	dɪrɪʒən
divide	dɪvaɪd	division	dɪvɪʒən
collide	kəlaɪd	collision	kəlɪʒən
incise	nsaɪz	incision	ɪnsɪʒən
misprise	mɪspraɪz	misprision	mɪsprɪʒən
revise	rɪvaɪz	revision	rɪvɪʒən

Here we see a verb and its corresponding noun. The verbs all end in a voiced alveolar obstruent, a /d/ or a /z/. Precisely what form we should assume for the suffix is not clear: in current English it has the form /ən/, but the spelling and the presence of a /ʒ/ both seem to imply that a form like /jən/ might be more helpful for explaining the forms that we find in the nouns.

 <5.28> Why would the outcome /ʒ/ suggest that there might be a /j/ in the suffix?

It might seem, then, that we could write a rule along the lines of (3), in the same way that we wrote a phonological rule above.

$$
(3) \quad \begin{bmatrix} C \\ +\text{Obstruent} \\ +\text{Voice} \\ \text{Coronal} \end{bmatrix} \rightarrow ʒ \,/\,\_\_\, j
$$

We would then need a subsequent rule deleting the /j/ following /ʒ/ to provide a suitable output. However, there are problems with (3). Most obviously, it is not a general phonological rule of English. While we have seen that a sequence of /zj/ may, in other places, give rise to /ʒ/, the same is not true of a sequence of /dj/, which typically gives rise to /dʒ/ (consider *would you, dune, produce*). Furthermore, although we may not find the sequence /aɪʒ/ in English, we have no evidence outside words like those in Data-set 5.19 that /aɪ/ is turned into /ɪ/ in this environment, and some evidence that this is not a relevant environment. In pairs like *divine/divinity*, *line/linear* we have a similar vowel alternation with no following /ʒ/. Rather what we seem to have is a change which is brought about by the particular sequence of base and suffix. The problem is not examples like *reside* and *exercise* (for which there happens not to be a corresponding *resision and *exercision in general usage) – their non-existence just means that we will not find them as examples that we can use in evidence. Rather the problem lies in a word like *accordion* where we do not get */əkɔːʒən/, apparently because we do not have a verb *accord* plus a nominalisation ending. Thus the phonological changes illustrated in Data-set 5.19 are not really

phonological rules at all; they are morphological rules, conditioned by the morphological structure of the words concerned. It seems we should really rewrite (3) as
something more like (4). The rule for the change between /aɪ/ and /ɪ/ is more complicated, but is equally determined by the morphology of the words concerned.

$$(4) \quad \begin{bmatrix} C \\ +\text{Obstruent} \\ +\text{Voice} \\ \text{Coronal} \end{bmatrix} \rightarrow \textit{ʒ} \, / \, \_\_ \, \{ion\}$$

> **<5.29>** You have been given some words where /aɪ/ and /ɪ/ alternate in morphologically
> related words, can you find any others? In order to create hypotheses about what might
> be going on in such cases, you have to be able to produce some relevant data, so this is
> an important skill for a linguist.

There are phonological generalisations to be made about the environment where
the alternation occurs, but the morphological environment is also crucial. You can try
the same exercise with the vowels /iː/ and /e/ (as in *serene/serenity*).

Because it is possible to write these rules in a format which considers the phonological environment alone (as in (2)) and because the change is a phonological one,
morphological rules are often made to look like phonological ones, and it requires
some care to note the distinction between them.

5.6 Compounds

A compound was defined earlier as a word composed of two or more potentially free
morphs: more precisely it could have been said that these were word-forms representing two lexemes. So a compound is a word composed of two constituent lexemes.
Precisely what form the constituent lexemes take depends on the languages
concerned. Consider the different forms of the verbs illustrated in (5) for instance.

(5)   English: *wash-cloth, washing machine*
      Danish: *vaske·bjørn* 'racoon'
      German: *Wasch·bär* 'racoon'
      French: *lave-vaiselle* 'dish-washer'

In English, we find that we sometimes have the base form of the verb and sometimes the *-ing* form, depending on the type of compound involved. In Danish, where
a racoon is literally called a 'washing bear' (from its habit of washing its food before
it eats it), we find the infinitive form of the verb meaning 'wash', *vaske*. In the closely-
related German, where the word for racoon is a literal translation of the Danish, we
find not the infinitive, but a verb stem, which could stand alone only if it were used
as an imperative. In the French example (which shows a compound of a rather different kind) the form of the element *lave* 'wash' is controversial. Historically it is proba-

bly an imperative, and some authorities like to call it an imperative in current French. The form could also be the first or third person singular of the present tense of the verb. It is probably best interpreted as a form which represents the lexeme while providing as little inflectional information as possible.

The moral to be drawn from this example is that when we say that a lexeme appears in a compound, the actual form it appears in is not necessarily predictable from general principles. When it is used in a compound, it may even appear in a form which does not appear elsewhere. However, in all of these cases, the form of the verb remains the same whether the compound as a whole is in the singular, plural or any other inflected form.

It was noted above that the compounds in (5) are not all of the same kind. A *vaske·bjørn* 'wash·bear = racoon' is a kind of *bjørn* 'bear' (at least in folk taxonomy, if not biologically). We can find many such cases, not only in Germanic, but also in a host of other languages. In Danish and German, languages which have grammatical gender, it is not only the case that *vaskebjørn* (or in German *Waschbär*) is a hyponym of *bjørn* (*Bär*) (see section 2.2 on hyponymy), but it takes its gender from the second element of the compound, too. *Bär* is a masculine noun, so *Waschbär* is also a masculine noun. The element which is the superordinate term in such compounds and which determines the gender (where relevant) is called the **HEAD** element. Just like the syntactic head (see section 6.3), it is the obligatory element in the compound: you could call a *wash-cloth* a *cloth*, but you could not call it a *wash*. Compounds like these are called **ENDOCENTRIC COMPOUNDS**, because their centre or head is inside the compound. Sometimes they are called **TATPURUSA COMPOUNDS**, following a Sanskrit classification, or **DETERMINATIVE COMPOUNDS**.

Data-set 5.20 Endocentric compounds in three languages	Literal gloss	Translation
Maori		
ipu·para	'container·waste'	'rubbish bin'
maarama·taka	'month·revolve'	'calendar'
roro·hiko	'brain·electricity'	'computer'
wai·mangu	'water·black'	'ink'
French		
blazer velours	'blazer velvet'	'corduroy blazer'
idée cuisine	'idea cooking'	'cookery suggestion'
timbre·poste	'stamp·post'	'postage stamp'
vendeur literie	'seller bedding'	'linen/bedding shop'
Vietnamese		
nhà nước	'establishment country'	'government'
nhà thương	'establishment be, wounded'	'hospital'
xe lửa	'vehicle fire'	'train'

 <5.30> Which word is the head in the examples above?

Although there is generally a pattern as to whether the left or rightmost element in a compound will be the head, a surprising number of languages (including French and Vietnamese) show compounds with both orders.

Now consider the words illustrated below:

Data-set 5.21
Non-
endocentric
compounds
in three
languages

	Literal gloss	Meaning or translation
English		
dreadnought		'type of war-ship'
egg-head		'intellectual'
hatch-back		'type of car'
red-eye		various meanings including 'cheap whisky'
French		
Alsace-Lorraine		'Alsace-Lorraine'
lave-vaisselle	'wash-dishes'	'dish-washer'
porte-drapeau	'carry-flag'	'standard-bearer'
rouge-gorge	'red throat'	'robin'
Vietnamese		
cây-cỏ	'plant-grass'	'vegetation'
quần-áo	'trousers-tunic'	'clothes'
sợ-hoảng	'be.afraid-be.panic.stricken'	'be terrified'

These words do not contain a head in the same way as those illustrated in Data-set 5.20. There is no word in the compound which can stand for the compound in a sentence, and there is no superordinate term: an *egg-head* denotes neither an egg nor a head, and so on. These are usually called EXOCENTRIC COMPOUNDS, because it is considered that their head is outside the compound itself. Some of them, like *egg-head*, *rouge-gorge* are termed BAHUVRIHI COMPOUNDS, following the Sanskrit classification: these are sometimes called POSSESSIVE COMPOUNDS, because they denote an entity which possesses a head like an egg or a red throat, and so on.

The French example *Alsace-Lorraine* and the Vietnamese examples are different again. They contain two items which are of equivalent status, and they have a number of names including COORDINATIVE COMPOUNDS, CO-COMPOUNDS and, following the Sanskrit classification, DVANDVA COMPOUNDS. Since *Alsace-Lorraine* is neither a hyponym of *Alsace* nor a hyponym of *Lorraine*, but denotes an area made up of the sum of the two areas named, these compounds are also exocentric. Note that the meanings of the various examples are different: the Vietnamese words meaning 'vegetation' and 'clothes' are made up of examples of the kind of thing that might count as 'vegetation' or 'clothes'; the word meaning 'be terrified', on the other hand, is made up of two words which are near synonyms. That is, there are a number of different kinds of co-compound, just as there are different kinds of exocentric and endocentric compound.

With noun + noun compounds, one of the features that has most caught the interest of linguists is that they appear to be a neutralisation of a lot of different semantic relationships. In some cases apparently parallel forms have radically different interpretations, in others the same form can have more than one interpretation. For instance, a *sleeping pill* is a pill which encourages sleeping, while a *sea-sickness pill* is a pill which discourages sea-sickness, and an *anti-histamine pill* neither encourages nor discourages anti-histamines, but contains them. If you are travelling from London to York by rail, you might say that you are on the *Edinburgh train* (meaning the train going to Edinburgh); but if you travel in the other direction, you might still travel on the *Edinburgh train* (now meaning the train coming from Edinburgh). In some American dialects, a *Jesus bug* is a bug which walks on the water (in the way that Jesus did), while in some northern English dialects, *Jesus boots* is the term used to refer humorously to sandals, that is, the kind of footwear that Jesus wore. All this raises the question of how speakers manage to understand compounds of this type when it seems that so little of the required information is spelt out in the compound. Various proposals have been made over the years, most of which present arguments that the amount of hidden information can be reduced to a small number of fundamental notions.

CONTROVERSY: The meanings of compounds

Just how many relationships might be possible between the elements of compounds, and how best to capture these notions, has long been controversial. Some scholars have argued for just one very general meaning relationship, others have argued for four, or a dozen, or over a hundred. Some have tried to relate the meaning involved to the meanings of prepositions or of grammatical cases. Some have argued that when the meanings of the two elements in the compound are considered, the number of possible readings of the compound is in fact reduced to no more than one in context: so given that *Edinburgh* denotes a place and *train* denotes a means of transport, the means of transport has to take something or somebody to or from that location, and which way the train is going will be clear from where the conversation takes place or from the wider context of the conversation in which the term *Edinburgh train* arises. Any particular proposal about the set of possible meaning relationships is therefore bound to be hotly contested, but the one that is used here is widely accepted as being one of the most useful classifications.

Data-set 5.22
Semantic relationships in compounds

Relationship	Example
N1 CAUSE N2	withdrawal symptom
N2 CAUSE N1	tear gas
N1 HAVE N2	lemon peel
N2 HAVE N1	picture book
N1 MAKE N2	snowball
N2 MAKE N1	silkworm
N2 USE N1	steam iron
N2 BE N1	soldier ant
N2 IS IN N1	field mouse
N2 IS FOR N1	arms budget
N2 IS FROM N1	olive oil
N2 IS ABOUT N1	tax law

While this classification is an extremely useful one, you may well find compounds which appear to fit into more than one of these categories, or perhaps into none at all.

 <5.31> Which relations do the compounds *flour mill*, *light year*, *milk tooth*, *spaghetti western* and *windmill* illustrate?

Part of the point about calling things 'compound lexemes' is that they are viewed as single lexemes, so that TAX LAW, for instance, has the forms *tax law* and *tax laws* (perhaps *tax law's*) just as LAW has the forms *law* and *laws*. But there is a real question as to how we know whether *tax law* is a single lexeme or a sequence of two lexemes, as *pale sky* is. In some languages there is evidence that compounds are single words; in English such evidence tends to be rather weak, based on the criteria for defining a word. The implication is that constructions which are built syntactically are made up of two (or more) lexemes, and are not compounds. While most sources seem to agree that there is a distinction between compounds and syntactic groups, precisely where the distinction falls, in English at any rate, is not clear. The spelling system and stress, often used as criteria when a decision has to be taken, are demonstrably inconsistent. For example, *toy factory* is stressed differently if it means 'a factory that makes toys' and 'a factory that is a toy', yet it is spelt as two words in both interpretations. *Coffee-pot* is pronounced with stress on the left-hand element, but is sometimes spelt *coffeepot* and sometimes *coffee pot*, apparently depending on the taste and fancy of the speller.

Consider two examples. If *black bird* is a sequence of two lexemes and *blackbird* is a single lexeme, what are we to make of *black bear*? Formally it is like *black bird*; in terms of its meaning, it is like *blackbird*, in that *a brown blackbird* and *a brown black bear* are not contradictions, while *a brown black bird* is. So is *black bear* a compound or a syntactic construction? If *tax law* is a compound, what about *commercial law*? Both are topics you might study as a part of a law degree, yet *commercial law* looks like a syntactic combination of adjective and noun. You might even say that *They studied tax and commercial law*, coordinating an adjective and a noun, which implies an equivalent status for the two. Some argue that this is sufficient to show that *tax law* is not a compound; others argue that *commercial law* works in precisely the same way as a compound.

Children learning English as their first language tend to learn to make compounds very early. They talk about a *bus man* instead of a *bus-driver* and a *bread man* instead of a *baker*. This suggests that compounds are easy constructions to manipulate. Yet the moment we consider them in detail, we discover that they are extremely complicated constructions to analyse and to explain.

5.7 Where do the affixes go? (Advanced)

The notion of head introduced in section 5.6 also has other implications in morphology, in particular for the placement of morphology. To see how this works, consider first the examples in overleaf:

Data-set 5.23
English

Possessive construction:	Kim's car
Sentence:	He saw her
	She saw him

❓ **<5.32>** How is the function of the noun phrases (*Kim, car, he, her, she, him*) shown in these examples?

❓ **<5.33>** What is the head in each of these examples?

The important thing for present purposes is that the possessive function is marked not on the head, but on the modifier; equally, the functions in relation to the verbs are marked not on the head (on the verb) but on the modifier. That is, in English, these constructions are marked not on the head but on the DEPENDENT, to use a slightly different terminology. So we want to ask, are there languages which mark this information on the heads? The answer is clearly 'yes'. In Swahili, for example, the subject and object are marked by agreement markers on the verb, and in Saliba (an Austronesian language of Papua New Guinea) inalienable possession is marked on the possessed noun. These are illustrated in below:

Data-set 5.24
Swahili and Saliba

Swahili:	a·li·ku·ona	3SG·PAST·2SG·see	's/he saw you'
	a·li·ni·ona	3SG·PAST·1SG·see	's/he saw me'
	a·me·ni·ona	3SG·PERFECT·1SG·see	's/he has seen me'
	Hamisi	H. 3SG·PERFECT·3SG·	'Hamasi has brought food'
	a·me·ki·leta	bring food	
	chakula		
Saliba:	sine natu·na	woman child·3sg	'the woman's child'
	niu wuwu·na	coconut root·3SG	'the root of the coconut'

To summarise, then, we have some languages which seem to mark the dependents in cases of possession, and others which seem to mark the head. Similarly, when it comes to marking subject and object functions, some languages mark these on the arguments of the verb (the dependents: the subject, object etc. See section 6.5 for further detail), while others mark them on the head (the verb itself).

Now consider the data presented in Data-set 5.25. Here we have data from two languages for comparison. The two languages are Russian and Tzutujil. The data-sets from the two languages match in terms of their English translations, so you need to look carefully at the glosses to see how the various constructions are being marked in the two languages. The Russian is presented in transliteration; that is, the letters of the Cyrillic alphabet have been turned into Roman letters, but this does not necessarily represent the pronunciation in any direct way.

Data-set 5.25
Russian and
Tzutujil

Possession 'my father's horse'	
Russian:	loshad' moego otsa
	horse my.GENITIVE father.GENITIVE
Tzutujil:	xʊn ruːkeːx nataʔ
	a his.horse my.father

Fundamental verb groups: 'I cured you/him'; 'I cure him'	
Russian:	ya vylechil tebya
	I cured 2SG.ACCUSATIVE
	ya vylechil ego
	I cured 3SGM.ACCUSATIVE
	ya lechu ego
	I cure 3SGM.ACCUSATIVE
Tzutujil:	ʃatnkuːnaːx
	ʃɪnkuːnaːx
	nkuːnaːx

More complex syntax

'The man cut the tree with the machete'

Russian:	chelovek srubil derevo machete
	man cut.PAST tree.ACCUSATIVE machete.INSTRUMENTAL
Tzutujil:	xarːaːʧɪ ʃuːʧoːj ʧeːʔ ʧeː maʧat
	the man it.he.cut tree with.it machete

'I gave a blouse to Juan'

Russian:	ya otdal rubashku kxuanu
	I gave shirt.ACCUSATIVE Juan.DATIVE
Tzutujil:	ɪnɪn ʃɪnjaʔ jun kɔtoːn ʧeː aː ʃwaːn
	I it.I.gave a huipil to.him youth Juan

Adpositional phrase: 'I am in the hole'; 'it is inside you'

Russian:	ya v yame
	I in hole.PREPOSITIONAL
	ono vnutri tebya
	it inside 2SG.GENITIVE
Tzutujil:	ɪn kʼɔ ʧpaːn xa xʊl
	I.ABS be inside-of-it the hole
	kʼɔ ʧaːpaːn
	be inside-of-you

 <5.34> Are Russian and Tzutujil head-marking or dependent-marking when it comes to the marking of possession?

 <5.35> How are the subject and object marked in relation to the verb in Russian and Tzutujil?

<5.36> So are these languages head-marking or dependent-marking in this regard?

In the sentence meaning 'The man cut the tree with the machete', we see the same thing. The subject and object are shown only by separate words in Russian, while in Tzutujil there are markers on the verb itself. We would probably normally say that the verb agrees with the arguments, but we might want to consider which way round the agreement goes. We also see something else. In the part meaning 'with a machete', we simply find an instrumental form of the noun in Russian, while in Tzutujil we find an adposition and a noun (on adpositions, see section 6.2). But the adposition in Tzutujil is glossed as 'with-it'. In other words, it appears that the adposition has a marker on it to showing agreement with the following noun.

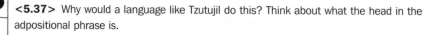 **<5.37>** Why would a language like Tzutujil do this? Think about what the head in the adpositional phrase is.

The other examples in the data-set confirm this general analysis: Russian shows dependent-marking, Tzutujil shows head-marking. We do not have enough information here to see precisely what the root in the Tzutujil adpositions might be and what the agreement markers might be, but we can get the general picture that adpositions in Tzutujil inflect for the person in the noun phrase complement of the adposition.

Those of us brought up on mainstream European languages are so used to thinking in terms of dependent-marked languages, that until we gain regular exposure to them, head-marked languages look rather odd. They are not. They are probably more common than dependent-marked languages.

Before we move on, there are two things to say about head-marking and dependent-marking. The first is that we cannot necessarily expect languages to be consistent in using head-marking or dependent-marking. Tzutjil has expressions like *xa kaq·a ʧe:ʔ* the red ATTRIBUTIVE tree 'the red tree' where the dependent and not the head is marked for the attribution function, and it also has four prepositions which do not inflect. It just so happens that Tzutujil is relatively consistently head-marked and Russian is relatively consistently dependent-marked. There are even languages which mark both participants in a construction: in Turkish, for example, both the possessor and the possessed noun are marked in a possessive construction. All we can say is that if you find head-marking in one place in a language, it is worth looking for it elsewhere.

The second point is that head-marking and dependent-marking can be taken further than has been shown here. You might like to consider what other constructions might show differences between the two sites for marking functions by morphological means.

5.8 Reduplication (Advanced)

In this section we will consider reduplication in rather more detail than previously. The idea here is not so much to tell you what the answers are in regard to reduplication (indeed, linguists do not agree on all the answers), but to explore some of the ways in which languages function with regard to reduplication and some of the things that the linguist needs to think about when describing reduplication in a particular language.

Although reduplication is not particularly common in English, in many languages it is extremely common. It is sometimes said to be a particularly ICONIC form of creating new words: the form of copying some (part of a) word is supposed directly to reflect the meaning that a word containing reduplication is given. Thus reduplication is often found in plural nouns, in intensive adjectives, and in verbs that indicate continuation or repetition of an action. Some examples of these will be given below. However, we find reduplication with so many meanings that it would be dangerous to assume that reduplication is going to have a restricted set of meanings in this way. When we look across a number of languages and language-families, reduplication can be found meaning plurality, distributedness, durativeness, iteration, repetitiveness, intensity, diminished intensity, too much, diminution, attenuation, similar to, full of ~, habituality, continuity, adverbialisation, adjectivalisation, nominalisation, verbalisation, transitivity, intransitivity, pretence and so on. In fact, reduplication may be used to indicate several of these in any one language. It is also the case that several patterns of reduplication may indicate the same meaning in a given language. Sometimes this will be obvious in examples below, when a given pattern may not appear to have a consistent meaning, or where several patterns are illustrated for a single language with apparently the same meaning. Although we do not know what limits there may be on such variability, the fact that it exists should not perturb you greatly.

We can begin with some straightforward data from Afrikaans, presented in Afrikaans orthography:

Data-set 5.26
Afrikaans

amper	'nearly'	amper-amper	'very nearly'
bal	'ball'	bal-bal	'a ball game'
bottels	'bottles'	bottels-bottels	'by the bottle'
brul	'roar'	brul-brul	'roaring repeatedly'
heuwels	'hills'	heuwels-heuwels	'numerous hills'
hier	'here'	hier-hier	'right here'
mooiste	'prettiest'	mooiste-mooiste	'really pretty'
sakke	'bags'	sakke-sakke	'bags and bags'
tien	'ten'	tien-tien	'ten at a time'
vat	'touch'	vat-vat	'tentatively feeling'

<5.38> Does the reduplication have a consistent meaning here?

<5.39> What is reduplicated in these examples?

<5.40> Does this example of reduplication show a phonological unit being reduplicated, a morphological one, or a syntactic one?

The data show an instance where we can tell what kind of unit is being reduplicated:

Data-set 5.27a
Dyirbal

bana	'water'	banaginay	'unpleasantly covered with water'	banaginayginay	'totally unpleasantly covered in water'
dʲudʲaɽ	'urine'	dʲudʲaɽginay	'unpleasantly covered in urine'	dʲudʲaɽginayginay	'totally unpleasantly covered with urine'
guna	'faeces'	gunaginay	'unpleasantly covered with faeces'	gunaginayginay	'totally unpleasantly covered with faeces'
bana	'water'	banaɲaŋgay	'without water'	banaɲaŋgayŋaŋgay	'totally without water'
baŋgay	'spear'	baŋgayŋaŋgay	'with no spear'	baŋgayŋaŋgayŋaŋgay	'with no spear at all'

Data-set 5.27b
Dyirbal

ɲalŋga·ŋgu	'girl·ERG'	ɲalŋgaɲalŋga·gu	'girls·ERG'
dʲadʲa·ŋgu	'baby·ERG'	dʲadʲadʲadʲa·gu	'babies·ERG'
biɲdʲiriɲ·u	'small lizard·GEN'	biɲdʲiriɲbiɲdʲiriɲ·u	'small lizards·GEN'

In Data-set 5.27a, two different suffixes are illustrated, one meaning 'covered with something unpleasant' and the other meaning 'without'. In both these cases, it is just the suffix which is reduplicated. In Dataset 5.27b we see that the ergative marker is not part of what is reduplicated (the allomorphy in the ergative marker depends on how many syllables there are in the stem). So in these instances, the part of the word that is reduplicated is defined in terms of its morphology. Note the contrast with the Afrikaans example.

<5.41> Is an alternative analysis of the data presented here feasible?

Another example where morphological structure clearly matters is in Data-set 5.28 from Creek.

The morphs are marked in Data-set 5.28, and you should be able to see that some of these morphs make a difference.

<5.42> What is the basic pattern of reduplication here? How much is reduplicated and where is it placed in the base?

Data-set 5.28
Creek

gloss	singular	plural
'precious'	a·cá:k·i:	a·ca:cak·í:
'sticking in'	cákh·i:	cakcah·í:
'sticking in and on'	oh·cákh·i:	oh·cakcah·í:
'sweet'	cámp·i:	camcap·í:
'split'	falápk·i:	falapfak·í:
'crooked'	fayátk·i:	fayatfak·í:
'white'	hátk·i:	hathak·í:
'broken off'	kálk·i:	kalkak·í:
'old'	lísk·i:	lislik·í:

There is more than one way in which this could be modelled. We could say that reduplication applies to the stem, or we could say that the suffixation happens after the reduplication process.

<5.43> Why might one of these be preferable to the other?

There are very many examples where the morphological make-up of the base does not seem to be relevant for the process of reduplication. Often this is because the REDUPLICANT (the affix formed by reduplication) is made up of just part of the base. In such instances, instead of looking for morphological guides to what form the reduplicant will have, we have to consider purely phonological structure. Other examples in this section will illustrate this, and lead us to consider how we are to isolate the reduplicant in phonological terms.

As a first example consider the reduplication below:

Data-set 5.29
Nukuoro

seni	'sleep, SG actor'	sseni	'sleep, PL actor'
huge	'open, PL goal'	hhuge	'open, SG goal'
ludu	'pick (trees) in a leisurely manner'	lludu	'pick (trees) frantically'

<5.44> What is the form of the affix illustrated?

Data-set 5.30
Nauruan

edegeri	'to follow'	ededegeri	'to chase away'
goro	'to run'	gogoro	'to run around'
ibua	'to catch'	ibibua	'to catch repeatedly, clap'
ake	'to fight'	akake	'to quarrel continually'
nab	'to grow bigger'	nanab	'to increase'
ure	'to pull'	urure	'to drag after'
kamae	'to roar'	kamaeae	'to make a noise'
buro	'to froth over'	buroro	'to froth over violently'
opaeo	'to make round'	opaeoeo	'to make completely round'
tiribo	'to vibrate'	tiribobo	'to undulate'

In Data-set 5.29 we have a kind of minimal reduplication: only one segment is reduplicated. We find longer strings reduplicated in Nauruan, as illustrated in Data-set 5.30.

<5.45> Which of these words have a reduplicant that is a prefix and which have a suffix? How is the prefix derived from the base? How is the suffix derived from the base?

Phonological structure still remains important here. Each of the reduplications appears to maximise the number of (C)V syllables in the output, even though Nauruan clearly allows syllable-final consonants (see the word for 'to grow bigger'). We do not have enough information to know why some of these words have prefixes and others have suffixes, nor even to be able to tell whether the distribution is predictable from general principles. The source of the data implies that it is not. However, it does seem as though the form of the reduplication is governed as much by the output as by anything else.

This contrasts with the situation illustrated below:

Data-set 5.31
Marshallese

takiŋ	'socks'	takiŋkiŋ	'wear socks'
kaɳir	'belt'	kaɳirɳir	'wear a belt'
hat	'hat'	hathat	'wear a hat'
wah	'canoe'	wahwah	'go by canoe'
tʲeweb	'soap'	tʲewebweb	'be soapy'
tʲehet	'shirt'	tʲehethet	'wear a shirt'
bahat	'smoke'	bahathat	'to smoke'

<5.46> Where does the reduplicant occur in this data-set? How much of the stem contributes to the reduplicant?

Another example which involves syllables can be seen below, though the argumentation is perhaps a little more complex in this case:

Data-set 5.32
Yaqui

base	habitual	gloss
vusa	vuvusa	'awaken'
chike	chichike	'comb one's hair'
hewite	hehewite	'agree'
ko'arek	koko'arek	'wear a skirt'
cho'ila	chocho'ila	'lasso'
vamse	vamvamse	'hurry'
chepta	chepchepta	'jump over'
chukta	chukchukta	'cut with a knife'
hitta	hithitta	'make a fire'
bwalkote	bwalbwalkote	'soften'

<5.47> Where is the reduplicated syllable placed in this example?

Such examples raise the question of whether other prosodic units are involved in reduplication, and that does seem to be the case. Consider first the data below:

Data-set 5.33
Tepecano

singular	plural	gloss
atoɛkar	aʔatoɛkar	'seat'
ɘɛ	ɘʔɘɛ	'corn field'
upp	uʔupp	'skunk'
nov	nonov	'hand'
duːr	duduːr	'ant'
tiuːpp	titiuːpp	'church'
bauv	babauv	'bean'

 <5.48> Where does the glottal stop occur in these examples?

For an example of a different prosodic domain being involved in reduplication, consider this data-set:

Data-set 5.34
Kambera

ài	wood	aiˈai	'various woods'
tau	'person'	ˈtauˈtau	'various people'
reu	'talk, chat'	ˈreuˈreu	'various talks'
ˈrama	'work'	ˈramaˈrama	'keep working'
ˈlaku	'walk, go'	ˈlakuˈlaku	'keep walking'
ˈndau	'shiver'	ˈndauˈndau	'keep shivering'
ˈtaŋaˌru	'watch'	ˈtaŋaˈtaŋaru	'keep watching'
ˈuruˌhu	'organise'	ˈuruˈuruhu	'keep organising'

To understand this transcription, we will need to know that the sequences of two vowel symbols illustrated above represent diphthongs and not sequences of vowels in separate syllables.

 <5.49> What is reduplicated here?

A similar solution appears to hold in the data below for an unrelated language:

Data-set 5.35a
Diyari

ˈkiɳṭaˌla	'dog'	ˈkiɳṭaˈkiɳṭaˌla	'puppy'
ˈkanku	'boy'	ˈkankuˈkanku	'little boy'
ˈwiḷaˌpina	'old woman'	ˈwiḷaˈwiḷaˌpina	'little old woman'
ˈmaḍa	'stone'	ˈmaḍaˈmaḍa	'little stone'
ˈpiṭa	'tree'	ˈpiṭaˈpiṭa	'small tree'

 <5.50> On the basis of the data, are we dealing with the reduplication of segments, moras or syllables here, and how can you tell? (For syllables, moras, etc. see sections 4.5.1, 4.7, 4.8.)

Adding a little more data in Data-set 5.35b makes the description of this language even more difficult:

Data-set 5.35b
Diyari

| ˈʈilparˌku | bird sp. | ˈʈilpaˈʈilparˌku | 'small bird' |
| ˈŋankaɳˌʈi | 'cat fish' | ˈŋankaˈŋankaɳˌʈi | 'small cat fish' |

 <5.51> What problem do these examples raise?

In these examples, we see that the prosodic or phonological word and the morphological word do not necessarily coincide, but we know that from other languages as well: for example in Finnish and Turkish, vowel harmony, whose domain is the word, functions separately over the two parts of a compound.

So far we have seen that the reduplicant can be defined either in terms of the morphology or in terms of the phonology (sometimes it may be difficult to decide which is the appropriate analysis). We have also seen that if it is phonologically determined, the relevant unit can be the segment, the mora, the syllable, the foot, or the word. So far, though, the examples we have looked at have all the material in the reduplicant being derived from the base. This is not always the case. Consider the examples in Dataset 5.36, which we have already seen in Data-set 5.7.

Data-set 5.36
Comox

gloss	singular	plural
'bear'	mɪχaɬ	məχmɪχaɬ
'land otter'	q'aːtl'	q'ətl'q'aːtl'
'horn'	sapaχos	səpsapaχos
'man'	tumɪʃ	təmtumɪʃ
'box'	χəsəm	χəsχəsəm
'house'	tl'əms	tl'əmtl'əms
'index finger'	ts'əmaːlah	ts'əmts'əmaːlah

 <5.52> Here it is difficult to determine precisely what is being reduplicated. How can we tell that neither one mora nor one syllable is being reduplicated?

 <5.53> Why is it not the case that the reduplicant is simply a copy of the first CVC of the base?

A more complex example is provided below:

Data-set 5.37
Hausa

gangā	'drum'	gangōgī	'an abundance of drums'
abōkī	'friend'	abōkōkī	'an abundance of friends'
tākālmī	'sandal'	tākālmōmī	'an abundance of sandals'
dōrinā	'hippopotamus'	dōrinōnī	'an abundance of hippopotamuses'

<5.54> What is fixed and what is reduplicated here?

If the phonology is important for the form of the reduplicant, we would also expect it to be important for the placement of the reduplicant. In most cases the reduplicant is placed initially or finally in the word, but we also find infixed reduplication, although less commonly. The examples below suggest that similar phonological environments are likely to be important for the placement of the reduplicant within the word.

Data-set 5.38
Quileute

| tsi'ko | 'he put it on' | tsitsko | 'he put it on' (FREQUENTATIVE) |
| tukô'yo' | 'snow' | tutkô'yo' | 'snow here and there' |

<5.55> There is a very limited set of examples here, but what is reduplicated and where is the reduplicant placed?

The examples below from Samoan seem rather more expected, because there the reduplicant appears contiguously to the copied form:

Dataset 5.39
Samoan

savali	'he travels'	savavali	'they travel'
malosi	'he is strong'	malolosi	'they are strong'
manao	'he wishes'	mananao	'they wish'
matua	'he is old'	matutua	'they are old'
punou	'he bends'	punonou	'they bend'
atamai	'he is wise'	atamamai	'they are wise'

<5.56> What is reduplicated here, and where is it placed?

This adjacency of copied material and the reduplicant seems to be the norm; the odd cases are those where either the material copied is discontinuous, or the reduplicant is not contiguous to the relevant part of the base. Such an example was seen in Data-set 5.37, but an even more unusual case is shown below:

Data-set 5.40
Semai

base	reduplicated form	gloss
dŋɔh	dhdŋɔh	'appearance of nodding'
cʔɛ:t	ctcʔɛ:t	'sweet'
bʔəl	blbʔəl	'painful embarrassment'
ghɨp	gpghɨp	'irritation on skin'
kmrʔɛ:c	kckmrɛ:c	'short, fat arms'

<5.57> How is the reduplicant formed here?

As a final example for this section, consider the data-set overleaf:

Data-set 5.41

St'a'timcets
(Lillooet)

s·qaiχaʔ	'dog'
s·qəi·qχaʔ	'pup'
s·qəχ·qəi·qχaʔ	'puppies'
s·qaiyxʷ	'man'
s·qaiy·qyəxʷ	'men'
s·qəi·qy'əxʷ	'boy'
s·qəy·qəi·qy'əxʷ	'boys'

<5.58> There are two types of reduplication involved here. What are they?

This is an extraordinarily complex set of operations. What we see, though, is the interaction of phonological processes and morphological marking. In order to understand reduplication, you need an understanding of phonology. With more advanced phonological theories, better explanations of what happens in reduplication are possible.

5.9 Summing up

Morphology deals with the meaningful internal structure of words. The elements which we can analyse within words are of two kinds: roots and affixes, and affixes can be positioned in various places relative to the root. In some cases, instead of a root taking an affix, we find that it is phonologically modified in some way, with an equivalent function. In a few cases, there may not be any change in form to reflect a change in function.

Affixes or processes of phonological modification are classed as being either inflectional or derivational. The difference is largely related to how far the morphological changes are used to mark syntactic function, and how far they are used to mark the creation of words for new concepts. The terminology of inflectional morphology is different from that of derivational morphology, but the processes involved are the same.

When morphs are placed side-by-side, various phonological processes of adjustment take place. Some of these are phonologically-driven; others are driven by the individual affixes involved.

The placement of inflectional morphs in words is related to the syntactic function of the words in larger constructions: in some languages or in some constructions the morphology which indicates the construction type is placed on the head of the construction, in other languages or constructions on the dependent.

The phenomenon of reduplication was investigated in some detail, showing that a wide variety of structures can be involved in reduplication, and how complex the process can be. Not only was it shown that a description of the morphological process of reduplication requires a good understanding of phonological structure, the question was also raised as to how far the final form of a word is determined by the requirements of the morphological process, and how far it is determined by overall constraints on the phonology of word-forms.

Technical terms introduced in this chapter

Ablaut	Inflectional
Accusative	Inflectional morphology
Affix	Inherent inflection
Allomorph	Instrument
Apophony	Internal modification
Attributive	Lexemes
Bahuvrihi compounds	Lexicalisation
Base	Monomorphemic
Bimorphemic	Morpheme
Circumfix	Morphologically complex
Citation form	Morphologically simple
Co-compounds	Morphophonemics
Composition	Obligatorily bound morph
Compound words	Parasynthesis
Compounding	Popular etymology
Compounds	Possessive compounds
Conditioning factor	Possible
Contextual inflection	Potentially free morphs
Conversion	Prefix
Coordinative compounds	Prepositional
Dative	Reduplicant
Derivational	Reduplication
Derivational morphology	Root
Derivatives	Root-and-pattern
Determinative compounds	Stem
Dvandva compounds	Suffix
Endocentric compounds	Synaffix
Established	Tatpurusa compounds
Exocentric	Unmarked
Folk etymology	Verb
Frequentative	Word-forms
Infix	Zero morph

Reading and references

There are a number of books which focus on morphology, and therefore give a lot more detail than it has been possible to give here. Of these I would recommend Bauer (2003), Haspelmath (2002), Katamba & Stonham (2006) and Lieber (2010). These publications provide different perspectives on the study of morphology and are accessible to relative novices.

For a well elaborated argument on the synonymy of the affixes *-ify* and *-ise*, see Plag (1999). He does suggest that these two are allomorphs of the same morpheme, but does not include the prefixes in his considerations. For an analysis of the French compound elements like *lave-* see Villoing (2009). The semantic relationships shown in Data-set 5.22 are from Levi (1978); other sources give more or less similar sets of meaning relationships. For arguments on the distinction between compounds and phrases in English see, for example, Levi (1978), Bauer (1998), Payne & Huddleston (2002), Giegerich (2004).

For details of and comment on the case of *coonass*, see Wray & Staczek (2005). For the girl who was surprised by orange juice, see Derwing (1973: 124 fn. 2). The term *synaffix* is from Bauer (1988). On meanings of reduplication see Bauer (2002) and Moravcsik (1978).

Data on individual languages comes from the sources identified below.

Afrikaans	Botha (1988)	Quileute	Moravcsik (1978)
Comox	Harris (1981)	Russian	Polina Kobleva (pers.
Creek	Riggle (2003)		comm.)
Diyari	Austin (1981)	Saliba	Mosel (1994)
Finnish	Karlsson (1999)	Samoan	Crowley *et al.* (1995)
Hausa	Taylor (1959)	Semai	Raimy (2000)
Icelandic	Thomson (1987)	St'a'timcets	Urbanczyk (2000)
Kambera	Klamer (1994)	(Lillooet)	
Khmer	Jacob (1968)	Swahili	Ashton (1947)
Lango	Noonan (1992)	Tepecano	Haugen (2005),
Malayalam	Asher & Kumari (1997)		Mason (1916)
Maltese	Aquilina (1965)	Tümpisa	Dayley (1989)
Marshallese	Bender (1971)	Shoshone	
Nauruan	Kayser (1993)	Tzutujil	Dayley (1985)
Nukuoro	Rubino (2005)	Yaqui	Haugen (2005)

6

Syntax

Grammar is language, and language is grammar.
(Samuel Taylor Coleridge 1817)

In Chapter 5 we looked at the ways in which words are made up from smaller parts. In this chapter we consider the way that sentences are made up of smaller parts, the words. We begin by looking at different kinds of words, and then the ways in which those words go together to form larger and larger units.

6.1 Why we need syntax

There is a lay perception of grammar that it consists of a number of pitfalls which must be avoided: ending sentences with prepositions, splitting infinitives, using double negatives such as *I never saw no car*, or using *that* to refer back to a human as in *The man that I saw yesterday* (depending on how old you are, where you live, and other such factors, you may not personally have met these particular potential pitfalls). The reality is much more complex, and much more interesting. There is a large amount of grammar that everyone agrees on, and that we are never overtly taught, and where there are no pitfalls. Consider an unobjectionable sentence such as (1).

(1) The princess kissed the frog.

Nobody makes a big fuss about the order of the words in this sentence, yet if we changed it to (2), we would completely change the message.

(2) The frog kissed the princess.

Moreover, the fact that the words come in that order is a specific fact about English that would not hold in other languages. For example in Hebrew, Maori or Welsh to provide the message in (1), you would have to say something that would translate literally as (3), while in Japanese you would have to say the equivalent of (4). Some languages permit greater freedom of order than others, too.

(3) Kissed the princess the frog.
(4) (The) princess (the) frog kissed.

So there are some fundamentals of the grammar of a language which are so fundamental that they are virtually invisible, yet they can make a big difference to how easily we understand our language. When Yoda, the character from the *Star Wars* movies, says (5), we have to pause to understand him because he disobeys a very fundamental rule of English syntax. **SYNTAX** is concerned with the ways in which sentences are made up of words, and how those sequences of words are interpreted.

(5)   Suffer your father's fate you will

With this example we see that syntax is absolutely fundamental in every sentence we speak. But syntax also takes us further than that. For example, there are sentences which look as though they should be parallel, but they are not. Consider the pairs in (6) and (7):

(6)   (a) The fire was lit by the maid.
      (b) The fire was lit by 6 o'clock.
(7)   (a) I was watching television for entertainment.
      (b) I was watching television for schools.

Quite often, we can even find sentences which are ambiguous, have two distinct meanings, despite having the same words in them. Consider the examples in (8).

(8)   (a) Hunting lions can be dangerous.
      (b) I bought the house in Paris.
      (c) I only injured the dog.

> **<6.1>** How are the sentences in (8) ambiguous? What distinct meanings does each have?

In each of the cases in (8), the ambiguity arises because there are two possible syntactic descriptions that can be associated with each of the sentences. So syntax can help explain where ambiguities arise. Some sentences can be multiply ambiguous. The celebrated example in (9) can be interpreted as being parallel to any of the examples in (10) (and, no doubt, others as well).

(9)   Time flies like an arrow.
(10) (a) Fruit flies like a banana.
      (b) Kill flies like a pest controller.
      (c) Study flies like any serious problem.
      (d) A glider flies like a hawk.

Even more interesting are the sentences like those in (11) which appear to have a similar string of words in them, but where the interpretation is so different that it is clear that the semantic relationships (and thus probably the syntactic relationships) between the words are completely different.

(11) (a) The students are easy to please.
      (b) The students are eager to please.

All of these examples show the importance of syntax. Of course, you can tell that, for example, the sentences in (8) are ambiguous without having studied syntax. But if you want to understand how they get to be ambiguous, what the structures in question are, and perhaps, in the longer term, how to make sure that computers do not get confused when they are given instructions in natural English, you really need to understand some syntax.

6.2 Substitution and word-classes

Consider sentence (12):

(12) The man sneezed.

If we consider this sentence as a string of words, then the words are not randomly chosen from the lexicon of English. For each of the words, we can substitute a number of others which will give us sentences of English (not synonymous sentences, but possible sentences of English), but there are a number of words which we cannot substitute. Consider (13) which presents some possible substitutions for each of the words in (12), and (14) which shows there are words which cannot be substituted in each of the available slots.

(13) The	man	sneezed
A	cat	died
Our	child	fainted
Some	professor	laughed
That	vicar	left
This	woman	snored

In (14) the asterisk (*) is used to indicate that replacing the relevant word in (13) with the marked word would lead to something which is not a sentence of English.

(14) The	man	sneezed
*man	*sneezed	*the
*on	*on	*on
*afraid	*utilise	*yellow

What the examples in (12), (13) and (14) show us is that words belong to different classes, and that words in the same class can substitute for each other in a sentence like (12). The words in these classes are sometimes called **SUBSTITUTION CLASSES** or just **WORD-CLASSES**. Some substitution classes (like those illustrated in (13)) are quite large. Others are quite small. For instance, if we think of words which will fit into the blank slot in (15), we will probably find a very small number of words.

(15) The ____ miaowed.

<6.2> What words can you find that fit into the blank slot in (15), and what do they have in common?

In some places, you may feel that you have no choice at all.

(16) They're all my kith and _____
Peter is Michael's boon _____
You can't escape from the long _____ of the law

 <6.3> What words would you use to fill the gaps in (16)?

The examples in (16) illustrate the smallest possible classes of words, but here we are really concerned with larger substitution classes, classes known as parts of speech or word-classes.

You probably already know from school that the words in the middle column of (13) are called NOUNS and those in the third column are called VERBS. What you may not know is how to recognise members of these word-classes in individual cases, what the choices are, or what defines the different word-classes.

The school definition of noun is that it is 'a naming word'. The word *noun* and its related adjective *nominal* are derived from the Latin word meaning 'name'. But unless we know how to interpret this, it is not much help. *Red* seems to name a colour in *My red book*, but is classified as an adjective, and *sleep* seems to name some action in *I always sleep for eight hours*, but is classified as a verb. What we need to realise is that categories like noun are best viewed as prototypes rather than as clear-cut categories defined by such criteria as 'being a naming word' (on prototypes, see section 2.3). Some nouns are better exemplars of the category than others are. So we can give a number of things which tend to be true of nouns, even if there are few or no nouns of which all are true, and say that things which fit the prototype most closely are nouns. If we are to take this approach, then we can give a list like the following of typical nominal characteristics.

(a) Nouns typically denote concrete objects like children, chairs, computers and carrots. There is probably a case for saying that the very best nouns denote people, but this wider characterisation will not cause problems.

(b) Nouns in English typically have a singular form and a plural form (like *pencil*, *pencils* or *Scotsman*, *Scotsmen*).

(c) In some languages (though not English) nouns typically belong to a particular gender-class or noun-class, and appear in a range of different case forms (on case see below in this section).

(d) Nouns can have a range of typical shapes; in English these include ending in suffixes like *-er*, *-ness*, *-ity*, *-hood*, *-dom*, and *-ship*.

(e) Nouns typically occur after the word *the*, sometimes with an adjective or a numeral between *the* and the noun.

(f) Nouns can typically occur in a frame such as *The ___ will be* ADJECTIVE. To use terms we will explain later, nouns can function in a phrase which is the subject of the sentence.

(g) Nouns can typically be turned into adjectives – in English by adding a suffix such as *-y, -ly, -al, -ish* (as in *watery, friendly, parental, waspish*).

These seven characteristics cover a number of different aspects of nouns: their meaning, their forms, further endings that can be added to them, and their function – the jobs they do. If we try to apply them to a range of words, we can see that some nouns are better than others in terms of these criteria, but things that are not nouns are even further from the prototype than the weaker nouns are. This is shown in Table 6.1, where the criteria are listed and those that apply to various words are ticked, those that do not apply are given a cross. The words above the line are generally taken to be nouns, those below the line are not.

Table 6.1
The nominal characteristics of some words

	(a)	(b)	(c)	(d)	(e)	(f)	(g)
girl	✓	✓	n/a	✗	✓	✓	✓
kindness	✗	✓	n/a	✓	✓	✓	✗
advancement	✗	✓	n/a	✓	✓	✓	✗
knowledge	✗	✗	n/a	✗	✓	✓	✗
around	✗	✗	n/a	✗	✗	✗	✗
destroy	✗	✗	n/a	✗	✗	✗	✗
lunar	✗	✗	n/a	✗	✓	✗	✗
with	✗	✗	n/a	✗	✗	✗	✗

 <6.4> Do you agree with all the ticks and crosses in Table 6.1?

You can see that *knowledge* is a pretty poor sort of noun, but it still a better noun than a word like *around*. One way of looking at this is that our language forces us to treat *knowledge* as though it denoted something concrete like *girl* does, even though in many ways it is different.

 <6.5> Are any of the following words nouns: *allergy, college, off, pretty, soup, vilify?*

We can carry out the same exercise for defining verbs. Verbs are called 'doing words' in school grammar, but *see* is a verb but not really something you do (If someone asks, *What are you doing?* how good an answer is it to say, *Oh, I'm seeing?*). *Forget* and *omit* are verbs, too, but they seem precisely to be words of not doing. Some fairly typical verbal characteristics are in the list below.

(a) A verb will typically denote an action, a state, an event or a process.
(b) A verb can take an *-s* ending if the person carrying out the action or in the state it denotes can be referred to as *he, she* or *it*, and it will lose that *-s* if the entity carrying out the action or in the state it denotes can be referred to as *I* or *we* or *they*. In languages other than English, it may be the case that there are different endings for a range of different persons carrying out the denoted action, so that there will be different endings on the verb if I do it or if you do it, and so on.

173

(c) A verb can indicate whether it refers to some general time or whether it refers to some time in the past, usually, in English, by adding an *-(e)d* ending to indicate the past. More generally (in the sense that this formulation will apply to more languages), verbs often carry markers for tense.

(d) A verb will occur with some material including a noun (in English, this material will typically come before the verb), and this material will denote the instigator of the action denoted by the verb. We can rephrase this by saying that a verb can occur in the context *The NOUN* _____.

(e) A verb can be turned into a noun by adding an ending such as *-ation, -al, -ment, -age*.

(f) Although not all verbs have typical endings, there are some which show a verb, such as *-ise* and *-ify*.

(g) In many languages, verbs may carry marking showing other categories such as ASPECT (e.g. whether the action/state is complete or still in train), CAUSATIVITY (whether someone is causing some action to take place), TRANSITIVITY (whether or not the action is affecting some other entity), REFLEXIVITY (whether the action affects its own instigator or not), and so on. Arguably, English uses *-ing* to show aspect, but does not mark the other categories listed here.

Table 6.2 illustrates the verbal characteristics of some words in the same way that Table 6.1 illustrated nominal characteristics.

Table 6.2
The verbal characteristics of some words

	(a)	(b)	(c)	(d)	(e)	(f)	(g)
kiss	✓	✓	✓	✓	✗	✗	n/a
pretend	✓	✓	✓	✓	✗	✗	n/a
visualise	✓	✓	✓	✓	✓	✓	n/a
seem	?	✓	✓	✓	✗	✗	n/a
around	✗	✗	✗	✗	✗	✗	n/a
girl	✗	✗	✗	✗	✗	✗	n/a
lunar	✗	✗	✗	✗	✗	✗	n/a
with	✗	✗	✗	✗	✗	✗	n/a

 <6.6> Do you agree with the ticks and crosses in Table 6.2?

Again, we see that while some verbs are 'better' verbs than others, the words above the line are clearly different from those below it.

 <6.7> Which of these words are verbs: *appear, off, pretty, purify, quickly, sleep*?

Every language we know about has nouns and verbs. The nouns and verbs may not be defined by precisely the set of characteristics that have been listed here, but they are likely to share at least some of the characteristics that have been listed here. Clearly, where particular endings have been specified for English above (like *-al*, or *-ify*) these will not transfer to other languages, but it is possible that there will be equivalent ways of marking nouns and verbs in other languages.

The next kind of word-class, and the last we shall deal with in as much detail, is the class of adjectives. There is a certain amount of disagreement about whether all languages have adjectives or not. It is certainly true that there are some languages in which most of the words which translate English adjectives look like verbs, for example in taking tense marking or in being able to make a sentence with *The* NOUN in front of it: in such languages we might say the equivalent of *The sky blues* meaning 'the sky is blue'. However, there are certainly many languages which have an identifiable class of adjectives, and they tend to have the characteristics listed below.

(a) Adjectives denote qualities. This is a standard phraseology, although it may be difficult to know what qualities are without reference to adjectives!
(b) Adjectives are typically gradable. This means that we can say that something is *rather* ADJECTIVE, or *very* ADJECTIVE, or *exceedingly* ADJECTIVE, or that something is *more* ADJECTIVE than something else. (In English we sometimes put *-er* on the end of the adjective rather than using *more* in front of it: e.g. *colder*.)
(c) Adjectives can typically occur between a word like *the* and a noun, so in the slot *The* _____ NOUN.
(d) Adjectives can typically occur in the slot *The* NOUN *is* _____.
(e) Adjectives end in a range of typical markers, including *-able, -al, -ar, -ish, -y*.
(f) Adjectives can be turned into nouns by adding *-ness* or *-ity* to them.
(g) Adjectives can typically be turned into verbs by adding *-en, -ise, -ify* to them.
(h) In some languages, but not in English, adjectives AGREE WITH the nouns they modify; that is, they share some kind of marking with the noun indicating things like gender, number, case. Compare Italian *il tavolo piccolo* 'the table little' with its plural form *i tavoli piccoli*, where the adjective meaning 'little' is masculine singular (*piccolo*) when agreeing with *tavolo*, but masculine plural (*piccoli*) when agreeing with *tavoli*.

These adjectival characteristics of several English words are indicated in Table 6.3, similar to the last two tables.

Table 6.3 The adjectival characteristics of some English words	(a)	(b)	(c)	(d)	(e)	(f)	(g)	(h)
silly	✓	✓	✓	✓	✗	✓	✗	n/a
afraid	✓	✓	✗	✓	✗	✗	✗	n/a
former	✓	✗	✓	✗	✗	✗	✗	n/a
lunar	✓	✗	✓	?	✓	✗	✗	n/a
around	✗	✗	✗	✗	✗	✗	✗	n/a
girl	✗	✗	✓	✗	✗	✗	✗	n/a
visualise	✗	✗	✗	✗	✗	✗	✗	n/a
with	✗	✗	✗	✗	✗	✗	✗	n/a

The question mark in column (d) for *lunar* is because we cannot say *The eclipse was lunar*, but we can say *The landscape was positively lunar*, when *lunar* is intended figuratively. *Lunar* also seems to be gradable in this example. Column (g) does not seem to be particularly helpful with the examples that have been chosen, but there are many adjectives for which it would work.

<6.8> Provide some examples of adjectives being turned into verbs in the relevant way.

 <6.9> Why doesn't *silly* get a tick in column (e)?

 <6.10> Why does *girl* get a tick in column (c)?

There is no set number of word-classes that languages must have. The three we have covered so far (nouns, verbs and adjectives) are some of the most important and most frequent, and virtually all languages will have some others. Depending upon the analysis to be undertaken it may or may not be important to distinguish all of the possible classes: after all, as we have already seen, if we push things too far, every word is in its own class, and this is not particularly useful for grammatical analysis. Some other recurrent classes will be described below, but in less detail than has been given so far. In principle, we could set up sets of prototypical characteristics for each of them in languages in which they occur, and the lists would agree to a large extent (but not perfectly) from language to language.

ADVERBS prototypically restrict the reference of verbs and adjectives, and answer questions such as when? where? how? why? The *italicised* words in the sentences in (17) are adverbs.

(17) She will take us to Winchester *tomorrow*.
  Mr Smith is *here* to see you.
  He smiled *sweetly* at me.
  That's a *really* pretty bunch of flowers.

In discussions of English, adverb very often becomes the category into which words are put if their word-class is unclear. So sometimes (though not always) you will see the highlighted words in the sentences in (18) called adverbs.

(18) (a) I am *not* going to Winchester.
  (b) He is on his way *out*.
  (c) *Yes*, you are right.
  (d) *Unfortunately*, he is delayed.

The highlighted adverb in (18a) is generally agreed to be an adverb, though it is so different from overtly marked adverbs like *closely, covertly, impossibly* and *strenuously* that it is hard to see much commonality. The highlighted adverb in (18b) is sometimes called a PARTICLE or an INTRANSITIVE PREPOSITION. The one in (18c) is sometimes called a PRO-SENTENCE, because it can stand in place of a whole sentence. That in (18d) is sometimes called a SENTENCE ADVERB, because it reports on the speaker's feeling about the whole sentence.

The easiest way to define a preposition is by showing some examples. PREPOSITIONS are words like *after, at, by, for, from, in, of, on, under, up* and *with* when these are followed by a noun or a piece of language whose main part is a noun, as in (19).

(19) John is *in* the garden.

We are all *under* observation *by* the authorities.

This piece *of* wood gets thinner *at* one end.

Prepositions are so called because they are placed or posed before (*pre-*) another word (a noun). This is true in English (to a certain extent, anyway – see (18b)), and in Latin from where we get the term. In some languages, though, things which correspond to English or Latin prepositions actually come after the noun they belong to. In such instances the term *preposition* seems inappropriate, and POSTPOSITION is used instead. Language typologists sometimes use the term ADPOSITION as the superordinate term for *preposition* and *postposition*.

Data-set 6.1 Postpositions in Turkish		
	bülbül gibi	'like a nightingale'
	onlar gibi	'like them'
	Hasan gibi	'like Hasan'
	vapur ile	'by boat'
	adam ile	'with the man'
	yolculuk için	'for the journey'
	Hasan için	'for Hasan'

Not all languages have adpositions, though most have at least a few. To translate English adpositions in some languages, you use endings on nouns. Examples are given from Finnish in Data-set 6.2. Some people use the term *postposition* in these instances as well, though many others view this as a matter of case. It is not always straightforward to distinguish between the two, and it is not necessary at this stage to be able to do so. **Case** is a marking on a noun of its function in the sentence.

Data-set 6.2 English prepositions translated by endings in Finnish			
talo	'house'	tuoli	'chair'
talon	'of the house'		
talossa	'in the house'	tuolilla	'on the chair'
talosta	'out of the house'	tuolilta	'off the chair'
taloon	'into the house'	tuolille	'onto the chair'

PRONOUNS are words which allow us to refer to people and other entities without repeating their entire descriptions again. So if I say *I saw a man wearing a heliotrope three-cornered hat last night*, I can, in the next part of the conversation, simply refer to that man as *he*: *He was juggling swords outside the cinema. He* is a pronoun. There are many types of pronoun, and *he* exemplifies the most basic sort, so we can begin here. In most languages these personal pronouns are distinguished according to **PERSON** and **NUMBER**. For number, let us provisionally simply assume that the options are singular and plural (more on that in a moment). Person requires a little more explanation.

For there to be an act of speaking, there has to be a person who is speaking. The speaker is fundamental to the whole notion. So the word which denotes the speaker is said to be in the **FIRST PERSON**. *I* is a first person pronoun. Once you have a speaker, the next basic requirement is somebody to talk to. The person you address is the **SECOND PERSON**. *You* is a second person pronoun.

<6.11> You could, of course, talk to yourself. Would you address yourself in the first person or in the second person?

For present purposes, we can say that anything else is something or someone being talked about, and they are all **THIRD PERSONS**. *She*, *he* and *it* are third person pronouns. All the pronouns mentioned so far have been discussed as referring to single individuals. But pronouns can also refer to more than one individual. Where there is more than one speaker (which is more often one speaker representing a group of individuals) we have the pronoun *we*; a group of listeners is still *you* in English (though you may know languages where the form would not be the same for the singular and the plural); and a group of third persons would be *they*.

So far we can present these pronouns efficiently in a table like that in (20).

(20)

	Singular	Plural
First person	I	we
Second person	you	you
Third person	she	they
	he	
	it	

There are languages which do not distinguish between *she*, *he* and *it* in the third person singular, but have the same form for all; there are languages which have similar distinctions in the plural; most languages have different forms for a singular second person and a plural second person (so did English until around the time of Shakespeare, and some regional dialects still have *thou* as a singular form); there are languages which have a separate polite form for the person you are speaking to – a form which may look like one of the other forms in the set, or may be distinct from all of them. There are many languages which distinguish between an **INCLUSIVE** and an **EXCLUSIVE** first person plural. An inclusive form means 'all of us, including you', and an exclusive form means 'all of us, but not including you'.

<6.12> Does the kind of English you speak distinguish between second person singular and second person plural?

Although the set in (20) provides only singular and plural forms (as reflects the Standard English usage), there are also languages which have **DUAL** forms (to refer to just two individuals) and, rarely, **TRIAL** forms (referring to precisely three). A few languages have other patterns, too.

You have probably already noticed that the set in (20) is only part of the story. While we may use *I* in some positions, we use *me* in others – in rather more places, in fact. And if we are talking in terms of possession we use *my*. In most languages these differences can be described as differences in **CASE**; while that description is dubious for English (see page 180), we can pretend that it works for English as well.

We then need to say that English has three cases, which, following usual custom, we can call NOMINATIVE (or *subjective*), ACCUSATIVE (or *oblique* or *objective*) and GENITIVE (or *possessive*). Many languages have more cases than this; some have none. A peculiarity of English is that it has two possessive forms, one that is used before a noun and one that is used in a context such as *That object is ____*. In traditional descriptions of English the latter is often called the 'strong' possessive, but in modern English the label *predicative* may be better. This gives us the entire set of personal pronouns in (21) for English.

(21)	Nominative		Accusative		Genitive (Attributive)		Genitive (Predicative)	
	Singular	Plural	Singular	Plural	Singular	Plural	Singular	Plural
1st	I	we	me	us	my	our	mine	ours
2nd	you	you	you	you	your	your	yours	yours
3rd	she	they	her	them	her	their	hers	theirs
	he		him		his		his	
	it		it		its		its	

Notice that there is a great deal of SYNCRETISM in this table, that is the same form recurs in a number of different slots (this would be – at least apparently – increased if we put *they* next to each of *she*, *he* and *it*, for example).

<6.13> The meanings of each of these pronouns has been given in terms of person, number and case, but are there are examples where these meanings do not fit?

DETERMINERS are a group of words which define nouns and help say what they refer to. The most obvious determiners are the ARTICLES, in English *the* and *a*. *The* is commonly described as the 'definite' article and *a* (or its alternate form *an*) as the 'indefinite' article because their main use is in co-occurrence with nouns which refer to entities which are definite or indefinite respectively. *The man* refers to a man we know about, *a man* refers to some man who has not yet been fully introduced into the discourse. Some languages do not have articles at all (Finnish and Russian are such languages); some languages change the form of the noun to indicate corresponding information.

CONTROVERSY: Does English have case?

In most languages which have a clear category of case, the case of a noun (or pronoun) depends on the function it plays in the sentence. So if you have a particular pronoun in *X played poker*, the other forms in the set will be ruled out in that position, and that form will always occur in that position. So in English we have *I played poker*, and we cannot have **Me played poker*. So far, so good. The problem arises if we add Sharon. Can we say *I and Sharon played poker, Sharon and I played poker, Me and Sharon played poker, Sharon and me played poker*? There might be politeness reasons for preferring one order over the other, but in a true case language the *I* forms would be acceptable, and the *me* forms would not be. In English there is variation, and the answers may be unclear. We get a similar problem with

a   Frances played poker with me and Sharon.
b   Frances played poker with Sharon and me.
c   Frances played poker with I and Sharon.
d   Frances played poker with Sharon and I.

There are different dialects of English, and the interpretations of these sentences will differ depending on the dialect. For some speakers (a) and (b) are acceptable (though (b) is politer) and (c) and (d) are impossible. This is the case solution. For some speakers (a) and (b) and (c) are possible, but (d) is the nicest or poshest way of saying this. This is no longer simply a matter of case.

Equally, there is a problem – and has been for at least four hundred years – with sentences of the form *It was X*. In some written forms of English you can find *It is she, It is I, It is we*, but these are odd in spoken English and, interestingly enough, not equally odd. *It is I* is probably rather more likely than *It is we* (e.g. *It is we who must take responsibility for this error*). So here we have an instance where different forms from the set can substitute for each other, again something that is not typical of case systems.

The English system is in a process of change; once there was case; now we have confusion; we cannot yet tell what will emerge.

Note that while most languages with case systems mark case on nouns as well as on pronouns, in English it is really only the pronouns that show these patterns. A thousand years ago, English had case on the nouns, too. English has been losing case for a long time, and the confusion with the pronoun forms appears to be a continuation of this long-time trend.

Other kinds of determiners are demonstratives (in traditional descriptions called demonstrative adjectives). In English the demonstratives are *this, that, these* and *those* (and in some varieties *yonder, this here, that there*). We can see that demonstratives can substitute for articles:

The	cat	saw	a	mouse
A			the	
This			this	
That			that	

Possessive pronouns, illustrated in (21) above where they are listed as attributive, can also act as determiners, and fit into the same slots, as do some quantifiers: *some, many, most*. Less obviously, possessive phrases like *George's* or *my downstairs neighbour's* also fit into the same slots, and are determiners:

The	cat	saw	some	mice
A			the	
This			these	
That			those	
George's			my	
Your			my downstairs neighbour's	

<6.14> Since we can also say *three mice* and *blind mice*, why don't we put *three* and *blind* in the same slot as *the* and *my*?

<6.15> What about *Our George's cat*? Isn't that a counterexample?

The final word-class we will consider here is the class of **CONJUNCTIONS**. Conjunctions join things together. In some instances the two things that are joined together are of equal status, and then we talk about **COORDINATING CONJUNCTIONS**. The major coordinating conjunctions in English are *and*, *but* and *or*. In *She was poor but she was honest*, *but* joins two sentences; in *You and I need to talk*, *and* joins two subject pronouns; in *The book is red or purple*, *or* joins two adjectives. You cannot join things with these conjunctions which do not match in some way: **He is here but a bully; *She was running or lazy; *The flowers are in the garden and blue*. Other conjunctions join a less important bit of language onto a more important one. They are called **SUBORDINATING CONJUNCTIONS**, or sometimes **COMPLEMENTISERS**. The prototypical complementiser is *that* (usually pronounced /ðət/): *I know that you are doing well; The bus that we caught broke down*. Other subordinating conjunctions are highlighted in (22).

(22) They came *because* I asked them to.
    When I arrived, he had already left.
    I haven't seen you *since* you were three years old.
    I need to know *if* the money is safe.

Notice that in each case here the more important part of the sentence (*They came, He had already left, I haven't seen you, I need to know*) makes sense alone, while the part introduced by the subordinating conjunction does not (**Because I asked them to, *When I arrived, *Since you were three years old, *If the money is safe*).

The word-classes we have considered here are not sufficient to allow you to assign every word in every sentence to a word-class, but they should be sufficient to allow you to make a very good start.

TRIVIA

Some non-linguists believe there to be precisely eight parts of speech (word-classes). These are usually given as noun, pronoun, verb, adjective, adverb, conjunction, preposition, article, and some would add a ninth, interjection. However, we have seen that there are several distinguishable kinds of conjunction, that not all languages necessarily have all of the word-classes we have mentioned, and that there may be an argument for seeing some adverbs, at least, as belonging to the same class as prepositions. The idea that there is a fixed and definite list of parts of speech comes from school teaching over several centuries based on the Graeco-Latin tradition, eight parts of speech being attributed to by Dionysius Thrax before the second century CE. There was plenty of development in views of the parts of speech both before that time and after it (at various stages, participles were seen as a separate part of speech, and adjectives and nouns were not distinguished). Insisting on precisely eight fixed parts of speech is simply ignorance of or a refusal to acknowledge the amount of thought that has been given to this topic for several thousand years, and the amount of development that has taken place in our understanding of classifying words.

 <6.16> Assign every word in the sentence *The owl looked up to the stars above and sang to a small guitar* to a word-class.

6.3 Sticking words together

We not only need to know what kind of words we are dealing with, but how they go together: *Fred sneezed* is a perfectly good sentence of English, while **sneezed bright* is not. To see how this works we need to continue the idea of substitution that was introduced in section 6.2, and see how sequences of words and single words can be substituted for each other and leave coherent constructions behind, so that complex constructions are elaborations of simple ones, but elaborations that hold to quite strict constraints.

As far as English is concerned, about the shortest statement we can come up with consists of two words, just like the example of *Fred sneezed* given above. It is true that under appropriate circumstances, you could manage with less than that. If someone asked you, 'Who sneezed?', then 'Fred' would be a perfectly acceptable answer, and if you were asked 'What did Fred do?', you might equally appropriately answer, 'Sneeze'. Those utterances, though, require the context to be appropriate. You would not walk into a room where your parents were sitting and announce, a propos of nothing at all, 'Sneeze' (probably not even if it was intended as a command – but recall that we are talking about statements). To make a complete sentence we need the two bits in *Fred sneezed*. The same is not true in all languages, but we will use English for this particular example.

Each of the bits in *Fred sneezed* can have a longer sequence of words substituted for it, in ways similar to the ways we saw in (13). Consider the various expansions suggested in (23) below.

(23) Fred   sneezed
    That man   ran off
    The bald man   ran to work
    The very tall model   ran to the town
    The very fit teacher of physics ran quickly to the secondary school

The importance of this is that we can find very complex sequences like *The very fit teacher of physics ran quickly to the secondary school* and discover its basic structure by substituting other words for the various **CONSTITUENTS** of the sequence, and so discover its fundamental structure.

> **<6.17>** What do you think the basic structure of the sentences *The cat in the hat came back* and *The woman at the centre of the controversy refused to answer our telephone calls* might be?

To show this structure, it is often useful to bracket the pieces of the sequence which belong together. So we might want to write *[The cat in the hat] [came back]* or *[The woman at the centre of the controversy] [refused to answer our telephone calls]*. Similarly, for *That man ran off*, we might want to write *[[That] [man]] [[ran] [off]]*. You can probably already see the disadvantage of this system: it becomes very difficult to read. In fact, it becomes even more difficult if we want to label the brackets so that we can see what word-class each word belongs to. If we put the labels on each of the matching brackets we might get something like (24)

(24) $[[_{Det}$That$]_{Det}$ $[_{Noun}$man$]_{Noun}]$ $[[_{Verb}$ran$]_{Verb}$ $[_{Adv}$off$]_{Adv}]$.

This very quickly becomes totally impossible to read or write. To make things easier, we usually use **TREES** instead. Trees provide precisely the same kind of information, but are easier to read. The tree for *That man ran off* would be (25).

(25)

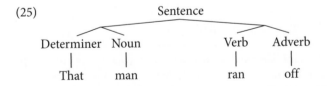

The tree makes clear that we have not yet provided a label for the sequences *that man* and *ran off*; we will do that soon. Apart from the fact that the whole construction has been labelled a Sentence, the tree in (25) provides precisely the same information as the bracketing in (24). Under normal circumstances we would abbreviate the various word-class labels in the tree. Rather than Sentence, we would just write 'S', and similarly we would write 'D' for Determiner, 'N' for Noun, 'V' for Verb and 'Adv' for Adverb ('A' would mean Adjective).

In order to see how sequences of words are built up, we will start by looking at adjectives. Imagine an adjective like *sweet* appearing in a sequence such as *The sweet coffee*. *Sweet* is an adjective, so we want to put an A above it in the tree, as in (26).

(26)   A
         |
       sweet

However, we also need to think of what else might occur in the same slot between *the* and *coffee*. One obvious thing that we could do is say *the disgustingly sweet coffee*. *Disgustingly* tells us about the degree of sweetness, and not about the coffee (it is not *the disgustingly coffee*) and not about the word *the*. So we are going to need a tree in which the *disgustingly* is linked to the *sweet*, as in (27).

(27)
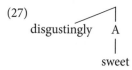
       disgustingly   A
                       |
                     sweet

It is easy to see that there is something missing in this tree. First, we need a label for the word *disgustingly*.

<6.18> What word-class does *disgustingly* belong to?

We also need a label for the whole sequence *disgustingly sweet*. We have already noted that we cannot replace *sweet* with *disgustingly*, but need the *sweet* (or some other adjective) in this phrase. This means that the adjective is the obligatory part of this sequence of words, so we will call it an **ADJECTIVE PHRASE** (AP for short), and we will call the adjective the **HEAD** of the adjective phrase. This gives us a label for the sequence *disgustingly sweet*, but we have not yet finished. The residual problem is that in place of *disgustingly* we could have had *rather disgustingly*.

<6.19> What word does *rather* tell us about in *rather disgustingly sweet coffee*?

<6.20> What word-class does *rather* belong to?

The point of this extra information is that although *disgustingly* is just an adverb, it is the obligatory word (the head) in what could have been an adverb plus its own modifier; that is, it is the head of an **ADVERB PHRASE** (AdvP). So rather than just having the adverb stuck directly on the tree, as we did in (27), we really need to see it as part of an adverb phrase, as in (28).

(28)   AP
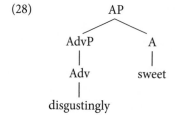
        AdvP   A
         | |
        Adv   sweet
         |
     disgustingly

From this example, we will take three generalisations, which we will use in future to help build up our trees.

i   The phrase is always named after its head, and each phrase has its head as one of its constituents (or, equivalently, every node of the tree labelled with a word-class must be immediately dominated by a phrasal node for which that word-class is the head).
ii   Anything that is not a head in a tree must be a phrase.
iii   As far as we have seen so far, all trees have just two branches coming from any one point.

We have not previously defined *node* or *dominated*, but their meaning can be deduced from their use in (i): a **NODE** is any point in a tree at which the branches of a tree could potentially or do diverge or the ends of the branches of the tree; the top node of a tree is called the **ROOT** of the tree; a node X **DOMINATES** another node Y if to get from Y to the root of the tree you have to pass through the X node, and it **IMMEDI-ATELY DOMINATES** Y if there are no intervening nodes.

CONTROVERSY: Heads in trees

Two kinds of trees are widely recognised. The first is the constituency tree that is presented in the main text. It is explicit about which bits go together in meaningful and grammatically important chunks – the constituents – but it does not overtly mark the notion of head. The second is the dependency tree, which overtly marks the head of a construction (by putting it further up the tree), but is less explicit about which bits belong together as constituents: anything depending on a head is taken to form a constituent with that head, and no phrasal nodes need to be specifically marked. The reason for presenting the constituency tree here is simply that it is by far the more widely accepted way of drawing trees, and thus the one you are most likely to meet once you start reading other materials for yourself. Some scholars prefer dependency notation, and it also seems to be useful for showing the structure of some languages. A dependency tree for the phrase *rather disgustingly sweet* is presented in below.

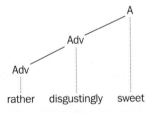

Let us now turn to what happens when we put adjectives into a larger construction. So now we pass from concentrating on *disgustingly sweet* to thinking about *sweet coffee*. We have already seen that we have to consider *sweet* to instantiate an AP (even though it is only made up of a single word, there is the theoretical potential for more).

<6.21> What word-class does *coffee* belong to?

<6.22> If we have a unit made up of a noun and an AP, what is that unit likely to be?

All this leads to a coherent view according to which we can present the construction as in (29).

(29)

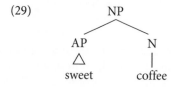

<6.23> What do you think 'NP' must stand for in (29)?

A new piece of notation has been introduced in (29). The triangle in the tree under AP is to say that we could be more specific about the content of this node if we wanted to be, but that it is not relevant for the point we are discussing at the moment. To be more precise, the tree should have been drawn as in (30), but we were not discussing the internal structure of the AP at this point.

(30)

We could add more to this NP. In particular, we could say *coffee from Brazil*. Here we have something after the head noun, but we have not learnt how to deal with a construction like *from Brazil* yet, so we will put this larger construction and its implications temporarily in abeyance.

Now we need to consider what happens if we look at the phrase *this coffee*. We have already seen that *coffee* represents an NP.

<6.24> What word-class does *this* belong to in *this coffee*?

Since the word *this* is a determiner, and co-occurs with a phrasal category, an NP, in a constituent, then from (i) and (ii) above we expect the whole thing to be a determiner phrase. Furthermore, we can replace the whole of *this coffee* with *this* (e.g. in *This comes from Brazil*). So let us say that *This coffee* is a DP, made up of a determiner and a noun phrase.

CONTROVERSY: Two branches to each node

It was said above that we work with a generalisation that we cannot have more than two branches dominated by any node. (We have seen that we can sometimes have just one.) This constraint is widely accepted, and certainly makes for tidier trees, but there is no particular reason to believe that our picture of syntax would be radically different if we flouted this convention. Indeed, many linguists do – and even more used to before the constraint was adopted as a general principle governing syntactic trees. There is at least one exception, though. Where constituents are coordinated we can have more than two branches at a node. So the tree below is the kind that is often drawn for the phrase *sweet and hot coffee*:

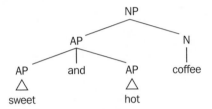

If we can have a structure here that is not **BINARY**, it means we have to be careful to justify the **BINARITY** where we do use it. Sometimes this is quite difficult.

The ultimate argument for binarity probably comes from information theory, from computing and from the (subsequently disproved) notion that neurons in the brain operate on a binary basis: either firing or not firing. Accordingly, binarity was assumed to be the easiest structure for a child learning a language to work with. Since adopting the binarity principle implies that you have to argue the case of which two branches go together most closely every time three constituents seem to co-occur, accepting this constraint is accepting a very restricting hypothesis on the form of a grammar.

Next we need to move on to constituents like *in the garden, on a white horse*.

<6.25> What word-class do *in* and *on* belong to?

<6.26> What are *the garden* and *a white horse*?

<6.27> Draw the tree for *a white horse*.

<6.28> If we have a preposition and then a DP making up a unit, what would you expect that unit to be called?

If that unit is a PP, we would also expect the preposition to be able to stand for the entire phrase. We can see this if we compare *She jumped on a white horse* and *She jumped on*. Here *on* is, as noted earlier, an intransitive preposition: it has no following DP. In some languages intransitive prepositions do not occur, but they are common in English. All this also provides a coherent picture, and we can call *in the garden* or *on a white horse* a PP, each made up of a P and a DP.

We are now in a position to go back and consider expressions like *coffee from Brazil* or *the cat in the hat*. In both these cases we have a noun (*coffee, cat*) which is immediately followed by a PP which provides further information about that noun. It seems we need a tree like that in (31).

(31)

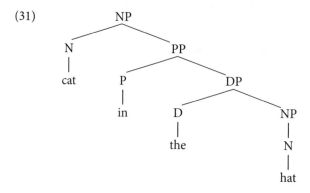

CONTROVERSY: The lack of controversy over DPs

The DP as it has just been introduced is remarkably uncontroversial in much modern linguistics, though it is a relatively new innovation. There are very good reasons for saying that this is a DP, in precisely the way that was explained, but there are some problems with the notion, too. First of all, what would have happened if the phrase chosen to introduce this notion had been *the coffee* and not *this coffee*? The argument about expecting a non-phrasal category to be dominated by a phrasal node with the name of the word-class in the phrase name would still have held, but it would not have been true that *the* could stand for the whole phrase. We cannot say **The comes from Brazil*. We might argue that this is an exception and something special about *the*, but there are other determiners which cannot replace the entire construction: *a, my, our* and so on. Indeed, in many constructions it is possible to have no determiner, as in *Coffee is horrible*. Do we have no DP in such sentences or do we have an empty determiner slot, and how does this fit together with the expectation that the head of a phrase should be able to stand for the phrase as a whole? Furthermore, if we look beyond English, we find that the homophony of what is traditionally called the demonstrative pronoun *this* and the demonstrative adjective *this* is a by-product of the history of English. In French we can say *Cette bière est d'origine alsacienne* ('this beer comes from Alsace') but not **Cette est d'origine alsacienne. Cette* can only occur where there is a following noun phrase. Another problem is that it is not entirely clear what happens with a determiner like *My sister's* in *My sister's coffee. My sister* is a phrase. In English, we might be able to claim that *'s* is the marker which turns the phrase into a determiner, but in a language like Russian or Latin which has case it is harder to separate out the genitive inflection to make just that the head of the construction, and in some languages possession is shown by simple juxtaposition, so there is no overt marker of possession. Then we have the problem with so-called pronouns. If *this* is a determiner, is *she* a determiner or a noun? Traditionally it is seen as a special kind of noun (hence the name). But *this* and *she* appear to be parallel in *She/this has just arrived*, and probably have to be treated as determiners. The real counterargument to all these points is that to try to do anything else with determiners is much messier!

The trouble with this is that we have already seen that where we have an adjective and noun construction we want to call that an NP, and we have also said that each node should have a maximum of two branches. So what happens if we get something like *hot cups of tea*? Can we have three branches under the NP node?

Before we accept such a departure, we should ask whether we have any evidence on whether these three elements are all at the same level or not. If we are going to stick with binary trees we have two possibilities: (a) [[hot cups] of tea] and (b) [hot [cups of tea]]. Are there arguments in favour of either of these? As it happens, there are. The first is the meaning, although this one may not be entirely clear. We need to ask whether *hot* describes the *cups of tea* (corresponding to (b)) or whether *of tea* explains what kinds of *hot cups* we are dealing with (corresponding to (a)). You will probably agree that (b) corresponds best with the meaning. Moreover, we can replace *cups of tea* with *ones*, which suggests that *cups of tea* is a constituent; there is nothing that we can use to replace *hot cups* in such a construction: we cannot say *them of tea* or *ones of tea*, for instance. So both of these pieces of evidence agree in suggesting that the structure in (b) is what we need. That is not quite the end of the question, though, because we still need to know what to call the node which dominates *cups of tea*. We said that NP dominates *sweet coffee*. NP must also dominate *cup of tea*. The evidence comes not so much from these particular examples as from ones like them, as in (32).

(32)   hot cups of tea   hot ones
       the large cups with broken handles   the ones with broken handles
                                                the large ones
                                                the large ones with broken handles

If *ones* can stand for a plural NP, then it seems to be the case that both *large cups* and *cups of tea* must be NPs, which implies that we can have NPs inside NPs. This is a break from what we have done previously, because now it seems that we can have an NP immediately dominating an NP. This feature is called **RECURSION**.

 <6.29> What is the implication of the last example in (32)?

At this point the tree for *the large cups with broken handles* (in (33)) is getting rather long and involved, and you might be asking yourself whether trees are really all that simple to read; the format of the trees follows from a few basic principles we have followed and the arguments we have put forward, and the trees are still easier to read than labelled brackets!

(33)

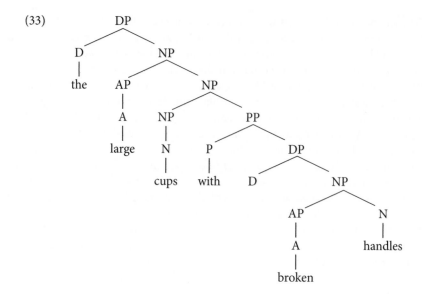

CONTROVERSY: Zero elements in trees

In (33) there is a DP with an empty D. What gives us the right to assume that there is a DP there, and not simply an NP?

The answer may be 'nothing': it depends on how we want to argue. If we want to look at the form alone, the form looks like an NP. Moreover, leaving the D empty adds to the multiplicity of zero elements that linguists postulate, and that we have previously criticised (see section 5.2). If that were all there is to consider, then we would be justified in calling this an NP and not a DP. The other side of the question is the semantic side. The expression *broken handles* seems to be referential: they are the handles on the cups in a higher NP. It would be equally possible in this sentence to have *with the broken handles* – in which case the whole problem might have gone unnoticed. Part of the difference between an NP and a DP is whether or not it refers: a DP does, an NP, generally speaking, does not. There are many languages in which all referring expressions must have determiners (English just happens not to be one of them).

So how we answer the question depends on whether we are looking at the form or the function. The tree was drawn with the function in mind; had the tree been drawn considering only the form, the DP node would have been omitted.

We will see another case a bit later where we do not know from the form whether to say we have a sentence or something larger than the sentence with an unmarked (zero) element. The same argument applies there: form argues in one direction, function in the other.

Now that the general pattern of these trees is established, we can move fairly rapidly on to other examples. Clearly an AdvP will be made up of a possible AdvP and an Adv, as in, for example, *rather stupidly*. A VP will be made up of a V and whatever kind of phrase might follow: a DP in *grew tomatoes*, a PP in *grew in the garden*, an AP in *grew very hot*, and nothing at all in *Topsy grew*.

We can have a verb phrase like *grew tomatoes*, but what do we do with a phrase like *will grow tomatoes*? Here *will* can stand for the phrase as a whole under appropriate circumstances (e.g. *Will you grow tomatoes? I will.*), and it goes together with a VP to make up a larger constituent, so we would expect *will* to be the head of the phrase. What this phrase is called is very variable in the literature. Some people call it a *predicate phrase*, some people call it a *tense phrase*, others an *auxiliary phrase*, but the most usual name – for reasons which it would take too long to explain here – is **INFLECTION PHRASE** (IP), so we will adopt that nomenclature here.

We now reach the stage when we want to put the IP together with an NP to make a larger structure like *The gardener will grow tomatoes*. We have previously called this a sentence (S), which is the traditional name, but now we have a problem. What is the head of the sentence? We have nothing that is not a phrase. The only way we have found of dealing with that in what has been said earlier is to put one phrase inside another phrase of the same kind, and let the head be the head of the lower (or internal) phrase. That was what we did, implicitly, in *the large cup with broken handles* in (33). If we do the same thing here, we will need to say that a sentence is a special kind of IP, and the tree for *The gardener will grow tomatoes* is as in (34).

(34)

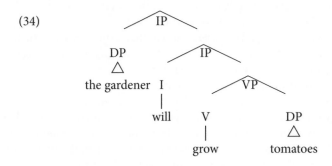

 <6.30> What would that imply that the head of the sentence in (34) is?

The reason for *will* being the head in (34) is not obvious on the basis of what you have been told. *Will* cannot stand for the sentence as a whole, nor is it an obligatory element in a sentence. The argument is that when the category I (inflection) is not filled by a modal like *will*, it is filled by the tense which gets attached to the verb. Tense does seem to be obligatory in a sentence which makes a statement (at least in Standard English). *Susan be a government official* is not a good sentence of Standard English, and neither is *John being here*. Each of these lacks tense. They could, of course, appear in larger sentences where there is a modal or tense to carry the sentencehood: *When will Susan be a government official?*, *John being here is no reason for ignoring Fred.*

There is another reason for finding the 'I = tense' argument to be convincing. First consider the sentences in (35).

(35) (a) Susan will come, will she?
    (b) John could come, could he?
    (c) Mary comes, does she?
    (d) Mary came, did she?

The little question tagged on the end of the sentence is called a TAG QUESTION. The examples in (35) do not illustrate the most typical tag questions, but they are perfectly possible given an appropriate intonation pattern and context. Where we have a modal in the main part of the sentence, that modal is repeated in the tag question (as in 35a, b); where there is no modal we find the verb *do*. Where the verb in the main part of the sentence is in the present tense, *do* is in the present tense (*does* in (35c)), where it is the past tense, *do* is also in the past tense. So it seems that the function of *do* in these sentences is to carry the tense where there is no modal: the modals and the tense seem to fit into the same slot. Note that this means that in a sentence like *Kim ate a very unripe banana and so did Lee*, the *did* carries the tense and the *so* is a pro-VP corresponding to *eat a very unripe banana*; that is, the *so* represents the VP but with no tense attached, just as the tree in (34) would predict.

To accept this argument, though, you have to accept that a slot in a syntactic tree can be filled by something which is not a word in the language being described. Implicitly we have presumed so far that the nodes at the ends of the branches in a syntactic tree are all words (though see the box about zeros in trees).

We could stick with the notion that what we have here is a sentence, and call it S, but this would carry with it the implication that a sentence is a construction which is different in type from every other construction we have considered. Calling it an IP makes it part of the general sequence of constructions, but raises these other questions. We will continue to use the term 'sentence' informally in what follows, since the term is widely used and understood, but you might like to think of the possibility that it is a rather non-technical term.

Let us end this section with a final construction, the one illustrated by *that gardeners will grow tomatoes* in the sentence (or IP) *I hope that gardeners will grow tomatoes*.

 <6.31> What word-class is *that* in this sentence?

The word *that* goes together with an IP to make up the larger construction, so although it is not obligatory in all cases and cannot stand for the entire construction, it is assumed to be the head of a complementiser phrase (CP), which means that the tree for *I hope that gardeners will grow tomatoes* is as in (36).

(36)

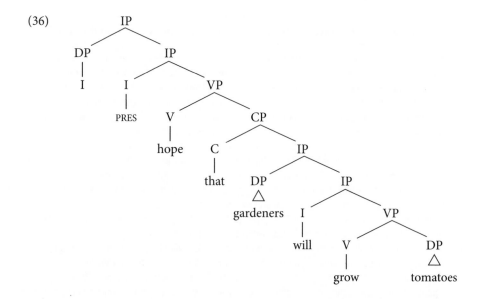

❓ <6.32> Is the complementiser obligatory in the construction illustrated in (36)?

❓ <6.33> Are there other places where the complementiser is obligatory?

6.4 Rules: Observed regularity returns

Just as in phonology, we can state regularity in syntactic patterning by means of rules. The notation used is much the same as it was in phonology, though slightly simpler. For example, corresponding to the fact that a DP is made up of a determiner and an NP, we could have the rule in (37).

(37)   DP → D NP

This can be read as an instruction to expand the category of DP into a sequence of two categories, D and NP.

Now we could set out a number of rules, parallel to (37), including, say, the rules in (38).

(38)   AP → A PP
        NP → N PP
        VP → V $\left\{\begin{array}{l} NP \\ AP \\ PP \end{array}\right\}$
        PP → P DP

❓ <6.34> We have not illustrated an AP containing an A and a PP. Can you think of one?

CONTROVERSIES: Interpreting a syntactic rule, and does it do too much?

The obvious interpretation of a rule such as (37) is an instruction: every time you find a category DP, do something to it (draw the tree, replace it by a sequence of two other things – however you wish to interpret the notion of 'expansion' mentioned but not defined above). In many of the earliest discussions of syntactic rules that seemed like an excellent interpretation. The grammar including such rules was seen as the kind of series of instructions you might give a computer if you wanted it to produce natural-sounding sentences of a particular language. It even seemed that there might be an abstract sense in which speakers might have rules like (37) in their heads, and some psycholinguists attempted to find behavioural patterns which might correspond to the brain's manipulation of such strings. However, it was clear from the start that there must be more to the story than that: you can understand a sentence as well as create one, so you must be able to work backwards from the sequence of D and NP to finding a DP, for example, despite the direction of the arrow used in the rule. So perhaps all that was needed was a two-headed arrow, and all would be well. A more sophisticated possibility is that the rules are not instructions, but statements of permissible patterns. A tree represents a grammatical sentence if and only if each of the branches in the tree is licensed by a rule. If our only rule expanding DP is the one illustrated in (37) and we find a tree that (in part) looks like (i) below, we know that the output cannot be a grammatical sentence.

(i)

This particular controversy has never, to my knowledge, been settled. It seems likely that there are other possible interpretations of rules as well.

Some scholars have pointed out that a rule like (37) does two things. First it tells you what categories the category DP dominates in the tree, and second it tells you what order the categories D and NP come in. That is, in the jargon, it gives information about **IMMEDIATE DOMINANCE** and about **LINEAR PRECEDENCE**. Some suggest that it might not be useful to merge these two kinds of information into a single rule, and that there might be generalisations about linear precedence that are independent of immediate dominance. This seems likely, but depends, among other things, on whether some branches in the tree are going to be allowed to dominate material which is not a word of the language concerned (as was suggested with tense above). Because different syntacticians have different beliefs about what the trees must look like, there has been no general agreement on such patterns.

There is a generalisation to these rules, which we could abbreviate as (39).

(39) XP → X YP

where X and Y are variables which can be any one of A, D, N, V (or indeed, C, I, which were not mentioned in (38).

We have also seen other types of construction in our trees which we can rephrase as general rules of a similar type. These include the rules in (40).

(40) XP → YP XP
      XP → YP X

Because a grammar of the type we have introduced here allows such generalisations, it sometimes referred to as an **X-BAR GRAMMAR** (we will not worry about the 'bar' here, but the X is simply a way of marking the generalisations over other categories in this way). Clearly the value of a grammar of this type is greater if we do not have to put constraints on the X or the Y. It is a much better generalisation to be able to say 'any phrase is made up of its head and a phrase of some other type' than to say 'any phrase except the following types can be made up of their heads and a following phrase' or 'any phrase can be made up of a head and any other phrase as long as it is not a VP'. The examples you have been given so far are certainly not sufficient to justify all the possibilities suggested by (40). But even if there are exceptions, and we have to put some restrictions on the generalising rules in (39) and (40), it does not prove that the enterprise is doomed to failure. It might be that the exceptions are ruled out for semantic or pragmatic reasons, not for strictly grammatical ones. Alternatively, it could be that some of the rules in (39) or (40) can apply only in particular syntactic environments. Such speculation takes us far beyond what we need to consider here.

NOAM CHOMSKY

X-bar grammar as described here is usually associated with the name of Noam Chomsky (b. 1928), although the basic idea of having the class of the phrase linked to the class of its head was not original to Chomsky, and although the whole notion has been developed by a number of other people as well. Chomsky is also one of the main figures behind the view of syntax as being rule-governed, as discussed in section 6.4. Chomsky has been a hugely influential linguist since his early work in the 1950s, and many modern linguistic insights stem from him. He argued that behaviourist psychological theories of the early twentieth century could not deal with the complexities of language, argued for a completely new view of language in which syntax has a privileged position in the centre of grammatical thinking, argued that children could not learn human language if they did not come specifically equipped for the learning of language, and that there must therefore be some form of Universal Grammar in the head of every human.

Not only has Chomsky revolutionised linguistics, he has had a profound effect in neighbouring disciplines such as philosophy and psychology, and he is one of the leading political dissidents in the United States.

6.5 Form and function: You look familiar, but what are you doing here?

You will have noticed that some of the phrasal categories we have mentioned occur in a number of different positions. DP can occur immediately dominated by IP with another IP to the right, or immediately dominated by VP with a V to the left, or immediately dominated by a PP with a P to the left; PP can be immediately dominated by a VP with a V to the left or by an NP with an N to the left. This is because we use the same building blocks to do different jobs in our sentences. Just as the same woman can sometimes act as a daughter, sometimes as a mother, sometimes as a customer and sometimes as a surgeon, so a single form can have a host of different functions in a sentence. Just as we have names for the different roles our woman can play in society, so we have different names for the functions that the different kinds of construction can display in the sentence.

Let us start by looking more closely at verbs. Verbs come in different kinds.

<6.35> Consider the three sentences below which contain many unfamiliar words (unfamiliar because they are nonsense words I have just made up). Despite this, you can tell which of the verbs *snored*, *touched* and *gave* fit into each sentence. How do you know this?

(i) The blingle spruffs ___ a cluther their farshy clougs.
(ii) Some trangets ___.
(iii) The foostles ___ the farshy clougs.

Note that which pattern a particular verb enters into is partly a matter of its meaning, but not entirely; it is also a matter of grammar. *Give* fits into pattern (i) in <6.35>, but *donate* means much the same as *give*, yet we cannot say *We donated them their presents*. Finally we have a type of verb not illustrated in <6.35>, the type that is like *become*. Like *touch*, *become* can take two DPs (*He became a rich man*), but here *he* and *a rich man* refer to the same entity, which is not the case for *I* and *the baby's nose* in *I touched the baby's nose*. All of these verbs require a DP to the left, that DP is called the **SUBJECT** of the IP in which the verb occurs; a verb like *touch* takes not only a subject, but a **DIRECT OBJECT** (*the baby's nose* is the direct object of *touch*); and a verb like *give* can take not only a subject and a direct object, but an **INDIRECT OBJECT** (*them* in *We gave them their presents*); verbs like *become* are said to take a subject and a **SUBJECT COMPLEMENT**. Each of these verb-types has a name, as set out in Table 6.4.

Table 6.4
Types of verb

Example	Takes a subject	Takes a direct object	Takes an indirect object	Takes a subject complement	Called	Alternative name
snore	✓	✗	✗	✗	intransitive	monovalent
touch	✓	✓	✗	✗	transitive	divalent
give	✓	✓	✓	✗	ditransitive	trivalent
become	✓	✗	✗	✓	copula	

No verb seems to take more than three DPs, in any language. If we want to associate more than three DPs with a particular verb, then we have to mark them in some extra way – in English with a preposition.

<6.36> Which of the following English verbs belongs in which category? *Seem, shampoo, show, sneeze.*

Here we have seen that a DP may have a number of different functions; but it is also possible for other forms to fulfil some of the same functions. For example, in *I became sleepy* we find an AP acting as the subject complement of a copula (and we can use it as a test of a copular verb that it can take an AP as well as a DP).

<6.37> Which of the following sentences contains a copular verb?

(i)   The gardener grew tomatoes.
(ii) The gardener grew impatient.
(iii) The doctor felt her pulse.
(iv) The doctor felt an idiot.
(v)   The doctor felt ill.

Note the difference between transitive verbs and copular verbs. Corresponding to (i) we can have *Tomatoes were grown by the gardener*, and corresponding to (iii) we can have *Her pulse was felt by the doctor*, but we cannot have, corresponding to (iv), where there is a copular verb, **An idiot was felt by the doctor.*

The role of subject is not necessarily filled by a DP. It can also be filled by a CP: *[That the plane arrived on time]*$_{CP}$ *surprised me.* Similarly, the role of direct object can be filled by a CP: *I know [that you will be pleased with our success]*$_{CP}$. Where there is no complementiser before the direct object clause, we might argue about whether we have a CP or an IP. In *I know [you will be pleased with our success]* is the bracketed portion a CP with nothing in the C slot, or an IP? As we saw in earlier (see p. 190) it may depend on whether we consider form alone or whether we consider function. Function suggests a CP. CPs used as subjects and objects are called **CLAUSES**, and specifically are called **NOUN CLAUSES** (because they play a role usually played by something containing a semantically salient noun).

<6.38> Are there any noun clauses in the following sentences, and if so, which part of the sentence is a noun clause?

(i)   The train leaving Paddington at 4:00 pm will be half-way to Bristol before you can decide that a long drink would be a good idea.
(ii) That they would say such a thing is hardly surprising when you realise they have had it in their policy documents for three years.

Neither of the object noun clauses illustrated in <6.38> is the object of the highest verb in the tree for its sentence (that is, the **MAIN VERB**), which may have misled you.

CPs can also give information on when, where, how, why and whether something happened. Examples are highlighted in (41), with the complementiser shown in bold.

(41)   ***When** the guests arrived*, they opened the champagne.
       ***If** you get here early*, we will have time for a little chat.

You mustn't do that ***because*** *you might hurt yourself.*
I haven't had a wink of sleep ***since*** *they got a noisy dog next door.*

Such clauses are given different names in different theories, but the terms **ADVERBIAL** and **ADJUNCT** are fairly neutral. Adverbials can also be PPs, as in (42).

(42) *After our arrival,* they opened the champagne.
  At that point, we will have time for a little chat.
  You mustn't do that *for your health's sake.*
  I haven't had a wink of sleep *since last Thursday.*

> **<6.39>** Look at the last example in (41) and the last in (42). Why is one said to contain a clause and the other a prepositional phrase? What is the implication with regard to the word-class of *since*?

Consider the pairs in (43).

(43) (a) He is taller **than** I am
  (b) He is taller **than** me.
  (a) She arrived **after** I left.
  (b) She arrived **after** me.
  (a) The sky was pretty **before** the sun set.
  (b) The sky was pretty **before** the sunset.

In each case, the highlighted word is a complementiser in the (a) sentence, and a preposition in the (b) sentence. In some cases, the same words can act as what are traditionally called adverbs, but which we might better term intransitive prepositions, too, as illustrated in (44).

(44) I haven't seen him **since**.
  The sky was pretty **before**.
  As they approached, I looked **up**.

Prepositional phrases have a number of other functions, too. They can be parts of NPs as in *the cat in the hat,* they can be parts of adjective phrases as in *dead to the world,* they can act as adverbials as in *I planted the tomatoes in the greenhouse,* and they can be subject complements as in *the car is in the garage.*

CONTROVERSY: Adverbial or subject complement; indirect object or adverbial

If we say

(a) The tomatoes are in the garden,

in the garden is a subject complement, but if we say

(b)   I planted the tomatoes in the garden,

in the garden is an adverbial. Is this distinction justified, or should they both be seen as adverbials on the grounds that the meaning is virtually identical in the two cases? Apart from the meaning, there is a grammatical reason for saying that what we have in (a) is not a subject complement. Nominal subject complements, such as that in

(c)   Susan is the CEO

are alternative descriptions of the same person as is referred to by the subject. Both *Susan* and *the CEO* refer to the same person. In (a), on the other hand, *in the garden* does not denote the same entity as *the tomatoes*: it tells us where the tomatoes are. The trouble with this argument is that where we have an adjectival subject complement as in

(d)   The tomatoes are red,

red describes rather than refers to *the tomatoes*, and (a) does not seem any different in principle from that.

On the other hand, if we said that *in the garden* in (a) was an adverbial, we would have to say that the verb *to be*, the copula which appears in all of (a), (c) and (d) takes a subject complement in (c) and (d) but not in (a), hence denying any parallel between (a) and (d). Furthermore, it is typical of adverbials (though there are some exceptions) that they can be deleted and leave a perfectly acceptable sentence behind. So if we delete *in the garden* from (b), we still have a good sentence in English. But if we deleted *in the garden* from (a) we would have a rather strange sentence. (Although it is perfectly possible to say *God is*, or *I don't know why, it just is*, it is unusual to use the verb *to be* without any subject complement.) So on the whole, calling *in the garden* in (a) a subject complement seems the best solution.

We face similar problems of indeterminacy with sentences like

(e)   We gave the presents to the children.

Is *to the children* in (c) an indirect object or an adverbial? The reason for thinking it might be an indirect object is that (e) is synonymous with (f) where *the children* is not marked by any preposition, and must be an object (an indirect one).

(f)   We gave the children the presents.

Also, note, it is awkward to delete *to the children* in (e). A verb like *give* seems to require either an indirect object with no preposition, or a *to*-phrase. This suggests that the *to*-phrase has the same function as the indirect object. The two are in complementary distribution.

If it is not an indirect object, it must be an adverbial. The first reason for preferring this alternative is that there are places where we can use a *to*-phrase but not an indirect object without a preposition. An example is in (g).

(g)   They donated the vase to the museum.

However, the unmarked indirect object and the *to*-phrase are still in complementary distribution here, so this is not a strong argument. The larger problem is in deciding when something is or is not an indirect object if we allow *to*-phrases to be called indirect objects. Consider the prepositional phrases in the examples in (h).

(h)   They walked to London.
      He ran to his son.
      They took the book to the library.
      He gave the book to his son.
      He showed the book to his son.
      He dedicated the book to his son.
      He delivered the book to his son.
      He posted the book to his son.

The first example in (h) illustrates what is presumably the basic meaning of *to*, a meaning which underlies the other examples as well. But if we agree that (g) contains the same kind of *to*-phrase as (e), it is not necessarily clear which of the phrases in (h) is also of the same type. We also have parallel problems with *for*.

(j)   He baked his son a cake.   He baked a cake for his son.
      He prepared his son a meal.   He prepared a meal for his son.
      He wrote his son a story.   He wrote a story for his son.
      He caught his son a trout.   He caught a trout for his son.
      ?He signed his son a cheque.   He signed a cheque for his son.
      ?He wrote his son a sonata.   He wrote a sonata for his son.
      ?He prepared his son a party.   He prepared a party for his son.
      *He sorted his son the books.   He sorted the books for his son.
      *He demolished his son a house.   He demolished a house for his son.
      *He lied his son.   He lied for his son.

In order to solve the problems raised here, one simple solution is to reserve the term indirect object for the cases where there is no preposition. The solution may not be theoretically extremely well-founded, but it is practical. However, you may well find scholars who come to a different conclusion.

Adverbials can be adverb phrases, prepositional phrases or CPs (which can be called adverbial clauses when they act as adverbials), as illustrated in (45).

(45)   I will see you [[soon]$_{Adv}$]$_{AdvP}$
       I will see you [in the morning]$_{PP}$
       I will see you [if I can get away]$_{CP}$

Another function which can be filled by several forms in English is **PREMODIFIER** to a noun, as illustrated in (46).

(46)   a [very bright]$_{AP}$ light
       a [stone]$_{NP}$ wall
       a [just-you-wait]$_{IP}$ look
       a [down-to-earth]$_{PP}$ approach

We can call the PPs which modify a noun and come after it **POSTMODIFIERS** (and some scholars use the term **QUALIFIER** for such constructions). CPs can also act as postmodifiers. They are called **RELATIVE CLAUSES**. Postmodifiers are illustrated in (47).

(47)   the bird [on the twenty-dollar note]$_{PP}$
       the bird [that we saw on the beach]$_{CP}$

The function that verbs fulfil is to act as **PREDICATOR**. There are languages which can have a predication without a verb, particularly where a subject complement is involved, but English is not one of them. Nothing else acts as a predicator.

To summarise this section, we can see that there are many functions and many forms, and that it is often not the case that one form corresponds to one function.

(48)   **Forms**   **Functions**

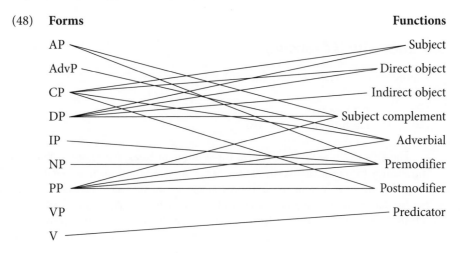

<6.40> You may be able to find some links between forms and functions that have been omitted in (48). Check that you can find examples of the links that are drawn and look for omissions.

<6.41> Can you find a relative clause with no complementiser?

6.6 Ergativity (Advanced)

Consider the sentences in (49) and (50).

(49)   The man snored.
(50)   The teacher watched the girl.

The DPs in these sentences have three different roles: *the man* is subject of an intransitive (monovalent) verb; *the teacher* is subject of a transitive (divalent) verb; *the girl* is object of a transitive verb. Although we seem to say that *the man* and *the teacher* have more similar roles by calling them both 'subjects', the meanings of intransitive verbs are often different enough from those of transitive verbs for us to be able to understand that some languages might want to distinguish these two functions. So it might not seem particularly surprising that we can find languages which mark these three DPs in different ways to indicate these different roles. An example is Diyari, as exemplified below:

Data-set 6.3
Diyari

'The man is going'		
nawu	kaṇa	wapa-ji
3SG	man[ABS]	go-PRS

'The snake watched the (two) girls'			
nulu	wanku-jali	mankada-wuḷa-ṇa	ṇaji-ṇaji-ji
3SG	snake-ERG	girl-DU-ACC	REDUP-see-PRS

Where the case is glossed as Abs(olutive), there is no morphological marker of that status; the subject of the transitive verb (the snake) is marked with an Erg(ative) suffix, and the object of the transitive verb is marked with an Acc(usative) suffix. We will see that the use of names for the different cases may vary from language to language, though these labels are fairly standard; what is clear is that when we have languages that show such distinctions, the label 'subject' is no longer sufficient. The usual convention is to label the subject of the intransitive verb 'S', the subject of the transitive verb 'A' (for 'agent') and the object 'O'. The difference between ṇawu and ṇulu in Table 6.7 is that the former introduces an S and the latter introduces an A.

Most languages do not overtly mark a three-way distinction between these roles in the way that Diyari does. More often, a two-way distinction is made. One type of two-way distinction is illustrated, from Latin below:

Data-set 6.4
Latin

'The girl is asleep'
puell-a   dormi-t
girl-NOM   sleep-3SG

'The farmer loves the girl'
agricol-a   puell-am   ama-t
farmer-NOM   girl-ACC   love-3SG

<6.42> Which of S, A and O are equated in Latin?

A system like the one in Latin is called a nominative-accusative system. To the extent that English has a case system at all (see the controversy box on p. 180), it has a nominative-accusative system, but only for pronouns. That is, *the dog* (a DP which is not a pronoun) has the same form in *The dog saw the rabbit* and *The rabbit saw the dog*, while some of the pronouns have different forms in these two functions, so that we say *I saw them* but *They saw me*.

<6.43> Why does it say 'some of the pronouns' in the last sentence? What is the nominative form of the first person singular pronoun, and what is the accusative form, in these examples?

A different two-way distinction is now illustrated:

Data-set 6.5
Dyirbal

'Father returned'
ŋuma   banaga-nʲu
father[ABS]   return-NONFUT

'Father saw mother'
jabu   ŋuma-ŋgu   bura-n
mother[ABS]   father-ERG   see-NONFUT

<6.44> Which two roles are treated the same way in Dyirbal, on the evidence of this data?

Dyirbal is known as an ergative-absolutive language. Languages like Diyari are rare, but nominative-accusative languages and ergative-absolutive languages are both common. However, not all ergative-absolutive languages show precisely the same set of characteristics. In fact, most of them show some degree of **SPLIT ERGATIVITY**, whereby only some part of the language shows the expected ergative-absolutive patterning.

Dyirbal provides a nice example. In Data-set 6.5 we saw what happens when we have full noun phrases acting as S, A and O, but when pronouns occur in these positions we get a different pattern:

Data-set 6.6
Dyirbal

'You guys returned'

nʲurra	banaga-nʲu
2PL-NOM	return-NONFUT

'We saw you guys'

ŋana	nʲurra-na	bura-n
1PL-NOM	2PL-ACC	see-NONFUT

? **6.45** How does the data presented contrast with the data in the previous data-set?

Split ergativity can be found in very different environments, depending on the languages concerned. In Mangarayi, some gender classes of noun inflect following a nominative-accusative pattern, while another inflects using the ergative-absolutive pattern. In Hindi, we find different patterns of case-marking in the perfect and in other aspects, as the material below illustrates:

Data-set 6.7
Hindi

'Raam had eaten bread' (perfective)

raam-ne	roṭii	khaajii	thii
Raam-ERG	bread(F)	eat-PFV.F	was.F

'Raam was eating bread' (imperfective)

raam	roṭii	khaataa	thaa
Raam(M)	bread	eat-IPFV.M	was.M

So far, it may seem that the distinction being illustrated here is purely a morphological one. Some languages use the nominative case for either A or S and the accusative case for O, while others use the ergative case for A and the absolutive for either S or O. However, consideration of the Hindi data indicates that more is at stake than this. In Hindi the verb appears to agree with highest rank (most subject-like) of the unmarked DPs. In the case where an ergative case is present, the highest unmarked DP is the direct object, while when there is no ergative case, and the subject is unmarked, the agreement is with the subject. While this is a matter of agreement and thus affects the morphological shape of the word, the determination of what should agree with what is a syntactic process. So ergativity is not merely morphological, but also syntactic.

Another very clear case of ergative syntax occurs when we find deletion under identity. The title 'deletion under identity' assumes that a sentence such as

(51)   Kim saw Chris and ran

'starts out' as

(52)   Kim saw Chris and Kim ran,

and the second *Kim* is deleted because it is identical with the first one. An alternative view of such sentences is that when we see a sentence like (51) we have to decide who it is that did the running: was it Kim or was it Chris (or, indeed, was it someone else entirely)? What might give us a clue? In English, we will probably agree that (51) must be understood as though it were (52), and cannot be interpreted as is shown in (53).

(53)   Kim saw Chris and Chris ran

The example in (53) is a perfectly possible sentence of English, it just cannot mean the same as (51). Since we have no case marking on names in English, we might want to say that we interpret (51) as meaning (52) because we are looking for a name which functions in the subject role, and the only relevant name in the linguistic environment is *Kim*. In a language like Latin, the case marking helps (see below).

Data-set 6.8
Latin

'The farmer came'				
agricol-a	veni-t			
farmer-NOM	came-3SG			
'The farmer saw the girl				
agricol-a	puell-am	vidi-t		
farmer-NOM	girl-ACC	saw-3SG		
'The farmer saw the girl and [?] came'				
agricol-a	puell-am	vidi-t	et	veni-t
farmer-NOM	girl-ACC	saw-3SG	and	came-3SG

The last of these examples is interpreted as meaning that the farmer came, because the listener is looking for a noun carrying the nominative case to be the subject of the verb *venit*, and the only relevant noun in the linguistic environment is *agricola*. So what will happen in an ergative language? Consider the examples in Data-set 6.9.

At this point, you should be making predictions about the interpretation of the bracketed question marks. Some examples from Dyirbal have already been presented in this section (Data-sets 6.5 and 6.6), and you can use them to help, if required.

 <6.46> When Mother saw Father and somebody returned (in Data-set 6.9), who do you think returned? Why?

To answer this question, you should think about the case-marking.

 <6.47> When we saw you all and somebody returned, who do you think returned? Why?

In Dyirbal, the logic of the case-marking is followed precisely in the syntax. Father returned, because we need an argument in the absolute case to act as the S

Data-set 6.9
Dyirbal

ŋuma	jabu-ŋgu	bura-n	
father[ABS]	mother-ERG	see-NONFUT	

'Mother saw father'

jabu	banaga-nʲu
mother[ABS]	return-NONFUT

'Mother returned'

ŋuma	jabu-ŋgu	bura-n	banaga-nʲu
father[ABS]	mother-ERG	see-NONFUT	return-NONFUT

'Mother saw father (and) [?] returned'

ŋana	banaga-nʲu
we[NOM]	return-NONFUT

'We returned'

ŋana	nʲurra-na	bura-n
we[NOM[	you[PL]-ACC	see-NONFUT

'We saw you all'

nʲurra	ŋana-na	bura-n	banaga-nʲu
we[NOM]	you[PL]-ACC	see-NONFUT	return-NONFUT

'We saw you all (and) [?] returned'

of the intransitive verb; we returned because with pronouns, we need an argument in the nominative case to act as the S of the intransitive verb.

Unfortunately, languages are more complicated that this suggests. Languages do not follow the general pattern set up in the comparison between Latin and Dyirbal above. Not only do we find languages which tend to avoid precisely the structures which might seem informative in this regard (e.g. West Greenlandic, which uses special forms in such contexts), it is also the case that we find examples like (54) from Chukchee.

(54) ətləg-ə   talaywə-nən   ekək   ənkʔam   ekwet-gʔi
      father-INS   beat-3SG3SG   son[ABS]   and   leave-3SG
      'The father beat his son and [?] left'

In this example, (54) can be interpreted as meaning either the father left or the son left. Similarly with (55) from Basque, which can be interpreted as meaning that either the father or the son went to class.

(55) aitak   semea   eskolan   utzi   eta   klasera   joan   zen
      father.ERG son.DET   school.in   leave   and   class.to go   AUX
      'The father left the son at school and [?] went to class'

What you should be thinking about now is that this is all extremely complicated, because it is. Ergativity is not simply a matter of case-marking, it also has reflexes in the syntax, but those reflexes are not found to the same degree in every language which shows ergative case-marking. Clearly there is room for plenty of research here. What other kinds of constructions might lead to similar problems of interpretation or places where we might predict that it would be difficult to allow conjunction? One such instance is the construction illustrated in *I wanted to go*.

<6.48> What type of verb is *want*? What type of verb is *go*? Why might this cause a problem in an ergative language?

There are other problems with this construction, though, not least the fact that to *go* is (at least in English) non-finite, and non-finite verbs do not take subjects the same way as finite verbs do.

Such constructions have been considered in some detail in the literature, and there is a lot of data available on the way in which different ergative-absolutive and nominative-accusative languages treat them.

Another question which all this brings up is the nature of the interaction between notions like 'nominative-marked phrase' and 'subject'. Is subject a unitary notion, or are there many aspects to what it means to be a subject? (There seems to be general agreement that it is not unitary.) If it is not unitary, the features of a subject can be spread round various phrases in a sentence, and phrases may not 'be subjects' but be 'more subject-like' than other phrases. This is entirely consistent with the idea that notions like subject are prototypes, but makes the analysis of any language a lot more challenging than we might have thought it would be.

6.7 The order of sentence elements (Advanced)

It was pointed out in section 6.1 that in order to say something corresponding to the English sentence in (56), speakers of some languages would have to say the literal equivalent of (57) or (58).

(56)   The princess kissed the frog.
(57)   Kissed the princess the frog.
(58)   The princess the frog kissed.

We are now in a situation to discuss rather more technically what the difference between these various orderings is. In each of the versions (56)–(58) there are two DPs and a verb acting as the predicator. The two DPs function as Subject and Direct Object of the verb. So in (56) we get the order Subject–Predicator–Object, in (57) we have the order Predicator–Subject–Object and in (58) we have the order Subject–Object–Predicator. Two questions immediately arise: (a) What about the other logically possible orders, are they ever found? (b) Does it matter? Does this order tell us anything about the structure of the languages involved?

6.7.1 Ordering of major constituents

Before we begin, we should note that although we have drawn a distinction between Predicator as a function and Verb as word-class, the discussion in the literature is largely carried out in terms of Subjects, Verbs and Objects, not Subjects, Predicators and Objects. So a language like English is usually referred to as an SVO language, one in which the normal, expected order of the elements is Subject, then Verb and then Direct Object. (Note that here *S* means 'subject' and not, specifically, intransitive subject, as it did in the last section. To avoid this ambiguity here, I shall refer to subjects using the abbreviation *Su*, but this is not the general usage in the field.)

The first question we need to ask is whether there is, for every language, a normal, expected order of sentence elements. In English, there clearly is. A sentence like (59), while possible, has an intonation break after the Object and could only be found in certain, quite narrowly specified, discourse situations. Moreover, although statements of this form are possible (see (60)), (59) is probably a question.

(59)   A frog, the princess kissed?
(60)   A kilt, I'll never wear.

 <6.49> What kinds of situation might (59) and (60) be found in?

That is, of course, not to say that all sentences of English must be SuVO. Consider the sentences in (61).

(61) (a) What did you catch?
     (b) There is a green hill far away.
     (c) Making a donation? You?
     (d) A garden is a lovesome thing, God wot.

 <6.50> In the sentences in (61), what order do the major constituents appear in? Is there anything not normal or unexpected about the context?

Not all languages have a normal ordering of Su, V and O in quite the way this implies. One type of divergence from the norm is provided by so-called 'V2' languages, where the verb always comes in second position but other arguments may freely occur before the verb. As an example, consider the data from Danish below. The following examples illustrate various possible and impossible orders of four constituents, each represented by a single word: *manden* 'the man', *købte* 'bought' *bilen* 'the car' *igår* 'yesterday'.

Dataset 6.10
Danish
word-order

(a)	Manden købte bilen igår
(b)	Igår købte manden bilen
(c)	Bilen købte manden igår
(d)	Købte manden bilen igår?
(e)	*Købte bilen igår manden
(f)	*Manden bilen købte igår

Except in a question (see (d)), the verb occurs in second position, and despite the lack of case-marking, (a) and (c) are both possible and are both said with a single intonational phrase. The variants (b) and (c) tend to occur when the time or the car is being brought into focus or made important in some way.

However, consider what happens in subordinate clauses.

(62) Jeg synes, at manden kˉøbte bilen igår.
      I think that the.man bought the.car yesterday

German is another V2 language, so that in German we can also have the variation shown below, corresponding to the Danish data in Data-set 6.10.

Data-set 6.11
German
word-order

(a)	Der Herr kaufte gestern das auto
	The sir bought yesterday the car
	'The man bought the car yesterday'
(b)	Das Auto kaufte der Herr gestern
(c)	Gestern kaufte der Herr das Auto

But while in main clauses there is a relatively good match with the Danish data, in subordinate clauses we find something different, as indicated by (63) in contrast with the Danish equivalent in (62).

(63) Mir scheint es, daß der Herr gestern das Auto kaufte.
      To.me seems it that the sir yesterday the car bought
      'I think the man bought the car yesterday'

In subordinate clauses the finite verb comes second in Danish, but finally in German, so that Danish subordinate clauses are SuVO while German ones are SuOV (there are many other complications in both languages, but we will not consider them here). So while both the languages are V2, they have different word-orders in subordinate clauses. Such languages seem to have two distinct word-orders.

<6.51> Which of the sentences in Data-set 6.10 do the sentences in Data-set 6.11 correspond to?

In other languages, it may be difficult to determine any basic word-order at all. Many Australian languages seem to have this property, and Warlpiri has been singled out for particular comment in this regard.

Consequently, it is dangerous to assume that all languages have a basic word-order, and any discussion of word-order and word-order variation should allow for the fact that there may be more than one possible order of elements or that there may not be any clear preference for order in particular languages. Nonetheless, there are useful correlations between the orders of various constituents to be found, and we turn to those now.

6.7.2 Word-order correlations

Consider the order of elements in the following sentences, each of which illustrates the basic word-order for the language concerned.

(64) Maori

Kei te		whāngai	a	Tamahae	i	ngā	kau
TENSE/ASPECT		feed	person	T.	OBJ.	DET[PL]	cow

'Tamahae is feeding the cows'

(65) Kham

no-e	chiti-ni	nehblo	ni-pərī:-ke-o
he-ERG	letter-DU	two	3D-send-PERF-3S

'He sent two letters'

(66) Hixkaryana

bɨryekomo	yothano	wosɨ
boy	she.hit.him	woman

'The woman hit the boy'

> ❓ **<6.52>** What is the basic word-order in each of these languages?

Here we have three other orders of Subject, Verb and Object. The basic word-order in Hixkaryana is rare, and was not known to exist until the 1970s. The other orders illustrated here, however, are all common. All possible orders of Subject, Verb and Object are found, but SuVO, VSuO and SuOV are the most common.

To get the benefit of this classification, we have to look at other constructions as well. Consider, for instance, the use of adpositions in the various languages, and how that correlates with the classification in terms of Subject, Verb and Object. In fact, to make sense of this parallel, we do not even need to worry about the positioning of the subject, just the relative position of the Verb and its Object. In principle we have the two options in (67).

(67)

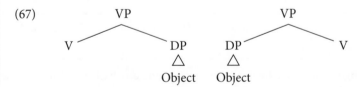

Where we have phrases with adpositions, we have the two possibilities of prepositional phrases or postpositional phrases, as in (68).

(68)

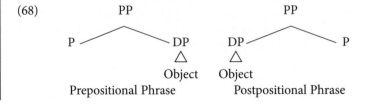

Prepositional Phrase   Postpositional Phrase

The obvious question is how well these two structures align in languages.

Before we look at the answer to this question, we need to consider the possible findings, and what they might mean. There are some statements which seem to be true of all languages. For example, in spoken languages (but not, for obvious reasons, in signed languages) it is true (as far as we know) that all languages have consonants and vowels. We can call this an ABSOLUTE UNIVERSAL. However, most of the patterns we discover in languages are not absolute universals. Rather we find them occurring sometimes, and not occurring other times. For instance, there are languages which use particles for asking questions, and sometimes these occur at the beginnings of sentences, sometimes they occur sentence-internally and sometimes they occur sentence-finally. If we look at the proportion of times they occur sentence-initially and sentence-finally, it seems to be about half and half. Where there are two possible patterns and each occurs half of the time then (unless there is something we have forgotten to consider) the two are occurring randomly. But what if something occurs considerably more than half the time? For instance, one such statement that is often made is that if a sentence has a fricative consonant, it has /s/ (see section 3.8). It is not true, because there are languages like Maori and Tiwi which break the rule. But it is overwhelmingly true; it is true far more often than it is false. As you can imagine, we could (within the limits of our knowledge) set up statistical tests to tell us just how unusual languages such as Maori and Tiwi are: what level of confidence we can have in the assumption that the next fricative-inclusive language we meet will have an /s/. Correspondingly, such statements are called STATISTICAL UNIVERSALS or UNIVERSAL TENDEN-CIES.

Often more informative than a universal tendency, is being able to correlate a universal tendency with something else. So we said earlier, in effect, IF a language is a spoken language THEN it will have consonants and vowels; IF a language has any fricative at all, THEN it has /s/. So, to return to the patterns in (67) and (68), we want to ask IF a language has VO, THEN can we predict the order of the adposition and its determiner phrase? To the extent that such predictions provide results which are more than random, results which allow us to make predictions with a great deal of confidence – even if not with 100 per cent confidence – we have a TYPOLOGY. In the case in hand, we are looking at a word-order typology.

So let us consider the answers for the order of adposition and its determiner phrase in the languages we have considered. Relevant examples are provided below in (69)–(72).

(69)   English (SuVO)
       in the house
(70)   Maori (VSuO)
       ki te pā
       to the pa ('fortified village')
(71)   Kham (SuOV)
       bahrət-lə
       India-in
       'in India'

(72)   Hixkaryana (OVSu)
       wewe   mahyaye
       tree   behind
       'behind the tree'

In these cases, there is a perfect correlation: VO languages have prepositions, OV languages have postpositions. The result arises from a fortunate choice of languages, because this IMPLICATIONAL UNIVERSAL TENDENCY is not absolutely true: there are both VO languages with postpositions and OV languages with prepositions. Consider the data in Data-set 6.12, which shows that some languages have both prepositions and postpositions, so that no absolute match can be expected. Nevertheless, the correlation seems to hold true over 85 per cent of the time, and where VSuO languages are concerned, seems to be absolute.

Data-set 6.12
Finnish

läpi	vuotisatojen
through	century.PL.GEN
'through the centuries'	

ilman	rahaa
without	money.PART
'without money'	

tunnin	jälkeen
lesson.GEN	after
'after the lesson'	

kirkkoa	vastapäätä
church.PART	opposite
'opposite the church'	

Given the trees in (67) and (68), you may have noticed that there are at least two possible explanations for why verb-object constructions and adpositional phrases should pattern in the same way: it could be that the position of the head is fixed in relation to the rest of the construction, or it could be that speakers prefer to deal with trees that branch in a particular direction. Both explanations have been proposed for the observed patterning. While statements in terms of the position of the head are more common in the literature, there is good evidence that the direction of branching is the more important variable.

<6.53> What kind of correlations could you consider to decide which of these two hypotheses is the better one?

This word-order typology is remarkably robust. The original work, which provided the fundamental patterns, was done on the basis of just 30 languages. Now that the correlations have been confirmed on a sample of over 600 languages, we have a rather more nuanced picture of what is going on, but many of the original patterns remain.

CONTROVERSY: The interpretation of patterns

What are the implications for such patterns for the storage of language in the brain and for historical change? Such questions are extremely difficult to answer. Clearly, an individual speaker cannot be supposed to 'know' in any sense what the patterns are across human languages in general. Where languages display discordant patterns they do not appear to be more difficult to learn than concordant patterns. But it is possible that there is a pressure towards a consistent head position or direction of branching which has a slow effect on language change, and that languages which – for whatever reasons – become discordant, gradually change so that they are once more concordant. Note that there does seem to be an implication that the head position or the branching pattern is something that is used by the human brain in processing language. It should not, however, be assumed that the human brain has a mental construct which corresponds in any direct way to the tree structure that linguists operate with; the tree is simply a way of representing a relationship which must, somehow, be exploited in human language processing. Such questions belong to the domain of psycholinguistics.

Other pairs of elements which seem to fit into this typology are the order of head noun and relative clause (*people who live in glass houses*), possessed noun and possessee (*land of our fathers*), adjective and standard of comparison (*faster than a speeding bullet*) and many more. With enough experience of such matters, the researcher starts to build up expectations about many facets of word-order, and can move on to ask the more difficult kind of question: why should individual languages deviate from the expected patterns?

6.8 Summing up

In this chapter we began by looking at the different kinds of words we find, and showing how they can be classified according to their form and their function. While form and function do not match precisely, in any given language we expect to find a relatively small number of different word-classes. Phrases form round word-classes, and the word-class of the head of the phrase is used to name the kind of phrase: a phrase headed by a noun is called a noun phrase, a phrase headed by an adverb is called an adverb phrase and so on. These phrases of various kinds eventually combine to form sentences or clauses (sentence-like elements in other sentences). We need to distinguish the labels used to denote the forms from the labels used to denote the functions those forms perform since each form may have many functions. We can write rules to show the way in which the elements of sentences are strung together, and use trees to diagram the structures of syntactic objects such as phrases and sentences.

Despite these basic principles, languages can differ in such fundamental ways as which of the three of the fundamental nominal functions in a sentence (the subject of an intransitive verb, the subject of a transitive verb, and the object of a transitive verb) are coded as being similar, and in the fundamental order in which the elements of a sentence are built up. Often we find patterns of co-occurrence in preferred orderings of different parts of the sentence.

Technical terms introduced in this chapter

Absolute universal
Accusative
Adjective
Adjective phrase
Adposition
Adverb
Adverb phrase
Article
Aspect
Binarity
Case
Causativity
Clause
Complementiser
Conjunction
Constituent
Coordinating conjunction
Copula
Determiner
Direct Object
Ditransitive
Divalent
Domination
Dual
Ergative
Exclusive
First person
Genitive
Head
Immediate dominance
Implicational Universal Tendency
Inclusive
Indirect Object
Inflection phrase
Intransitive
Intransitive preposition
Linear precedence
Main verb
Monovalent
Node
Nominative

Noun
Noun clause
Noun phrase
Number
Particle
Person
Postmodifier
Postposition
Predicator
Premodifier
Preposition
Prepositional phrase
Pro-sentence
Pronoun
Qualifier
Recursion
Reflexivity
Relative clause
Root (of a tree)
Second person
Sentence adverb
Split ergativity
Statistical universal
Subject
Subject complement
Subordinating conjunction
Substitution
Tag question
Tense
Third person
Transitive
Transitivity
Tree
Trial
Trivalent
Typology
Universal tendency
V2
Verb
X-bar grammar

Reading and references

There are many good introductions to syntax, but most of them are introductions to a particular model of how syntax works. Matthews (1981) is more eclectic, but not easy; Brown & Miller (1980) is much more approachable, but now rather out-dated. Miller (2008), while more recent and non-evangelistic, deals only with English.

On word order in Australian Aboriginal languages in general, see Dixon (1980: 441) and Blake (1987: 154). On Warlpiri in particular see Nash (1986: Chapter 5).

The original work in the area of word-order typology is Greenberg (1963); for a more recent discussion see Dryer (1992). Dryer has some observations on how to organise language samples and how to interpret the outcome from them which can be used even with relatively small and manageable language samples. A good introductory text on this material is Croft (2003).

Information on the various languages mentioned has been taken from the sources mentioned below:

Basque	Hualde & Ortiz de Urbina (2003)	Kham	Watters (2002)
		Mangarayi	Merlan (1982)
Chukchee	Nedjalkov (1979)	Maori	Harlow (2007);
Diyari	Austin (1981)		Bauer (1997)
Dyirbal	Dixon (1994)	Turkish	derived from Lewis
Finnish	Karlsson (1999)		(1967) and Kornfilt
Ghomala	Saxena (2004)		(1997)
Hindi	Laka (2006)	West	Fortescue (1984)
Hixkaryana	Derbyshire (1979)	Greenlandic	

7

Pragmatics

'Actions speak louder than words' may be an excellent maxim
from the pragmatic point of view, but betrays little insight into
the nature of speech.

Edward Sapir (1933)

In this chapter we see that what you say may not be quite what you mean and that listeners have to interpret what is said in the light of their own beliefs and the context in which it is said. In order to be polite you may have to be less direct than might seem ideal, and even how you address someone is tied to politeness in many ways.

7.1 The interface with the world

What is the purpose of language? This is a very difficult question to answer, and accordingly many answers have been offered. One is that we have language in order to be able to lie. Dogs show you they're happy when they're happy; chimpanzees have great difficulty in not telling their neighbours when they have found some food (even if it is to their own disadvantage). Humans have the ability to lie.

If that suggestion sounds too cynical, then you may agree with another suggestion that is frequently made, that we have language in order to communicate information. Superficially at least, this sounds more reasonable. Even a boring sentence such as *The cat sat on the mat* tells us something about the cat and about the mat; it makes explicit the relationship between the two at some time in the past. In that sense, it appears to be communicating information.

If that is one thing that language does, though, it is not the only thing that language does. If you say, 'Where are the toilets?', you are not so much communicating information (except perhaps that you need some guidance), as indicating precisely what information you would like your interlocutor to provide for you. If you say, 'Close the door!', you may inadvertently communicate that the door is open, but you are really attempting to make some other person behave in a particular way.

So rather than say that the purpose of language is to communicate information, we might be better to say that language allows us to communicate information, among other things.

However, there are times when we appear, on the face of it, to be communicating information, when we are not really communicating the ostensible information derivable from what we say. In *The Virginian* (1929), Gary Cooper says to someone who calls him a rude name, 'If you wanna call me that, smile.' If someone says, 'You're a sonofabitch', are they providing you with information? Cooper's reply suggests, accurately, that in any case there are (at least) two ways of saying this sentence, one of which is not an insult. So not only may an apparently information-bearing sentence not actually provide information, but the way in which you say it may moderate the kind of message it transmits.

Even more confusing are the instances where what we say does not appear to match the message that we impart. Suppose someone walks into a room and says, 'It's a bit cold in here.' Depending on who else is present, and what the relationship between the people present is, this could mean any of 'Shall I close the window?', 'I'd like you to close the window,' 'I suspect that you don't have enough money to pay your power bills' or 'I told you that this house wasn't properly insulated'.

This chapter looks at the relationship between what we say and what we mean. It looks at instances where saying is doing, instances when you do not answer questions and instances when an important bit of what you mean is hidden away.

7.2 Speech acts

If you say something like (1), then saying it does not make it true.

(1) I like to eat tripe.

Sentence (1) may be true, or it may be false, depending upon who *I* refers to and the time at which it is uttered. If, on the other hand, you say (2), it is not clear that it can be fairly characterised as either true or false.

(2) I promise to eat tripe.

While (1) merely describes a situation, (2) performs an action: (2) is itself the promise, while (1) does not in itself constitute the liking. Whether or not you keep the promise that is made by saying (2), the promise is made, because you perform a promise by using the verb *promise* in this way.

There are many **PERFORMATIVE** verbs of this kind in English. Some examples are given in (3).

(3) (a) I name this ship 'Lollipop'.
     (b) I bet you a dollar that Chris is late.
     (c) I now pronounce you man and wife.
     (d) I sentence you to 10 years' imprisonment.
     (e) I declare this fête open.
     (f) I resign.
     (g) I dare you to go bungee jumping.

For any of these to work, certain **FELICITY CONDITIONS** or **HAPPINESS CONDITIONS** have to be met. For example, (3d) does not work as a performative unless the speaker is a judge.

<7.1> What felicity conditions can you think of that have to hold for (3a) to function as a performative? Are any of them generalisable to the other situations illustrated in (3)?

<7.2> Why would it be odd to answer (3b) by saying 'No, you don't', although it would be perfectly possible to answer (1) in that way?

We can distinguish between several types of performative verb according to the kind of act they denote, but the important thing is that there is a vital difference between performatives on the one hand and CONSTATIVE sentences which simply produce a statement about a state of affairs. This difference, however, is not marked grammatically. There is no difference in the grammatical structures of (1) and (2). So the same declarative form, apparently the same LOCUTIONARY ACT or utterance of a particular sentence may have a different ILLOCUTIONARY FORCE of stating, warning, asking, offering, promising, and so on, on different occasions. We can add to that that any locutionary act also is a PERLOCUTIONARY ACT, that is, it brings about an effect on the listener which may or may not be what was intended: uttering (1) could make you feel nauseous, for instance.

The notion of illocutionary force immediately takes us much further, though. We have already seen that a sentence like (4) may, under appropriate circumstances, mean 'Please close the window'. So although it has a declarative form, its illocutionary force under such circumstances is to act as a request. An interrogative grammatical structure, such as that in (5), may have as its illocutionary force an indication of politeness (utterances of this type, which do not provide real information, but which indicate a social purpose, a sort of social grooming, are sometimes termed PHATIC COMMUNION). And an imperative grammatical structure such as that in (6) may not have a command as its illocutionary force.

(4)   It's cold in here.
(5)   How are you today?
(6)   Let the good times roll!

For this reason, we need to make two sets of distinctions. First we need to distinguish between a DIRECT SPEECH ACT and an INDIRECT SPEECH ACT. Example (4) might be the indirect speech act corresponding to the direct speech act *Shut the window!* Second, we must distinguish between DECLARATIVE, INTERROGATIVE and IMPERATIVE grammatical patterns, and the STATEMENTS, QUESTIONS and COMMANDS (the illocutionary forces) they might be supposed to instantiate. While it may be the default for a declarative form to indicate that a statement is being made (and so on), there is no necessary match between the two. It can be very annoying when people interpret sentences like (5) or (7) 'literally', that is without regard to the illocutionary force that that the speaker had intended. We usually interpret such behaviour as being deliberately obtuse (though some mental conditions can lead to difficulty in interpreting the real illocutionary force behind such utterances).

(7)   Can you pass the salt?

<7.3> Here is a short passage from a novel.

'[D]o you want to tell me what happened?'
'Not particularly.'

The psychiatrist clasped his fists and levelled his forefingers at Acland's heart. 'It wasn't an invitation, Charles, it was an instruction . . . and don't test me because I'm not in the mood . . .' (Walters, 2007: 56)

Reformulate what is happening in terms of grammatical structures and illocutionary forces.

The distinction between performative and constative verbs (or the utterances containing them) is actually less clear than the presentation above implies. Consider a child who asks an aunt, 'Will you come to my birthday party?' and gets the response in (8). We would probably feel that the child was justified in reporting this as in (9), even though there is no overt performative.

(8)   I'll be there.
(9)   She promised to come to my party.

So the illocutionary force of a declarative sentence can be a promise, even in the absence of the relevant verb. Similarly, (10) might be the equivalent of (11).

(10)   There are no monsters in the cupboard.
(11)   I assure you there are no monsters in the cupboard.

While (10) looks like a constative statement, (11) is a performative. It seems that just as (8) performs a promise without an overt performative verb, so (10) could be seen as performing an assurance with no overt performative verb. At this point, any constative statement, it seems, can be analysed as a performative, and the clear distinction simply breaks down. Everything becomes a performative, although we have the power to emphasise the performativity by using the word *hereby* (for example, 'I hereby pronounce you man and wife'). It remains true, though, that some verbs are inherently performative, while others are not, even if it is true that utterances containing non-performative verbs may take on an illocutionary force equivalent to that of a performative verb in particular contexts. The felicity conditions still have to be right.

7.3 Gricean principles

Part of the reason that 'Yes' is not a good answer to (7) is that it fails to recognise that a conversation is an exercise in cooperation. The people taking part in the conversation have to work together to make the conversation effective, and listeners will draw conclusions from apparent breaches of the cooperative principle.

The **COOPERATIVE PRINCIPLE** was introduced by H.P. Grice, who set it out as a number of sub-principles, or **MAXIMS**, as in (12).

(12) The cooperative principle

  Quantity Make your contribution as informative as is required.
        Do not make your contribution more informative than is required.
  Quality Do not say what you believe to be false.
        Do not say that for which you lack adequate evidence.
  Relation Be relevant
  Manner Avoid obscurity of expression.
        Avoid ambiguity.
        Be brief.
        Be orderly.
        Speak idiomatically unless there is good reason not to.

(The last clause of the maxim of manner above is added by Searle.) We can illustrate the existence of these principles by showing what happens when one of them is broken. For example, if a speaker says

(13) Edward's meeting a woman this evening.

We will assume that the woman concerned is not a close relative, otherwise more information would have been given (following the first clause of the maxim of quality). So (13) would be considered misleading if the woman concerned was Edward's mother. Of course, it is always possible that the speaker does not know that Edward is actually meeting his mother, and that (13) is all that can be honestly said under the maxim of quality, but the listener is still likely to interpret (13) as meaning that the woman is not Edward's mother/wife/sister/daughter. That's why the old exchange in (14) contains a kernel of truth, although it ends up denigrating the speaker's wife.

(14) A: Who was that lady I saw you with last night?
    B: That was no lady; that was my wife.

To see the value of the second clause in the maxim of quality, consider (15), which we have to interpret as meaning something other than the violinist played the piece of music.

(15) The violinist played each note of Bach's Air on a G String in order.

<7.4> What interpretation does (15) get, and why?

The maxim of relevance means that we interpret all kinds of things as being relevant, even when there is no obvious connection. Consider (16), where the two sentences apparently have no common topic.

(16)   A: They're showing 'Gone with the Wind' on Friday.
        B: My mother's coming at the weekend.

Although A's utterance in (16) is declarative, its illocutionary force is readily interpreted as being an invitation or (as appropriate) a suggestion that A and B should go to the cinema on Friday. On the face of it, B does not respond to the invitation, but makes a statement about some other event. However, A will interpret B's utterance as being relevant, and will thus assume that because B's mother is coming at the weekend, preparations need to be made, and that these preparations will take up the relevant time on Friday (or perhaps, even, that the maternal visit will coincide with the time of the proposed excursion to the cinema). Thus B's utterance is interpreted as a rejection of the covert invitation in A's utterance.

If we really cannot see the relevance of an utterance, we have fixed phrases such as (17) we can use to get an interlocutor to make the relationship explicit.

(17)   What's that got to do with the price of fish in China?

It is perhaps easier to think of cases where the maxim of manner is broken than cases where it is clearly adhered to: we all know people who talk for too long or who are not clear in what they say, either deliberately or because they are not good speakers. Jokes and headlines set out to be ambiguous. And presenting material in an orderly manner is a skill which people need to practise if they are to get it right. The fact that we notice these cases, though, implies that there are many more cases which we do not notice and which achieve these aims.

<7.5> Here are some headlines from newspapers. Why do they fail the maxim of manner, and what is the effect?

Churchill flies back to front.
Miners refuse to work after death.
If strike isn't settled quickly it may last a while.
Diet of premature babies affects IQ.

In fact, all of these maxims are regularly contravened, but what happens when they are contravened is instructive. The least useful utterances in terms of the maxim of quantity should be a tautologous sentence, one which is self-evidently true. Yet we have already seen (see section 2.4) that equatives which contain the same referent but with a different sense may be informative, as in (18) which might be interpreted as meaning that 'The Right Honourable X is the Right Honourable X', and even equatives with the same term in the subject and the predicate are taken as meaningful, as in (19).

(18)   My father is the Minister of Justice
(19)   News is news.

 <7.6> Under what circumstances might someone say (19), and what would it communicate?

The principle of quality is regularly broken in figures of speech such as irony or metaphor (see (20) and (21) respectively). In such cases we say things which we know to be false, and then assume that our interlocutors will recognise them as being false, and make an appropriate interpretation of the utterance in that light.

(20)   It's so nice to see a united family. (Said when the children are fighting)
(21)   This crossword's a pig.

 <7.7> What kinds of 'appropriate interpretation' do (20) and (21) demand?

Even cases which seem to flout the cooperative principle, really underline the fact that we generally function within the kind of framework that the cooperative principle envisages.

AUSTIN AND GRICE

John L. Austin (1911–1960) was Professor of Philosophy at Oxford University until his early death from liver cancer. He was one of the leading 'ordinary language philosophers' of his period. His most famous work, *How to Do Things with Words*, in which he develops the idea of constative and performative verbs, is a collection of lectures given at Harvard in 1955. While in Cambridge, Austin got to know Noam Chomsky (see p. 195).

Although Austin's work was seminal in the development of what is now called Speech Act Theory, Austin himself did not live long enough to answer the criticisms of his ideas, and it was left to his pupil, Grice, to take them further.

H. Paul Grice (1913–1988) was a philosopher who made a profound impression on the study of language. He is one of the scholars who made pragmatics a major part of linguistics. While he is known both in philosophy and linguistics for his work on conversational implicature (see below, section 7.5.3), his work in philosophy was much wider than this might seem to imply, including work in ethics and on the philosophy of Kant.

Speech Act Theory has also developed into the more recent Relevance Theory, introduced by Dan Sperber and Deirdre Wilson.

7.4 Being polite

We might think that there is another maxim in the cooperative principle which we have not yet discussed, namely, be polite. We can certainly see a lot of our behaviour as being driven by such a principle. But being polite is not simply a matter of behaving in a consistent way, and often seems to lead to breaches of the cooperative principle as we have discussed it.

7.4.1 Don't be too direct

If you speak English, unless you are a commanding officer in the armed forces or dictatorial ruler, the one thing you should never do if you want people to do something for you is tell them directly to do it. The command in (22) is more likely to get a rude response than the desired result.

(22)   Fetch my new suit from the tailor's.

The example in (22) has been chosen not to be the kind of order a child might make. English-speaking children are often asked, 'What's the magic word?' to get them to mitigate orders of this type into requests with the word *please*. So the very least you can do with something like (22) is add a *please* to it. However, (22) probably involves some considerable effort on the part of the person who is to do the fetching, so that it is more likely that a speaker will make a considerable effort to make the request more polite. Typically, at least in English, the way of making a request more polite is to make it less direct. This can be done linguistically, by turning the order into a question format (and thus leaving the illocutionary force of the utterance to be deduced by the hearer). In general, we also make the request more polite by making it more removed from the here and now. One way we do that, in English, is to use part tense verbs rather than present tense ones (although no past action is implied by this). So in (23) we have a number of possible versions of (22), each of them more polite than (22), and generally more polite the less direct they are.

(23)   Can you fetch my new suit from the tailor's?
       Could you fetch my new suit from the tailor's?
       I wonder if you could fetch my new suit from the tailor's.
       I wondered if you could fetch my new suit from the tailor's.

Another way to make an order appear less abrupt is to make the task sound less of an imposition on the hearer. Some examples are in (24).

(24)   Could you possibly fetch my new suit from the tailor's?
       I wonder if you could, like, fetch my new suit from the tailor's.
       Could you perhaps just fetch my new suit from the tailor's?
       While you're in the High Street, could you fetch my new suit from the tailor's?
       Could my new suit be fetched from the tailor's?

<7.8> Why does the last of the examples in (24) make the request sound like less of an imposition on the hearer?

The theory behind all of this is concerned with the notion of FACE. We have, the theory goes, two kinds of face: positive face and negative face. POSITIVE FACE is the desire of the individual to be liked, to be part of the group, and to share the needs of interlocutors. NEGATIVE FACE is the desire to be free and be able to act independently and of one's own volition, rather than at someone else's behest. The examples that have been given above are ways of mitigating a threat to negative face: they are ways of making it seem that the order or request is less of an imposition on the hearer, less constraining upon the individual. However, in principle we can gain similar effects by exploiting positive face, as is done in (25).

(25)   Could you be a dear and fetch my new suit from the tailor's?
       Chris, my old friend, could you fetch my new suit from the tailor's for me?
       If you can fetch my new suit from the tailor's for me, I'll put up that shelf you've been asking me to fix.

Some of these may sound a little exaggerated, but parallel examples are found in requests in everyday interaction.

Another approach to similar data works again on the basis of maxims, and suggests that there are six maxims of politeness, as set out in (26).

(26) | Tact | Minimise cost to other | Maximise benefit to other |
       |---|---|---|
       | Generosity | Maximise cost to self | Minimise benefit to self |
       | Approbation | Minimise criticism of other | Maximise praise of other |
       | Modesty | Maximise criticism of self | Minimise praise of self |
       | Agreement | Minimise disagreement between self and other | Maximise agreement between self and other |
       | Sympathy | Minimise difference between self and other | Maximise sympathy between self and other |

The first four of these maxims are pairs of mirror images, while the last two are distinct. The examples that have already been given in (23)–(25) can be seen as providing examples for some of these, but these also imply that you can be polite by running yourself down, and appealing to common feelings. Examples are given in (27).

(27)   I'm so stupid, I forgot to fetch my new suit from the tailor's. Could you possibly do it if you're passing that way?
       I know you'd like me to look my best for the wedding, so could you fetch my new suit from the tailor's for me?
       If you can fetch my new suit from the tailor's I'll be a real credit to you when we visit your parents.
       You're much better at remembering these things than I am, so could you possibly fetch my new suit from the tailor's?

 <7.9> Which maxims do the examples in (27) make appeal to? What about the examples in (25)?

Somewhere in all of this, you may feel that we are leaving politeness behind and moving into an area of manipulation. Nevertheless, people do use strategies like these in order to be polite. We should note, however, that strategies of politeness vary from culture to culture, and what has been described here, while suitable for English, is not necessarily what happens in other languages. This leads into the area of cross-cultural pragmatics, a fascinating area, but not one which will be dealt with here.

7.4.2 Calling people the right thing

Imposing on people by asking them to do something is not, of course, the only place where you have to be polite. In some societies (e.g. Belgium or Singapore) you can show politeness by your choice of language. In many more you can show politeness by the way you address people or the way you refer to yourself.

Thai is a language which has a number of different pronouns for referring to the speaker (see Data-set 7.1), depending on whether the speaker is male or female, whether the interlocutor is of lower or higher status than the speaker, how intimate the conversation is or how formal the context is.

Data-set 7.1
Some Thai first-person pronouns

khâaphacâw	♂ or ♀ in formal writing or, decreasingly, in public speech
kraphŏm	♂ in formal situations, when addressing a high-ranking person
dìchán	♀ in formal speech
phŏm	♂ speaking to superiors or equals, especially, but not exclusively, in a formal setting
chán	♂ or ♀ in mid-level formality, such as between friends
raw	♂ or ♀ use this for 'we', but young speakers increasingly use it for 'I', and superiors may use it for 'I' to inferiors
kháw	used especially by young ♀
tua eeŋ	used especially by young ♀
kan	♂ to close ♂ friends
kuu	very informal, used more often by ♂
nǔu	by child to older sibling or adult

Data-set 7.2
Basque

Different ways of saying 'I remain' depending on the addressee and the speech situation	
nagozu	polite
nagok	familiar to a male
nagon	familiar to a female
nagoch	intimate nago neutral form

Even in English we have seen a rapid evolution in terms of address over the past few decades. In British universities in the 1960s professors were addressed as *Professor*, and other teachers were addressed as *Dr/Mr/Mrs/Miss X*, as appropriate. Students were addressed as *Mr/Miss X*. These days, in very many institutions, everyone is addressed by their given name, independent of their status as staff or student, or their place in the hierarchy.

In Germany in the 1970s it was still normal to address an unmarried woman as *Fräulein* ('Miss'), but these days that would be considered rather impolite, because it makes specific reference to her marital status. A similar change has affected the use of *mademoiselle* in France.

The use of family names and given names in addressing a person has also changed rapidly. In the British mixed secondary school attended by the author in the 1960s, boys were addressed by their family names, and girls by their first names. In the army, and in many workplaces at the time, men addressed each other by family name alone. The following passage from a novel makes a specific point about the use of given names in direct address, linking that to social values.

> I have recorded Ruth saying, 'It's our life, Michael, not theirs.' The significant word here is my own name, 'Michael'. In Britain, the interpolation of an inter-locutor's name is uncommon among the educated classes: it is usually heard from the mouths of working class criminals in a tight spot. They think it gives credence to some preposterous lie. In the United States, on the other hand, such an interpolation is ubiquitous. (Read, 1997: 218)

While this particular passage does not reflect the results of academic research, and may be exaggerated in its claims, nevertheless it does illustrate that the use of given names can be interpreted according to social norms, which can vary even within the English-speaking world. Getting such things right is part of being polite in the relevant society.

<7.10> Which of the following people would you expect to address you by your given name, and are there any of them for whom it would be rude to address you by your given name? Can use of your given name have any other implications? Is the use of given names reciprocal? That is, do you call all those people who use your given name by their given name?

Your sister, your grandmother, a classmate at school, another student at university, a shop assistant, a policeman, an insurance salesman, your landlord/landlady, your employer, a judge in court.

Such usage of names is usually driven – albeit in different ways in different societies – by questions of power and solidarity. Where there are power relationships (e.g. between an employer and an employee, between a judge and a plaintiff) what works in one direction will not necessarily work in the other. You might use given names in one direction, but title and family name in the other, for instance, or title in one direction, and family name in another. Use of expressions like *sir, madam, your honour, your majesty* are most usually not used reciprocally. Where there is reciprocal usage, there is equality, and thus solidarity.

In some languages, though not in English, there is pronoun choice for addressees to consider as well. French, German, Italian, Spanish and many other languages have polite pronouns and intimate pronouns. Following the French system, where the polite pronoun is *vous* and the intimate one is *tu*, these are often called T and V forms even where, as in German, they begin with different letters. It might look as though it is possible to set up translational equivalents between the second person pronouns in these languages, as in (28). However, such a table fails to take into account the different ways these pronouns are used in the various cultures of which they are a part. In some of these cultures, the use of such forms is changing as rapidly as the use of titles or given names. In the late twentieth century, for instance, it looked as though the Danish polite form might disappear entirely, though it was current twenty-five years earlier. At one stage, for an adult male to use *tu* to an adult female from outside his own family in French was tantamount to a confession of intimacy, but that is no longer the case.

(28)	Language	T-form	V-form
	Danish	du	De
	Dutch	je	U
	French	tu	vous
	German	du	Sie
	Italian	tu	Lei
	Spanish	tu	Usted
	Swedish	du	Ni

You cannot necessarily guess from (28) which pronoun a speaker of the language will use when addressing God, a customer in a shop, a university student, and so on. In some cultures there are quite complex traditions for moving between one and the other: in general, once you use the T form to someone, you cannot move back to the V form without giving offence.

Names and pronouns are not the only way of marking solidarity between people. In English, swearing is one of the things that can mark solidarity. On the whole you cannot use swearing to someone senior to you in an organisation, because that is not 'polite'. You cannot swear to a subordinate, because that is not professional and is too emotionally involved to be appropriate in most business contexts. So the only people you can swear to are your equals. Accordingly, the use of large numbers of swear words usually indicates that you feel yourself to be on an equal footing with your interlocutor, and so it can be interpreted as a statement of solidarity.

7.5 Drawing conclusions

We spend our lives drawing conclusions by 'reading between the lines' of the things that are said. For example, if you fly into Manchester from Chicago, and before you're even out of the airport someone says to you, 'It's nice to see the sun, isn't it?', you will infer that it is currently sunny and that it has not been sunny for at least several days. The weather for the past few days has not been explicitly mentioned. If someone asks you whether you enjoyed the play last night, you will infer that they saw you at the play and that therefore they too were there (you could be wrong: they might just have seen you coming out with the crowd). And if someone addresses you, saying, 'Gidday, mate', you will infer they come from Australasia. There are many kinds of inferences that can be drawn from what people say, some of which are given special names. In this section we look at some of these. The word *infer* (or *inference*) will be used – as it has been here – as a neutral term without any special implication.

7.5.1 Presupposition

A **PRESUPPOSITION** is something that you take for granted or appear to take for granted when you produce an utterance. Because it is simply taken for granted, negating the sentence in which the presupposition occurs does not negate the presupposition. For example, (29) and (30) are mutually incompatible, but both of them presuppose (31).

(29) A tow-truck crashed into our house.
(30) A tow-truck did not crash into our house.
(31) We have a house.

The sentences in (32) all have presuppositions in the same way.

(32) The film we saw last week got a bad review.
      I'd forgotten that you gave me a copy of *War and Peace*.
      The computer is not useful for this task.

<7.11> What is presupposed in each of the sentences in (32)?

It can be difficult to say that someone who presupposes something told you that thing. For instance, in relation to the second sentence in (32), it is not obviously true to say of the person who utters it, that:

(33) She told me that I had given her a copy of *War and Peace*.

We are much more likely to say something along the lines indicated in (34):

(34) $\left.\begin{array}{l} \text{She implies} \\ \text{She seems to believe} \\ \text{She must think} \end{array}\right\}$ that I gave her a copy of *War and Peace*.

Denying presuppositions in questions is even more difficult. That is why the traditional trick question in (35) is so difficult to deal with.

(35) Have you stopped beating your wife yet?

Because presuppositions persist even when the entire sentence is negated, and saying *Yes* in answer to (35) implies (35a), and saying *No* implies (35b), whatever answer we give, we still have the presuppositions in (35c).

(35a) I have stopped beating my wife.

(35b) I have not stopped beating my wife

(35c) I have a wife.

       At some time in the past I beat (*possibly*: was in the habit of beating) my wife.

If we want to deny the presuppositions in a question like (35), we have to address them directly, as in (36), and that is impossible if we are only allowed to answer with *Yes* or *No*.

(36) I don't even have a wife.

      I have never beaten my wife.

7.5.2 Entailment

Inferences we draw through entailment are opposed in kind to presuppositions in a number of ways. An **ENTAILMENT** is a conclusion which links two propositions (that is, the semantic content of a simple sentence) in such a way that if the first is true the second must also be true. So, for example, (37) entails (38) and (39) entails (40).

(37) I saw an oak.

(38) I saw a tree.

(39) I killed the spider.

(40) The spider is dead.

Notice how entailment is different from presupposition. First of all, the inference of (38) from (37) is true only if (37) is true. If instead, it turns out to be the case that I did not see an oak, then we cannot conclude that I saw a tree. In presupposition, in contrast, the presupposition holds even when the first statement is negated. Second, if I say (37) this could justifiably be reported as (41).

(41) He $\left\{ \begin{array}{l} \text{said} \\ \text{told me} \end{array} \right\}$ that he had seen a tree.

There would be no need to resort to expressions such as *he seems to believe* to describe the state of affairs. Third, we saw above that you can deny presuppositions, but you cannot deny entailments (at least not if you want to remain logically coherent). So having said (39), I cannot then credibly continue with (42), given the normal acceptation of the words involved, our normal assumptions about the world, and assuming that the same spider is involved.

(42) The spider is not dead.

<7.12> Which of the statements below is a presupposition, and which an entailment, of the proposition that *Paul married Frances last week in the town hall* (on the assumption that *Paul* is not the name of the officiating functionary).

There is one relevant town hall.
Frances exists.
Frances is Paul's wife.

7.5.3 Conversational implicature

CONVERSATIONAL IMPLICATURE deals with the kind of inferences we make as a result of Grice's cooperative principle. Some of the examples used in section 7.3 illustrated conversational implicature, although the term was not used. Let us return to a sentence that has been used before. Assume that Evelyn says (43) to Sam.

(43)   It's cold in here.

Following the principle of quality, this is almost certainly true (although, of course, *cold* is a relative term). Evelyn will have evidence from his own senses. According to the principle of relevance, it must be relevant to the interaction. Just how it is relevant may not be explicit – this could, for example, be the first sentence in this particular interaction – but Sam must assume it to be relevant. Sam must also assume that she has been given enough information to interpret this declarative sentence, because of the principle of quantity. Thus, Sam must assume that she knows enough to work out what Evelyn means by (43). The requisite information could be in (43), that is, Evelyn could mean no more than to comment on the temperature in a particular place. It could, for instance, be a prelude to adding something like *I'd better go and get a jersey* or *Do you mind if I turn the heater on?* But if nothing more is forthcoming, and there is other information available to Sam, she can interpret (43) in the light of that other information. Perhaps someone came to fix the central heating yesterday. In that case, Sam will have to reason (a) that the central heating is supposed to be fixed, (b) that Evelyn still thinks it is cold in here, (c) that if the central heating was working properly it would not be cold in here, so (d) Evelyn thinks that the central heating repair was not carried out properly. According to circumstances, any of the sentences in (44) might then be an appropriate response.

(44)   He's still waiting for a part.
       I haven't turned it on yet.
       I thought it was warm enough.

The point to notice in all of this is how complex the deduction processes are, and that Sam, if she responds as in one of the options in (44), is equally leaving a great deal for Evelyn to deduce, for instance about who *he* is or what *it* is. Terminologically, we need to note that, under the appropriate circumstances, (43) can **IMPLICATE** that the repairs were not properly done.

One of the most celebrated examples of the potential complexity of implicatures comes from a hypothetical job reference. Suppose Lee asks Pat to write a letter of reference for her, because Lee is applying for a job in a university, and Pat writes (45).

(45)   Lee has very neat hand-writing and attended all the tutorials in the courses I taught.

Superficially Pat is doing all the right things: saying only positive things about the job candidate, and obeying the principles of manner by writing in a clear and straightforward manner. However, nobody will appoint Lee on the basis of a reference like (45), because it is such a poor recommendation.

<7.13> Why is the conversational implicature of (45) that Lee is not suitable for the job?

7.5.4 Conventional implicature

A **CONVENTIONAL IMPLICATURE** is something that can be inferred on the basis of the semantics of a particular word or expression. Conventional implicatures are sometimes seen as a special case of conversational implicatures. Two fairly standard examples will be given below.

(46)   Camilla is a linguist, but she is rich.
(47)   Marjorie hasn't phoned yet.

The sentence in (46) states that two propositions are true, namely that Camilla is a linguist and also that she is rich. It implies, by the use of *but* rather than *and*, that it is unexpected for linguists to be rich. This is a fixed effect associated with the use of *but*, namely that there is a contrast between the two conjuncts. The sentence in (47) seems to be true under the same conditions that *Marjorie hasn't phoned* is true, but the *yet* adds the implicature that the speaker expects this to happen. Note the oddity of (48a) as opposed to (48b).

(48)   (a) ?I don't expect her to phone, and Marjorie hasn't phoned yet.
       (b) I don't expect her to phone, and Marjorie hasn't phoned.

7.5.5 'Conceptual baggage'

At the vaguest end of things that can be inferred from what is said is what has been termed 'conceptual baggage'. Conceptual baggage is a collection of miscellaneous information which we more or less take as following from the use of a particular word, even though there is no logical reason why it should, and even real-world experience does not automatically confirm it. Consider a conversation like that in (49), for example.

(49)   A: Where does that guy live?
        B: He's Jane's husband, you know.

We seem to be intended to infer that 'that guy' lives with Jane. But not all married people live together (and not all those who live together are married), so there is no logical reason for the assumption. This particular instance is fairly bland: it is obvious what we are meant to deduce, and it is probably true given that the speaker provides us with this guideline in answer to the direct question. But we probably all have conceptual baggage associated with terms like *Englishman*, *American* or *Frenchman*, terms like *aunt* or *grandfather*, *student* or *professor*, and so on. In many cases such information can be pernicious; we may not even be aware of the baggage we have surrounding such everyday terms, but make judgements of people, things, actions, and so forth, depending on the labels attached to them simply because we associate particular things with the labels.

7.6 Texts

Given how hard we all appear to strive to find the relevance in any two adjacent statements, it may seem surprising that there comes a point when we all give up. Some sequences of sentences cohere into a text, others do not, however hard we may try. Consider the text in (50).

(50)   Goldilocks got lost in the forest. When she was very tired, she found a pretty house. She went in, and found three bowls of porridge there on the table. She ate one of the bowls of porridge, and then went upstairs, where she found three beds. She tried them all, but found the smallest one was the most comfortable, and fell asleep on it.

Without making any of the sentences ungrammatical, it should be possible to turn this into a sequence of sentences which do not produce a text. An attempt is provided in (51).

(51)   In the forest Goldilocks will get lost. A pretty house was found by her, after she grew tired. Three bowls of porridge were on the table here, and Goldilocks went in. Upstairs she went, and a serving of cereal was eaten by her and three beds had been found by Goldilocks. It was the most comfortable, she thought, and she fell asleep on the smallest one.

There are a number of reasons why (50) is a better text than (51), and they are generalisable to all texts. We shall consider only a few of the kinds of factors which play a role in making a text coherent, but sufficient to give you something of the flavour of the kinds of things that are relevant.

7.6.1 Deixis

DEIXIS is concerned with those spatio-temporal aspects of language which are anchored in the setting or context of the utterance itself. Some of these are fairly obvious, some are less obvious.

An obvious one is the use of the pronouns *I* (*me*) and *you*. Who *I* refers to depends on who is speaking, and who *you* refers to must change with the speaker, since it usually excludes the speaker (the *usually* in this sentence is to take account of the instances when the speaker is talking to him- or herself). Third person pronouns also change with the individual utterance, since the person referred to by *she* in one sentence may not be the same person as is referred to by *she* in another. Within a sentence, there are rules as to which person pronouns can refer to; and to some extent these spread over sentence boundaries. Compare (52) and (53), for instance, where the subscripted indices are to show which noun phrases are intended to be interpreted as having the same referent.

(52) $John_i$ said that Mary had paid him_i

(53)   *He_i said that Mary had paid $John_i$.

We can do the same with separate sentences.

(54) $John_i$ told me a secret. Mary has paid him_i.

(55)   *He_i told me a secret. Mary has paid $John_i$.

If we want (53) or (55) to be possible the *he* has to refer to someone other than John. The examples within a sentence can be explicated in terms of grammatical rules; but since the phenomenon spreads beyond the sentence, it takes us beyond sentence grammar into textual grammar.

Pronouns can be of three kinds. They can be **ANAPHORIC**, when they refer back to some entity already mentioned in the text. The *him* in (52) is anaphoric. Its **ANTECEDENT** is *John*. Pronouns can also be **CATAPHORIC**, when they refer forwards to some entity which will be mentioned in the text, as the *her* in (56). Or they can be **EXOPHORIC**, in which case they refer to some entity not otherwise mentioned in the text, but where the reference is simply to some real world entity. If it were said in isolation from everything else, (57) would be an example of this.

(56)   When I saw her, Christine was at the bar.

(57)   He's late again.

Some scholars see the main division here as being one between pronouns whose referent is explicit in the text and those whose reference has to be deduced from the setting, and these scholars do not distinguish between anaphoric and cataphoric, but simply call all such pronouns *anaphoric*.

Of course, not all languages use pronouns in the way in which they are used in English. Many languages provide sufficient information in the inflection of the verb to make the presence of an overt pronoun unnecessary in a large number of instances. Thus Julius Caesar wrote in one of his letters, *Veni, vidi, vici* (with no overt pronouns, but the verb showing that he was speaking of himself), which has to be translated into English with pronouns, 'I came, I saw, I conquered'.

As can be seen from examples like (52)–(55), there are rules about when a pronoun can be related to a particular antecedent, and one of the common difficulties that writers and speakers encounter is making sure that their pronouns refer to the right entities. One of the things that goes wrong in (51) is that it becomes difficult to assign a referent to the pronouns, and in section 7.5.3, there was deliberate manipulation of the pronouns to provide a surprise (*Evelyn* and *Sam* are both names that can be applied to males or to females, but *Evelyn* is usually applied to females and *Sam* usually to males, so that the converse situation is unexpected). Making sure that it is clear what pronouns refer to is one way of writing a clearer text.

Another example of deictics is provided by words such as *here* and *there*. The position of *here*, meaning 'close to the speaker' clearly varies with the speaker and the occasion. The same speaker can use *here* to mean Vienna one week and Sydney the next. Closely related to these are *now* and *then*, which have a similar function, but with reference to time rather than to place. Similarly *this* and *that* (with their corresponding plurals *these* and *those*) point to things which are close (PROXIMAL, near the speaker) or DISTAL (away from the speaker). Consider the set from rather old-fashioned English in Data-set 7.3, where we find allatives (direction to which) and ablatives (direction from which) as well as the straightforward locatives.

> **7.14** *There* and demonstratives such as *this* and *that* can be used exophorically. Give examples of such use. Can *here* and *now* and *then* also be used in this way?

Data-set 7.3
English

	ablative	locative	allative
proximal	hence	here	hither
distal	thence	there	thither

While standard English has only two sets of words like this, some non-standard varieties retain the form *yon(der)*, meaning 'away from both speaker and listener'. Many other languages have similar sets, as is shown below:

Data-set 7.4
Deictics in
several
languages

	Latin	Maori		Japanese
Near speaker	hic 'this'	nei 'here'	teenei 'this'	kono 'this'
Near listener	iste 'that'	naa 'there'	teenaa 'that'	sono 'that'
Away from both	ille 'yon' raa	'yonder'	teeraa 'yon'	ano 'yon'

Given that *now* and *then* are deictic, it also follows that tenses are deictic. The use of the present tense in (58) can turn into the past tense in (59) after a few hours.

(58) She is on the beach.
(59) She was on the beach.

Similarly, of course, there are a number of other deictic expressions: examples include *today, tomorrow*; German *Übermorgen* 'the day after tomorrow'; French *voici, voilà* 'here is, there is'; *the former* and *the latter*; *come* and *go* (*come* means something like 'move towards here' and *go* 'move towards there'). These can be interpreted only with respect to the situation in which something is said. Such expressions can be extremely difficult to interpret, especially for children, as is shown by the two common sayings given in (60).

(60)   The rule is, jam tomorrow and jam yesterday – but never jam today.
        Tomorrow never comes.

Even adults can have problems with deixis. Note, for instance, that American speakers of English, on picking up the phone, usually say (61a), indicating that they perceive the speaker as being close to them (presumably, in the phone itself), while British speakers are much more likely to use (61b), indicating that they perceive the speaker as being distant. American speakers of English and British speakers of English may also use *bring* rather differently.

(61)   (a) Who's this?
        (b) Who's that? / Who's there?

 <7.15> *She went to the store, but she forgot to bring her purse.* This sentence was found on a blog called 'Learn American English Online' for November 2009. It would not be possible in British English, and it is all a matter of deixis. Why do British speakers use *take* rather than *bring* here, and why can some Americans apparently do the opposite?

7.6.2 Sequencing events

If we say that we have a cat and a dog, we merely claim that both animals belong to us. The truth of (62a) is no different from the truth of (62b), each equivalent to *Kim owns a cat and Kim owns a dog.*

(62)   (a) Kim owns a cat and a dog.
        (b) Kim owns a dog and a cat.

It might seem, therefore that *and* just links together equivalent pieces of text, and that their order is unimportant. However, consider the sentences in (63).

(63)   (a) Kim got drunk and crashed the car.
        (b) Kim crashed the car and got drunk.

In both (63a) and (63b) the same two events took place, but they almost certainly happened in a different order. In (63a) getting drunk came before crashing the car (and was probably the cause of crashing the car), while in (63b) Kim got drunk after crashing the car. In other words, here the order of the two things conjoined has become meaningful.

One of the big differences between written and spoken language, is that we tend to use *and* a lot more in spoken language. Consequently, we tend to narrate events in the order in which they happened. In writing, we are much more likely to use overt means of ordering content: *after, before, while, since* and, with a causative implication, *because, since, for, therefore, thus* (note that *since* appears in both lists). One of the problems in (51) is that events are not related in the order in which they occur, and the story breaks down as a result.

<7.16> Provide unambiguous examples of *since* in its two different meanings.

As causes precede their effects, order can also be used to show not only temporal order but, by implication, causation, as we have already noted with respect to (63a). In (64) the implication is clearly that clicking on the button causes the file to be deleted, and not just that the two things were independent of each other as in (65). Note that while such implications are strongest when we have a single sentence with two coordinated parts, the implication can remain when two sentences are juxtaposed (as in (66)), so that this is a matter of drawing inferences about what is happening in the world, rather than strictly a grammatical matter within the sentence.

(64)   He clicked on the button and deleted his file.
(65)   He spat on the ground and deleted his file.
(66)   He clicked on the button. He deleted his file.

7.6.3 Making the information flow

On the whole, the flow of a sentence in English tends to go from known material, or knowledge which the speaker assumes that the listener also shares, to new material. So the typical opening to a children's story given in (67) starts from what we know, that we are now telling a story, and that when you do that it is about things that have already happened, and moves on to something new, that this story is about a bear.

(67)   Once upon a time, there was a bear.

Typically, as in (67), the intonational focus will be on the new information, here on the word *bear*, and typically, as in (67), the new noun will be introduced with an indefinite article, here *a*. In the next sentence, the fact that we are talking about a bear has moved from being new information to being information which speaker and listener share, and we expect some new information about the bear. Note that the determiner with *bear* will typically now shift to being a definite determiner, because now we know there is one bear in the discourse, and we can refer to that bear unambiguously. So we get a following sentence like (68).

(68)   The bear was very fond of honey.

This flow from established to informative is usually discussed in terms of GIVEN and NEW information.

It goes without saying that this picture is greatly simplified, and there are many reasons why you may find that it is not followed in a text. In particular, while this accounts for a great deal of the variation between *a* and *the* in English, you should not assume that this is the only factor leading to a choice between those two words. It is just one factor among many. Nevertheless, this provides a neutral background and we can talk about how this background affects the way we talk, and why we might break away from it.

> **<7.17>** Consider the sentence: *Once upon a time, I saw the moon.*
>
> *Moon* is new information in the sentence, but has a definite determiner. Why? Why should the usual expectation be overruled in this particular case?

Sometimes we have to change the syntax of a sentence in order to keep the flow of information correct. Consider, for example, the sentence (69) and the possible following sentences in (70).

(69)   The Great Fire of London destroyed St Paul's cathedral.
(70)   (a) It was rebuilt by Sir Christopher Wren.
       (b) Sir Christopher Wren rebuilt it.
       (c) The rebuilding was done by Sir Christopher Wren.
       (d) Sir Christopher Wren rebuilt the cathedral.
       (e) The cathedral was rebuilt by Sir Christopher Wren.

Of the sentences in (70), the best one to continue (69), other things being equal, is (70a). In (70b, d) the new information comes first rather than last. In (70c) we assume that we know that it was rebuilt, while (70a) makes no such assumption. And (70a) is better than (70e) because it uses a pronoun for the shared given information, which is more efficient than using the full noun phrase again as in (70e). Note that the pronoun is definite, just as the phrase *the cathedral*, but it avoids the need for repetition. The best options in (70), then, are all passive. Making them passive allows us to move the given information to the beginning of the sentence, and let the new information fall at the end of the sentence. This is despite the fact that many style manuals will suggest that you should avoid the passive. The passive has a number of functions, one of which is allowing an efficient flow of information, as seen here.

The distinction between given and new information sometimes supports and sometimes cuts across another distinction, that between theme and rheme (sometimes, more or less equivalently, called topic and comment). The THEME of a sentence is what you are talking about in the sentence, and the RHEME is what you say about the theme. In (69) the theme is *The Great Fire of London*, and the rheme is that it destroyed St Paul's cathedral. In (70a) the theme is *it* (namely, Saint Paul's cathedral) and the rheme is that it was rebuilt by Sir Christopher Wren. In (70a) the theme is the given information, and the rheme is the new information, and that pattern is often found. However, the two need not support each other in this way.

Consider the question in (71), and the two possible answers in (72).

(71)   What is your favourite Shakespeare play?
(72)   (a) My favourite play is *Much Ado About Nothing*.
         (b) *Much Ado About Nothing* is my favourite play.

In (72a) the theme and the given information are both *my favourite play*. In (72b), though, the given information remains *my favourite play*, but the theme is *Much Ado About Nothing*. Just as we have syntactic ways of making the distinction between given and new information flow smoothly, so we have syntactic ways of making something the theme of the sentence. Some examples are given in (73).

(73)   (a) As for *Much Ado About Nothing*, it's my favourite play by Shakespeare.
         (b) *Much Ado About Nothing*, that's my favourite play by Shakespeare.
         (c) It's my favourite play, *Much Ado About Nothing*.

Notice, in particular, the use of intonation to mark given and new where these may differ from theme and rheme. In (74) the intonational focus is shown with underlining.

(74)   (a) *Much <u>Ado</u>* is my favourite play.
         (b) *Much Ado* is my <u>favourite</u> play.

In (74a), *Much Ado* is new information and the theme, while in (74b) *Much Ado* is given information and the theme.

Although intonation is not available in written text, so that other ways have to be found of doing the same thing in writing, intonation can be used to structure a whole speech event in speech. Completely new topics are frequently introduced by an intonational rise to a new peak, dividing the interaction up into what are sometimes called **PARATONES** (like paragraphs). When we look at language on the page, it is easy to forget that we have many prosodic devices available to us to allow us to comprehend how the information is being structured, but that these are a vital part of our repertoire.

 <7.18> If you add a parenthetical remark to something you are saying, you frequently mark in speech by one or more prosodic devices, perhaps the speech phenomena that the parentheses or dashes try to reproduce in writing. Consider, for instance, the possible utterance:

The silly idiot (I'm sure you know who I mean) had forgotten to take his pills again.

What prosodic devices might you use to delimit the parenthetical remark?

7.6.4 Holding it together

As well as getting the flow of information right through a text, texts become text-like by being cohesive, that is the various parts stick together properly. Again, there are numerous ways of doing this, not just one. Some of these grammatical features are things that we have already considered from other points of view, so that they are potentially multifunctional in a text.

The first of these features is vocabulary. The words we use say what we are talking about, and provide links between clauses, sentences, paragraphs and even distant parts of a text. Sometimes the same vocabulary item is repeated, but often we find a hyponym or superordinate (see section 2.2 on hyponymy), or a derivative or a compound fulfilling precisely the same function. Some examples are provided below, with the links specifically highlighted.

(75)   Last week I got a <u>collie pup</u> for the kids. They love that <u>dog</u> already.

(76)   Takes two for <u>blackmail</u>. The <u>blackmailer</u>, Kettle, ... And the <u>blackmailee</u>, skimming Supa-Spa profits, and unmasked by Kettle. (Kenyon, 1986: 138)

(77)   I saw a <u>woman</u> standing in the lighted kitchen, leaning back against a counter. In her left hand was a bottle of <u>tequila</u> . . .
[100 pages]
The <u>tequila woman</u> almost certainly lived in the house.
(Laymon, 2001: 51–152)

We have already seen that determiners help hold a text together. In singular contexts in English, *the* implies that there is just one item which can easily be identified in the context of the utterance, and very often that identification is possible through the preceding linguistic context. In other cases, though, the individual which a noun phrase with *the* picks out is there by implication, or is there in the general knowledge of the interlocutors. Consider the range of examples in (78).

(78)   (a) I need a new car. The vehicle must be no more than three years old.
       (b) They walked into the room. The light was still on.
       (c) We passed Buckingham Palace today. We didn't see the Queen.
       (d) The sun is very hot today.

<7.19> The rule for *the* above was phrased in terms of singular noun phrases; how are plural noun phrases different, and how are they the same?

<7.20> What kinds of factors make the definite noun phrases with *the* in (78) easily identifiable to the listener?

Like definite noun phrases, pronouns refer to some entity or entities which the listener can identify, and have the advantage of economy: they avoid repetition of sometimes clumsy noun phrases. If the listener cannot assign proper reference to a pronoun, communication breaks down, as Lewis Carroll reminds us.

(79) '"Stigand, the patriotic arch-bishop of Canterbury, found it advisable –"'
'Found *what*?' said the Duck.
'Found *it*,' the Mouse replied rather crossly: 'of course you know what "it" means.'
'I know what "it" means well enough, when *I* find a thing,' said the Duck: 'it's generally a frog or a worm. The question is, what did the archbishop find?' (Carroll, 1865: Ch. 3)

The joke here is that the *it* in *found it advisable* is not a referring *it* at all, but the animals, being unfamiliar with the expression, try to interpret it as though it were, just like most cases of *it*.

> **<7.21>** Can you think of any other example of an *it* which does not refer?

One of the main ways of organising a text, and relating the various bits of it to each other, is by way of adverbials of different kinds. This includes many prepositional phrases and subordinate clauses introduced by various conjunctions. So, for example, *after that, next, once she had finished her tea, a long time ago, during the Vietnam war, after the goldrush,* all locate the events related in the text in time, and thus, relatively speaking, to each other. *In the garden, closer to home, nearby, out of sight* locate events in space (sometimes metaphorically). *Because you are too big, due to the forces of gravity* provide reasons, and so on. We have already seen that *and* can imply a temporal or a causal relationship, and that *but* implies some kind of contrast. Equally, misuse of connectives or adverbs can cause misunderstandings or confusion. *We passed Buckingham Palace today so we didn't see the Queen* is either total nonsense, or requires us to work overtime on working out what the conversational implicature is meant to be: perhaps the speaker and listener have an in-joke whereby they only ever see the Queen when she is abroad, and never in England, for instance.

7.7 Doing gender (Advanced)

A number of languages are reported as having distinct forms for men and women. For instance, in Koasati, there are certain differences in some verbal paradigms, as illustrated below:

Data-set 7.5
Koasati

Female form	Male form	Gloss
lakawtakkṍ	lakawatakkós	'I am not lifting it'
lakawwã́	lakkawwá:s	'he will lift it'
taʧilwân	taʧilwâ:s	'don't sing'
iltoʧihnôn	iltoʧihnô:s	'don't work'

Chiquito is reported to have an affix to refer to men only in men's speech, as shown overleaf.

Data-set 7.6

Chiquito

yebotii ti n-ipoostii	'he went to his house'
yebotii ti n-ipoos	'he went to her house'
yebo ti n-ipoostii	'she went to his house'
yebo ti n-ipoos	'she went to her house'

The distinctions above are made in men's speech. In women's speech, the last form can have any of the meanings illustrated.

While such reports are certainly dramatic, and make a valid point, it is usually the case that one of the two forms indicated is more innovative than the other, and that the innovative form is, at the time of observation, used largely by one sex or the other. Other types of difference are less time-dependent. It is often said that women use a wider pitch range in their intonation patterns than do men, and that by doing so, they show more emotion than men. Partly this is a reflection of the use of an average voice pitch which is higher than men use. Transgendered men in Tonga are said to be recognisable by the same features. Some of this is obviously biological; at the same time it should be noted that pre-pubertal children also show sex-based differences in pitch which are not biologically-determined, so that there is a cultural component even to voice pitch. The former British Prime Minister, Margaret Thatcher, is said to have been taught to deepen the pitch of her voice so that she would sound more authoritative (read: less feminine).

In other ways, too, women speaking English might be said to speak a different language from men. Most women feel comfortable with a term like *turquoise*, and know what colour it denotes (how far they agree is perhaps less clear). Most men tend to avoid the term, and prefer to use either *blue* or *green* (perhaps *greeny-blue*). Similarly most men avoid terms like *lavender, heliotrope, lilac, magenta, mauve, puce*, and may not even know what shades these denote; they call all of these colours *purple*. Here, even women may be less secure, but they are likely to have a better feel for the words than men do.

There are other words that women are said to use but men to avoid, but often these vary depending on the dialect of English spoken and the age of the women concerned. Examples might include *darling* (as an adjective), *divine* (again as an adjective), *dreamy, super* (as an expression of approval). And it has been suggested that women sound less sure of themselves, use more tag questions like *don't you, aren't they, shouldn't we*, more hedges like *sort of, like*, use *so* as an intensifier (*I think he's so great*), and that they interrupt other speakers less than men do, but talk more.

Most of these differences have been shown in subsequent research to be based on impressions gathered from a consideration of too small a sample. In particular, they pay no attention to the context of situation. Neither women nor men behave the same way in all contexts, and some of these features depend upon the context. So if you were to put a woman who was an expert on her subject in a conversation on that subject with a man who knew little about it, you might find that woman did not use tag questions or hedges, but did talk more. The context is a vital ingredient in the mixture, and you cannot make generalisations about the way 'women' or 'men' will speak without reference to the situation in which the speech occurs.

Nevertheless, some stereotypes emerge which, while they are stereotypical for good reason, can always be overridden. A list is given in (80).

(80) **Other things being equal,** **Other things being equal**
women tend to: **men tend to:**
be indirect be direct
be conciliatory be facilitative
be confrontational be competitive
be collaborative be autonomous
provide supportive feedback provide aggressive interruptions
be person or process oriented be task or outcome oriented

Note that some of the items in (80) like the question of (in)directness and the matter of whether or not you provide aggressive interruptions (the *aggressive* is important) suggest that women will, again stereotypically, appear more polite than men.

What the list in (80) suggests is that gender is not something you just have, but is something you work at, and that you work at differently in different contexts. It has been suggested that academic men, for example, use more 'women's language' than men in general. In terms of the list in (80) this could be that all teachers are trained not to provide aggressive interruptions, but to provide supportive feedback, and also to be collaborative. At the same time, successful academics, whether they are male or female, have to remain relatively task-oriented, or books would never be written, the marking would never be completed, and so on. In other words, the nature of the task determines to some extent the way in which language is used to achieve the task. At the same time, individuals are free to choose how best to deal with a task, so that everyone, male or female, can opt to be more or less collaborative or confrontational, more or less direct, more or less competitive in the way in which they approach a task. If, instead of *a task* in the last sentence, we substitute *life*, we can see that how 'masculine' or 'feminine' your approach is remains a social construct, which you can deliberately or unconsciously manipulate. Being 'masculine' or 'feminine' is not a strict divide, nor is it a genetically given distinction: there are degrees of masculinity or femininity in language which can be exploited by the individual to construct a personal style. This style is more masculine or more feminine, the more the traits in (80) align with sex and are perceived as being characteristic of gender groups. In principle, though, if men and women started to use the traits in (80) simply on the basis of the task they were undertaking and not on the basis of their sex, 'gendered language' would cease to exist, and we would have context-based language instead. Some scholars suggest that this is what is already happening, at least in western societies. The traits associated with 'men's language' or with 'women's language' would be better associated with 'powerful' language and 'powerless' language, and women have been conditioned by generations of powerlessness to use certain techniques, while men, conditioned by generations of powerfulness tend to use others. Modern social conditions lead to a lot of variation in power relations, and these affect the language that is used, but there are still traces of the old correlations left, which is why the kinds of stereotypes given in (80) have some validity.

7.8 Summing up

What we have seen in this chapter is that while language can be described in terms of its own systems, these systems interact with the real world and are influenced by it. There are reasons why a particular structure may be used on a particular occasion; grammatical structures may be exploited to allow the speaker to gain a particular effect – implying something, being polite, and so on. We cannot know how a given language works without knowing about the systems; phonetic, phonological, morphological and so forth, that make up the language; but at the same time, unless we know how those systems are exploited in actual usage, we see only part of the picture.

Clearly, only a superficial introduction to all of this has been given here. Several distinct technical areas have grown up within what we have here loosely called 'pragmatics', including politeness theory, text linguistics, conversational analysis, speech act theory and so on, and many specialist books have been written on all of them.

 Technical terms introduced in this chapter

Anaphoric	Implicate
Antecedent	Indirect speech act
Cataphoric	Interrogative
Comment	Imperative
Constative	Locutionary act
Conventional implicature	Maxim
Conversational implicature	Negative face
Cooperative principle	New
Declarative	Paratone
Deixis	Performative
Direct speech act	Perlocutionary act
Distal	Phatic communion
Entailment	Positive face
Exophoric	Presupposition
Face	Proximal
Felicity conditions	Rheme
Given	Speech act
Gricean principle	T and V forms
Happiness conditions	Theme
Illocutionary force	Topic

Reading and references

On performative verbs, see Austin (1962). For Grice's cooperative principle, see Grice (1975). On politeness maxims, see Leech (1983). On Tongan transgendered men, see Besnier (2003). On conceptual baggage, see McConnell-Ginet (2008). For an early and provocative approach to language and gender – one from which I have taken several examples here – see Lakoff (1975). The list in (80) comes from Holmes & Stubbe (2003) but is not the complete set of distinctions given by that source.

Information on the various languages mentioned has been taken from the sources mentioned below:

Basque	Anderson & Keenan (1985: 274)	Koasati	Haas (1944)
		Latin	Lyons (1977)
Chiquito	Jespersen (1922: 240)	Thai	Hudak (1990); Smyth (2002); Iwasaki & Ingkaphirom (2005)
Japanese	Anderson & Keenan (1985: 285)		

8

Conclusion

We are at the commencement of a philological age, everyone studies languages: that is, everyone who is fit for nothing else.

(George Borrow, 1851)

In this chapter we look back at where we have been and consider where the material covered in this book can lead us.

8.1 A summing up and a new start

This chapter is different in nature from the others in this book. Here the idea is to bring together the various bits we have examined independently, and then to look ahead to ways in which the information that has been learned from this book might be employed. Linguistics is at the service of language description, and language description is at the service of the users of the descriptions, whether they are foreign language learners, computer scientists, sociologists, philosophers or medical people. So far we have been looking at the principles underlying the linguistics. In doing so we have, of necessity, provided fragments of language description. Mostly, though, we have not shown how those bits of description might be of value to the community – or, rather, the communities – that linguistics, as a discipline, serves. It has been assumed that having a good description is a goal in its own right.

For many linguists, this might, indeed, be the only goal they have. A solid description of any facet of any language is remarkably difficult to produce. Linguists are led to seek new ways of framing those descriptions as a result of their expectations (based on their experience of languages and the lessons they learn from linguistics) and advances in linguistic theory. New ideas about phonology, morphology or syntax can lead to new questions about the way in which language behaves, and the answers to these questions can illuminate aspects of language use which have previously been obscure. A better description is always desirable.

This raises the question of what 'better' means in this context, of course. Is a better description a more economical one (one that can be written in less space), is it one which gives rise to further testable hypotheses about human linguistic behaviour or is it one that makes sense to someone who wants to analyse the language for their own non-linguistic ends? It could be any one of these or no doubt other things, too.

We will start this chapter by looking at two of the major problems linguistics faces, and at questions concerning the goals and methods used in linguistic description. We will then go on to look at the way in which the various modules we have described fit together, before looking at the potential uses of linguistic descriptions.

8.2 Some fundamental problems in linguistics

There are many large problems facing linguistics, and there may be disagreement about which of these problems is most likely to yield to investigation or to provide valuable insights into human linguistic behaviour. Many linguists are, for example, concerned with the way in which language arose in humans: how and why did humans evolve into a language-using species? The difficulty with that question traditionally has been that it had led to speculation without evidence. Below we consider two other problems that affect the things we think linguists should be looking at.

8.2.1 Plato's problem

How do children learn such a complex phenomenon as language in such a short period of time? It is usually said that children, by the age of five, know all the fundamentals of their language (though they continue to learn new vocabulary all their lives). This may be a slight exaggeration, but certainly they are – except in pathological cases – able to use language fluently and effectively to communicate by that age. Moreover, they know things that no adult has taught them explicitly.

For example, consider a sentence like (1).

(1)   Do you think that Suzy saw Owen?

If we want to make this into a question about Suzy, we can say

(2)   Who do you think saw Owen?

Or we could ask about Owen, and ask

(3)   Who do you think Suzy saw?

For this last sentence there is an alternative

(4)   Who do you think that Suzy saw?

But for the first question, there is no corresponding possibility with *that*:

(5)   *Who do you think that saw Owen?

Children know not to say things like (5) without having been taught them. What is more, in general they hear rather bad examples of language: people add hesitations to their speech, make false starts, correct themselves, use wrong words, fail to finish what they were going to say and so on. Given that input, given that there is an infinite number of sentences in English (or any other natural language) so that no child can have heard them all, how do they manage to learn language so well?

The answer given by Chomsky and his supporters is that the child's brain must be pre-programmed to be ready to learn a language, and must have some information about what is or is not possible in language. Whatever it is that is built in to the minds of humans is called Universal Grammar (often abbreviated to UG): universal because it must allow us to learn any human language – we are not genetically programmed to learn Chinese or Moseten, we are only programmed to learn a language, and we learn whatever language is spoken in the community we grow up in.

If that is the case, then a really interesting question is what that UG looks like: what kind of information does it contain and what do we learn from our experience of language once we are born? This is the question that many linguists try to solve.

Others prefer to attack the question from the other end. If we look at the languages we know about, they ask, how much is really common to all languages and what principles drive the range of variation that can be found? If there is something that is found in all languages, then it is a candidate for something that might be pre-programmed in the human brain. This does not prove that it must be pre-programmed, of course. There are many reasons why all languages might have things in common, to do with the way in which humans use languages, the way humans are constructed and the laws of physics. A language in which the normal intonation of a sentence started with low pitch and rose gradually to very high would be unusual because we would have to overcome the physics and physiology of the way in which air is expelled from the lungs, which normally means that it is easier to have falling intonation patterns.

Whichever way we look at the problem, the fundamental question of how the brain can cope with language is a fascinating one.

PLATO

Plato (ca. 427–347 BCE) was a student of Sophocles and a teacher of Aristotle. The problem that Plato faced, and that is picked up in the name 'Plato's problem', was not specifically anything to do with language. Rather, Plato was worried about how people knew things that they had not been taught (in his case, geometrical principles). He concluded that they must know such things from previous lives.

Plato was also concerned with the nature of names. Are names conventional (and can the names of things thus be changed at will), or are they in some way naturally linked to whatever they name? He realises that a single individual cannot change the name of some object, because we cannot have a horse being termed a *man* by one person and a *horse* by everyone else. He assumes that names must once have been natural, but over time have become conventionalised as they have been corrupted. Because some words have been borrowed from other languages, we cannot know the etymologies of all names, and thus cannot uncover their original natural meanings.

Not until the time of Saussure (see p. 89) did it become generally accepted that the relationship between the form of a word and its meaning is, as a general rule, arbitrary.

8.2.2 Where are the borders of language and linguistics?

How much should we try to describe in linguistics, and where should we just say that we have gone beyond the bounds of what linguistics is about? Chomsky raised the question with reference to a now celebrated (or perhaps notorious) example given in (6).

(6)   Colourless green ideas sleep furiously.

The question is whether our grammar should provide an account of the oddity of (6), or whether our grammar should treat (6) just as if it were (7).

(7)   Motherless black children sleep deeply.

It might take some imagination to suggest a set of circumstances in which it would make sense for someone to say or write (7), but it seems to be 'part of English' in a way that (6) does not.

We can suggest many reasons why (6) is odd: sleeping is something that is done only by animate entities, and ideas are not animate; only concrete entities can have colour, and ideas are not concrete and so cannot be green; the words *colourless* and *green* are incompatible, and so on. We can also find counterarguments. There is a book called a *dictionary of green ideas* (Button, 1988), so it is clear that ideas can be green, and so that *green* and *colourless* (which can also mean something like 'uninteresting') need not be incompatible. Poems have been written which incorporate the line in (6), so it clearly can be made meaningful.

It is certainly true that (6) strikes us as being odd; but at the same time we say many things which are odd, apparently with sincerity:

(8)   As I was going up the stair
      I met a man who wasn't there.
      He wasn't there again today.
      I wish that man would go away.

We could equally find reasons why (8) is impossible, but to do so would be to miss the point. Sometimes, it seems, we want to say things that are wrong, unusual, ridiculous or internally inconsistent and our language does not prevent us from doing that.

The issue was brought into focus very nicely by the linguist who pointed out that if someone were to say (9), we would not conclude that they required remedial grammar lessons.

(9)   My toothbrush is alive and is trying to kill me.

Accordingly, we must conclude that the oddity of (9) is not grammatical. The conclusion is supported by the fact that *I dreamt that my toothbrush was alive and was trying to kill me* is perfectly unobjectionable.

Next, consider a very different kind of example. In (10) we have part of a familiar nursery rhyme.

(10)   This is the dog
       that chased the cat
       that caught the rat
       that ate the malt
       that lay in the house
       that Jack built.

Corresponding to *the dog that chased the cat* we can in English turn the sentence round and say, equivalently, *the cat that the dog chased*, and it is possible to miss out the word *that* to give *the cat the dog chased*. We can put *the cat the dog chased* in a sentence, to give (11).

(11)   The cat the dog chased caught the rat.

But what if we now want to start with the rat? Following the same principles as before, we should get (12).

(12)   The rat the cat the dog chased caught (ate the malt)

Most speakers of English fail completely to understand (12). So should we consider (12) to be part of the language we are trying to describe? And what if we continue to (13)?

(13)   The malt the rat the cat the dog chased caught ate (lay in the house that Jack built)

Some linguists have suggested that a sentence like (13) is part of English and we should include it in what we have to describe; to exclude (13) while allowing (11), they claim, would be to put an arbitrary limit on the application of a grammatical rule. Possibly. On the other hand, if speakers cannot produce or understand (13) without using paper and pencil, is the decision to omit it really arbitrary?

There are other kinds of language which popular perception tends to damn as being somehow not proper language. This includes things like the examples in (14).

(14)   (a) We might could finish in time.
      (b) I was like wow! You know?
      (c) He er was um not very pleased, really.
      (d) The f—ing bastard idiot f—ing well forgot!

The sentence in (14a) belongs to a non-standard dialect of English; double modals of this kind (here meaning 'might be able to') are found in parts of Northumbria in England, southern Scotland and in some of the southern states of the United States. The rule here is that different dialects or varieties may require different rules or statements about the patterns that are found in them, but that each dialect can be described as a system in its own right, and that linguistically speaking there is nothing special about standard varieties of a language which make them more worthy of description than others.

CONTROVERSY: The lack of primacy for standard dialects

It is part of the credo of linguists that no dialect is linguistically superior to any other, and that none should be given pride of place by virtue of being a standard variety. This runs directly counter to the lay position that the standard variety of any language is the 'best' variety of that language. Part of the difficulty here is that there is some equivocation about the nature of 'good English' (or 'good Japanese', etc.). For the linguist, 'good' simply means that it is well-suited to allowing communication between the people who speak it; for the lay person, a variety is 'good' if it confers social prestige. A variety may do one of these things without doing the other. Linguists also tend to prefer to talk of different varieties as being 'appropriate' in different contexts, rather than as being 'good' or 'bad'. The variety illustrated in (14a) may be appropriate in certain parts of the world among local speakers, but not among other speakers; the variety illustrated in (14d) may be appropriate from a person of a certain age, sex, social class (etc.) in a certain social environment, but not appropriate in a court of law or a discussion during a university lecture. Having said all that, there is usually one predictable difference between standard varieties of a language and non-standard ones: the standard varieties generally allow less variation than the non-standard ones. Whether that is 'good' or not, and in what sense, is an open question.

Sentences (14b, c) are more likely to be found in spoken English than in written English. The two are very different, and must be described as having different syntactic rules and different fixed phrases. Similarly (14d) illustrates another spoken variety of English: swearing may or may not be socially acceptable (depending on the social circumstances), but it has its own grammar and its own vocabulary. None of these alternative varieties is excluded from the field of linguistic description; we just have to realise that we are dealing with different objects of description in the various cases.

This leads linguists to the position where they frequently say that linguistics is a matter of **DESCRIPTION** (saying what the language is like) rather than **PRESCRIPTION** (saying how the language should be spoken). One of the major misunderstandings between linguists and lay people rests on this point. Lay people want linguists to tell them what is right; linguists know that what is right changes with time, and that what is right changes from environment to environment.

8.3 Some problems of doing linguistics

As well as problems concerned with the subject matter of linguistics, there are problems concerned with the way in which we do linguistics. Two such problems are addressed briefly here.

TRIVIA

We might not think of swearing as having its own grammar, but it does. Part of the reason that foreigners often have difficulty with swearing is that the grammar is so difficult. To prove the point, consider that we have a whole lot of verbs which we can swear with, usually (in English) denoting bodily functions or sexual activity. We also have a number of constructions that these verbs can enter into: *piss off* means 'go away', and we can replace *piss* with some of these verbs, but not all. *Sod all* means 'nothing at all', and *sod* can be replaced by some of these verbs, but not by all. *Screw up* means 'make a mistake' and again *screw* can be replaced with some other verbs, but not all of the relevant ones. Even if you are not a person who swears a great deal, you will, if you are a speaker of English, recognise the grammar. You can make a table with verbs down the left and constructions across the top and look for patterns.

You will also be aware that *Screw you!* is grammatical swearing, but **Go screw you!* is not. It has to be *Go screw yourself!* Why, then, does it not have to be *Screw yourself*? That would seem to be more in line with the grammar of the rest of English, where you have to say, for example, *Pinch yourself!* and not **Pinch you!*

If you are not a native speaker of English, you would be wise to avoid all these expressions because their pragmatics as well as their grammar is so difficult to work out, and you can easily give offence.

8.3.1 Realism versus instrumentalism

What are linguists trying to create when they provide a description of linguistic material? One answer is that linguists are trying to produce a maximally economical description of the language data, with the greatest possible degree of generalisation. Another answer is that linguists are trying to produce a description that reflects the structure of that linguistic material in the human mind. In the philosophical literature, these are termed INSTRUMENTALISM and REALISM respectively; in the linguistic literature they are often referred to as hocus-pocus linguistics and God's truth linguistics.

It might seem obvious that a description which mirrors the structures in a person's head would be better (and certainly, no instrumentalist would refuse the evidence if it turned out that the structures and processes they were proposing had some measurably behavioural correlate), but that is not necessarily the case. We cannot necessarily know, for instance, that all speakers have the same structures in their heads – we know that speakers have differing abilities to use language for various effects such as to persuade, to amuse or to create literature. And in a few cases, it seems fairly clear that the hocus-pocus solution is not in people's heads.

Consider the case of adjectives in French. Adjectives in French agree in gender with nouns, and there are two genders, masculine and feminine. The masculine is used in any instance where there might be doubt, while use of the feminine form specifically marks places where there is agreement with a feminine noun. Some typical examples are given in Data-set 8.1.

Data-set 8.1
French
adjectives

masculine	feminine	gloss
blɑ̃	blɑ̃ʃ	'white'
fʁɛ	fʁɛʃ	'fresh'
gʁɑ̃	gʁɑ̃d	'big'
gʁo	gʁos	'fat'
œʁø	œʁøz	'happy'
pti	ptit	'small'

The question here is how to predict the form of the adjective from a base. If we start with the masculine form, we can see that we have to add a consonant to get the feminine form, but it seems to be unpredictable which consonant will be added. If, on the other hand, we start with the feminine form, we can predict the masculine form: subtract the last consonant. It appears, though, that French speakers learn the masculine form and which consonant to add to make the adjective feminine rather than the other way round. The easy solution is not the one that is apparently in people's brains.

8.3.2 Getting data

How do we know what a language looks like? How do we know what the generalisations are? The questions need rather different answers depending on whether we are speakers of the language concerned or not.

Field linguists go out to places in the world where there are undescribed languages, and live among the relevant population, learning the language and talking to speakers about their language. They take tape-recorders (these days) and notebooks and note down what people say, recording stories and speeches, asking people whether they could say the same thing some other way or not. Gradually, as they learn more about the language, they are able to make better generalisations about the patterns they hear.

People who speak the language concerned may be able to consult their own intuitions about what is or is not possible in their language. So we can ask speakers of English, or you can ask yourself if you are a speaker of English, whether (6) is a good sentence of English or not. However, intuitions are fallible. If we say them often enough, sentences like (6) or (12) start to sound reasonable; in other instances we may not even know whether something sounds right or not. In any case, one individual only knows about some bits of English, and we may want to know more than is in the head of a single individual: for example, 'which of these two structures is more common?'

At this point we turn to electronic CORPORA (singular: corpus). A corpus is a representative body of language collected and filed in some kind of electronic database so that it can be analysed by linguists. Questions that you can answer on the basis of corpus evidence include things like: Do speakers of English ever actually say things like *The house must have been being painted at the time*, even if it is part of the system of English? When do speakers end sentences with *and stuff*? Is *by* more often a marker of location or a marker of agency? Is the suffix -able added to nouns as well as to verbs? The development of electronic corpora of many millions of running words of text is, of course, a relatively recent phenomenon; prior to the advent of humanities computing, linguists used to read large numbers of texts and copy out relevant examples and then look for generalisations across the examples they had found. In either case, the linguist needs to be able to analyse carefully examples of genuine usage and draw conclusions based on the various examples that are available.

8.4 Some links between modules

In this book, phonetics has been presented as separate from phonology, phonology separate from morphology and so on. Yet it will have been obvious from time to time that these various modules of linguistic behaviour are in many ways interlinked. It would take us much too far to consider all the links that might possibly exist, but it is important to notice that there are links between the various modules, some more than others.

Although the question was raised in Chapter 1 as to whether phonetics was really part of linguistics at all, there have been other writers who have speculated as to whether phonetics is separable from phonology at all (and if so, how). Both deal with the sounds of language in various ways. Both can be influenced by the articulatory possibilities of humans. Many questions can be observed from a more-or-less phonetic angle or a more-or-less phonological angle. For example, although the question of what sounds a language has was dealt with in this book in section 3.8 as part of phonetics, implicitly we were dealing with phonemes, which are part of phonology.

We saw in section 5.5 that phonology and morphology overlap in the whole area of morphophonemics, where the sounds of a language change depending on the morphological environment in which they find themselves. We had examples like *electric* (with final /k/) but *electricity* (with /s/ before the suffix -ity), for instance.

Morphology and syntax meet up in the study of inflection, where morphological form is used to indicate syntactic function. Phonetics is sometimes said never to influence syntax (and certainly any examples are rare and controversial), but phonology does. We saw an example in Data-set 4.10, where words with a particular phonological structure in Maori required an extra syntactic particle in vocatives and imperatives.

Semantics and pragmatics seem to meet up with every other feature. We might have a word like *scary*, but if we phonetically make it longer (and say something like [skeːːːːːːəri]), it has the pragmatic effect of increasing the scariness. Semantics and phonology meet up in the whole notion of iconicity, where it is sometimes claimed, for instance, that close front vowels are used in words denoting proximity (like words for 'here'), while opener vowels are used in words denoting greater distance (like words for 'there'). The vowels concerned are virtually always considered in phonological terms, but the relationship is often assumed to be phonetic, with an iconic relationship between the distance of the tongue from the roof of the mouth and the distance denoted by the relevant words. Most such claims are controversial, but some are relatively well attested.

Morphology is explicitly concerned with the interface between form and meaning. Although there are examples of forms which appear to have no meaning or meanings which arise despite forms, the general rule for morphology is that the meaning must follow the form. This is why we cannot divide *misled* as *misle* + *d* but must divide it as *mis* + *led* (and similarly with *spoonfed*): *mis* and *led* both have relevant meaning attached to them – meaning which is reflected in the meaning of *misled*; there is no meaning at all, let alone relevant meaning, attached to *misle*.

Syntax and semantics are very tightly tied together; the difference between *The cat ate the snake* and *The snake ate the cat* is a syntactic difference which has effects on the semantic interpretation of the sentence. Sentences are all about building up coherent messages from meaningful elements whose relationship to each other has to be made explicit. Verbs are central in relating elements to each other.

Pragmatics always takes some kind of linguistic structure and deals with the way in which that structure becomes interpreted in context, and why it might mean more than we would want to attribute to the meaning of the element itself. For example, *water* might mean something we could gloss as 'H_2O', but if a desperate man comes up to you in the middle of the Sahara Desert and gasps 'Water!', you will interpret that as meaning more than just 'H_2O'.

In the final analysis, anything you say will have a phonetic aspect, a phonological aspect, a morphological aspect, a syntactic aspect, a semantic aspect and a pragmatic aspect, even if it is something as simple as *Nuts!*

8.5 Where to go?

If you know some phonetics, some phonology, some morphology, some syntax and so on, how can you use it? Where does it all take you?

One obvious thing to say is that in a course such as the one you have undertaken, the amount of information about these topics that you can be introduced to is very limited. There is a lot more to learn about each of these areas as subjects in their own right. Some people find a career in trying to increase the depth of our knowledge about these areas. However, we will move on and look at other areas where linguistics has a role to play.

We have seen that as linguists we can be realists or instrumentalists. But there is a more specific question as to how the brain copes with language. How do we store linguistic knowledge, and how do we access it? For example, is there a word *prefamularity*? I would guess that you have answered with a negative very quickly, but how can you tell? You might have a vocabulary of some 60,000 words, so if you checked ten of those words every second it would take you over one-and-a-half hours to exhaust them, so how are you so sure so quickly you don't know *prefamularity*?

CONTROVERSY: How many words do you know?

The figure of 60,000 words in a vocabulary is a fairly standard estimate, but is based on some rather dangerous assumptions. There are estimates of half that and estimates of twice that. Partly it depends on what you count as a word (word-forms or lexemes? How many words are there in *brain child*?), partly it depends on what you mean by 'know' a word: is it enough to recognise it vaguely or do you have to be able to use it in your everyday conversation? So if we use the word *jeroboam*, do you 'know' it if you know what kind of thing it is or do you only 'know' the word if you know what a *jeroboam* is made of and how much it contains and what it contains? Many language teachers do not count words, but word families, whereby *book, bookish, book-learning, bookshop* and *textbook* are all part of the same **WORD FAMILY**. The puzzle of how you access all these words still remains, whatever number you come up with, but there are very different ideas about precisely what the number of items you remember might be.

Not only do we want to know how you store all this material, we want to know how you produce sentences in real time, apparently without effort, in which you recall all the words, put them together according to all the rules of phonology and morphology and syntax, and choose precisely the right ones to give the meaning you want to express (or correspondingly, how you understand sentences produced in this manner by someone else). In other words, as well as questions about storage there are questions about processing linguistic data. If we knew all of this (and we have only the first inklings), then we could work out how we learn language as children, and what goes wrong when the brain is damaged and language is affected. All of this is dealt with under the heading of **PSYCHOLINGUISTICS**.

If you hear someone speaking your first language you may be able to tell where they come from, how old they are, and what social class they are. If you listen for long enough you may be able to tell a doctor from an engineer. If you just read a transcript of someone's utterance, you might be able to decide whether it had been said by a man or a woman. In other words, the language you use tells other members of your speech community a lot about your social position in society. There is plenty of evidence that we find this feature of language a very important one: we define our own in-group in terms of the way we speak, and we mock people who do not speak like us. To a certain extent we also manipulate the picture we present of ourselves by adapting our language, so that we do not talk to our grandmothers in the same way as we talk to our partners, and we speak differently again when interviewed for the television cameras.

In most places in the world, people do not just manipulate a single language to deal with those around them, they use two or more languages. Sometimes states get involved in determining what language will be used for specific purposes such as higher education or for use in parliament. Some religions use a specific language for their meetings and ceremonies. All this interaction between language and the society in which the language is used is studied under the heading of **SOCIOLINGUISTICS**.

There are many ways of applying linguistic knowledge to real-life situations. When people talk about '**APPLIED LINGUISTICS**' they are normally talking about the overt knowledge that underlies successful language teaching: the description of language, ways of teaching the relevant patterns and items, ways of introducing a variety of tasks into the language classroom, and so on. But there are also other applications of linguists.

One of these is SPEECH AND LANGUAGE THERAPY, where overt intervention from skilled professionals is used to correct speech defects arising from physical or psychological problems such as treating stammers or retraining speech after stroke damage to the brain.

Another is FORENSIC LINGUISTICS, where linguistics is used in the service of the law. This may involve matters as disparate as trying to decide whether a particular document (whose authorship is in doubt) was written by a person who has written another document whose authorship is known, saying whether voices on different tape recordings belong to the same person or not, saying whether a recording has been tampered with so that words have been added or excised, or determining where a speaker on a recording comes from. All of these things involve very specialised knowledge, but start from linguistic analysis of some kind.

Another application of linguistics, specifically of sociolinguistics, is LANGUAGE PLAN-NING, when the state makes policies concerning the way in which language will be used in government or in the country more widely. The adoption of English as an official language in post-colonial India and South Africa, the adoption of Hebrew in Israel, have been matters of overt planning and policy decisions. The status of minority languages and sign languages for the deaf are often matters of policy – questions such as whether these languages can be used in education, in the legal system, in parliament, in the broadcast media. Bad policy can lead to the relevant groups feeling marginalised in or estranged from the state in which they live.

Yet another application of linguistics is in LEXICOGRAPHY, the writing of dictionaries. Although they require skills in writing definitions that are not derived specifically from linguistic principles, dictionaries are meta-linguistic constructs, and a training in linguistics is often invaluable in helping lexicographers think about the structure of the dictionary and the type of information a dictionary needs to include.

Finally, all the questions we have looked at so far have dealt with language at a given point in time (usually right now). But languages change through time. Just as Latin changed and turned into French, Italian, Spanish, Portuguese and Romanian so English is likely to change over time and turn into a new set of mutually incomprehensible languages. Some might say that this has already happened.

When languages change, the particular features that change usually seem fairly random, but the paths of change that are followed can be seen recurring from language to language and from period to period. We might not be able to predict what the next word to mean 'really good' will be, but we can predict that it will change relatively soon. We cannot predict whether any language that has a sequence of vowel + [t] + vowel in words will change; but if it does, a change to vowel + [d] + vowel seems a very likely change, while a change to vowel + [p] + vowel seems very unlikely. We know that very often languages which have a word like *not* and then a verb change to add something to strengthen the *not* (perhaps something equivalent to *not never* VERB) and then tend to lose the original *not* (so that we end up with *never* VERB).

Part of the fascination of studying the history of languages is that it gives an insight into the way in which people learn and use their languages, and how they perceive the patterns in their languages.

8.6 Envoi

Even the information presented in this chapter has done no more than scratch the surface of the kinds of areas that a sound knowledge of linguistics can help with. A knowledge of linguistics can be useful in areas as disparate as anthropology, computer science, literary studies, philosophy, psychology and sociology. A knowledge of linguistics can facilitate foreign language learning (and foreign language learning can make it easier to appreciate some of the problems that are faced by linguistics). Perhaps most of all, a knowledge of linguistics can help you appreciate just how difficult using language must be, and therefore how much we all achieve when we learn our first language. So whether you are watching your own (or other people's) children acquire their first language, watching children learning to read and write, watching stroke patients struggle with the difficulties that language suddenly puts in their way, or teaching yourself better literacy skills, linguistics can help.

Enjoy the new power that linguistics gives you.

 Terms introduced in this chapter

Applied linguistics	Prescription
Corpus	Psycholinguistics
Description	Realism
Forensic linguistics	Sociolinguistics
Instrumentalism	Speech and language therapy
Language planning	Word family
Lexicography	

References and further reading

There are many textbooks available on different aspects of linguistics. On corpus linguistics, see Lindquist (2009), on historical linguistics, see Campbell (2004), on psycholinguistics, see Aitchison (1992), on sociolinguistics, see Holmes (2008). On field linguistics read Dixon (2011).

On sentence (9), see McCawley (1971). On French adjectives see Royle & Valois (2010) and works cited there.

Appendix A

Glossary

Ablative   Ablative is the name of a CASE meaning 'moving away from' or just 'from', or a semantic relationship indicating motion away from.

Ablaut   Ablaut (also called apophony) is the marking of certain morphological relationships by an alternation in vowel sound: the vowel change in *sing, sang, sung*, which marks the infinitive, the past tense and the past participle, is a case of Ablaut.

Absolute universal   An absolute universal is something that is true of all languages.

Absolutive   Absolutive is the name given to the CASE used for the subject of an intransitive verb and the object of a transitive verb in a language which shows ergative case marking.

Accusative   Accusative is the name given to the CASE used for the object of a transitive verb in a language which shows nominative case marking.

Active   In an active sentence the agent is used as the subject of the verb (contrast PASSIVE). *Her parents saw the girl* is an example of an active sentence.

Active articulator   The active articulator is that part of the vocal tract which moves in order to produce a particular sound. Active articulators are attached to the lower jaw.

Adjective   An adjective is a word like *fruitful* which can typically be used both to modify a noun (*a fruitful relationship*) and in predicative position (*Their relationship was very fruitful*), can be submodified by *so* and *very*, and so on.

Adjective phrase   An adjective phrase is a phrase which has an adjective as its HEAD or main word.

Adjunct   Adjunct is another name for an ADVERBIAL.

Adposition   Adposition is a cover term which includes both PREPOSITIONS and POSTPOSITIONS.

Adverb   An adverb is a word like *fully*, which is typically used to modify a verb (*He answered the question fully*) or an adjective (*She is fully awake*). In English, many adverbs have an *-ly* suffix.

Adverb phrase   An adverb phrase is a phrase which has an adverb as its HEAD or main word.

Adverbial   (also adjunct) Any unit which functions as an ADVERB in a sentence is an adverbial.

Affix   An affix is an OBLIGATORILY BOUND MORPH attached to a BASE.

Affricate   An affricate is a consonant that has two phases: first a stop phase, and then a fricative phrase, where the stop and the fricative are HOMORGANIC.

Agreement   Two words agree when they share morphological marking for some category, or when one of them imposes a marking on the other.

Allative   Allative is the name of a CASE meaning 'moving towards' or just 'to', or a semantic relationship indicating motion towards.

Allomorph   An allomorph is a conditioned variant of a MORPHEME.

Allophone   An allophone is a conditioned variant of a PHONEME.

Alveolar   A consonant is said to be alveolar if it is articulated with the tongue touching or close to the ALVEOLAR RIDGE.

Alveolar ridge   (also teeth ridge) The alveolar ridge is the hard, bony structure into which the upper incisor teeth are set, which can be felt immediately behind the top teeth.

Ambisyllabic   A consonant is ambisyllabic if it is analysed as belonging to the two syllables on either side of it simultaneously.

Amplitude   The amplitude of a wave is the distance it moves away from its baseline. With sound waves this corresponds to perceived loudness.

Anaphoric   A PRONOUN shows anaphoric reference if it refers to some entity mentioned earlier in the text (contrast CATAPHORIC).

Antecedent   The antecedent of the pronoun is the entity referred to in the text to which the pronoun refers. In 'The King of the Scots vowed that he would hold back the English', *the King of the Scots* is the antecedent for the pronoun *he*.

Apical   An apical consonant is one produced using the TIP of the tongue.

Apophony   see ABLAUT.

Applied linguistics   'Applied linguistics' normally means language teaching, but can be used more widely to refer to any practical application of linguistic knowledge.

Approximant   (also frictionless continuant, semivowel, glide) An approximant is a consonant articulated with the articulators so far apart that there is no friction between them.

Arbitrary   It is generally accepted in modern linguistics that in most cases the relationship between the form of a word and its meaning is arbitrary, that there is no particular reason why *house* (rather than, perhaps, *casa* or *starp*) should mean 'house'.

Argument   An argument of a VERB is a piece of information which obligatorily accompanies the verb.

Article   Articles are a word-class containing words such as *the* (the definite article) and *a/an* (the indefinite article). They are a sub-class of DETERMINER.

Arytenoid cartilage   The arytenoid cartilages allow the opening and closing of the vocal folds.

Aspect   Aspect is the morphological marking of information on the internal temporal make-up of the action of the verb (e.g. whether it is on-going, completed, habitual, etc.)

Assimilation   Assimilation is making two sounds more similar to each other so that they are easier to pronounce together.

Association lines   Association lines are lines drawn by the analyst to show the link between TONES and TONE BEARING UNITS.

Attributive   A modifier which appears immediately before a noun is in attributive position.

Back   (1) A back vowel is one articulated with the back of the tongue in proximity to the VELUM. (2) The back of the tongue is that part of the tongue which lies opposite the VELUM when at rest.

Bahuvrihi compound   (also possessive compound) A bahuvrihi compound is a type of EXOCENTRIC COMPOUND which superficially denotes something which the entity actually denoted by the compound has or owns. For example, *greenback* is a bahuvrihi compound meaning 'US dollar'.

Base   A base is some word or part of a word to which an AFFIX can be added.

Bilabial   A bilabial sound is one made with both lips.

Bimorphemic   A MORPHOLOGICALLY COMPLEX word which contains precisely two morphological elements may be termed bimorphemic. Examples are *un·sound* and *kill·er*.

Binarity   Binarity is a feature of systems in which there are precisely two choices at any point in the system: on and off, + and -, left or right, etc.

Blade   The blade of the tongue is the part of the tongue which, when at rest, is immediately under the ALVEOLAR RIDGE.

Bound variant   A bound variant of a unit is a variant which occurs only in a particular environment. See ALLOMORPH, ALLOPHONE.

Broad transcription   A broad transcription is one that includes relatively little phonetic detail, and uses relatively simple symbols.

Bronchus (pl. bronchi)   The bronchi are the air passages that lead from the TRACHEA to the lungs.

Case   Case is morphological marking on elements of the noun phrase to indicate the relationship between the noun phrase and other elements in the sentence (e.g. the verb, prepositions, other noun phrases).

Cataphoric   A PRONOUN shows cataphoric reference if it refers to some entity mentioned later in the text (contrast ANAPHORIC).

Causative   (1) adj. A causative verb is one which denotes causation.
(2) noun. A causative is something which marks causation in a sentence.

Causativity   Causativity is the system for marking causation in a language, or the abstract quality of being causative.

Central   A central vowel is a vowel articulated between a front vowel and a back vowel, with the tongue rising towards the transition point between the hard and the soft palates.

Circumfix   A circumfix is an AFFIX made up of two parts, one of which appears before the BASE and the other of which appears after the base.

Citation form   The citation form of a LEXEME is the form in which the lexeme is typically mentioned or listed in printed dictionaries. For example, the citation form of a French verb is the infinitive (e.g. *aimer*) while the citation form of a Latin verb is the first person singular of the present tense (e.g. *amo*).

Clause   A clause is a sentence-like structure which is a part of a larger sentence.

Close   A close vowel is a vowel pronounced with the tongue very close to the roof of the mouth.

Closed   A closed syllable is one which ends in one or more consonants.

Close-mid   A close-mid vowel is one pronounced with a vowel height between close and mid, as for example, the French vowel [e] in *été*.

Cluster   A cluster of consonants is a sequence of consonants within the same syllable.

Co-compound   (also coordinative compound, dvandva) A co-compound is a compound like *Alsace-Lorraine* where the two elements are of equivalent standing in the construction.

Coda   The coda of a SYLLABLE is made up those consonants which occur after the vowel in the syllable.

Cognate   Two words from closely related languages are cognate if they have arisen historically from the same source. *Hund* 'dog' in German and *hound* 'hunting dog' in English are cognate words, as are English *starve* and German *sterben* 'to die'.

Cohyponym   Two words are cohyponyms if they share the same superordinate term: *samba* and *waltz* are cohyponyms of *dance*.

Collocation   A collocation is a set of two or more words that regularly occur together in texts.

Command   A command is an utterance which gives an order; it is usually, but not always, of IMPERATIVE form.

Comment   see RHEME.

Complementary distribution   Two items are in complementary distribution if they are mutually exclusive in their distribution.

Complementary terms   Two terms are complementary within a domain if the negation of one implies the assertion of the other and vice versa.

Complementation   Complementation deals with the grammatical patterns that individual verbs carry with them. For example, both *hear* and *audit* allow a noun complement (*hear something, audit something*), but only *hear* allows a *that*-clause (*hear that she is teaching the German class*).

Complementiser   A complementiser is a word which introduces a clause, e.g. *that* in *I know that you are in there*.

Complementiser phrase   A complementiser phrase is a construction which has a complementiser as its HEAD or main word.

Complex wave   A complex wave is a WAVE corresponding to a sound comprised of TONES (1) of different pitches.

Componential analysis   Componential analysis is a semantic analysis of words which uses semantic features to specify the meanings of the word concerned.

Composition   (also compounding) Composition is the formation of compounds.

Compound (word)   A compound is a LEXEME whose immediate constituents are also lexemes.

Compounding   see COMPOSITION.

Conditioning factor   A conditioning factor is something that determines which of a number of forms in COMPLEMENTARY DISTRIBUTION will be found in a particular word. For example, the regular past tense marker -ed is pronounced /ɪd/ only when /t/ or /d/ immediately precedes, so the preceding alveolar plosive is the conditioning factor.

Conjunction   A conjunction is a word which joins together elements of sentences. There are two kinds, SUBORDINATING and COORDINATING.

Connotation   A connotation is an emotive or stylistic signification of a word, over and above its DENOTATION.

Consonant   A consonant is a sound which, in a given language, acts like the majority of CONTOIDS in that language.

Constative   A constative or constative verb merely asserts that something is occurring rather than being itself part of the event (contrast PERFORMATIVE).

Constituent   A constituent is a part of a unit which acts as a smaller unit inside a larger piece.

Constriction   When the ACTIVE ARTICULATOR comes close to the PASSIVE ARTICULATOR in the articulation of a sound, it provides a constriction between the two by which the smooth flow of air is interrupted.

Contextual inflection   Contextual inflection is INFLECTION which is determined by some other element in the linguistic environment, for example, in languages where determiners agree with their nouns for number, the inflection on the determiner is contextual.

Contoid   A contoid is a speech sound produced with some interruption to the free flow of air through the vocal tract (contrast VOCOID).

Contrast   Two elements contrast if replacing one of them with the other changes the message.

Convention   Any transcription is made up of a text and the conventions for interpreting that text. These include such things as [uː] usually indicates a slightly diphthongised vowel in Australian English, and that [p] is aspirated in various positions in the English word.

Conventional implicature   Conventional implicatures are things that can be deduced on the basis of the use of a particular word or phrase. The difference between *I saw it and ran away* and *I saw it but ran away* is that any notion of causation between the two parts of the sentence is overruled by the *but*, which implies that there is a contrast between the seeing and the running away.

Conversational implicature   Conversational implicatures are implications that are drawn on the basis of what is said and the application of Grice's cooperative principle: *Were you born in a barn?* may be understood by conversational implicature as meaning that you should close the door.

Converse terms   Converse terms are opposites in the sense that they denote the same reality, but view it from a different angle. *Buy* and *sell* are converse terms; they differ in that the focus is on the purchaser in the one case and on the person from whom something is purchased in the other, but the same transaction can be viewed from either angle.

Conversion   (also zero-derivation) This is the change of word-class of a particular form without any concomitant change of form such as AFFIXATION or APOPHONY. The change between *empty* and *to empty* and *an empty* illustrates conversion.

Cooperative principle   This is a principle, set out by H.P. Grice as a series of MAXIMS, which says that participants in a conversation generally attempt to cooperate, e.g. by telling the truth.

Coordinating conjunction Coordinating conjunctions are those which link items of equal status and function: in English they are *and*, *or* and *but*.

Copula A copula or copular verb is a verb which links the subject with the subject complement: the most typical copula is the verb *to be*, although there are others such as *become*, *grow* (e.g. *big*), *look* (e.g. *pretty*) and so on.

Corpus (pl. corpora) A corpus is a collection of texts put together in a format which allows it to be searched by computer for linguistic purposes.

Countable A noun is used as countable if it can be used in its plural form with numbers (e.g. *two chairs*), and if it can take the determiner *many* rather than *much* (*many chairs*, **much chair*). See also UNCOUNTABLE.

Cricoid cartilage The cricoid cartilage is the ring of cartilage shaped like a signet-ring which is found at the top of the TRACHEA.

Dative Dative is the CASE which marks the person to whom something is given.

Declarative A sentence of declarative form is one which one would expect, other things being equal, to make a statement.

Defective distribution A particular element has a defective distribution if it is not found in some particular position in which other members of the same class regularly occur, and there is no particular reason for this unusual behaviour.

Definite A noun phrase is definite if it can be used to pick out a single individual, typically because it contains a name or, in English, begins with the definite article, *the*.

Deixis /daɪksɪs/ The system whereby reference to the here and now is embodied in language.

Denotation (1) The system whereby words represent real-world entities, actions or states, so that *dog* denotes any member of the set of canine quadrupeds, for example. (2) What a particular word denotes (so that the denotation of *dog* is a member of the set of canine quadrupeds).

Denote A word denotes a particular set of real-world entities, so that *university* can be used to denote any one of a set of appropriately designated tertiary institutions.

Dental A dental sound is one produced by putting the tongue in close proximity to the (front incisor) teeth.

Dependent A dependent is something that modifies a HEAD.

Dependent-marking There is dependent-marking in a particular construction when the morphological material which indicates the nature of the construction is on the DEPENDENT (contrast HEAD-MARKING).

Derivation Derivation is the production of new LEXEMES by morphological means (contrast INFLECTION).

Derivative A derivative is a word produced by DERIVATION.

Description Linguistics provides a description of some set of language data, telling you what actually occurs and is possible (contrast PRESCRIPTION).

Determinative compound A determinative compound is one in which one element (the HEAD) is a superordinate term for the compound as a whole, and the other element identifies the particular subtype involved. For instance, a windmill is a kind of mill, and *wind* tells us which kind of mill.

Determiner Determiners are a word-class which include ARTICLES, demonstratives and possessive PRONOUNS among other things.

Determiner phrase A determiner phrase is a phrase which has a determiner as its HEAD or main word.

Diaphragm The diaphragm is a muscle shaped like an inverted bowl, which separates the thorax from the abdomen. Contraction of the diaphragm causes air to be drawn into the lungs.

Diphthong   A diphthong is a vowel sound in which the tongue moves from one vowel target to another within a single SYLLABLE. The vowels in the English words *pie* and *pay* are diphthongs when pronounced with an RP accent.

Direct object   The direct object of a verb is the phrase which denotes the entity affected by the action of the verb, e.g. *my hard disk* in *The virus wiped my hard disk*.

Direct speech act   A speech act whose form reflects in a straightforward way its illocutionary force.

Distal   A distal form refers to objects which are away from the speaker (sometimes, more specifically, close to the hearer). This includes words like *that, there* (contrast PROXIMAL).

Distinctive feature   A distinctive feature is the smallest element of a linguist's analysis of a set of sounds or meaning relationships.

Ditransitive   (also trivalent). A ditransitive verb is one which takes two objects, as, for example, *give*, in *Kim gave the boy the book* where *the boy* is one object (the indirect object) and *the book* is another (the direct object).

Divalent   see TRANSITIVE.

Dominance   Node X dominates node Y in a tree if node X lies between node Y and the root of the tree. It immediately dominates node Y if there are no intervening nodes.

Dorsal   A dorsal sound is one articulated with the BACK of the tongue.

Double articulation   A consonant has a double articulation when it has two constrictions of equal weight. Such a consonant is [w], which has a labial and a velar constriction.

Dual   A dual is a particular morphological marker which indicates that precisely two entities are involved.

Durative   A durative is a morphological marker which shows that a verb shows an action persisting in time.

Elsewhere   The word 'elsewhere' is used in rules to say where the default or 'elsewhere variant' occurs.

Endocentric compound   An endocentric compound is one where the compound is a hyponym of one of its own elements (the HEAD element). A blackboard is a type of board, so *blackboard* is an endocentric compound.

Entailment   An entailment is a link between two propositions such that if the first is true the second must necessarily be true.

Environment bar   The environment bar is the marking in a rule formulation (usually shown by an underscoring) of the environment in which the rule applies. In a rule of the form A → B / C ___ D the environment bar between C and D indicates that the rule applies only when A occurs between C and D.

Ergative   Ergative is the name given to the case which is used to mark the subject of a transitive verb in languages where the subject of an intransitive verb and the direct object of a transitive verb are marked the same way (see ABSOLUTIVE).

Established word   An established word is one which is familiar to speakers of a particular speech community; it may occur in dictionaries, for instance.

Exclusive   First person plural exclusive pronouns denote a group made up of the speaker and at least one other third person, but not including the hearer (contrast INCLUSIVE).

Exocentric compound   An exocentric compound is a compound which is not a HYPONYM of its HEAD (contrast ENDOCENTRIC COMPOUND).

Exophoric   An exophoric pronoun is one which refers to an entity which is not mentioned in the text.

Expiration   Expiration is breathing out.

Face   Face is made up of POSITIVE FACE and NEGATIVE FACE. Any utterance which threatens someone's face threatens their self-perceived social standing and prestige in some way.

Feature   see DISTINCTIVE FEATURE.

Felicity condition   (also happiness condition). A condition which must be met before a SPEECH ACT can be successful.

First person   The first person is the speaker. The first person plural is a group of two or more people including the speaker.

Flap   A flap is a consonant which is pronounced with the active articulator briefly hitting the passive articulator in the course of the articulation.

Floating tone   A floating TONE (2)associated with a syllable is one which is not audible on that syllable, but is heard on an adjacent syllable when there is one.

Folk etymology   (also popular etymology). The supposed but factually incorrect origin of words, particularly as shown by the reanalysis of an unfamiliar word into more familiar MORPHS.

Foot   A foot is a phonological unit made up of a stressed syllable and associated unstressed syllables.

Forensic linguistics   Forensic linguistics is concerned with the application of linguistic knowledge to the resolution of problems in the service of the law.

Formant   A formant is a band of energy which can be seen on a SPECTROGRAM when a SONORANT is pronounced.

Free variation   Two elements are in free variation where either can be replaced by the other in any utterance without any change to the message.

Frequentative   A frequentative form marks something that recurs frequently or repeatedly.

Fricative   A fricative is a consonant articulated with the ACTIVE ARTICULATOR so close to the PASSIVE ARTICULATOR that the air-flow is made turbulent.

Front   (1) A front vowel is one articulated with the front of the tongue against the HARD PALATE. (2) The front of the tongue is that part of the tongue which lies opposite the HARD PALATE when at rest.

Fundamental frequency   The fundamental frequency of any part of an utterance is the frequency with which the VOCAL FOLDS vibrate.

Geminate   A geminate consonant is a consonant with extended duration of the articulation such that it might be perceived as a sequence of two identical consonants.

Gender   Gender is a classification of nouns in some languages. In a language like English, gender is determined largely by real-world sex: the difference between calling a dog *he* and calling it *she* depends on knowing its sex. But in many languages, nouns are assigned to gender sets for other reasons – sometimes phonological, sometimes semantic, and the gender assignment may look relatively arbitrary. For instance, the word meaning 'moon' is masculine in German, but feminine in French. Some linguists prefer the term 'noun class', which has wider application, to 'gender'.

Genitive   Genitive is the name of the case used to mark, among other things, possession. In the Latin phrase *nōmen rēgis* 'the name of the king' the word *rēgis* 'of the king' is in the genitive case.

Given (information)   Given information is information which is shared between the speaker and addressee, frequently because it is present in the preceding text.

Gloss   A gloss is a word-by-word (or morpheme-by-morpheme) translation of foreign language data in order to show the structure of the foreign language.

Glottal stop   A glottal stop is a consonant made by closing the vocal folds together so as to interrupt the airflow coming from the lungs.

Glottalisation   (also laryngealisation) Glottalisation is a narrowing or closing of the GLOTTIS at the same time as the production of another sound.

Glottis   The glottis is the space between the vocal folds, which is open for quiet breathing, in VIBRATION when there is voicing, and closed for a GLOTTAL STOP.

Gradable antonym   Two words are gradable antonyms if they designate end-points of some scale so that each can be defined as the negation of the other: *deep* and *shallow*, *long* and *short* are examples.

Grapheme   The spelling equivalent of the PHONEME in the spoken language. A grapheme is a contrastive unit of the written language. To extend the terminology, <H> and <h> are allographs of the same grapheme.

Gricean principles   Gricean principles or maxims are principles of cooperation in interaction first enunciated by Paul Grice.

Grundbedeutung   'Basic meaning': the central and irreducible SENSE of a word or other meaningful item.

Happiness condition   see FELICITY CONDITION.

Head   The head of a construction is the major element in the construction which typically (where appropriate) can stand for the construction as a whole, is a superordinate for the construction as a whole, is obligatory in the construction, and characterises the construction (e.g. in terms of word-class).

Head-marking   There is head-marking in a particular construction when the morphological material which indicates the nature of the construction is on the HEAD (contrast DEPENDENT-MARKING).

Heavy syllable   A syllable which contains either a long vowel or a short vowel and a coda consonant is said to be heavy in English; in each case the syllable is bimoraic.

Homonym   Two items are homonyms if they have the same form but not the same meaning. For instance, *duck* 'aquatic bird' and *duck* 'lower one's head quickly' or *flee* and *flea* are pairs of homonyms.

Homonymy   The relationship holding between two HOMONYMS.

Homophone   Any two items that sound the same are homophones.

Homorganic   Two sounds are homorganic if they are pronounced in the same place of articulation.

Hypernym, hyperonym   see SUPERORDINATE.

Hyponym   A hyponym is a word which denotes a sub-type of its superordinate term. For example, *cat* and *dog* are hyponyms of *animal* (and *animal* is the SUPERORDINATE term).

Hyponymy   The relationship holding between a HYPONYM and its SUPERORDINATE.

Iconic   Any form which in some ways reflects the meaning of the form is said to be iconic. The reflection is often very abstract, even as vague as more form corresponding to more meaning.

Illocutionary force   The illocutionary force of an utterance is the way it is interpreted as opposed to the literal meaning of the words and constructions within it. So the illocutionary force of *It's hot in here* may not be a statement about the temperature in a particular place, but an instruction to open the window.

Immediate dominance   see DOMINANCE.

Imperative   A sentence of imperative form is one which one would expect, other things being equal, to act as a command.

Inclusive   First person plural inclusive pronouns denote a group made up of the speaker and the listener and possibly some other people (contrast EXCLUSIVE).

Indirect object   The indirect object of the verb is a noun phrase with no prepositional marking which denotes the person for whose benefit or to whom the subject of the verb carries out the action of the verb on the direct object. In *I gave Billy six dollars*, the indirect object is *Billy*.

Indirect speech act   A speech act which does not say directly what is intended, but leaves the ILLOCUTIONARY FORCE of the speech act to be deduced by the listener.

Inference   An inference is anything which is not said overtly but which can be deduced from what is said.

Infix   An infix is an affix which is attached inside its base, specifically in such a way as to split a single morph.

Inflection   (1) Inflection is the production of new WORD-FORMS of given LEXEMES by morphological means (contrast DERIVATION). (2) Inflection may also be the morphological material used to do this. (3) In X-bar grammar I(nflection) is the name given to the node which used to be called S(entence). Its head is the tense marking on a verb.

Inflection phrase   An inflection phrase is another name for a sentence; it is a construction whose HEAD is the tense on the finite verb.

Inherent inflection   Inherent inflection is that part of inflection which is not determined by agreement.

Inspiration   Inspiration is breathing in.

Instrument   An instrument is something with which some action is performed. In *She opened the case with a hammer*, *a hammer* is the instrument. Where the instrument is indicated by specific morphology, that is termed instrument marking. For example, the *-er* in *(telephone) receiver* is an instrument marker. Where a language has a particular CASE for indicating instruments, this may be called the instrument(al) (case).

Instrumentalism   Instrumentalism is the philosophy that a linguistic description should be governed by criteria of economy and generality (contrast REALISM).

Intensity   The intensity of a sound is a measure of its perceived loudness.

Internal modification   Internal modification is any non-additive change in the phonological make-up of a word which signals some morphological information. For instance, the difference between *foot* and *feet* is a case of internal modification.

Interrogative   A sentence of interrogative form is one which one would expect, other things being equal, to ask a question.

Intervocalic   A consonant is intervocalic if it occurs between vowels.

Intonation   Intonation is the melody of language.

Intransitive   An intransitive verb is one which has a subject but no direct object or subject complement. In *Lee laughed*, *laughed* is an intransitive verb.

Intransitive preposition   One possible analysis of a word like *down* in *They looked down* is that it is a preposition with no following DP, and so is intransitive, whereas the *down* in *They looked down the drain* the preposition has the expected following DP and is transitive.

Killer language   A killer language is the name given to a language which speakers regularly use in place of the minority language which they originally grew up speaking. When too many people stop speaking a minority language and start speaking the language of a larger group, the minority language 'dies'. The term 'killer language' elaborates on this metaphor, but the incoming language does not directly cause the death of the minority language.

Labial   A consonant which is articulated with the lips is labial.

Labial-palatal   A doubly-articulated consonant which is articulated both with the lips and at the hard palate is called labial-palatal. The sound [ɥ] at the beginning of the French word *huit* 'eight' is labial-palatal.

Labial-velar   A doubly-articulated consonant which is articulated both with the lips and at the velum is called labial-velar. The sound [w] at the beginning of the French word *oui* 'yes' is labial-velar.

Labialisation   Labialisation is lip-rounding added to any consonantal articulation.

Labio-dental   A labio-dental sound is articulated with the top incisors forming a constriction with the lower lip.

Laminal   A consonant is laminal if it is articulated with the BLADE of the tongue.

Language   (1) The facility which allows humans to communicate by a system of vocal (or signed) symbols. (2) A particular system of vocal or signed symbols viewed as an entity (e.g. *the French language*).

Language game   A language game is any way in which speakers play with the form of their language, either simply for fun, or in order to disguise their meaning.

Language planning   Language planning is the development of policy regarding language matters.

Laryngealisation   see GLOTTALISATION.

Larynx   (also Adam's apple, voice box) The larynx is the construction of cartilage hinged onto the top of the TRACHEA within which the VOCAL FOLDS are located.

Lateral   In the articulation of a lateral consonant, the air from the lungs flows out over one or both sides of the tongue.

Lexeme   If we say that *consume, consumes* and *consumed* are 'all the same word', we mean that they are all realisations of the same lexeme (contrast WORD-FORM).

Lexical gap   A lexical gap is a place where we might expect a word to exist, but none is current.

Lexicalisation   A morphological structure becomes lexicalised as its original structure becomes opaque to the user, either through changes in form or through changes in meaning.

Lexicography   Lexicography is the compiling of dictionaries.

Lexicon   (1) The mental dictionary presumed to be in every speaker's head; some model of that mental dictionary. (2) The words of a LANGUAGE.

Light syllable   A syllable which contains a short vowel with no following consonant is said to be light in English; the syllable contains only one MORA.

Linear precedence   A constituent structure TREE gives information on two things: DOMINANCE and linear precedence. Linear precedence is which branch of the tree precedes the other, corresponding to the order in which items are spoken in real time.

Linguistics   The scientific study of LANGUAGE.

Liquid   Liquid is a rather impressionistic term to cover all different kinds of 'r' and 'l' sounds.

Locutionary act   A locutionary act is the act of uttering some series of sounds which can be perceived as words and sentences and which has an ILLOCUTIONARY FORCE.

Lung   The lungs are the organs from which air for speaking is expelled.

Main verb   A main verb is a verb which contains lexical information as well as grammatical information. In *Lee may be being forced to act against our interests, force* is the main verb, and *may be being* are all auxiliary verbs. Where a sentence has multiple clauses, the main verb is the verb in the matrix sentence.

Mass   see UNCOUNTABLE.

Maxim   One of the subparts of Grice's COOPERATIVE PRINCIPLE.

Median   A median consonant is one which is articulated with the air from the lungs flowing over the centre of the tongue, and not over the sides of the tongue (contrast LATERAL).

Meronym   A word denoting some part of a whole item.

Meronymy   A classification in terms of parts of wholes.

Metaphor   A figure of speech in which one names a referent by naming something which the referent is supposed to resemble.

Metonymy   A figure of speech in which one refers to something by naming something closely associated with the referent.

Mid   A mid vowel is one that is articulated with the tongue height approximately half-way between close (high) and open (low).

Middle voice   This is a construction which allows the agent of an action to remain unspecified without being passive in form (the way in which specifying the agent is usually avoided). In English, we have examples like *This car drives well*, where someone must drive the car, but we are not told who that is.

Minimal pair   A minimal pair is provided by two parallel examples which differ only in one element but which provide distinct messages (which CONTRAST). So *sap* and *tap* provide a minimal pair indicating that the two initial consonants contrast, *employer* and *employee* provide a minimal pair showing that the two suffixes contrast, and *I saw him* and *You saw him* provide a minimal pair showing that the two subject pronouns contrast. On the other hand, *She saw Mike and I* and *She saw Mike and me* do not provide a minimal pair, because the message is the same in both instances.

Monomorphemic   (also simple) A monomorphemic word is one which contains only one morpheme, and therefore cannot be analysed morphologically: *far* and *elephant* are monomorphemic words of English.

Monophthong   A monophthong is a vowel sound which maintains its quality or tongue position and lip position throughout its duration.

Monosemy   The property or principle of having a single meaning.

Monovalent   see INTRANSITIVE.

Mora   A phonological unit intermediate in length between a phoneme and a syllable.

Morph   A recurrent element of a word-form with constant form and constant meaning.

Morpheme   An abstract element of linguistic analysis represented at the concrete level by one MORPH or by several morphs in COMPLEMENTARY DISTRIBUTION.

Morphologically complex   A word which is made up of more than one morphological element and is thus morphologically analysable is said to be morphologically complex. Examples include *windmill*, *unlikely*, *photographic*, *hatefulness*.

Morphologically simple   see MONOMORPHEMIC.

Morphology   (1) The study of the relationship between the formal make-up of words and their meaning. (2) The elements of words in which form is related to meaning.

Morphophonemic alternation   Two PHONEMES are in morphophonemic alternation if each appears in a different ALLOMORPH of the same MORPHEME in corresponding positions. For example, in *house* /haʊs/ and *house·s* /haʊzɪz/, /s/ and /z/ are in morphophonemic alternation.

Morphophonemics Morphophonemics is the study of the patterns of morphophonemic alternation found in a language.

Narrow transcription   A narrow transcription is one which provides more than the minimum amount of information to allow the transcription to be read unambiguously.

Nasal   A nasal is a sound pronounced with air flowing through the nose and not through the mouth.

Nasalisation   A sound is nasalised if the air from the lungs passes through the nose as well as through the mouth.

Natural class   A natural class of sounds is a group of sounds which behaves similarly in terms of some phonological process.

Near-close   A vowel sound which is near-close is pronounced with a tongue-height between close and close-mid, such as the RP English [ɪ].

Near-open   A vowel sound which is near-open is pronounced with a tongue-height between open and open-mid, such as the RP English [ʌ].

Negative face   To threaten someone's negative face implies putting a direct imposition on them so they are obliged to conform.

Neutralisation   Two elements are neutralised if they usually CONTRAST, but fail to contrast in a relevantly specified environment.

New (information)   New information is information which is not shared between speaker and addressee.

Node   A node in a TREE is a point at which two (or more) branches of the tree meet.

Noise   Noise is sound without periodic structure.

Nominative   Nominative is the name given to the CASE which marks both the subject of a transitive verb and the subject of an intransitive verb in languages which mark these differently from the object of a transitive verb.

Noun   A noun is word like *cat* which can typically be used to denote a discrete object in the real world, and which can be used in various functions, including in the subject and direct object of a verb.

Noun clause   A noun clause is a clause which fulfils the same role as a DP. In *That he finished his degree is surprising*, *that he finished his degree* is a noun clause, functioning as the subject of the verb, *is*.

Noun phrase   A noun phrase is a phrase which has a noun as its HEAD or main word.

Nucleus/nuclear syllable   (1) A stressed syllable in which there is concomitant change of pitch; the most prominent syllable in an intonational phrase. (2) The nucleus of a syllable. See PEAK.

Number   Number is a morphological system, usually marked on the noun or pronoun, but often also in agreement on the verb or adjective, which provides information on how many entities are involved. In English, the division is between singular (just one) and plural (more than one), but other languages may have a DUAL (precisely two) or a trial (precisely three).

Obligatorily bound morph   An obligatorily bound morph is a MORPH which can occur only when attached to another element, such as the *-ed* in *killed* or the *geo-* in *geography*.

Obligatory Contour Principle   The hypotheses that adjacent elements in any tier of description must be distinct (i.e. may not be identical).

Obstruent   Any plosive (or other stop), affricate or fricative is an obstruent (contrast SONORANT).

Onset   The onset of a SYLLABLE is made up of any consonant or consonants which occur before the vowel in the syllable.

Open   (1) A vowel is open if it is pronounced with the tongue as far from the roof of the mouth as possible, and with the widest opening of the vocal tract. (2) A syllable is open if it has no consonants in CODA-position.

Open-mid   An open-mid vowel is one pronounced with a tongue-height between OPEN and MID, as for example the standard Italian vowel /ɔ/ in *cuore* 'heart' /kwɔre/.

Palatal   A consonant (or vowel) is said to be palatal if the tongue forms a constriction with the hard PALATE in producing it.

Palatalised   A consonant is palatalised if the front of the tongue is raised towards the PALATE during its articulation, even though it is not primarily a palatal sound.

Palate (hard palate)   The palate, or hard palate, is the hard bony structure at the peak of the roof of the mouth.

Paradigm   (1) A paradigm is a set of contrasting elements, any one of which could be substituted for any other with a consequent change in meaning. (2) A morphological paradigm is a set of forms (usually WORD-FORMS of the same LEXEME) illustrating a particular pattern of morphological structure in a given language.

Parallel distribution   Two elements are in parallel distribution if each can occur in at least one identical environment as the other with a consequent change of meaning. A MINIMAL PAIR is proof of parallel distribution, and shows CONTRAST.

Parasynthesis   Parasynthesis occurs when two or more formal elements, usually not contiguous to each other in the word, are used together to mark a morphological category.

Paratone   A paratone is the intonational equivalent of a paragraph in writing.

Particle   A particle is a word-class made up of words which have a grammatical usage (i.e. they are not lexical in nature), and which typically are short and morphologically simple.

Passive   In a passive sentence, the undergoer of the action is used as the subject of the verb, and the agent is put in a grammatically subordinate position or omitted (contrast ACTIVE). *The girl was seen (by her parents)* is an example of a passive sentence.

Passive articulator   The passive articulator in the articulation of a consonant is the one which does not move, typically the articulator attached to the upper jaw.

Peak   The peak of a syllable is the most sonorous part of the syllable.

Performative   A performative (verb) is one whose felicitous utterance is itself the undertaking of the action it describes, e.g. *I now pronounce you man and wife.*

Periodic   A WAVE is periodic when its structure is regularly repeated.

Perlocutionary act   The effect, intended or not, of a speech act on a listener: saying *Come to my office immediately* may have the effect of making the listener come to the speaker's office (intended) or scaring the listener (possibly unintended).

Person   Person is a morphological category which marks who took part in a particular action: the first person (the speaker or some set of people including the speaker), the addressee(s) (second person), or some external party or parties to the discourse (the third person).

Pharyngeal   (also pharyngal). A pharyngeal consonant is pronounced with the tongue drawn back so as to cause a constriction with the back wall of the PHARYNX.

Pharyngealisation   A consonant is pharyngealised if the root of the tongue is drawn back towards the rear wall of the PHRAYNX during its articulation, even though it is not primarily a pharyngeal sound.

Pharynx   The pharynx is that part of the vocal tract between the vocal folds and uvula.

Phatic communion   Phatic communion is that function of language which establishes bonds between interlocutors, rather than transferring information.

Phonatory system   The phonatory system is that part of the vocal tract which causes phonation or voicing, that is, the part in the LARYNX.

Phone   A phone is a SPEECH SOUND.

Phoneme   A phoneme is a unit in the linguist's analysis of the contrastive sound elements in a language, constituted by a number of phonetically related phones which are in complementary distribution.

Phonemic transcription   A phonemic transcription is a transcription in which the units transcribed are PHONEMES.

Phonetic similarity   Two speech sounds are phonetically similar to the extent that they share phonetic characteristics.

Phonetic transcription   A phonetic transcription is any transcription which uses phonetic symbols (so that it may be a PHONEMIC TRANSCRIPTION), but also, more specifically, one which provides more phonetic detail than is given in a phonemic transcription. See also NARROW TRANSCRIPTION.

Phonetics   The study of speech sounds in their physical manifestation.

Phonology   The study of the patterning of speech sounds in a language.

Phonotactics   Phonotactics deals with the ways in which PHONEMES are concatenated within larger units.

Plosive   A plosive is a stop consonant in which air coming from the lungs, is blocked from entering the nasal passages, and where there is a brief complete blockage of the vocal tract in the utterance of the sound.

Polysemy   A linguistic element is said to be polysemous if it has two or more meanings.

Popular etymology   see FOLK ETYMOLOGY.

Positive face   If you threaten someone's positive face, you make it seem that the person is not really part of the group and does not share the needs of other members of the group, or that their ideas are not of interest.

Possessive compound   see BAHUVRIHI.

Possible word   A possible word is one which is not an existing word of the language, but which is perfectly grammatically constituted.

Post-alveolar   A post-alveolar sound is one in whose articulation the tongue approaches the roof of the mouth immediately behind the ALVEOLAR RIDGE.

Postmodifier   A postmodifier is any element which comes after the HEAD which it modifies. In 'proud of his daughter', *of his daughter* is a PP acting as a postmodifier to the head *proud*.

Postposition   A postposition is an **ADPOSITION** which follows its NP. In Japanese *Namida ga deta* 'tears NOM came.out = tears came to my eyes' the subject marker *ga* follows its NP, and is a postposition.

Postvocalic   A consonant is postvocalic if it occurs after a vowel.

Potentially free morph   A potentially free morph (often abbreviated to a *free morph*) is one which can occur on its own as a **WORD-FORM**.

Pragmatics   Pragmatics deals with the interpretation of language in context.

Predicator   The predicator in a sentence is the element which performs the function usually filled by a **VERB**, namely to create a clause and link the nominal arguments.

Prefix   A prefix is an **OBLIGATORILY BOUND MORPH** which is added before (to the left of) a **BASE**.

Premodifier   A premodifier is any element which comes before the **HEAD** which it modifies. In 'extremely proud', *extremely* is an adverb acting as a premodifier to the head *proud*.

Preposition   A preposition is an **ADPOSITION** which precedes its DP. In English 'In the garden', *in* precedes its DP *the garden*, and is a preposition (contrast **POSTPOSITION**).

Prepositional phrase   A prepositional phrase is a phrase which has a preposition as its **HEAD** or main word.

Prescription   If you prescribe about language you say what it should be like (contrast **DESCRIPTION**).

Presupposition   A sentence S presupposes X if X is true whether S is negated or not. For example *The Newcastle metro is very efficient* has as one of its presuppositions that there is a Newcastle metro.

Prevocalic   A consonant is prevocalic if it occurs before a vowel.

Primary articulation   The primary articulation of a consonant is the narrowest or strongest constriction in the articulation of the consonant.

Primary stress   Primary stress is the most important stress in a word.

Pro-sentence   A pro-sentence is an element such as *yes* which stand in place of a whole sentence.

Pronoun   A pronoun is an element such as *him*, *hers* or *those* which can stand in place of a noun phrase.

Proposition   The semantic content of a simple sentence.

Prototype   A prototype is a mental image of some category which has less or more typical members. A prototypical house may be different in Scotland and Zimbabwe, yet mansions and cottages are still types of house.

Proximal   A proximal form refers to objects which are close to the speaker. This includes words like *this*, *here* (contrast **DISTAL**).

Psycholinguistics   The study of the ways in which language is dealt with in the brain.

Qualifier   A qualifier is a post-modifier to a head noun. In *the man of the moment*, *of the moment* is the qualifier.

Question   A question is an utterance used to elicit information, usually, but not always, by means of an **INTERROGATIVE** form.

Radical   A radical sound is produced when the **ROOT** of the tongue is articulated against the back wall of the **PHARYNX**.

Realism   Realism is the philosophy that linguistic description should reflect the way in which the material is dealt with in the mind (contrast **INSTRUMENTALISM**).

Recursion   Recursion is the ability of a particular constituent type to occur within another constituent of the same type (NP within NP, IP within IP, for example).

Reduplicant   The reduplicant is that part of the word which is copied from the base in **REDUPLICATION**.

Reduplication   Reduplication is the repetition of material from the base of a word to produce some morphological effect. In Indonesian, *anak-anak* is the plural of *anak* 'child', a case of full reduplication.

Refer   What a REFERRING EXPRESSION does in order to pick out an entity.

Reference   The system whereby REFERRING EXPRESSIONS pick out real-world entities.

Referent   The entity picked out by a REFERRING EXPRESSION.

Referring expression   A referring expression picks out a particular real-world entity. For example, *Abraham Lincoln* picks out the former American president.

Reflexivity   A reflexive action is one which the subject of the verb carries out on him/her/itself: typically, things like brushing the teeth, shaving or stubbing one's toe. Reflexivity is the system of marking such phenomena in a given language.

Relative clause   A relative clause is a clause which modifies a noun. In *The woman who bought the ticket had a yellow purse*, *who bought the ticket* is the relative clause.

Relative pronoun   A word which introduces a relative clause, such as *who* in *The woman who paid was Lisa's mother*.

Resonance   Resonance is the phenomenon whereby a particular body responds to sounds at particular pitches with the effect of amplifying those pitches.

Retroflex   A sound is retroflex when it is articulated with the tongue tip curled back behind the ALVEOLAR RIDGE.

Rheme   The rheme of the sentence is what it says about the THEME.

Rhyme   The rhyme of the syllable is made up of the peak of the syllable and any following consonant(s). In the syllable /fʌnd/, the rhyme is /ʌnd/.

Root   (1) The root of a tree is the point of origin on the tree, from which all the branches spring. (2) The root of a word is what is left when all affixes have been removed. (3) The root of the tongue is the part of the tongue opposite the back wall of the PHARYNX.

Root-and-pattern   In root-and-pattern morphology, the root of a word is made up of a small number of consonants, while the vowels which are intermingled with these consonants provide other morphological information. The result is that both the root and the affixes are discontinuous.

Rounded   A vowel is said to be rounded if it is pronounced with the lips close to each other (and usually, with the corners of the lips drawn in).

RP   RP stands for Received Pronunciation, the standard pronunciation of the southern English of England.

Rule   A rule is a statement, usually presented in some notational shorthand, or an observed regularity of linguistic behaviour.

Second person   The second person in an interaction is the person addressed, hence the second person pronoun is *you*.

Secondary articulation   A secondary articulation is an articulation present during the pronunciation of a consonant which allows more airflow through the mouth than the concurrent PRIMARY ARTICULATION.

Secondary stress   Secondary stress is a level of stress less prominent than PRIMARY STRESS, but still associated with a rhythmic beat.

Semantico-syntactic feature   A feature such as [± Human] which has both syntactic and semantic value (semantic because it distinguishes people from other creatures, syntactic because it distinguishes entities of which one can ask *Who?* from those of which one should ask *What?*).

Semantics   The study of meaning.

Sense   The sense of a word or expression is its internal meaning, contrasted with its REFERENCE.

Sentence adverb   A sentence adverb is an adverb that modifies the whole proposition encapsulated in the sentence. In *Unfortunately, he did not arrive on time*, the whole thing means 'That he did not arrive on time was unfortunate', and *unfortunately* modifies the rest and is a sentence adverb.

Sine wave   A sine wave is a WAVE corresponding to a TONE (1) at a single pitch.

Sociolinguistics   Sociolinguistics is the study of the interaction between language and society.

Sonorant   A sonorant is any sound which is not an obstruent; nasals, lateral approximants, taps, trills, approximants and vowels are all sonorants.

Sonority   The sonority of a sound is its carrying power.

Spectrogram   A spectrogram presents a picture of the acoustic energy present in sounds, showing relative timing, pitch and INTENSITY.

Speech act   Speech acts are actions performed by using words.

Speech and language therapy   The application of linguistic and other kinds of knowledge to the resolution of pathological problems in language use.

Speech sound   A speech sound is a minimal element of an utterance.

Split ergativity   Split ergativity refers to the (common) situation where a language does not behave like a prototypical ergative language in terms of both its morphology and syntax, but has some features of a nominative-accusative language.

Spread   (1) (also unrounded) A vowel is said to be a spread vowel or to be pronounced with spread lips if the lips are not ROUNDED, and the corners of the lips remain as far from each other as possible given the vowel height. (2) A TONE is said to spread from one TONE BEARING UNIT to another when its phonetic exponent is copied onto an adjacent TBU.

Statement   A statement is the presentation of information, usually, but not always, in the form of a DECLARATIVE sentence.

Statistical universal   Something which is known to be true in most languages, but not in all.

Stem   A stem is the BASE to which an INFLECTIONAL affix is added. The word 'stem' is used by some authors to denote an obligatorily bound base.

Stop   A stop is a consonant sound which is articulated with a complete blockage of the oral tract.

Stress   Stress is an increase in prominence associated with variation in pitch, length and intensity, such as distinguishes *billow* [ˈbɪləʊ] from *below* [bɪˈləʊ].

Subject   Every declarative sentence is made up of a subject and a predicate which says something about it. Alternatively, we can define the subject as the DP immediately dominated by IP.

Subject complement   The ARGUMENT of a COPULAR verb which refers back to the subject of the sentence.

Subordinating conjunction   A subordinating conjunction attaches a clause inside a sentence, introducing a noun clause, relative clause or adverbial clause.

Substitution   Substitution of one item for another in a construction creates a PARADIGM in which the substitute elements share some quality.

Suffix   A suffix is an obligatorily bound morph which is added after (to the right of) its BASE.

Superordinate   (also hypernym, hyperonym) A word which has two or more HYPONYMS. *Dance* is a superordinate for *foxtrot, samba, waltz*, etc.

Syllabification   Syllabification is division into SYLLABLES.

Syllable   A syllable is a unit of sound structure made up of a sonorous peak and associated material in a way which differs from language to language.

Synaffix   A synaffix is a name given to two or more, usually discontinuous, pieces of form which together make up a single morpheme. The term PARASYNTHESIS is usually preferred.

Syncretism   Syncretism is the occurrence of the same form in different parts of the PARADIGM (e.g. *her* as either an accusative or a genitive pronoun).

Synecdoche   Synecdoche is a figure of speech in which an entity is named by something which is a part of it, as in *100 head* (meaning not just the head, but the whole beast) or calling a ship *a sail*.

Synonym   Synonyms are words or other linguistic elements which have the same meaning.

Synonymous   Two elements are synonymous if they mean the same thing.

Synonymy   There is synonymy between two elements if they both mean the same thing.

Syntactic atom   A syntactic atom is the smallest element of linguistic structure recognised in the syntax. This is usually taken to be a definition of 'word' in one of its senses.

Syntax   The way in which sentences are built up from words, or the study of this part of linguistics.

T and V forms   Pronouns used in many languages to distinguish between an addressee with whom the speaker is intimate (T) as opposed to one to whom the speaker wishes to remain polite and more distant (V).

Tag question   A tag question is a minimal question added to the end of an otherwise declarative sentence, often for pragmatic purposes. Following the sentence *She's coming today* we might get any of the tag questions *isn't she?*, *innit?*, *eh?*, depending on the age and social origins of the speaker.

Tap   A tap consonant is articulated with a rapid movement of the active articulator up to the passive articulator and away again, with a minimal duration of the contact.

Tatpurusa compound   See DETERMINATIVE COMPOUND.

Tautology   A tautology is a statement which is necessarily true, such as *This tree is a tree*.

Tense   Tense is a morphological feature which gives information about the time at which the action of a verb takes place. In English there are two tenses, non-past and past.

Theme   The theme of a sentence is what the sentence is about.

Third person   The third person is the entity talked about in the interaction, and referred to by *he/him, she/her, it,* or if plural, *they/them.*

Thyroid cartilage   The thyroid cartilage is the large ('door-like') cartilage at the front of the larynx.

Tip   The tip of the tongue is that vertical face of the tongue which lies behind the front incisors when the tongue is at rest in the mouth.

Tonality   Tonality is concerned with the number of intonational phrases into which a particular utterance is divided.

Tone   (1) A tone is a periodic sound with a regular structure. (2) A tone is one of a set of distinctive pitch elements which can be used to distinguish segmentally identical syllables.

Tone Bearing Unit (TBU)   A TBU is the segmental material with which a TONE (2) is associated.

Tone language   A tone language is a language which uses TONES (2) in its phonological structure.

Tonicity   Tonicity is concerned with the placement of the NUCLEUS in an intonational phrase.

Topic   see THEME.

Trachea   (also windpipe) The trachea is the windpipe, running from the larynx down into the chest, where it splits into the two bronchi, one feeding each lung.

Transitive   (1) A verb is transitive if it takes a subject and a direct object. In 'I see the moon', *see* is a transitive verb. (2) A relation is transitive if, when it holds between A and B and between B and C, it also holds between A and C.

Transitiviser   A transitiviser is a morphological marker which is added to an intransitive verb to make it transitive. The prefix *be-* in English can be seen as a transitiviser which changes intransitive *muse* into transitive *bemuse*.

Transitivity   Transitivity is the system affecting verbs which determines how many ARGUMENTS they take.

Tree   A tree is a directed graph, thought to resemble an inverted tree, used to represent the structure of linguistic constructions.

Trial   A language is said to have trial number when it has specific pronouns or other markers which are used when just three entities are involved.

Trill   (also roll) A sound is called a trill when one or both of the articulators vibrate in the stream of air coming from the lungs.

Trivalent   see DITRANSITIVE.

Truth Conditional Semantics   A theory of meaning which assumes that knowing the meaning of a sentence is equivalent to knowing the situations under which the sentence is true.

Typology   A typology is a set of predictions about language structure that follow from a particular premise.

Uncountable   (also non-count, mass). A noun is used as an uncountable if it cannot be used in a plural form with a numeral (e.g. *two knowledges*), and if it requires the determiner *much* rather than many (*much knowledge*, *many knowledges*). See also COUNTABLE.

Universal tendency   see STATISTICAL UNIVERSAL.

Unmarked   If a word has no morphological marker for a particular category, the word is unmarked for that category. If no word has a marker of the category, the category itself is unmarked.

Uvula   The soft, flexible end of the velum, which hangs down at the back of the mouth.

Uvular   A sound is said to be uvular if it is articulated with approximation of the back of the tongue and the uvula.

V2   A V2 language is one, like German, in which the verb regularly occurs in second position in the sentence.

Valency   The valency of a word (usually a verb) is a measure of the number of obligatory arguments it is linked with.

Velar   A sound is said to be velar if it is articulated with the back of the tongue causing a constriction with the VELUM.

Velarised   A sound is said to be velarised if, apart from its primary articulation, it has a SECONDARY ARTICULATION in which the back of the tongue forms a stricture of open approximation with the velum.

Velum   (also soft palate) The velum is the soft part of the roof of the mouth found immediately behind the hard PALATE.

Verb   A verb is a word like *admire, be, disappear* which in English can be marked for past tense or for the third person singular of the present tense, which takes a subject (and in some cases an object or subject complement), and which is central in a clause.

Verb phrase   A verb phrase is a phrase whose head is a verb.

Vibrate/vibration   The vocal folds are said to vibrate when they are forced apart by air coming from the lungs, and then spring back together again, fast enough to form a tone.

Vocal folds   (also vocal cords) The vocal folds are bands of muscle stretched across the top of the trachea at the larynx. They function as a valve to let air into and out of the lungs.

Vocalise   A consonant sound is vocalised if it is replaced by a vowel sound. The process is called vocalisation.

Vocoid   A vocoid is any segment which is articulated without an interruption to the stream of air coming from the lungs, whether it is phonologically a vowel (e.g. /æ/) or a consonant (e.g. /w/ in English).

Voice Onset Time (VOT)   This is the relative displacement of the end of a closure for a stop consonant at the beginning of voicing for a sonorant immediately following that stop.

Voiced   A voiced sound is one articulated with concurrent vibration of the vocal folds.

Voiceless   A voiceless sound is one articulated without any vibration of the vocal folds.

Vowel   A vowel is a SPEECH SOUND which is not a CONTOID and which is part of the PEAK of a syllable.

Vowel harmony   Vowel harmony is a phenomenon whereby all the vowels in a phonological word must agree for some particular feature (e.g. backness or rounding).

Wave   A wave is a pattern of compression and rarefaction of some medium through which the wave travels.

Wavelength   The distance in which a WAVE repeats its structure.

WH-question   A question which starts with a *wh*-word: *who, what, why, when, where, how.*

Word-class   (also part of speech) A word class is a substitution class at a high level of abstraction. Proper noun and noun are both word-classes, but one is more specific than the other.

Word-family   All the words which share a common base belong to the same word-family. So *man, postman, manly, unman, man-eater* are all part of the same word-family.

Word-form   If we say that *consume, consumes* and *consumed* are 'all different words', we mean that they are all distinct word-forms (contrast LEXEME).

X-bar grammar   The name given to a system of phrase structure grammar in which phrases headed by nouns, verbs, adjectives and prepositions are dealt with as parallel constructions, with binary-branching trees.

Zero morph   This term presents an oxymoron, since a morph is a form but if it is zero there is no form. A zero morph is a hypothesised morphological element with no form, whose function is to create a parallel with other words in the language where an overt morph occurs.

Data on individual languages comes from the sources identified below.

Indonesian   Kwee (1965)

Japanese   Kaiser et al. (2002)

Appendix B

Languages mentioned in this book

Language	Spoken in	Language family	Closely related to	Approximate number of speakers
Afrikaans	South Africa	Indo-European	Dutch	5 million
Alabama	Texas (Unites States)	Moskogean	Koasati	100
Amahuaca	Peru, Brazil	Panoan	Kashinawa	300
Amuesha (Yanesha')	Peru	Arawakan	Guana, Chamicuro	10,000
Arabic	Saudi Arabia, Algeria, Iraq, Jordan, Lebanon, Morocco, Syria, Tunisia, United Arab Emirates, etc.	Afro-Asiatic	Aramaic	221 million
Aranda (Arrente)	Northern Territory (Australia)	Australian	Areba, Warlpiri	1,000
Armenian	Armenia, Azerbaijan, Bulgaria, etc.	Indo-European	Albanian	6 million
Bakpwe (Mokpwe, Bakwiri)	Southwestern Cameroon	Niger-Congo	Swahili	32,000
Bandjalang	New South Wales (Australia)	Australian	Areba, Dyirbal	10 (almost extinct)
Bardi	Western Australia	Australian	Gagadu, Dyirbal	380

Language	Spoken in	Language family	Closely related to	Approximate number of speakers
Basque	France, Spain	Isolate	–	700,000
Beembe (Kibeembe)	Congo	Niger-Congo	Swahili	3,000
Bella Coola	Southwestern Canada	Salishan	Salish, Squamish	20 (almost extinct)
Burmese	Myanmar, Bangladesh, Malaysia	Sino-Tibetan	Chinese	32 million
Caddo	Western Oklahoma (United States)	Caddoan	Pawnee, Wichita	25 (almost extinct)
Campa (Nomatsiguenga)	Peru	Arawakan	Arawak, Guana	6,000
Cantonese (Yue Chinese)	Canton, Hong Kong (China)	Sino-Tibetan	Mandarin Chinese	55 million
Cayapa (Chachi)	Ecuador	Barbacoan	Totoro	9,500
Chinese: see Cantonese, Hakka, Mandarin				
Chiquito (Chiquitano)	Bolivia	Macro-Ge	Bororo	5,500
Chukchee (Chukchi)	Northeast Siberia	Chukotko-Kamchatkan	Alutor, Chukot	7,500
Comox	British Columbia, Vancouver Island (Canada)	Salishan	Salish, Squamish	400
Cree – macro-language	Canada	Algic	Shawnee	90,500
Creek (Muskogee)	Oklahoma (United States)	Muskogean	Alabama, Mikasuki	7,000
Croatian	Croatia	Indo-European	Serbian	5 million

Language	Spoken in	Language family	Closely related to	Approximate number of speakers
Dan	Côte d'Ivoire	Niger-Congo	Defaka, Obolo	1 million
Danish	Denmark	Indo-European	Swedish	5 million
Daur	China, Inner Mongolia	Altaic	Mongolian	96,000
Diyari (Dieri)	South Australia	Australian	Dyirbal, Aranda	<10 (extinct)
Dutch	The Netherlands, Belgium	Indo-European	German	21 million
Dyirbal	Queensland (Australia)	Australian	Aranda	40 (almost extinct)
Efik	Nigeria	Niger-Congo	Obolo	400,000
English	United Kingdom, United States, Australia, Canada, New Zealand, South Africa, India, etc.	Indo-European	Dutch	300 million
Even	Siberia	Tungusic	Evenki	7,500
Éwé	Ghana	Niger-Congo	Yace, Igbo	3 million
Finnish	Finland	Finno-Ugric	Estonian	5 million
French	France, Belgium, Switzerland	Indo-European	Italian	67 million
German (standard)	Germany, Austria, Switzerland, etc.	Indo-European	Dutch	90 million
Ghomala	Cameroon	Niger-Congo	Bafut	260,000
Greek (Ellinika)	Greece, Greek Macedonia, Albania, Australia, etc	Indo-European	Macedonian	11 million

Language	Spoken in	Language family	Closely related to	Approximate number of speakers
Greenlandic (Inuktitut)	Greenland	Eskimo-Aleut	Yupik, Aleut	57,000
Hakka	China	Sino-Tibetan	Mandarin	30 million
Hausa	Nigeria, Cameroon, Ghana	Afro-Asiatic	Gwandara	25 million
Hawai'ian	Hawai'i (United States)		Austronesian, Maori	1,000
Hebrew	Israel	Afro-Asiatic	Arabic	5 million
Hindi	India, Nepal, South Africa, Uganda	Indo-European	Bengali	181 million
Hixkaryana	Brazil	Carib	Carib, Waiwai	600
Icelandic	Iceland	Indo-European	Faroese	230,000
Igbo	Nigeria	Niger-Congo	Obolo, Ika	18 million
Irish (Gaelic)	Ireland	Indo-European	Scottish Gaelic	390,000
Italian	Italy, Switzerland	Indo-European	French	61 million
Japanese	Japan	Japonic	Okinawan	122 million
Kambera	Indonesia	Austronesian	Javanese	235,000
Kham	Nepal	Sino-Tibetan	Chinese	50,000
Khasi	India	Austro-Asiatic	Vietnamese	865,000
Khmer (Central)	Cambodia	Austro-Asiatic	Northern Khmer (Thailand), Vietnamese	13.5 million
Kiowa	Oklahoma (United States)	Kiowa-Tanoan	Tiwa, Jemez	1,000
Kisi	Tanzania	Niger-Congo	Zulu	10,000
Koasati	Louisiana, Texas (United States)	Muskogean	Alabama, Muskogee	200
Koiari	Papua New Guinea	Trans-New Guinea	Yareba	1,500

Language	Spoken in	Language family	Closely related to	Approximate number of speakers
Kpelle – macrolanguage	Liberia, Guinea	Niger-Congo	Éwé	795,000
Kunjen	Queensland (Australia)	Australian	Dyirbal, Aranda	20
Kurdish – macrolanguage	Iraq	Indo-European	Farsi, Pashto	16 million
Lak	Dagestan (Russian Federation), Azerbaijan, Georgia, Kazakhstan, etc.	North Caucasian	Chechen	164,000
Lango	Sudan, Uganda	Nilo-Saharan	Turkana	38,000
Latin	Formerly in Italy, Spain, France, etc. Now Vatican State	Indo-European	Italian	No estimate available, revival under way
Lezgian (Lezgi)	Dagestan (Russian Federation) Azerbaijan, Kazakhstan, etc.	North Caucasian	Chechen	783,500
Louisiana (Creole) French	Louisiana, Texas (United States)	Creole – French based	Haitian, Saint Lucian, Creole French	70,000
Malayalam	India, Kerala, Bahrain, Fiji, Malaysia, etc.	Dravidian	Tamil	36 million
Maltese	Malta	Afro-Asiatic	Arabic	387,000
Mandarin	China, Singapore, Taiwan	Sino-Tibetan	Gan Chinese, Hakka Chinese	845.5 million
Mangarayi	Northern Territory (Australia)	Australian	Gagadu	50 (almost extinct)

Language	Spoken in	Language family	Closely related to	Approximate number of speakers
Maori	New Zealand	Austronesian	Tahitian	60,000
Marshallese	Marshall Islands, Nauru	Austronesian	Kiribati	50,000
Maung	Northern Territory (Australia)	Australian	Wurrugu, Gagadu	240
Moseten	Bolivia	Isolate	–	1,000
Moxos (Mojos, Trinitario)	Bolivia	Arawakan	Ignaciano	5,500
Mura (Múra-Pirahã)	Brazil	Mura	–	360
Nauruan	Nauru	Austronesian	Kiribati, Marshallese	6,000
Navajo	Arizona, New Mexico, Utah (United States)	Na-Dene	Apache	150,000
Nengone	Mare, Loyalty Islands (New Caledonia)	Austronesian	Dehu	6,500
Ngiti (Bindi)	Democratic Republic of Congo	Nilo-Saharan	Bendi, Lendu	100,000
North Frisian	Germany	Indo-European	English, German	10,000
Norwegian (Bokmål)	Norway	Indo-European	Danish	4.5 million
Nukuoro	Caroline Islands	Austronesian	Tuvaluan	900
Nunggubuyu	Northern Territory (Australia)	Australian	Gagadu	360
Old English	England, Scotland	Indo-European	Old Frisian	evolved into Modern English

Language	Spoken in	Language family	Closely related to	Approximate number of speakers
Pashto, (Pushto) – macrolanguage	Pakistan, Afghanistan	Indo-European	Kurdish	20 million
Passamaquoddy (Maliseet, Malecite)	Canada, Maine (United States)	Algic	Cree, Shawnee	2,000
Pitta-Pitta	Queensland	Australian (Australia)	Arabana, Dieri	< 10 (extinct)
Pukapukan (Pukapuka)	Cook Islands	Austronesian	Samoan	2,000
Punjabi (Panjabi)	India, Kenya	Indo-European	Gujarati	28 million
Quileute	Washington State (United States)	Chimakuan	–	10 (almost extinct)
Rukai	Taiwan	Austronesian	Javanese	10,500
Russian	Russian Federation	Indo-European	Polish	143 million
Saliba	Papua New Guinea	Austronesian	Suau	2,500
Samoan	Samoa, American Samoa	Austronesian	Tokelauan	370,000
Semai	Malaysia	Austro-Asiatic	Khmer	44,000
Serbian	Serbia	Indo-European	Croatian	7 million
Serbo-Croatian – macrolanguage	Formerly in Yugoslavia	Indo-European	Croatian, Serbian, Bosnian	16 million
Shambaa, (Shambala, Kisambaa)	Tanzania	Niger-Congo	Swahili	664,000
Shona	Zimbabwe, Botswana, Zambia	Niger-Congo	Sotho	10.5 million

Language	Spoken in	Language family	Closely related to	Approximate number of speakers
Shoshone (Shoshoni)	Nevada, Idaho, Wyoming, Utah (United States)	Uto-Aztecan	Hopi	3,000
Spanish	Spain, Argentina, Chile, Colombia, Ecuador, etc.	Indo-European	Portuguese	328 million
St'a'timcets (Lillooet)	Canada	Salishan	Thompson	200
Swahili	Tanzania, Democratic Republic of Congo, Kenya, Mozambique, Somalia, etc.	Niger-Congo	Shambala	730,000
Swedish	Sweden, Finland	Indo-European	Danish	8 million
Tagalog	Philippines, Guam, etc.	Austronesian	Filipino	23 million
Tariana	Brazil	Arawak	Guajiro	100
Tepecano	Mexico	Uto-Aztecan	Tepehuan	< 10 (extinct)
Thai	Thailand	Tai-Kadai	Lao	20 million
Tigre	Eritrea, Sudan	Afro-Asiatic	Amharic	1 million
Tiwi	Northern Territory (Australia)	Australian	Dyirbal, Umbugarla	1,500 (nonfluent)
Tucano	Brazil, Colombia	Tucanoan	Arapaso	4,500
Turkish	Turkey, Bulgaria, Cyprus, Greece, Romania, Uzbekistan	Altaic	Azerbaijani	50.5 million

Language	Spoken in	Language family	Closely related to	Approximate number of speakers
Tzutujil	Guatemala	Mayan	Achi'	50,000
Urdu	Southern Pakistan, India, Bangladesh, South Africa, etc.	Indo-European	Hindi	60 million
Vietnamese	Viet Nam, Cambodia, China, etc.	Austro-Asiatic	Khmer	68.5 million
Wari' (Pakaásnovos)	Rondônia (Brazil)	Chapacura-Wanham	Torá	2,000
Warlpiri	Northern Territory (Australia)	Australian	Dyirbal, Aranda	2,500
Welsh (Cymraeg)	Wales	Indo-European	Breton	500,000
Wichita	Oklahoma (United States)	Caddoan	Pawnee	1,000
Yaqui	Mexico	Uto-Aztecan	Aztec	14,500
Yurak (Nenets)	Northwest Siberia (Russian Federation)	Uralic	Saami	31,000
Zulu	Zululand (South Africa), Botswana Lesotho, Malawi, Mozambique, Swaziland	Niger-Congo	Xhosa	10 million

Source: Much data from Lewis (2009).

Appendix C

Answers to questions

Chapter 2

<2.1> On one level it seems as though we might be claiming that *beanz* is another word for *Heinz*; on another it is being claimed that where you meet *beanz* there is a high correlation with meeting *Heinz* (just as in the *clouds mean rain* example).

<2.2> Both (3a) and (3b) could describe precisely the same situation, with the same woman involved, so the denotation of *slender* and *thin* is the same; but (3a) makes us feel decidedly positive about the woman, while (3b) is neutral or possibly even slightly negative. *Slender* has positive connotations, while *thin* has neutral or rather negative connotations in this context.

<2.3> You may not be familiar with the word *glabrous*, but can possibly guess that it is likely to be a technical, scientific term, while *hairless* is everyday language. *Glabrous* is often used to describe leaves with no hair, but may also be used humorously to describe a bald person or a man without facial hair. Again we can see differences in connotations.

<2.4> There are many such instances that you might think of. *Keyboard* and *piano* might be synonyms in a musical context but not in a computer context, for example.

<2.5> The superordinate term is *move*.

<2.6> Answered in the text.

<2.7> It depends on the way in which the words are being used. It might be referring to people of a certain age (would you claim that a baby was a non-smoker?); it might be referring to railway carriages (at least in a historical context); you may be able to think of other contexts as well.

<2.8> It is not a complementary term because English has no word which is its complementary. We can only say *not pregnant*. Complementary terms divide the relevant domain into two parts. *Pregnant* labels only one of the two parts. You might like to speculate about the reasons why English might not have a use for a word meaning 'non-pregnant', but given the gap, we do not have complementarity here.

<2.9> They are called complementary terms because they complement each other in dividing up the domain in which they apply, that is, between them they cover the complete domain.

<2.10> In ordinary usage, there are many types of things called 'opposites': *man* and *woman*, *come* and *go*, *here* and *there*, *in* and *out*, *rise* and *fall*, *heaven* and *hell*, *build* and *destroy*, and a whole lot more. Some of these may fit into the categories already discussed, but many will not.

<2.11> You may not be sure in all cases, but you should be able to find examples of both kinds. A tyre is part of a wheel and a wheel is part of a car and *the car's tyres* seems perfectly acceptable; a nail is part of a toe, a toe is part of a foot, but *a foot's nail* seems odd.

<2.12> In general, *little* is more affective and *small* is more neutral in its stance, so that *a little child* is perceived as nice, while *a small child* may not be. *Little* is also used to carry other emotional overtones: *He acts like a little Hitler* or *You little rotter!* may not make reference to physical size so much as to emotional attitude (in these cases, negative attitude).

<2.13> The question is phrased as whether these plants (or the edible parts of them) are in the set of vegetables; but we could also ask whether you would use the term *vegetable* to cover them, and the answer may be different. If you said *Pass the vegetables, please*, would you feel aggrieved or pleased if someone passed you potatoes or tomatoes? Does the term *roast vegetables* include roast potatoes? Does *meat and two vegetables* include or exclude potatoes as one of the vegetables? You may find that people disagree about some of these things. Brookes (2006) defines a tomato as a fruit.

<2.14> If the example had been *I saw my cousin yesterday and she/he gave me £10* we would have had to conclude that we were making reference to real-world information and not to lexical information. The same is true with things like *My sister's got a new baby. She's/He's really cute*, and with *Rover's a really good dog, isn't he/she?* Some children seem to simplify matters by assuming that all cats are feminine and all dogs masculine, but that is not the way the language or the world works. English also allows ships, cars and other machines to be referred to as *she* or as *it*.

<2.15> *Porridge* is a countable noun in that example, and the point is that many nouns can be either countable or uncountable depending on the context, and that speakers manipulate this grammatical feature to provide different shades of meaning: in this particular example, *porridges* probably means something like 'types of porridge'.

<2.16> By saying that *porridge* is neither masculine nor feminine, we imply that it is neuter. There are many complexities of dealing with systems of features which we cannot go into in detail here, although some will be taken up below. As to whether something could have plus values for both masculine and feminine, we could argue about the desirability of this. However, consider the case of the noun *Mädchen* 'girl' in German. It is of neuter gender, and has to have a neuter article or a neuter adjective: *das Mädchen, ein schönes Mädchen* ('the (N) girl', 'a beautiful (N) girl'). However, while it is possible in German to refer to a girl as *it*, in line with the noun's grammatical gender, it is also possible – indeed, probably more usual – to refer to a girl as *she*, reflecting real-world sex. So perhaps it is possible for a noun to have apparently contradictory marking for gender.

<2.17> The problem is the lack of marking for the gender features for the non-adult classes. It seems that we could leave those cells in the matrix blank (as is done in Data-set 2.6), or put '±' in them, but that in either case we would no longer have a strictly binary system, where values are either plus or minus. How much this matters depends on your view of what these features are doing, and how they work. You may have found other problems with the matrix, some of which will be discussed soon, but this seems to be a major one.

<2.18> *Duck*, *goose* and *hen* are words for female creatures or for any creature of the species; as with cows, it is the female which is economically exploited by humans. There is an old-fashioned use of *man* to mean any human. *Leopard*, *lion* and *tiger* are words for the male used for members of the species generally, as well.

<2.19> The difficulty is that every word in the lexicon except *eunuch* will have the negative value of this feature, and of most other such features, so that the componential analysis of any word risks becoming cluttered with a host of irrelevant features.

<2.20> Your definition might make reference to a number of features of birds: being alive, warm-blooded, laying eggs, having wings, having feathers, building nests and so on. To these defining characteristics, we might add some features that birds typically have: they are relatively small, they fly about and sing songs at dawn and dusk, they eat spiders, and so on.

<2.21> The phrase can fail to refer because the listener does not understand the words. The knowledge of the interlocutors is a factor in successful reference.

<2.22> The answer may depend on what has been said just before this: if it has been prefaced with 'As Oscar Wilde said', then the *I* may refer to Oscar Wilde, but it is more likely to refer to the speaker, taking on the role of Oscar Wilde.

<2.23> A famous one comes from a cricket commentator, who announced 'the bowler's Holding, the batsman's Willey'. This depends upon the homonymy of proper names and other words.

<2.24> **Countable**

Countable	**Uncountable**
Three beers, please.	Add some beer to the batter.
I'd like a chocolate cake.	I'd like some chocolate cake.
The clouds are very threatening	The valley was covered in cloud.
She is the love of his life.	Love makes the world go round.
I've had a thought.	That will take some thought.

<2.25> The question may come down to a matter of how far there is intention involved. If you stack up bricks, and there is a gale and one of the bricks is blown off the pile and hits a chicken, as a result of which the chicken dies, have you killed the chicken? There is a sense in which what you did has caused it to die, but what you did may not be an act of killing. The distinction becomes clearer, perhaps, where you do not do anything. If, as a result of my failing to remove a brick from an unstable pile, the chicken dies as above, have I killed the chicken by failing to act? Having said that, you may be happy with both *Hunger killed the refugees* and *Hunger caused the refugees to die* or *Lack of water killed the refugees* and *Lack of water caused the refugees to die*. Is there some personification involved here?

<2.26> (i)   I hired/leased/rented the car from Hertz.

(ii)   Hertz hired/leased/rented $\left\{ \begin{array}{l} \text{the car to me.} \\ \text{me the car.} \end{array} \right\}$

In some non-standard forms of English *borrow* and *learn* may work the same way.

<2.27> My solution is as below; it is quite different from the equivalent noun table.

	to call	to visit
a person	✓	✓
a place	✗	✓
from a person	✗	✗
of a period of time	✗	✗
on a person	✓	✗
to a person	✓	✗
for a period of time	✗	✓
with a person	✗	✓[1]

Note: [1] This may depend on the variety of English you speak.

<2.28> lion, 'a brave person'

litany, 'any recited list'

moan, 'to complain, a complaint'

peach, 'something which is good of its kind'

peacock, 'a boastful and proud person, especially one with little to be proud of'

scallop 'curved edges of, for example, a curtain'.

<2.29> *chair*, of a meeting, of a committee, is the person who sits in the chair.

head, of a school, institution, etc., is the person who leads that institution.

headache, 'a problem' is something associated with giving you a headache.

pot is a sum of money staked, in poker, which is viewed as having been put into a (metaphorical?) pot.

<2.30> *divine*, 'wonderful' (? informal), 'godlike' (? formal)

frog, 'amphibian' (neutral), 'Frenchman' (informal, offensive)

gas, 'neither liquid nor solid' (technical), 'great fun' (informal, slang)

grope, 'feel around blindly' (slightly formal), 'to touch someone in a sexually aggressive manner' (informal)

sustain 'to keep alive' (neutral), 'to uphold a claim' (formal, technical legal)

<2.31> *Flat* collocates at least with *battery, denial, drink, face, fare, joke, note, on one's face, out, plate, race, roof, tyre, voice, vowel, ware.* Here it is difficult to give a *Grundbedeutung.* 'Having a level surface' (see the *OED*), seems fundamental, but does not account for the musical *flat,* or for the phonetic *flat,* nor for the flat battery.

Rough collocates at least with *and ready, draft, guess, handling, hands, manners, ride, sea, texture, time, voice.* Many of the meanings shown here can be derived from something like 'not finished to the highest possible standards' and from there, 'having a surface which appears not to be finished, but has irregularities typical of something which has not been polished'. How many 'meanings' that makes is, of course, an open question.

<2.32> There is a cat.

The cat is black.

There is a mat.

The cat carries out an action of sitting.

The sitting occurs on (*or* at the top surface of) the mat.

The sitting is occurring at the time of utterance of the sentence.

Chapter 3

<3.1> Answered in the subsequent text.

<3.2> We might have to define 'successfully', of course, but unless you are extremely talented, the answer is almost certainly that you cannot. You might be able to imitate some aspects of the other accent, aspects which you find particularly striking, but you are likely to make so many mistakes that you will sound odd to speakers of the accent you are trying to copy. Even talented actors have difficulties with unfamiliar accents.

<3.3> This example shows that habits of pronunciation are not only present in making us say things in a particular way, they also influence the way in which we perceive speech sounds.

<3.4> It is true to say that under most circumstances; but if you want to keep breathing out for longer than normal, or using more air than normal, you might then have to work to breathe out. In circumstances which will be discussed immediately below, you might also have to work to keep the flow of air gradual.

<3.5> If you breathed in at the same rate as you breathe out, we would have to wait a long time for the next bit of the message every time you took a breath. The fact that we can breathe in quickly and breathe out slowly allows us to speak relatively smoothly.

<3.6> The two are identical, but a cough is not thought of as part of speech.

<3.7> Of these sounds, only [θ] is produced without vibration of the vocal folds.

<3.8> If you rest your fingers lightly on the Adam's apple, you should feel that it is higher in throat for [iː] than for [ɑː]. The vowel with the higher larynx (i.e. the one in *fee*) will probably sound as though it is on a higher pitch. This corresponds with point (1) just above.

<3.9> Normally the [ɑː] in *art* would be produced with vibration of the vocal folds, that is, with voicing. A whisper removes the vibration. Thus, the [h] in *heart* and the vowel in *art* are articulated in very similar ways indeed: your tongue and lips are probably in precisely the same position. Nevertheless, you may feel that the [h] has greater air-flow than the vowel does, since the glottis is not as open for a whispered vowel as it is for something which is totally voiceless.

<3.10> The answer is provided in the preceding text.

<3.11> [ʃ] is post-alveolar, [ŋ] is velar, [s] is alveolar and [ɹ] is alveolar or slightly post-alveolar, with the tongue-tip slightly curled up.

<3.12> In (a) only [d] is not dental (it is alveolar, at least in English); in (b) only [g] is not alveolar (it is velar); in (c) only [j] is not velar (it is palatal); in (d) only [t] is not post-alveolar (it

is alveolar); in (e) only [v] is not bilabial (it is labio-dental), and in (f), only [ʧ] is not alveolar (it is post-alveolar).

<3.13> You are asked what *you* do, and this might be different from what your neighbour does. Some native speakers of English (e.g. those from England) typically have an apical [θ], while others (e.g. those from California and New Zealand) typically have a laminal one.

<3.14> The answers are provided in the preceding text.

<3.15> You almost certainly have a dental [n] in *tenth*, but it might be apico-dental or lamino-dental, depending on how you answered <3.13>.

<3.16> You should get a [ʃ].

<3.17> You should get [h]. The consonant [h] can be seen as a voiceless version of the vowel that follows it.

<3.18> The passive articulator should be the (hard) palate, and if you thought of the English sound [j] as at the beginning of *yacht*, you should find your expectation confirmed.

<3.19> [t] is probably an apical-post-alveolar consonant. It may, alternatively, be articulated with the underside of the blade as the active articulator. Occasionally, the palate may be the passive articulator. The articulators for [ʔ] are the vocal folds: 'active' and 'passive' seem like irrelevant labels in this case. And [w] has two active and two passive articulators: the lower lip and the back of the tongue are the active articulators, the upper lip and the velum are the passive articulators.

<3.20> (a) [d, k], (b) [ŋ, m], (c) [r], (d) [j, w, ɹ], (e) [l] ([ɬ] would be described as a lateral fricative rather than just as a lateral), and (f) [ɫ].

<3.21> (a) the sounds are all plosives; (b) they are all alveolar; (c) they are all labio-dental; (d) they are all approximants; (e) they are all palatal; (f) they are all uvular; (g) they are all lateral; (h) they are all alveolar; (i) they are all palatal and all voiced; (j) they are all voiced.

<3.22> (a) all except [f] are bilabial (it is labio-dental); (b) all except [ʟ] are voiceless; (c) all except [ʀ] are alveolar (it is uvular); (d) all except [ɲ] are alveolar (it is palatal); (e) all except [ʕ] are glottal (it is pharyngeal); (f) all except [ɢ] are fricatives (it is a plosive); (g) all except [ç] are voiced; (h) all except [ʕ] are plosives (it is a fricative); (i) all except [j] are post-alveolar (it is palatal); (j) all except [ɣ] are approximants (it is a fricative).

<3.23> (a) all except [ɯ] are front vowels (it is back); (b) all except [ɜ] are close-mid vowels (it is open-mid); (c) all except [ɒ] are front vowels (it is back); (d) all except [ɞ] are spread (it is rounded); (e) all except [ɯ] are rounded.

<3.24> You probably labialise the initial consonants in *ship*, *chip* and *rip*, which you could write as [ʃʷ], [ʧʷ] and [ɹʷ] respectively.

<3.25> (a) reˈfer; ˈreference; refeˈree (b) imˈply; ˈimplicate; impliˈcation (c) ˈcharacter; ˈcharacterise; characteˈristic (d) ˈpopular; ˈpopulous; popuˈlarity (e) ˈdurable; duˈration; duraˈbility

<3.26> (a) ˌinterˈpolar; inˈterpoˌlate; interˈrupt (b) preˈrogative; ˌpreserˈvation; ˈpremature (or ˌpremaˈture) (c) ˈuniˌverse; uniˈversity; ˌuniversal ˈjoint (d) ˈsubjuˌgate; ˌsubˈcontract (*noun*); suˈblime (e) ˌdisapˈpoint; disˈhonour; ˈdisˌcharge (*noun*)

<3.27> (c), since '5' indicates the highest pitch level.

<3.28> Not without knowing more about Even. The transcription [uu] could mean 'long [u]' or it could mean a sequence of two syllables. (In fact, it means a long vowel, but that is the extra information that you need in order to be able to read the transcription.)

<3.29> No, it does not. A geminate is simply a way of writing the greater length, and there is no necessary implication that the geminate is precisely twice the length of the non-geminate consonant.

<3.30> Because the play is assumed to be background knowledge for both speaker and hearer.

<3.31> The former might be said if the previous turn was, 'What kind of audiences are you expecting for the play?' and the latter if the previous turn was, 'Are you expecting large audiences for the play?'

<3.32> Frequently under such circumstances the questions come in the form of statements, with no special marking as questions at all: 'You are Fred Smith.' 'Yes.' 'You live at 63 Rawhiti Road.' 'That's correct.' 'On the evening of 26th June last year you were working in your garden.' 'That's right.'

<3.33> Because the lips are closed, no air is coming out of the mouth, and none is emerging from the nose, either. Thus, the only acoustic energy comes from the voicing, which is relatively muffled. You can see the voicing in the black bar at the beginning of the closure for the /b/.

<3.34> On this graph, /u:/ looks as though it is more open than /ɔ:/, which is contrary to the general expectations set by the IPA vowel chart. It is because the vowel /u:/ is a lot closer in RP than the vowel /ɔ:/, but that is not true in New Zealand English, where the vowel we transcribe as /ɔ:/ is a lot closer.

<3.35> Given that F1 for the American speaker was close to 800Hz, it appears to be a lot more open than the New Zealand vowel. This is true, though it is dangerous to draw too definite a conclusion given that the value for American speakers was taken from a single woman and the values for New Zealanders taken as an average over several men.

<3.36> If we believe that there is cause and effect operating here, then it is because by rounding the back vowels they have more acoustic space to distinguish them from the front vowels: unrounded back vowels (and rounded front vowels) would be represented on the chart closer to the centre line.

<3.37> As long as the labels [i], [u] and [a] are taken as naming the extreme values, it is fine; but you might expect the central values of these vowels to be slightly nearer the centre if the balloon analogy were completely accurate.

<3.38> The question asks for your opinion; since we saw in the answer to <3.37> that there is some room for variation in interpretation, these will fit more or less. They cannot, though, all fit equally well.

<3.39> Presumably, not particularly well, though we might argue that if each of the vowels comes from a different area, then the predictions of dispersion are met.

Chapter 4

<4.1> *Exxon* starts like *excel* and finishes like *meson*; *frug* starts like *frog* and finishes like *rug*; *scag* starts like *scan* and finishes like *rag*; and *Yaris* starts like *yak* and finishes like *Paris*. *Frug* 'kind of dance' and *scag* 'heroin', although their origins are not clear, appear to be deliberately invented words, just like the trade names.

<4.2> You will probably agree that it is a voiced approximant. You may have had some difficulty with the place of articulation. It is articulated with the tip of the tongue either close to the back part of the alveolar ridge or just behind the alveolar ridge. Let us agree to call it alveolar for the purposes of the current exercise.

<4.3> This time you should be able to agree that it is alveolar, and that it is still voiced. You should discover, however, that it is a fricative, or that if it is not entirely a fricative, a lot of it is. Note that although it is a voiced alveolar fricative, it is not a /z/ because it does not have the groove in the tongue which is characteristic of a /z/.

<4.4> Like the sound in *drew*, this is an alveolar fricative, but this time it is not voiced, or not completely voiced. We must be dealing with a voiceless alveolar fricative.

<4.5> This one is harder to predict, since it is more dependent on the kind of English you speak. You may have a sound which is not easily distinguishable from one of those we have already met, or you may find that the tongue tip/blade touches the alveolar ridge very rapidly for this sound. If so, you probably have a voiced alveolar tap, transcribed [ɾ].

<4.6> There are many examples you could have discovered, but some relevant examples are *seal/zeal, bussing/buzzing, lice/lies, hence/hens*. Note that the [s] and [z] can occur in different positions in the word; all that matters is that substituting one for the other gives rise to a different word.

<4.7> Your broad transcriptions should be /druː/ and /θruː/, respectively, while the narrow transcriptions should be [dɹuː] and [θɾuː], respectively. Note the difference in the brackets surrounding the transcriptions.

<4.8> Dental and alveolar [l]s go together in /l/ and dental and alveolar [n]s go together in /n/. The two [l]s are more phonetically similar to each other than dental [l̪] is to alveolar [n] or vice versa.

<4.9> From the first two examples it might appear that [t] appears before [a], while [tʲ] appears before [i]. This would make sense, since the palatal (front) quality of the vowel must be prepared before the consonant is finished, and so can easily accompany the consonant. (If the vowel were not ready for articulation before the end of the consonant, we would always have a vowel that moved into position during its articulation.) However, the third example shows that [tʲ] can also occur where there is no following vowel. Then we also see that [tʲ] can occur with a following [a], so the preliminary hypothesis is shown to be false, and speakers must overrule the natural tendency to put the vowel quality in the consonant. Similarly, a hypothesis that [t] occurs word-initially and [tʲ] word-finally is quickly dismissed as contrary to the information provided. Both seem to appear before the same vowels and word-initially, and while we have no evidence of a word-final [t], this is not sufficient to prove complementary distribution. Again we might consider the vowels appearing before the consonants, but since both can occur word-initially, this seems a futile task. At this stage we might suspect that the two are not in complementary distribution at all, but in PARALLEL DISTRIBUTION. If they are in parallel distribution there is the possibility of contrast between them. Finally, however, the last two words in the table prove contrast, because they provide a minimal pair. At this stage we can say that [t] and [tʲ] cannot be allophones of the same phoneme in this language, but must belong to separate phonemes.

<4.10> This implies that speakers will hear the distinction between [t] and [tʲ] clearly, and consider them to be two very different sounds.

<4.11> You would need one symbol for each for an ideal writing system. Otherwise people might feel that the writing system was confusing (as the English system is when the words we write *earthy* and *worthy* do not rhyme because one contains [θ] and the other [ð]).

<4.12> Here we quickly see that [b] occurs at the beginning of words, while [β] does not, and [β] occurs at the ends of words, while [b] does not. We can draw a table like the one below to make the point:

Initial	Medial	Final
b	b, β	β

This is not enough to prove complementary distribution, however, since – as the table shows – both of them occur in the middle of words. If we look at the distribution inside words, though, we discover that while [b] is always preceded by a consonant, [β] is always preceded by a vowel. Again we can draw a table:

b occurring medially	β occurring medially
nbu	aβt
	aβi
	əβə

We can generalise over these two sets of observations by saying that [β] is always immediately preceded by a vowel in the same word, while [b] never is. In other words, because we have given a way to predict which will occur in any given environment, we have set up a statement which shows complementary distribution.

The other thing that is required is that the two allophones should be phonetically similar. In this case both are voiced and bilabial, and that is probably enough to guarantee that they are phonetically similar enough to be allophones. However, because phonetic similarity is a matter of more or less rather than yes or no, we can check that there is nothing that might be more similar to either [b] or to [β] than the other member of the pair. We have no evidence of a [v], for instance, which might have clouded the issue. So because we have two sounds in complementary distribution which are also more phonetically similar than other sounds we can find in the language, we can conclude that we are dealing with allophones of the same phoneme.

<**4.13**> This implies that speakers of Daur will probably hear [b] and [β] as being 'the same', and they may be unaware of any difference between the two sounds.

<**4.14**> You would need only a single symbol for the two sounds.

<**4.15**> You will probably have /bɑl/ and /xəb/ respectively. The slashes round the transcription indicate that it is a phonemic transcription (i.e. that the phonetic details of allophones have not been marked in the transcription). In order to read the transcription, you will need to understand the **CONVENTION** that /b/ in post-vocalic position is pronounced [β]. There are reasons for not having /βal/ and /xəβ/, but those reasons have not yet been introduced, so that if you have this result, it is valid at the moment.

<**4.16**> The sound [ŋ] is a voiced velar nasal (stop), and [s] is a voiceless alveolar fricative.

<**4.17**> We can start with the question of phonetic similarity, here. The plosives [p] and [b] are both bilabial, but differ in voicing. They are certainly phonetically alike, but are they sufficiently phonetically alike to be allophones of the same phoneme? We have no evidence in Data-set 4.3 of any segment which is more like [b] than [p] is, or more like [p] than [b] is, so it seems safe to say that they could be allophones of the same phoneme on that criterion alone. However, we also need to prove complementary distribution. If we go through the data, and for every word write down what precedes the [p] or [b] and what follows it, we should begin to see a pattern. The voiced [b] can occur at the beginning of a word followed by a vowel, at the end of a word preceded by a vowel, or in the middle of a word with a vowel on each side. The voiceless [p] can occur at the beginning of a word followed by a consonant, or in the middle of a word with a consonant on at least one side of it. We have no evidence that it can occur at the end of a word. We can summarise that by saying that [p] occurs when there is an adjacent consonant, [b] occurs **ELSEWHERE**. In other words, there is complementary distribution.

<**4.18**> It implies that speakers of Passamaquoddy will think that [p] and [b] are the same sound, and that they may not be able to hear a difference between them.

<**4.19**> You would only need one letter to represent the two sounds.

<**4.20**> Phonetically the two words are [kpidin] and [nidab]. Either the answer will be /gbidin/ and /nidab/ or it will be /kpitin/ and /nitap/. Is there anything to choose between these two versions? There are two ways of arguing, and here they happen to give different answers. The first is that we should always use the default or **ELSEWHERE VARIANT** as the symbol for the phoneme. That would mean /b/ in this case. The other is that since obstruents in most languages are preferentially voiceless and sonorants preferentially voiced, we should mark unpaired obstruents as voiceless and unpaired sonorants as voiced if there is any reason to do so. That would mean /p/ in this case. In most instances these two criteria would give the same result. Where they clash, the choice is fairly arbitrary.

<**4.21**> The name of the language makes it look as though voiceless obstruents are represented differently from voiced ones in the spelling, because it contains both <p> and <dd>. It is, however, likely that this is an English representation, not one devised for the language concerned. Since it begins with <p> with no adjacent consonant, we may speculate either that the English name was taken from some different dialect of the language, or that the

language name begins with [ph] in the original version, which would sound like an initial /p/ to English ears. We have no direct evidence on this matter.

<4.22> There are quite a few, including *fecund, Kenya, lever, Megan, plenary, scenic*.

<4.23> There are some, such as *incapacitate* whose first consonant may be either /n/ or /ŋ/, *nephew* which has either /f/ or /v/, *thither* which starts with either /θ/ or /ð/ and so on.

<4.24> If it were lexically conditioned suspension of contrast, we might expect to find both pronunciations of a word like *look*, which we do not. If it were neutralisation we might expect it to occur following other short vowels (or other vowels in general), but *bag* and *back* provide a minimal pair, and if you cannot provide minimal pairs for other vowels, you can probably find words which end in V + k and in V + g for any given V[owel]. This leaves defective distribution. It seems to be pure chance that [ʊg] does not occur, rather than a pattern built in to English phonology. That is the hallmark of defective distribution.

<4.25> It shows that the link between phoneme and its spelling equivalent, the letter or GRAPHEME, is not one-to-one. In less technical terms, the English writing system is not systematic in the way it represents sounds – which is why transcription is so useful.

<4.26> Let's assume that you think these are distinct phonemes, though I have come across small children who pronounce adult /j/ as [ʒ].

Some speakers have what may look like minimal pairs in words like *due* and *Jew*. But while there is a /j/ in *due* (for those speakers), there is arguably no /ʒ/ in *Jew*, since /dʒ/ is typically treated as a separate phoneme in English, not as a sequence of two (and there are arguments to support this position). In some systems of transcription, *player* might be transcribed as /plejə(r)/, which would then be a minimal pair for *pleasure* /pleʒə(r)/ (see section 4.3): but we have not used such a transcription system, so we have transcribed *player* as /pleɪə(r)/, where there is no minimal pair. Otherwise, the closest we seem to get, for speakers who have the word *genre* and pronounce it /ʒɒnrə/ is to compare that with *beyond* /bɪjɒnd/ where the stressed syllables are largely the same.

<4.27> Phonetic similarity (or the lack of it, given an intervening /z/) should lead you to suspect that these are not allophones of the same phoneme. A pair like *beige* and *bathe* /beɪʒ/, /beɪð/ will work for most speakers, though the number of minimal pairs is small because neither /ð/ nor /ʒ/ is frequent in English.

<4.28> Not only is it devoiced, it is also palatalised (assuming the British RP system).

<4.29> There is a lot of variation among English speakers on this point. Typically, in isolation, final voiceless plosives will be aspirated ([flæpʰ], [flætʰ], [flækʰ]), but some people have a glottal stop instead of aspiration or instead of the entire plosive. So you can also find [flæʔp], [flæʔt] and [flæʔk] or [flæʔ] for all of these words. The variants with glottal stop may be more likely in more common words, before consonants, or in less formal varieties. Some speakers resyllabify the plosive in an expression like *stop it*, to give [stɒ pʰɪtʰ], etc. Others treat the plosive here as intervocalic, so that you find [wɒɾɪf] for *what if*. You will need to think about your own pronunciation.

<4.30> It is often assumed that the best phonemic system is the most economical phonemic system in the sense of the system that employs the smallest number of symbols. Even here there may be problems of interpretation: is [iː] a single symbol or a series of two, for example? The most common answer – at least when it comes to measuring economy – seems to be that it is a sequence of two. On the other hand there clearly are advantages to a lack of economy on occasions: to avoid ambiguity, to act as better mnemonic symbols, to be of maximum use to the most diverse set of users, to draw attention to different phonological classes.

<4.31> Leading on from the last question, if we consider the alternatives of /ii/ and /iː/ for the vowel in *fleece*, we might argue that the double-vowel transcription becomes ambiguous in the transcription of a word like *being*, because /biiŋ/ could indicate [bɪiːŋ] or [biːɪŋ]. If the

supposed economy leads to ambiguity, it might be an insufficient system for other reasons. This fails to challenge the idea that few symbols = good for transcription systems. The only way to do that would be to try to discover how real speakers perceive these sounds and provide a transcription system which reflects it. Some phonologists would not accept this as relevant information, however (see section 8.3.1).

<4.32> Suggestions using the RP transcription used elsewhere in this book are provided below. The transcriptions are broad: it would be possible to add more detail.

aɪ ˈgəʊ tə ði ˈɒprə weðər aɪ ˈnɪd ðə sliːp ə ˈnɒt

ˈmædəm ‖ ˈdəʊnʧuː həv ˈeni ʌnɪksprest ˈθɔːts

ˈwaɪz əˈbriːvieɪtɪd sʌʧ ə ˈlɒŋ ˈwɜːd

meni ˈθæŋks fə jə ˈbʊk ‖ aɪ ʃəl weɪst ˈnəʊ ˈtaɪm in ˈriːdɪŋ ɪt

ə prəˈfesər ɪz ˈsʌmwʌn huː ˈtɔːks ɪn ˌsʌmwʌn ˈelsɪz ˈsliːp

ɪf ˈmen laɪkt ˈʃɒpɪŋ ðeɪd ˈkɔːl ɪt rɪˈsɜːʧ

ɪf jə ˌθɪŋk ˈskwɒʃ ɪz ə kemˈpetɪtɪv ækˈtɪvɪti ‖ traɪ ˈflavər əˌreɪndʒmənt

maɪ ˈhæmstə daɪd ˈjestədeɪ ‖ fel əˈsliːp ət ðə ˈwiːl

ˈwɒts əˈnʌðə ˈwɜːd fə θɪˈsɔːrʌs

ði ˈɜːli ˈbɜːd meɪ ˈkæʧ ðə ˈwɜːm ‖ bət its ðə ˈsekənd ˈmaʊs ðə? ˈgets ðə ˈʧiːz

aɪm ɒn ˈtuː ˌdaɪɪts ət ðə ˈməʊmənt ‖ bɪkəz jʊ ˈsɪmpli dəʊŋ ˌget ɪˌnʌf tʊ ˈiːt ɒn ˈwʌn

ən aɪˈdɪə ɪznt rɪˈspɒnsɪbl fə ðə ˈpiːpl hu bɪˈliːv ɪn ɪt

ˈlɪtrəʧə ɪz ˈməʊsli əbaʊt hævɪŋ ˈseks ‖ ən ˈnɒ?p mʌʧ əbaʊt hævɪŋ ˈʧɪldrən ‖ ˈlaɪf ɪz ðiː ˈʌðə weɪ ˈraʊnd

ˈwaɪ ɪz ðiː ˈælfəbet in ðæt ˈɔːdə ‖ ɪz ɪ? bɪˈkɒz əv ðe ˈsɒŋ

ˌwen aɪ get ə ˌlɒt əv ˈtenʃən ən ˈhedeɪks ‖ aɪ ˈduː wɒt ɪt sez ɒn ðiː ˈæsprɪn ˌbɒtl ‖ ˈteɪk ˈtuː əŋ ˈkiːp əweɪ frəm ˈʧɪldrən

ˈsʌm ˌpiːpl ˈkʌm baɪ ðə ˌneɪm əv ˈʤɪnjəs in ðə ˈseɪm ˌweɪ əz ən ˈɪnsekt ˌkʌmz baɪ ðe ˌneɪm əv ˈsentɪˌpiːd ‖ ˈnɒt bɪkɒz ɪt hæz ə ˈhʌndrəd ˈfiːt bət bɪkɒz ˈməʊs ˌpiːpl kɑːŋ ˈkaʊnt əbʌv fɔːˈtiːn

<4.33> The obvious answer is that they belong to the class of voiceless plosives. But this makes some assumptions: that there is no [ʈ] or [c] in the language concerned. Otherwise we would expect these also to be members of the set. If they existed but were not members of the class, we would have to specify the class much more carefully.

<4.34> The statement given earlier should work. If it does not, check your transcription carefully! You may say *garage* with final /ʒ/, or perhaps have the possibility of a noun *beige* (*How many different beiges are there in your paint range?*). I can think of no clear noun ending in /ð/. You might like to check that it is not the case that the vowel used in the words makes a difference.

<4.35> People from Scotland or the North of England may know the word *gowk* 'cuckoo', or *loup* 'leap, dance', and New Zealanders who have no /l/ in the relevant words may think that *twelve*, which they then pronounce as something like [twæʊv], is a counter-example. The wording given above was phrased to indicate that these examples fell outside the intended area of the generalisation.

<4.36> Since English does not have retroflex consonants, it is not possible to illustrate any English words that contain them. The closest we can get is the quality of /r/ in some North American varieties (although /r/ in British varieties is usually treated as alveolar) and that was included in the list.

<4.37> Many speakers, even non-conservative speakers of RP, say /pɪtiː/, or else they have a vowel which is neither clearly /ɪ/ nor clearly /iː/ in this position, something which is transcribed as /i/ in this book. However, since the argument is based on speakers who do have /ɪ/ in this position, all that is important is that there should be such speakers. As well as RP speakers, there are some North American speakers and some Yorkshire speakers who do the same thing.

<4.38> As long as you did not choose nouns with irregular plurals like *alumni*, *children*, or *oxen*, the predictions should be correct. You may, of course, have chosen plurals with the third possible variant, which would not be relevant here, either.

<4.39> We have words lie *spray, stray, scramble, splay, sclerosis, sputum, stupid, skewer, square*. Sequences of /tl/ and possibly /pw/ are ruled out by other constraints, but the non-existence of /stw/ seems to be an accidental gap, given that /tw/ is found in words like *twin*.

<4.40> It's not relevant for those speakers who have only two consonants at the start of this word, either because they say /stu:pɪd/ or because they say /stʃu:pɪd/ (with /ʃtʃu:pɪd/ as another possibility).

<4.41> Your answer should be [u, l, n, t].

<4.42> Since the nasal is now shown to be voiceless, we might expect it to behave more like a voiceless obstruent than like a voiced sonorant as far as sonority is concerned, and so we might expect this word to fit neatly into the predictions for monosyllabic words made by the sonority hierarchy.

<4.43> In colloquial speech you might very well says [sɪks:] and [twels:] with a long [s:], but only two final consonants. This implies that different styles of English might have different phonotactic constraints; we could extend this observation to any two varieties of English (or any other language) – their phonemic systems might differ and their phonotactics might differ. In general it is easier to predict reduced varieties from full varieties than vice versa. Given [sɪksθs] we can predict that we have to delete the middle two consonants and extend the [s], but given [sɪks:] we cannot predict which two middle consonants to reinsert: if we chose the wrong ones we might get *[sɪkfθs].

<4.44> The constraint was stated as involving a 'stop' in second position, and /m/ is a stop, albeit a nasal stop. If the constraint had been phrased in terms of a plosive, it would have had to be modified. However, since nasals in this position are so rare, we might wonder whether /s/ + plosive + approximant might not be a better generalisation for most speakers. The only other regularly cited word which has a nasal stop instead of a plosive is *snew*, a rare dialectal word meaning 'snowed'.

<4.45> Relevant words include *spare, stem, scowl, sphere, svelte* (if that is different; see above), and other words with the same initial clusters. Note that words like *ship, pterodactyl, tsunami* or *Dvořák* do not begin in clusters in most people's pronunciations of English. The examples given above all begin with /s/. Some speakers may use words like *shtuk* /ʃtʊk/ 'trouble', borrowed from Yiddish, which are exceptional, but provide a second pattern for some speakers.

<4.46> The morphological analysis would give [teɪst.ɪŋ]. If we maximise onsets, we get [teɪ.stɪŋ]. If we consider the allophones, either of these makes sense, but we must not split the medial /s/ and /t/, otherwise we would expect to find *[teɪs.tʰɪŋ], which does not seem to occur. The solution is still inconclusive, but the problems are not quite the same that we find with *testing*.

<4.47> There is no reason to believe that the phonology of *tester* ('a person who tests') is any different from that of *tester* ('a pillow'), though the morphology (which Hanks calls the 'etymology') is different. The fact that Hanks provides different syllabifications suggests that he is not looking at anything 'phonetic' here.

<4.48> Since both moras are reduplicated, we would expect *paruparu*.

<4.49> The first set of words has a heavy penultimate syllable, which can carry the stress. The second set of words has a light syllable in the penultimate syllable, and so the stress goes back to the antepenult.

<4.50> The allophone [ɾ] occurs only before the front vowels [i] and [e], while the allophone [l] occurs before the central vowel [ɐ] and the back vowels [o] and [u].

<4.51> The rule will be

t → ts / ___ ɯ

<4.52> The rule should be

$$V \rightarrow [+ \text{stress}] / \_\_\_ \text{(C) (C) (C) (ə) \#}$$

<4.53> $\left[_{\text{FOOT}} \begin{bmatrix} \text{-continuant} \\ \text{-voice} \end{bmatrix} \underset{\substack{\downarrow \\ h}}{\varnothing} \right.$

We need some way to mark that this occurs at the left edge of the foot, and that is what the opening square bracket shows (if we had an /s/ between the left edge of the foot and the plosive, the aspiration would not occur). I have used the 'Ø becomes something' notation used earlier, though if aspiration were treated as a feature, we could simply add that feature to the features marking the voiceless plosive.

<4.54> mawe magana mana na miloŋgo mine '440 stones'

stones hundred four and forty

magí mágána matátú ná mílóŋgo mine '340 eggs'

eggs hundred three and forty

Precisely how the 'forty' is made up is not clear from this data alone.

magí mágána   matátú ná mílóŋgo mine '340 eggs'

There must be two phonological words, the first ending on the last syllable of *mágána*.

<4.55> If it turns out that the general pattern is as in (21), for both tones to survive, then saying the same thing in (20) would be to gain a generalisation. It would also seem relatively natural for a sequence of two highs to merge when there is only one TBU, since there is no way to show that there are two unless either there is pitch movement or there are several TBUs.

<4.56> There are no doubt several ways, but one simple one is with ordering. If the segments are deleted before the association lines are put in place, the tones are not also deleted; if the deletion rule takes place after association lines have been put in place, both tone and associated TBU are deleted.

<4.57> If the OCP applies at the segmental level, geminates and long vowels must arise from the spreading of appropriate features into a position whose phonetic or phonological form is underspecified. That is, a geminate like /ss/ must arise from a single /s/ and an underspecified consonant, and a sequence like /oo/ (representing [oː]) must arise from an /o/ and an underspecified vowel.

<4.58> If the noun following the prefix 'with' has high tones throughout, all those highs become lows following the high tone on the prefix.

Chapter 5

<5.1> *Carriage* comes from *carry*. It first meant 'carrying' (as *coverage* means 'covering'), then 'something carried' (as *luggage* means 'something lugged'), and eventually 'something in which people are carried'. A *floodlight* must have been viewed as something which floods a place with light, that is, provides an over-abundance of light, just as too much rain provides an over-abundance of water. *Health* is related to *heal* (and also to *hale* and *whole*). If you are hale and hearty, you have your health. A *hedgehog* must have been viewed as a pig-like creature, no doubt on account of the noise it makes. And *sensual* is related to *sense*, because if something is sensual, it appeals to the senses.

<5.2> The name *woodchuck* is borrowed from the native American name for the creature, possibly from the Cree word *otchek*, having nothing to do with either wood or chucking. A polecat is a cat-like animal (actually related to the ferret) which eats chickens (modern French *poule*).

<5.3> You should have analysed *hospitalise* into *hospital* and *-ise*, and found parallels like *institutionalise* and perhaps *italicise* 'put into italics'.

<5.4> Although we can recognise the shapes *car* and *pet* in *carpet*, there is no meaning of either in *carpet* (and even the pronunciation suggests that there is no *pet*), so this is a single morph. *Decentralise* is analysed as *de·centr·al·ise*. We can find the meaning of *de-* from other words such as *de·classify*, *de·sensitise*. The meaning of *-al* is something vague like 'relating to' and can be found in *parent·al* and *trib·al*. The *-ise* part meaning, more or less, 'make' can be found in words like *legal·ise*, *pagan·ise*. Note that the spelling (and pronunciation) of *centre* has changed, but that this is not crucial as long as we can still see the connection and the meaning. *Distressing* must be *distress·ing*. It cannot be *dis·tress·ing* because it has nothing to do with *tresses*; the meaning does not allow us to discover *di·stress·ing* here, either. *Sensitivity* must be *sens·itiv·ity*. You are *sensitive* because you can *sense* something, the *-ity* we can find in words like *fertil·ity* and *practical·ity*, only the *-itiv(e)* is hard to justify. It also comes up in a few words like *compet·itive* and *defin·itive*. You might want to split it into two, but it is hard to find a meaning for the *-it-* part. *Tarragon* cannot be split into smaller meaningful elements.

<5.5> The answers are *bird·cage*, *cage·bird*, *bird·song*, *song·bird*. All of these morphs are potentially free.

<5.6> In Data-set 5.2 the suffix has the form /ssɑ/. It appears to mean 'in the', but in fact the 'the' is simply what we would say in English: Finnish has no word or morph corresponding to English *the*, and the suffix /ssɑ/ just means 'in'.

<5.7> *Pullo·t* contains the base *pullo* 'bottle' and the suffix *-t* 'plural'.

<5.8> *Ma·elezo* is analysed into morphs as shown, with the base *elezo* 'explanation'. The morph *ma-* means 'plural'.

<5.9> Thus the base for the word meaning 'speech' is /sdɤy/, with the affix /ɔm/ added after the /s/.

<5.10> The infix is *-p-*, determined by doubling the final consonant in the base.

<5.11> The rules here are much more complex, but if you look carefully, you can see that the plural is marked by a prefix in which the vowel is always /ə/, and where any consonants before the vowel are copied from the onset of the first syllable of the base; the prefix also contains one more consonant, the consonant which immediately follows the first vowel in the base.

<5.12> The form meaning 'I said' is cognate with old-fashioned English *quoth*. You might also have recognised *bear*, *drink*, *eat* (and *ate*), *give* (and *gave*) and *get*. You should have come up with a process something like 'change the <e> in the base to an <a> and delete the suffix'. (You might not have realised that this data is presented in Icelandic orthography; the phonology masks the relationship to a certain extent, though we could produce a more complex version of the same thing on the basis of the phonology.)

<5.13> You should find that the bases do provide lexical information and the affixes provide grammatical information.

<5.14> You could probably list the affixes as /ʃən/ (or possibly /ən/ if that was the form you decided on), /əl/ and /ɪst/. None of them is an infix, they are all suffixes. The reason is simple: none of them interrupts another morph, although some of them do fall between other morphs. So we see here words containing a sequence of suffixes. The meanings of the first two are rather abstract. For the first we might want to say the meaning is something like 'noun created from VERB' where VERB is the verb in the base. Similarly, the second affix probably means something like 'adjective pertaining to NOUN'. The third suffix is a bit easier to give a meaning to, perhaps, in this data, something like 'person philosophically inclined towards NOUN'. It is unusual, but not excessively so, that the meaning of the word in *-ist* seems to relate to the noun rather than to the adjective from which it is derived in formal terms.

<5.15> The base in *educationalist* is *educational*: that is the form to which the last suffix was added. Correspondingly, the base in *educational* is *education* and in *education*, the base is *educate*.

<5.16> You can find the singular form in the middle of the plural form of these words, so that seems to be the base. Then you have to add the suffix /(a)mmuɪ/. It is not clear from the examples we have when you have to insert the /a/ and when you do not. It might have to do with the individual words. However, that is not all. The plural forms contain a prefix as well. The prefix is formed by reduplication. First we need the first CV of the base, and then we need an extra copy of the first C. So the prefix part is made up of $C_1 V_1 C_1$ of the base (where the subscripts simply number the consonants and vowels of the base starting at the left-hand edge of the word).

<5.17> As well as the prefix, we have the loss of a vowel in this pattern. We can view vowel loss of this type as a type of internal modification, a kind of Ablaut or apophony.

<5.18> There is a generalisation here that the transitive verb must end in a low tone. This use of tone to indicate grammatical categories can be seen as a type of internal modification. There is also a process of reduplication or gemination of the last consonant of the base. The two appear both to be necessary for the verb to be transitivised.

<5.19> Although we can sometimes express transitivisation by some form of periphrasis (e.g. the use of 'cause to' in the examples above; 'periphrasis' means that the category is marked by syntactic means), on the whole English does not mark transitivisation at all. So we can say *The milk boiled* or *Kim boiled the milk*, *His head was pounding* and *Kim pounded the table to get silence*.

<5.20> There is no simple answer to this question. It seems relatively clear that a process should not be viewed as morphological in one language just because it is in another. We would not want to say that future marking with *will* in English (*I will see you tomorrow*) should be viewed as morphological just because Italian has a morphological future.

<5.21> For an answer, see the text below <5.21>.

<5.22> The root in *rejections* is probably *reject*. If you said it was **ject* you need to consider whether your answer is really valid for English or only for Latin, from which the word *reject* was ultimately borrowed. The root is not a stem here, because we have the derivational affix *-ion*, and so the inflection, the plural, is added to *rejection*, which accordingly is the stem.

<5.23> In the present and future we can isolate base and suffix quite easily, so that in the first example we will get *ceyy-* as the base and *-um* as the suffix for the future, and *-unnu* as the suffix for the present. You might think that the *-u-* which I have attributed to the suffix should be part of the base, but comparison with the forms of the past suggests that this is not so. However, when we look at the past forms, things are not as simple. First, the forms of the base are subtly different: there is no geminate <y> in the word for 'do', and a short vowel rather than the expected long vowel in the form for 'see'. Moreover, the suffix meaning 'past' has three different forms, depending on which base it is attached to. With only four verbs to consider, we have no idea how regular or otherwise these patterns are, but on the basis of the data we have here we might start to build up some hypotheses about what is going on.

<5.24> The affixes are *be-* and *en-* (both prefixes) and *-ise* and *-ify* (both suffixes). We could argue that they all take a noun and turn it into a verb, and that this change in word-class is the meaning they share. Alternatively, we could be more specific and find at least two meanings here: 'put into a NOUN' and 'treat as a NOUN' (itself ambiguous between treating it as if it is a NOUN and treating it as a NOUN would). The lack of form in common, and the very fact that we have prefixes and suffixes here, might deter some scholars from trying to class these together as a single morpheme. Note also that this is derivational morphology, where less leeway is given because the categories are not so well specified.

<5.25> You should have found that the words on the left of the table keep the same number of syllables in their past tense form, while those on the right add an extra syllable. What is the difference between the two columns which causes this difference? (Think about it before you are given the answer!) It is simply a matter of the words on the right ending in /t/. We can easily explain why this should be. The suffix for the past tense is /t/, and English does not allow us to pronounce /tt/ at the end of a word, and so we need to put something between the plosives to keep them apart. (Why the plosive is then voiced is a more elaborate question, though one which we could answer. Answering it involves looking at far more verbs than the small subset we have considered here.)

<5.26> The phenomenon illustrated in a small way in Data-set 5.19 has far more widespread effects in Finnish than we can see here. The phenomenon is called VOWEL HARMONY. In languages with vowel harmony, vowels match for certain features in a given domain. Here we can take the domain as being the word. If you look carefully at Data-set 5.19 you will see that six vowels are illustrated in the data: the back vowels, /ɑ, o, u/ and the front vowels /æ, œ, y/. Any given word contains vowels from only one of these sets.

<5.27> You could choose to write it with a T or, if you wished, as ED, in the way the writing system does. Most linguists would choose to write it with a D, but this is because they would consider more data than we looked at in Data-set 5.18.

<5.28> Because there are other places in English where an alveolar consonant followed by a /j/ gives rise to a post-alveolar consonant (although not always /ʒ/). *Tune*, which is conservatively pronounced /tjuːn/ is often pronounced /ʧuːn/ in colloquial speech, and in some varieties of English, *presume* is pronounced /prɪʒuːm/ (sometimes in variation with /prizjuːm/). Even a phrase like *his yacht* can be pronounced with an /ʒ/ at the end of *his*.

<5.29> Some examples are presented below. Finding such examples is not a trivial task, and you should feel free to use dictionaries, reverse dictionaries, and any other reference works you find useful.

saline/salinity	benign/benignant	crime/criminal	conspire/conspiracy
futile/futility	malign/malignant	mine/mineral	divide/division
fragile/fragility		reside/residual	sign/signature

<5.30> The underlined word in each example is the head: it is the element of which the compound is a hyponym. There is a generalisation in these languages that it is the left-hand element.

<u>ipu</u>·para
<u>maarama</u>·taka
<u>roro</u>·hiko
<u>wai</u>·mangu
<u>blazer</u> velours
<u>idée</u> cuisine
<u>timbre</u>·poste
<u>vendeur</u> literie
<u>nhà</u> nước
<u>nhà</u> thương
<u>xe</u> lửa

<5.31> The following are suggestions; you may disagree. One of the problems with the system is that if users disagree, or if a single user is unsure, there is no way of settling the dispute. Another is that some examples do not fit easily into the system at all.

flour mill	N2 make N1
light year	Unfair question: this is an exocentric compound.
milk tooth	N2 is for N1? N1 cause N2?
spaghetti western	Nothing seems to fit: 'a western made by people who can be characterised by their eating of spaghetti'
windmill	N2 use N1

<5.32> The function of possession is marked by the -'s on the possessor NP; *car* is unmarked for any function in the example given. The functions of subject and object are marked by the forms of the pronouns and by the order of the pronouns and the verb.

<5.33> The head in the possessive construction in the possessed noun, *car*, and the head in the sentential constructions is the tensed verb. This is because it is the tensed verb which gives the sentence its quality as a sentence.

<5.34> Russian is dependent-marking, just like English. It has a genitive ending on the possessor. Tzutujil, in contrast, is head-marking. The marker which shows that the horse belongs to my father is on the word for 'horse', not on the word for 'father'.

<5.35> Russian has separate words for the subject and the object, and those separate words, the pronouns, carry case (the nominative is not specifically mentioned in the glosses, although the gloss 'I' implies a subject form; for the direct objects, the accusative is specifically glossed). In Tzutujil we can only see that there is a single verb-word, which appears to carry marking for subject and object. We do not have enough information in Data-set 5.26 to allow us to segment those word-forms, but it looks as though the root comes towards the end of the word.

<5.36> Again Russian is dependent-marking and Tzutujil is head-marking.

<5.37> If Tzutujil is consistently head-marked, then marking the arguments in the construction on the head of the adpositional phrase – that is, on the adposition – would make sense. In Russian, the function is marked by the case on the noun, that is, by a dependent, which is again consistent.

<5.38> You will probably decide that there is no consistent meaning here, though the author who presents this data goes on to argue that there is some cohesion to the meanings that arise. Although no attempt will be made to convince you of this cohesiveness here, what this shows is that we have to take care in specifying what 'the meaning' of a particular process of word-formation might be: translations can be deceptive.

<5.39> The expected answer is that whole words are reduplicated. Although some of the words are apparently uninflected, some of them carry inflectional affixes (or apparently so, given that we cannot be completely sure that plural and superlative marking will necessarily be inflectional in all languages). So it looks as though word-forms are reduplicated.

<5.40> Ironically, given that we have defined this in terms which are used within morphology rather than within phonology or syntax, we cannot tell. A word-form is a morphological unit, but it often corresponds to a phonological unit and it is a syntactic element (sometimes called a syntactic atom: the smallest element that is dealt with in syntax). We cannot necessarily tell which of these aspects of the word-form is the crucial one for the reduplication process. This is not always the case.

<5.41> It could be that the last two syllables of the word are reduplicated rather than the suffixes; unfortunately, the suffixes that allow reduplication in Dyirbal are two syllables long, so we cannot distinguish between the two hypotheses – although it is rather strange if it is simply a matter of two syllables being reduplicated that it should happen only when those two syllables make up a suffix. The same kind of analysis does not seem to be viable for the plural-marking reduplication.

<5.42> The basic rule here is that the initial CV of the base is copied to immediately before the final consonant. However, it seems that prefixes do not count. So it is the first CV of the stem which is copied. Again, morphological structure is important for the reduplication process.

<5.43> Which of these is preferable would probably depend on your overall picture of how reduplication works – either in one specific language, or in general. For instance, if you were trying to support a notion that material for reduplication always comes from one edge of the word-form, you would prefer the second solution (we will have examples below which show such a hypothesis to be untenable as a general principle, but the point is that a particular analysis might fit well with a particular theoretical position).

<5.44> The affix has the form C where the C is the same as the first consonant of the base. Note that we cannot tell which of the two consonants is the original and which the copy: this probably does not even make sense. Phonetically the gemination is probably simply a lengthening of the consonant concerned.

<5.45> The first six of these words show prefixed reduplicants and the rest show suffixed reduplicants. In every case the affix is made up of precisely two segments, whether these are consonants or vowels. It may be tempting to say that a single syllable is involved in each of these cases, but that cannot be right. In the first place, in a form like *ake* the expected syllabification would be /a.ke/, with the /k/ in the second syllable, following the rule of maximising onsets. So if the first syllable were reduplicated, we would expect to find **aake* instead of the attested *akake*. Then if we look at the suffixed forms, we have *kamae* and *opaeo*. It is not clear from the data we have whether the final /ae/ and /eo/ represent diphthongs or series of vowels. But if /ae/ is a diphthong we would expect the final syllable to be /mae/, yet we do not get **kamaemae*; if, on the other hand, /ae/ is a sequence of vowels, we would expect the last syllable to be made up of just /e/, in which case we might expect to find **kamaee*. It seems that the reduplication here is simply a matter of two segments, independent of how they function in syllable structure.

<5.46> Although it would be strictly correct to say that the final three segments of the base are copied for the reduplicant, which appears as a suffix, this time those three segments do appear to have important structure: they are always CVC, and they are always the final syllable of the base. So this time it appears that the reduplication process does not just copy a number of segments, but that it copies a phonological structure, namely the syllable.

<5.47> Here we see the reduplicated syllable being prefixed to the base. We can see that where there is only one intervocalic consonant, it is not taken as part of the reduplicant, but where there are two, the first is taken as part of the reduplicant. Thus the reduplicant is an entire syllable, including a coda when there is one.

<5.48> In Data-set 5.34 we see reduplication of the first consonant of the base if there is one, and a short vowel of the quality of the first vowel of the base. If there is no consonant, then a glottal stop is inserted to keep the resultant two vowels apart. We might want to summarise this as (C)V, but that is not sufficient, because given the base form CV:, the reduplicant has the form CV with a short vowel (see the word meaning 'ant'). So what is copied is something equivalent to a short vowel with an onset consonant where that occurs. This is precisely what a mora is. Basically we have three options:

V is copied as V

CV is copied as CV

CVV (i.e. a long vowel) is copied as CV

(It might also be that VV is copied as V, but we have no evidence of that type, though we would expect that if there are words in this language with initial long vowels, this is what would happen.) The epenthetic [ʔ] can be explained as an automatic filling of an onset position when two vowels occur adjacent to each other. So this seems like a clear example of mora-reduplication.

<5.49> Where we have a base with a single syllable, the entire base is reduplicated. All these examples have two moras, so it is difficult to see what the pattern might be so far. Where there are two syllables in the base, both are reduplicated. Given that we have no consonant clusters intervocalically in the bases (and indeed the apparent cluster [nd] acts as a single consonant in Kambera, equivalent to [d] in the closely related Indonesian), we cannot tell whether it is important that it is two moras or two syllables that are reduplicated in these words. The fact that we can state a generalisation over monosyllables and disyllables, if we talk in terms of moras, might tempt us to use that terminology. However, it is when we look at bases with three syllables that things become interesting. Only the first two syllables are

reduplicated. Again we could count in syllables or in moras, but the bit that is copied goes from one stressed syllable to the next. That makes it precisely a foot, which seems like the best generalisation.

<5.50> We are probably not dealing with segments, since there are different numbers of segments reduplicated in different words; neither do we appear to be dealing with moras, for the same reason. In the words for 'dog' and 'boy' three moras are reduplicated, while only two are reduplicated in the other words. So it looks as though we are dealing with reduplication of syllables. But there is a better answer than that here, and that is that we are dealing with the reduplication of the first foot in the word, since in every case the first stressed syllable and the following unstressed syllable is reduplicated. However, when we add just a little more data, this hypothesis is shown to be incorrect as well.

<5.51> In these examples we see that not all of the second syllable is reduplicated: the reduplication stops at the vowel. In order to explain this, we need to know more about Diyari. In Diyari, although syllable-final consonants occur word-medially, they never occur word-finally. Furthermore, the smallest word of Diyari is two syllables long. So what is reduplicated is just sufficient to make a minimal prosodic word. There is apparently phonological evidence that a new phonological word starts after the reduplicant, in terms of the allophones that are found.

<5.52> Since the consonant following the vowel is reduplicated, we would expect that to be more than one mora, not just one. However, we cannot be dealing with a single syllable, because we would expect the [χ] in the word for 'bear' to be the onset of the second syllable, not the coda of the first. At the same time, we cannot be dealing with a sequence of two moras, since a syllable-onset consonant is not usually considered moraic. So we must be dealing with a sequence of CVC, as long as [tl'] is a single consonant.

<5.53> In this case, however, the vowel of the reduplicant is always [ə], whatever the vowel in the base is. So we have a case of reduplication, but with one part of the reduplicant being phonologically fixed rather than copied. Notice that the vowel in the reduplicant is [ə] whether the vowel in the original word is long or short, and whether it is [ə] or not.

<5.54> In this case the suffix is mostly fixed, with the form <ōCī>, which replaces the last vowel of the base. However, the nature of the consonant is variable, apparently copied from the last consonant of the base. So the consonant is reduplicated, while the rest of the suffix is fixed.

<5.55> It seems that the initial consonant of the word is reduplicated (assuming that [ts] counts as a single consonant in Quileute, just as [tʃ] does in English), and that it is placed immediately after the first mora/syllable (we do not have enough information to determine which is important). If you suggested before the second syllable, that is equally true.

<5.56> The second syllable is reduplicated (possibly the second mora), and it is placed adjacent to the copied syllable. We cannot tell whether the copy comes before or after the copied syllable.

<5.57> The reduplicant is formed from the initial and final consonants of the base, and the two consonants then act as a prefix. This is an extremely unusual case because of the discontinuity involved. Although discontinuity is found elsewhere in morphology and syntax, it is nearly always a typologically unusual phenomenon.

<5.58> Here we see that there is reduplication used to mark the diminutive. In this reduplication the initial consonant of the root is reduplicated, and there is a fixed vowel /ə/. The reduplicant comes immediately before the root in the examples we have. When this reduplication takes place, the first vowel of the root is deleted (there seems to be some later addition of [ə] in one case). The plural reduplication takes the first CVC of the root, and replaces the vowel with a /ə/. It precedes the diminutive reduplication when both are present. The nature of the /s/ prefix is left unexplained in the data in this table, though the decimal point indicates that it is a prefix.

Chapter 6

<6.1> The two readings of (8a) can be seen if you contrast *Hunting lions is dangerous* and *Hunting lions are dangerous*. In one case the lions are being hunted, in the other they are doing the hunting. The two readings of (8b) can be seen in the paraphrases *I bought the house that is in Paris* or *(When I was) in Paris, I bought the house*. In the second case, the house may or may not be in Paris. (8c) is ambiguous in writing, but not in speech – which is why this type causes difficulties. It can either mean that I didn't kill the dog but only injured it, or it can mean I did not injure people as well, only the dog. In speech, these two are differentiated by where the stress falls: on *injured* or on *dog*. *I injured only the dog* would be unambiguous.

<6.2> You will probably find some words like *cat*, and then *tom, kitten, moggy, Siamese* all of which are hyponyms of *cat*. You might have thought of *car*, but it would be odd to say it miaowed without adding something like *down the road*.

<6.3> If you know all these expressions, you will probably agree that the missing words have to be *kin, companion* and *arm*. Such restricted substitutions are called COLLOCATIONS, and are vitally important in determining the way we use individual words.

<6.4> You might think we should have a tick in (g) for *knowledge* because of *knowledgeable* (though -*able* is rarely added to nouns), and you might wonder whether *with* has a noun-like ending because of words like *warmth* and *truth* (although *warm* means something by itself, while *wi* does not). In general, though, I hope you agree.

<6.5> You should decide that *allergy, college* and *soup* are nouns and the other words are not. If you are in doubt, check the criteria.

<6.6> You might argue that being a girl is a state, and so have wanted a tick in column (a) for *girl*, but if you think about it, you will see that it is not *girl* which is the state, but *being a girl*. So I hope you will agree with the ticks and crosses. I put a '?' in column (a) for *seem* because, although I did not think seem was an action (*She seems very clever* is not a good answer to *What is she doing?*), I could not decide whether it was a state or not.

<6.7> You should find that *appear, purify* and *sleep* are verbs.

<6.8> Examples are *humidify, legalise* and *stiffen*, but there are many other examples you might have thought of.

<6.9> Although *silly* ends in -*y*, it is not like adjectives such as *fishy, mighty, speedy* where removing that final -*y* leaves a word behind. The cases that are relevant are those where the -*y* is an ending. A way of talking about such cases was introduced in Chapter 5: it depends on whether the -*y* represents a morpheme {-y} or not.

<6.10> *Girl* is ticked in column (c) because you can have phrases like *a girl guide*, where *girl* occurs before a noun. It is not uncommon for words other than adjectives to occur in this position in English; some nouns can also occur in a position for column (d), for example in 'That man is president', *president* is a noun.

<6.11> You probably agree that you would address yourself in the second person: *You should make a break*; *You have to stop behaving in this way*; and so on. In other words, you treat yourself, when you are the only listener, as a listener.

<6.12> You may speak a variety of English (as opposed to write one) where the plural form is *yous, y'all, you guys, yous guys, you fellows, you lot* or some other similar form. If not, you may know some group of people who use one of these. Speakers who know only the standard variety are frequently confused by such usages, and often fail to see that they may be totally systematic.

<6.13> The answer is yes, but these deviations are usually considered marginal and pragmatically determined. You may not agree. For example, there is the so-called 'royal plural' whereby a monarch refers to himself or herself as *we*, presumably on the grounds that the

monarch represents all the people ruled by the monarch, and not just a private individual. There are also cases such as *We're not going to do anything silly, now, are we?* which really means 'You had better not try to do anything silly'.

<6.14> The point with *three* and *blind* is that they can follow *the* (*the three mice, the blind mice*); none of the other items we have listed can do this (and nor can they precede *the* and *my*: **the my mice, *George's that cat, *the my downstairs neighbour's cat*). So *three* and *blind* must belong in slots which are between the determiner slot and the noun slot in the chart above.

<6.15> No, it is not a counterexample, because in this instance it means 'the cat of our George', and the *our* goes with *George* rather than with *cat*, just as the *my* in *my downstairs neighbour* tells you about the neighbour, and not about the cat.

<6.16> *The* is an article (and hence a determiner), *owl* is a noun, *looked* is a verb, *up* is an adverb, *to* is a preposition, *the* is an article, *stars* is another noun, *above* is another adverb, *and* is a coordinating conjunction, *sang* is a verb, *to* is a preposition, *a* is an article, *small* is an adjective and *guitar* is noun.

<6.17> These both have the same basic structure as *Fred sneezed*: *The cat in the hat / came back* and *The woman at the centre of the controversy / refused to answer our telephone calls*. In fact, in these particular cases, we can substitute a single word for each constituent and still retain the meaning of the original: *He returned* and *She refused*.

<6.18> *Disgustingly* is an adverb, and so we need to label it as such in the tree.

<6.19> *Rather* tells us about the degree of disgustingness, so it tells us about the word *disgusting*.

<6.20> *Rather* is another adverb. This time, the adverb is telling us about another adverb.

<6.21> *Coffee* is a noun.

<6.22> Given the rules that were set out above, any noun must be a part of a noun phrase, and since the other element we are trying to put with the noun represents a phrasal category, there is no conflict here. We can also see that we can replace *disgustingly sweet coffee* by *coffee* but not by *sweet*, so that *coffee* is the obligatory element in this construction.

<6.23> NP stands for 'noun phrase', just as AP was the abbreviation of adjective phrase and AdvP was the abbreviation of adverb phrase.

<6.24> *This* is a determiner in this construction.

<6.25> *In* and *on* are prepositions.

<6.26> These are both DPs, the difference is that in *a white horse* the NP contains an AP filled by the adjective *white*, while there is no adjective in the DP *the garden*.

<6.27>

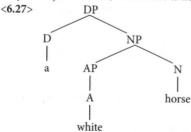

<6.28> We would expect it to be a prepositional phrase (PP for short).

<6.29> The last example in (32) implies that the plural noun must also be an NP. It is an NP because we could have something like *the hot cups of tea with broken handles*, where **ones of tea* does not seem to work, but *ones with broken handles* is perfectly all right. We will not go into the implications of this here, but you might like to think about them.

<6.30> The implication is that the head of the sentence in (34) is *will*.

<6.31> *That* is a complementiser (also called a subordinating conjunction).

<6.32> No it is not. *I hope gardeners will grow tomatoes* would be just as good.

<6.33> Yes, in a sentence like *That gardeners will grow tomatoes is my dearest hope* we cannot omit the complementiser: **Gardeners will grow tomatoes is my dearest hope* is not a sentence of Standard English.

<6.34> Phrases such as *proud of her children, sick of essays, afraid of spiders* are relevant examples.

<6.35> You should immediately be able to tell that *gave* fits in (i), *snored* fits in (ii) and *touched* fits in (iii). You know this because *snore* is a verb which takes only one DP (and *some trangents* looks like a DP): **Some sleepers snored a plank* is a very weird sentence, probably not ordinary English, even though you might think that it is trying to blend *snoring* and *sawing a plank*. On the other hand, *touch* requires two DPs. We can say *I touched the baby's nose*, but not **I touched*. We need to know what has been touched. *Give* has the possibility of taking three DPs: *We gave them their presents*.

<6.36> *Seem* is a copular verb (also just called a **COPULA**), *shampoo* is transitive, *show* is ditransitive and *sneeze* is intransitive (except in expressions like *He sneezed a sneeze*). Note the implication here: individual verbs can belong to more than one of these classes. In *We walked down the street*, *walk* is an intransitive verb, in *We walked the dog*, *walk* is a transitive verb; in *I gave at the office*, *give* is being used as an intransitive verb (though you might like to consider whether what you gave and who you gave it to are somehow implicit in the intransitive usage).

<6.37> Sentences (ii), (iv) and (v) contain copulas, while sentences (i) and (iii) contain transitive verbs.

<6.38> In (i) *that a long drink would be a good idea* is a noun clause, and in (ii) there are two noun clauses, *that they would say such a thing* and *they have had it in their policy documents for three years*.

<6.39> In *since they got a noisy dog* there is an IP following the *since*, so *since* is acting as a complementiser; in *since last Thursday* there is a DP following since, so *since* is a preposition. Either *since* represents two homonymous words or words can shift between the categories of complementiser and preposition, depending on what follows them. The fact that we find other words which work the same way suggests that the second of these possibilities is the right one.

<6.40> No answer.

<6.41> English allows these, as in *the man I saw yesterday* alongside *the man that I saw yesterday* or *the man who(m) I saw yesterday*.

<6.42> S and A are marked in the same way, with O marked differently in Latin.

<6.43> The pronoun *you* has only one form, whether it is subject or not: *You smiled; I saw you. I* and *me* are, according to the statement given here, nominative and accusative forms respectively of the same first person singular pronoun.

<6.44> In Dyirbal as illustrated here, A is marked differently from S and O, which are marked in the same way (here they carry no morphological marking).

<6.45> Where the full DPs were concerned in Data-set 6.5 we had ergative-absolute marking; where we find pronouns we have nominative-accusative marking.

<6.46> Since the person who is in the same case as the one who returned is the father, that is the right answer. Note that this runs counter to our intuitions as English speakers, because we do not have a syntactically ergative language.

<6.47> Here, where the pronouns are marked as nominative and accusative, it is the pronoun marked as the nominative which is assumed to be the subject of the verb return, so *we returned*. This is in line with what we would expect in English.

<6.48> *Want* is a transitive verb (someone has to want something) and *go* is an intransitive verb. Therefore, in an ergative-absolutive language, we would expect the subject of *want* to be in the ergative case, but the subject of *go* to be in the absolutive case. That being true, we would expect it not to be possible for the subject of one of these verbs to be able to do service for both verbs.

<6.49> (59) is probably found in response to a statement which either you didn't hear properly or you did not believe. (60) is likely to be found in a situation where there has already been discussion of dressing in different types of garment, but where the kilt is being discussed for the first time (see further section 7.6).

<6.50> (61a) has O–Auxiliary–Su–V and is a question. (61b) has a formal subject, there, then V–Su–SC (or possibly adverbial, see the controversy panel on p. 190). (61c) has V–O–Su, but is split over two written sentences, and clearly has an intonational break in the middle. (61d) has O–Su–V (God knows something, namely that a garden is a lovesome thing), but *God wot* is an old fashioned expression, probably no longer understood by many modern speakers, and there is an intonational break in the middle of the sentence.

<6.51> Sentence (a) in Data-set 6.11 does not correspond directly to any sentence in Data-set 6.10, since the order of object and adverbial is different. This is a complication we will not discuss here. Sentence (b) in Data-set 6.11 corresponds to (c) in Data-set 6.10. Sentence (c) in Data-set 6.11 corresponds to (b) in Data-set 6.10.

<6.52> Maori is a VSuO language, Kham is a SuOV language, and Hixkaryana is an OVSu language.

<6.53> You would have to look for cases where the dependent is not a branching structure, so things like German *geht nicht* 'works not = does not work', or English *very tall*. Here *nicht* and *very*, respectively, are the dependents, *geht* and *tall* are the heads, but neither of the dependents is readily expandable. Cases with expandable heads ought to be impossible, except under coordination: *very tall and strong*.

Chapter 7

<7.1> You have to be the appropriate person on the appropriate occasion (if you have a rehearsal and say 'I name this ship "X"', that will not really count, and if I shout out in the middle of a launching 'I name this ship "X"', everyone will ignore me. So more generally, only a person who is somehow empowered to perform the action may do so, and then only on a relevant occasion: a judge cannot say to her errant son 'I sentence you to five years hard labour' with the same effect that the same thing can be said in court.

<7.2> It would be odd because, by saying (3b), the speaker has already done it.

<7.3> Although the first speaker's utterance has an interrogative grammatical form, its illocutionary force is a command. When the respondent answers the superficial grammatical form instead of answering the intended illocutionary force, the questioner gets annoyed.

<7.4> Because of the maxim of quality, if the musician played the piece of music, we would expect the person to say that the piece of music was played. Because they say that each note was played in order, there is an implication that this is all that can be said, and that this is something less than that the piece was played. Therefore, the sentence can be interpreted as meaning that the musician played each of the notes, but that somehow this did not equate to playing the piece of music, so they were doing other things wrong (e.g. not taking account of the rhythm or the phrasing).

<7.5> Each of the headlines is ambiguous, and thus fails to avoid obscurity of expression. Because one of the interpretations in each case is wildly inappropriate, and incongruous in the serious context, it strikes us as being funny – possibly an intended joke.

<7.6> You might say this if something has been reported in the news that affects someone you know closely. You might mean that something which is news will be reported as news, whatever effect it may have on individuals.

<7.7> Since the family is clearly not acting in a united way, (20) is interpreted as being ironic, and thus as meaning something like 'It would be nice to see a united family'. (21) has to be interpreted as metaphorical, so as saying that the crossword reminds one of a pig in some way. Since wallowing in mud is probably not an appropriate association, being particularly difficult to deal with is a suitable interpretation.

<7.8> By not specifying who will actually do the fetching, it implies (probably falsely) that the addressee will not necessarily be the person doing the fetching, and so implies that this is not a major task for the addressee.

<7.9>

I'm so stupid, I forgot to fetch my new suit from the tailor's. Could you possibly do it if you're passing that way?	Modesty
I know you'd like me to look my best for the wedding, so could you fetch my new suit from the tailor's for me?	Tact
If you can fetch my new suit from the tailor's I'll be a real credit to you when we visit your parents.	Tact
You're much better at remembering these things than I am, so could you possibly fetch my new suit from the tailor's?	Approbation
Could you be a dear and fetch my new suit from the tailor's?	Approbation, sympathy
Chris, my old friend, could you fetch my new suit from the tailor's for me please?	Agreement, sympathy
If you can fetch my new suit from the tailor's for me, I'll put up that shelf you've been asking me to fix.	Tact, generosity

<7.10> Since the question makes reference to your own personal experience, clearly there is not a single 'right' answer to it. Nevertheless, it would be odd if all the usages were entirely reciprocal. If a police officer addresses you by your given name, it can be a way of controlling you, and speaking down to you; addressing a police officer by their given name in a formal situation, assuming you knew the given name, could be interpreted as cheeky, and therefore as rudeness.

<7.11>

Statement	Presupposition
The film we saw last week got a bad review.	We saw a film last week.
I'd forgotten that you gave me a copy of War and Peace.	You gave me a copy of War and Peace.
The computer is not useful for this task.	There is a computer which we both know about.

<7.12> That Frances is Paul's wife is an entailment; the others are presuppositions.

<7.13> The maxim of quality says that we must not say anything which we believe to be false; but in a reference, to be helpful, one must say everything positive that one can say about the candidate. Thus, what one says is assumed to be the most one can truthfully say about the candidate that is positive. Since writing neatly and attendance at class are not likely to be the most desirable features in a new employee (although they may well be desirable), the implication is that there is nothing else positive to say. Therefore this is a bad reference.

<7.14> I saw a ghost just <u>there</u>.
  Watch <u>this</u> carefully.
  I've never seen anything like <u>that</u> before.

Each of the above requires something outside the text to make sense of it. Since *here* and *now* refer to the place and time of speaking, we could argue that they refer to something external to the text, or we could say that the place and time at which it is uttered is a part of the text. It is hard to use *then* simply to point to a time, but if you imagine yourself watching CCTV footage of someone walking through a city, you might say *He was carrying his coat then*, where *then* would refer to the point in the CCTV footage.

<7.15> Britons perceive themselves as standing where they are now and moving towards a distant store; Americans perceive themselves as standing at the position they would be in at the time the event happened.

<7.16> I haven't seen Randy since he was last in Basingstoke. (Temporal: that is the last time). I haven't seen Randy, since he does his best to avoid me. (Reason: this is why I haven't seen him)

<7.17> Because (on Earth) there is only one moon, it can be definite all the time. This uniqueness overrules other factors which determine article use.

<7.18> At least different speed and different volume (intensity) are possible ways of marking the parenthesis; it may also be marked by a different pitch (typically lower that the main information).

<7.19> With plural nouns, *the* picks out a known set, rather than a known individual. So in 'I saw the cars', *the cars* refers to a known set of more than one car.

<7.20>

(a)	I need a new car. The vehicle must be no more that three years old.	*The vehicle* is identified by the text in the form of *a new car*.
(b)	They walked into the room. The light was still on.	There is an assumption that there is one light for a room.
(c)	We passed Buckingham Palace today. We didn't see the Queen.	There is only one Queen who resides at Buckingham Palace.
(d)	The sun is very hot today.	There is only one sun in our world.

<7.21> The most obvious example is the *it* that occurs with weather words like *It is raining*. There is no suitable answer to the question 'What is raining?'

Appendix D

Assignments and study questions

1. Choose six nouns at random from a published dictionary, and determine what strategies are used for defining those words. Are the same strategies used to the same extent in defining verbs?

2. Consider the sentences below. You may consider that some of them make sense while others do not. In any case, there is a reading on which they may appear not to make sense. Whatever your reaction to the sentences, discuss their potential oddity in technical semantic terms, showing what could be considered odd or why there is a perfectly reasonable reading of them.

   (a) This potato isn't cooked, it's boiled.
   (b) She jogged round the lake without running.
   (c) He hurt his toe, not his foot.
   (d) She won her freedom, but not her liberty.
   (e) The Alsatian bitch had kittens.

3. Look up one of the following words in a published dictionary. How many homonyms does it have according to the dictionary, and how many polysemes? Do you agree with the dictionary on this subject? If not, why do you differ? Try to convince other members of a small group that you are right. How would the writer of the dictionary argue?

   dog, grub, hooker, mean, plot, stay

4. *Rose* and *tulip* are hyponyms of *flower*, and *rose* is incompatible with *tulip*: anything which is a rose cannot simultaneously be a tulip. How far is this a necessary truth about co-hyponyms, and how far is it a result of the particular example chosen? You might wish to consider hyponymy in verbs and adjectives as well as in nouns.

5. For each of the pairs of words below, explain what they mean, being careful to make clear the distinction between them, and provide suitable illustrations.

   affricate, fricative
   palatal, palatalised
   primary articulation, secondary articulation
   syllable-timed, stress-timed
   velar, velic

6. Explain in detail how the consonants in the middle of each of the following words are produced. Consider the function of the lungs, the larynx, the velum, the (different parts of the) tongue and the lips at every stage.

    ajar, allay, annoy, atone, betray, over

7. In standard British or American English, [p] and [tʰ] are in complementary distribution: roughly, the distribution can be characterised as [p] occurs following an [s] and syllable-finally; [tʰ] occurs syllable-initially. Both [p] and [tʰ] are voiceless plosives. Are they allophones of the same phoneme or not? Explain how you reach your decision.

8. Tol, a language of Honduras, has six vowel phonemes, namely /i, e, ɨ, a, u, o/. In this language, [β] and [w] are in complementary distribution, as determined by the following vowel and illustrated in the data below. What symbol would you use for the phoneme and why? Write a rule to provide an account of these allophones.

βia	'up'	tloβa	'you (pl) went'
βaka	'cow'	pʰʃel	'her arm'
βis	'tooth'	wolas	'fruit'
kaβaju	'horse'	βetseβets	'weevil'
wuku	'mix'	pβela	'plays'
kuβis	'I come'	βiste	'last night'

9. Below is a phonological rule of Greek. The phonemic structures for a number of words are provided in (a) – (d). What is the actual pronunciation of these words after the rule has applied?

$$\begin{bmatrix} + \text{obstruent} \\ + \text{dorsal} \end{bmatrix} \rightarrow \begin{bmatrix} - \text{dorsal} \\ + \text{coronal} \end{bmatrix} / \underline{\hspace{1cm}} \begin{bmatrix} +\text{syllabic} \\ + \text{coronal} \\ - \text{low} \end{bmatrix}$$

   (a) efkolo   'easy'
   (b) vɣazo   'take off'
   (c) evangelio   'gospel'
   (d) xino   'pour'

10. In Mandan, any sequence of a consonant followed by a /w/ or an /r/ (which are the only two sonorant consonants in this language) is interrupted by an epenthetic vowel which is a front, non-nasalised version of the vowel immediately following the sonorant. Thus, /wrĩ/ is pronounced [wirĩ] and /wro/ is pronounced [wero], and /wɑʔkrãk/ is pronounced [wɑʔkærãk]. There are only six vowels in this language: /i, e, æ, u, o, ɑ/, some of which may be contrastively nasalised. Write a rule to produce the epenthetic vowels. You will need to use features to write the rule. The vowels are distinguished in terms of the features [± high], [± low], [± round], [± nasal], and their place of articulation, which may be seen in terms of [± coronal] and [± dorsal].

11. Allophones of phonemes are predictable in their environments, which leads some people to suggest that a phonemic transcription is one without any redun-

dancy, because allophones provide redundant information. However, sometimes phonemes are, at least to some extent, predictable. Consider places where phonemes are predictable or partly predictable. Is the predictability in these instances different in nature from the predictability of allophones?

12. How are the terms *morph* and *phone*, *allomorph* and *allophone*, *morpheme* and *phoneme* parallel and how do they differ?

13. Consider in detail whether the English words *mobile*, *momentum*, *motion* and *move* can be said to contain a morpheme in common.

14. For each of the sets of words below, say whether each word is morphologically analysable or not. Where the words are morphologically analysable, divide the word into morphs and morphemes, giving parallels with other words containing the same affixes. If the morphology gives rise to phonological processes, comment and show whether the processes are consistent.

preamble, prejudge, prelude, pressure
disappear, disinter, dismiss, distress
actress, caress, governess, witness

15. Is the suffix *-ly* in a word like *quickly* inflectional or derivational? You might like to consider points such as

the extent to which the meaning of this affix is regular
the extent to which this affix is productive
whether it changes word-class or not
how it is ordered in relation to other affixes
the extent to which it is obligatory in context
the extent to which it provides syntactic information

16. There is some dispute as to whether the suffix *-able* which occurs in the words in column A below represents the same morpheme as the *-able* which occurs in the words in Column B. Provide **three** arguments which consistently provide evidence **either** in favour of them being the same morpheme **or** in favour of them being different morphemes. State clearly whether your arguments support the one-morpheme solution or the two-morpheme solution.

A	B
comfortable	acceptable
honourable	agreeable
knowledgeable	commendable
marriageable	desirable
objectionable	reliable

17. In each of the following sentences, what is the subject of the sentence? Provide evidence to support your point of view.

A good man is hard to find.
A puppy with long floppy ears was licking my shoes.

I saw the boys eat the cake.

Responsibility for the explosion was claimed by a splinter opposition party.

That *Avatar* should have grossed more than *Titanic* surprises me.

The cattle that had been roaming all over the road now seemed to cluster tightly round our car.

Whatever you think about Philip, he can play basketball.

18. Consider the words below and discuss whether or not there is a class of adjectives in English.

    afraid, big, black, former, Parisian, polar, unique

19. Draw X-bar phrase structure trees to show the two meanings of the ambiguous sentence:

    Lee told the girl that Kim knew.

20. What is the difference, if any, between a noun class and a gender class? Look for definitions and discussions in technical works, but also consider the way these terms are used in descriptions of individual languages.

21. Look up the construction for expressing comparison in the grammars of a number of diverse languages. You should look for a structure which means 'more X than Y', as in English *prettier than a picture*. In English the adjective (*prettier*) precedes the standard (*a picture*), while in Turkish *kurşun-dan ağır* (literally lead-from heavy, 'heavier than lead') the standard precedes the adjective. Does the order of adjective and standard correlate with the basic order of verb and direct object in the languages you consider? What factors might play a role in determining your outcome?

22. Choose a short text from a newspaper or a piece of fiction, and examine all the figures of speech that are used in it. How might you go about teaching a computer to interpret the figure of speech?

23. Take a simple expression in English, and enter it into any Internet translation site. Take the output of the translation, and get the site to translate it back to English. Repeat twice. Is the message as it comes back to you comprehensible? If so, does it mean what you intended to say in the first place? If not, what has gone wrong in the process? Is it lexical, syntactic, pragmatic, semantic? Try with several sentences (proverbs work well!). What kinds of sentence cause the most problems?

24. Make a list of the things you are called by different people: your parents, your siblings, your teachers, your partner, your nieces and nephews, shopkeepers, your friends, customs officers, and so on. How do factors such as age, relationship, sex affect the term of address? Does any of this mimic the use of T and V pronouns in languages which have them?

25. How would you ask the head of your old school to write a reference for you? How would you ask your best friend to help you wash the car? What kinds of linguistic differences are there in the two requests? How do these reflect general strategies for politeness?

26. Is the best description of some linguistic phenomenon (say the use of irregular past tense forms of verbs or the use of the passive voice) one which reflects the

way in which the knowledge about this phenomenon is stored in a native speaker's brain or not? In most cases we do not know (or have conflicting information about) precisely what is stored in the brain. Does this matter for a linguist describing a language?

27. It might seem that *cricket* 'type of insect' and *cricket* 'name of a sport' are homophonous and thus easily confused. Consider the grammar of sentences in which these words occur, and decide whether they are actually easily confused in use. What kinds of clue can be found in the environment as to which of these two meanings is intended? Repeat the exercise with any other pair of homonyms or polysemes.

Bibliography

Aaltio, Maija-Helikki 1964. *Finnish for foreigners*. Helsinki: Otava.

Abercrombie, David 1967. *Elements of general phonetics*. Edinburgh: Edinburgh University Press.

Adams, Douglas 1979. *The hitchhiker's guide to the galaxy*. London: Pan.

Aikhenvald, A.Y. 2006. Evidentiality in grammar. In K. Brown (ed.), *Encyclopedia of language and linguistics*. Vol. 4. Oxford: Elsevier: 320–5.

Aitchison, Jean 1992. *The articulate mammal: an introduction to psycholinguistics*. 3rd edn. London and New York: Routledge.

Anderson, Stephen & Edward L. Keenan 1985. Deixis. In Timothy Shopen (ed.), *Language typology and syntactic description*. Vol. 3. Cambridge: Cambridge University Press: 259–308.

Aquilina, Joseph 1965. *Maltese*. Sevenoaks, Kent: Hodder and Stoughton.

Armstrong, Lilias E. 1964. *The phonetics of French*. London: Bell.

Asher, R.E. & T.C. Kumari 1997. *Malayalam*. London and New York: Routledge.

Ashton, E.O. 1947. *Swahili grammar*. 2nd edn. Harlow: Longman.

Austin, J.L. 1962. *How to do things with words*. Cambridge, MA: Harvard University Press.

Austin, Peter 1981. *A grammar of Diyari, South Australia*. Cambridge: Cambridge University Press.

Basbøll, Hans 2005. *The phonology of Danish*. Oxford: Oxford University Press.

Bauer, Laurie 1983. *English word-formation*. Cambridge: Cambridge University Press.

Bauer, Laurie 1988. A descriptive gap in morphology. *Yearbook of Morphology 1*. Dordrecht: Springer: 17–27.

Bauer, Laurie 1993. *Manual of information to accompany the Wellington Corpus of written New Zealand English*. Wellington: Victoria University, Department of Linguistics.

Bauer, Laurie 1998. When is a sequence of two nouns a compound in English? *English Language and Linguistics* 2: 65–86.

Bauer, Laurie 2002. What you can do with derivational morphology. In S. Bendjaballah, W.U. Dressler, O.E. Pfeiffer & M.D. Voeikova (eds), *Morphology 2000*. Amsterdam and Philadelphia: Benjamins: 37–48.

Bauer, Laurie 2003. *Introducing linguistic morphology*. 2nd edn. Edinburgh: Edinburgh University Press.

Bauer, Laurie & Paul Warren 2004. New Zealand English: phonology. In Bernd Kortmann, Edgar W. Schneider, Kate Burridge, Rajend Mesthrie and Clive Upton (eds), *A handbook of varieties of English*. Berlin and New York: Mouton de Gruyter: 580–602.

Bauer, Laurie, John Dienhart, Leif Kvistgaard Jakobsen & Hans Hartvigson 1980. *American English pronunciation*. Copenhagen: Gyldendal.

Bauer, Winifred 1993. *Maori*. London and New York: Routledge.

Bauer, Winifred 1997. *The Reed reference grammar of Māori*. Auckland: Reed.

Bender, Byron W. 1971. Micronesian languages. In Thomas A. Sebeok (ed.), *Linguistics in Oceania* (Current Trends in Linguistics 8). The Hague and Paris: Mouton: 426–65.

Besnier, Niko 2003. Crossing genders, mixing language. In Janet Holmes & Miriam Meyerhoff (eds), *The handbook of language and gender*. Malden, MA: Blackwell: 279–301.

Blake, Barry 1987. *Australian Aboriginal grammar*. London: Croom Helm.

Bohn, Ocke-Schwen 2004. How to organize a fairly large vowel inventory: The vowels of Fering (North Frisian). *Journal of the International Phonetic Association* 34: 161–73.

Booij, Geert 1995. *The phonology of Dutch.* Oxford: Oxford University Press.

Botha, Rudolf P. 1988. *Form and meaning in word formation.* Cambridge: Cambridge University Press.

Brookes, Ian (ed.) 2006. *The Chambers Dictionary.* 10th edn. Edinburgh: Chambers Harrap.

Brown, E.K. & J.E. Miller 1980. *Syntax: A linguistic introduction to sentence structure.* London: Hutchinson.

Button, John 1988. *A dictionary of green ideas: vocabulary for a sane and sustainable future.* London and New York: Routledge.

Campbell, Lyle. 2004. *Historical linguistics: an introduction.* 2nd edn. Edinburgh: Edinburgh University Press.

Carroll, Lewis 1865. *Alice's adventures in wonderland.* London: Macmillan.

Catford, J.C. 1977. *Fundamental problems in phonetics.* Edinburgh: Edinburgh University Press.

Chapallaz, Marguerite 1979. *The pronunciation of Italian.* London: Bell and Hyman.

Childs, G. Tucker 1995. *A grammar of Kisi.* Berlin and New York: Mouton de Gruyter.

Childs, G. Tucker 2003. *An introduction to African languages.* Amsterdam and Philadelphia: Benjamins.

Clark, Eve V. 1993. *The lexicon in acquisition.* Cambridge: Cambridge University Press.

Croft, William 2003. *Typology and universals.* Cambridge: Cambridge University Press.

Crowley, Terry, John Lynch, Jeff Siegel & Julie Piau 1995. *The design of language.* Auckland: Longman Paul.

Cruse, D.A. 1986. *Lexical semantics.* Cambridge: Cambridge University Press.

Crystal, David 1985. *Linguistics.* 2nd edn. London: Penguin.

Crystal, David, & Hilary Crystal 2000. *Words on Words: Quotations about Language and Languages.* London: Penguin.

Davies, Mark. (2008) The Corpus of Contemporary American English (COCA): 425 million words, 1990–present. Available online at www.americancorpus.org

Dayley, Jon P. 1985. *Tzutujil grammar.* Berkeley: University of California Press.

Dayley, Jon P. 1989. *Tümpisa (Panamint) Shoshone grammar.* Berkeley: University of California Press.

Delattre, Pierre 1981. *Studies in comparative phonetics.* Heidleberg: Groos.

Derbyshire, Desmond C. 1979. *Hixkaryana.* Amsterdam: North Holland.

Derwing, Bruce 1973. *Transformational grammar as a theory of language acquisition.* Cambridge: Cambridge University Press.

Dixon, R.M.W. 1980. *The languages of Australia.* Cambridge: Cambridge University Press.

Dixon, R.M.W. 1994. *Ergativity.* Cambridge: Cambridge University Press.

Dixon, Robert M.W. 2011. *I am a linguist.* Leiden and Boston: Brill.

Dryer, Matthew S. 1992. The Greenbergian word order correlations. *Language* 68: 81–138.

Dutton, Tom E. 1996. *Koiari.* München and Newcastle: Lincom Europa.

Easton, Anita & Laurie Bauer 2000. An acoustic study of the vowels of New Zealand English. *Australian Journal of Linguistics* 20: 93–117.

Everett, Daniel & Barbara Kern 1997. *Wari'.* London and New York: Routledge.

Fortescue, Michael 1984. *West Greenlandic.* London: Croom Helm.

Fry, D.B. 1979. *The physics of speech.* Cambridge: Cambridge University Press.

Gahl, Susanne 2008. *Time* and *thyme* are not homophones. *Language* 84: 469–96.

Giegerich, Heinz 2004. Compound or phrase? English noun-plus-noun constructions and the stress criterion. *English Language and Linguistics* 8: 1–24.

Greenberg, Joseph H. 1963. Some universals of grammar with particular reference to the order of meaningful elements. In Joseph H. Greenberg (ed.), *Universals of language*. Cambridge MA: MIT Press: 73–113.

Grice, H.P. 1975. Logic and conversation. *Syntax and Semantics* 3: 41–58.

Gronnaum, Nina 2001. *Fonetik og fonologi*. 2. Udgava, København: Akademisk.

Gussenhoven, Carlos & Haike Jacobs 1998. *Understanding phonology*. London: Arnold.

Haas, Mary R. 1944. Men's and women's speech in Koasati. *Language* 20: 142–9.

Hanks, Patrick (ed.) 1979. *Collins dictionary of the English language*. London and Glasgow: Collins.

Harlow, Ray 2007. *Māori: a linguistic introduction*. Cambridge: Cambridge University Press.

Harris, Herbert Raymond 1981. A grammatical sketch of Comox. Unpublished PhD dissertation, University of Kansas.

Haspelmath, Martin 1993. *A grammar of Lezgian*. Berlin and New York: Mouton de Gruyter.

Haspelmath, Martin 2002. *Understanding morphology*. London: Arnold.

Haspelmath, Martin, Matthew S. Dryer, David Gil & Bernard Comrie (eds) 2005. *The world atlas of language structures*. Oxford: Oxford University Press.

Haugen, Jason D. 2005. Reduplicative allomorphy and language prehistory in Uto-Azecan. In Bernhard Hurch (ed.), *Studies on reduplication*. Berlin and New York: Mouton de Gruyter: 315–49.

Herbst, Thomas, David Heath, Ian F. Roe & Dieter Götz 2004. *A valency dictionary of English*. Berlin and New York: Mouton de Gruyter.

Hinds, John 1986. *Japanese*. London: Croom Helm.

Holmes, Janet 2008. *An introduction to sociolinguistics*. 3rd edn. Harlow: Longman.

Holmes, Janet & Maria Stubbe 2003. 'Feminine' workplaces: Stereotype and reality. In Janet Holmes & Miriam Meyerhoff (eds), *The handbook of language and gender*. Malden, MA: Blackwell, 573–99.

Householder, Fred W. 1966. Phonological theory: A brief comment. *Journal of Linguistics* 2: 99–100.

Hualde, José Ignacio & Jon Ortiz de Urbina 2003. *A grammar of Basque*. Berlin and New York: Mouton de Gruyter.

Hudak, Thomas John 1990. Thai. In Bernard Comrie (ed.), *The major languages of South-East Asia*. London and New York: Routledge: 29–47.

Hyman, Larry 1975. *Phonology*. New York: Holt, Rinehart and Winston

Iwasaki, Shoichi & Preeya Ingkaphirom 2005. *A reference grammar of Thai*. Cambridge: Cambridge University Press.

Jacob, Judith M. 1968. *Introduction to Cambodian*. London: Oxford University Press.

Jakobson, Roman 1971 [1959]. On linguistic aspects of translation. In *Roman Jakobson: Selected writings Vol II*. The Hague and Paris: Mouton: 260–6.

Jespersen, Otto 1922. *Language*. London: George Allen & Unwin.

Johnson, Keith 1997. *Acoustic and auditory phonetics*. Cambridge, MA and Oxford: Blackwell.

Kaiser, Stefan, Yasuko Ichikawa, Noriko Kobayashi & Hilofumi Yamamoto 2002. *Japanese: A comprehensive grammar*. London and New York: Routledge.

Karlsson, Fred 1999. *Finnish: an essential grammar*. London and New York: Routledge. Trans. Andrew Chesterman. Previously published 1983. *Finnish grammar*. Helsinki: WYSO.

Katamba, Francis & John Stonham 2006. *Morphology*. 2nd edn. Basingstoke: Palgrave.

Kayser, Alois 1993. *Nauru grammar*. Yarralumla ACT: Embassay of the Federal Republic of Germany.

Kenstowicz, Michael 1994. *Phonology in generative grammar*. Cambridge, MA: Blackwell.

Kenyon, Michael 1986. *A healthy way to die*. London: Hodder.

Klamer, Marian 1994. *Kambera, a language of Eastern Indonesia*. Amsterdam: Holland Institute of Generative Linguistics.

Kornfilt, Jaklin 1997. *Turkish*. London and New York: Routledge.

Krauss, Michael E. 1992. The world's languages in crisis. *Language* 68: 4–10.

Kwee, John B. 1965. *Indonesian*. London: English Universities Press.

Ladefoged, Peter 1975. *A course in phonetics*. New York: Holt, Rinehart and Winston.

Ladefoged, Peter & Ian Maddieson 1996. *The sounds of the world's languages*. Oxford and Cambridge MA: Blackwell.

Laka, Itziar 2006. Deriving split ergativity in the progressive. In Alana Johns, Diane Massam & Juvenal Ndayiragije (eds), *Ergativity*. Dordrecht: Springer: 173–95.

Lakoff, George & Mark Johnson 1980. *Metaphors we live by*. Chicago: University of Chicago Press.

Lakoff, Robin 1975. *Language and woman's place*. New York: Harper & Row.

Lass, Roger 1984. *Phonology*. Cambridge: Cambridge University Press.

Laver, John 1994. *Principles of phonetics*. Cambridge: Cambridge University Press.

Laymon, Richard 2001. *Night in the lonesome October*. London: Headline.

LDCE5 2009. *The Longman dictionary of contemporary English*. 5th edn. Harlow, Essex: Pearson Education.

Leavitt, Robert M. 1996. *Passamaquoddy-Maliseet*. München and Newcastle: Lincom Europa.

Leech, Geoffrey 1983. *Principles of pragmatics*. London and New York: Longman.

Lenneberg, E.H. 1967. *Biological foundations of language*. New York: Wiley.

Levi, Judith N. 1978. *The syntax and semantics of complex nominals*. New York: Academic Press.

Levin, Beth & Rappaport Hovav, Malka 1994. A preliminary analysis of causative verbs in English. *Lingua* 92: 35–77.

Lewis, G.L. 1967. *Turkish grammar*. Oxford: Oxford University Press.

Lewis, M. Paul (ed.), 2009. *Ethnologue: languages of the world*. 16th edn. Dallas, TX: SIL International. Available online at http://www.ethnologue.com/

Lieber, Rochelle 2010. *Introducing morphology*. Cambridge: Cambridge University Press.

Liljencrants, Johan & Björn Lindblom 1972. Numerical simulation of vowel quality systems: The role of perceptual contrast. *Language* 48: 839–62.

Lindquist, Hans 2009. *Corpus linguistics and the description of English*. Edinburgh: Edinburgh University Press.

Lojenga, Constance Kutsch 1994. *Ngiti: a central Sudanic language of Zaire*. Köln: Köppe.

Lyons, John 1968. *Introduction to theoretical linguistics*. Cambridge: Cambridge University Press.

Lyons, John 1977. *Semantics*. Cambridge: Cambridge University Press.

Mackridge, Peter 1985. *The modern Greek language*. Oxford: Oxford University Press.

Maddieson, Ian 1984. *Patterns of sounds*. Cambridge: Cambridge University Press.

Malchukov, Andrei L. 1995. *Even*. München and Newcastle: Lincom Europa.

Malécot, André 1977. *Introduction à la phonétique française*. The Hague: Mouton.

Mason, J. Alden 1916. Tepecano, a Piman languae of Western Mexico. *Annals of the New York Academy of Sciences* 25: 309–416.

Matthews, P.H. 1981. *Syntax*. Cambridge: Cambridge University Press.

McCawley, James D. 1971. Where do noun phrases come from? In Danny D. Steinberg & Leon A. Jakobovits (eds), *Semantics*. Cambridge: Cambridge University Press: 217–31.

McConnell-Ginet, Sally 2008. Words in the world: how and why meanings can matter. *Language* 84: 497–527.

Melnar, Lynette R. 2004. *Caddo verb morphology*. Lincoln and London: University of Nebraska Press.

Merlan, Francesca 1982. *Mangarayi*. Amsterdam: North Holland.

Miller, Jim 2008. *An introduction to English syntax*. Edinburgh: Edinburgh University Press.

Moravcsik, Edith A. 1978. Reduplicative constructions. In Joseph H. Greenberg (ed.), *Universals of human language*. Stanford: Stanford University Press: 297–334.

Mosel, Ulrike 1994. *Saliba*. München and Newcastle: Lincom Europa.

Nash, David 1986. *Topics in Warlpiri grammar*. New York and London: Garland.

Navarro Tomás, Tomás 1926. *Manual de pronunciatión española*. 3rd edn. New York: Hafner.

Nedjalkov, V.P. 1979. Degrees of ergativity in Chukchee. In Frans Plank (ed.), *Ergativity*, London: Academic Press: 241–62.

Noonan, Michael 1992. *A grammar of Lango*. Berlin and New York: Mouton de Gruyter.

Payne, John & Rodney Huddleston 2002. Nouns and noun phrases. In Rodney Huddleston & Geoffrey K. Pullum (eds), *The Cambridge grammar of the English language*. Cambridge: Cambridge University Press: 323–523.

Plag, Ingo 1999. *Morphological productivity*. Berlin and New York: Mouton de Gruyter.

Raimy, Eric 2000. *The phonology and morphology of reduplication*. Berlin and New York: Mouton de Gruyter.

Read, Piers Paul 1997. *Knights of the cross*. London: Weidenfeld & Nicolson.

Riggle, Jason 2003. Nonlocal reduplication. In Keir Moulton & Matthew Wolf (eds), *Proceedings of NELS 34*. Amherst MA: Graduate Linguistic Student Association: 485–96.

Rosch, Eleanor 1978. Principles of categorization. In Eleanor Rosch & Barbara L. Lloyd (eds), *Cognition and categorization*. Hillsdale, NJ: Erlbaum: 27–48.

Royle, Phaedra & Daniel Valois 2010. Acquisition of adjectives in Quebec French as revealed by elicitation data. *French Language Studies* 20: 313–38.

Rubino, Carl 2005. Reduplication: form, function and distribution. In Bernhard Hurch (ed.), *Studies on reduplication*. Berlin and New York: Mouton de Gruyter: 11–29.

Russell, Bertrand 1905. On denoting. *Mind* 14: 479–93.

Russell, Bertrand 1948. *Human knowledge: Its scope and limits*. London: Allen & Unwin.

Sakel, Jeanette 2004. *A grammar of Moseten*. Berlin and New York: Mouton de Gruyter.

Salisbury, Mary C. 2002. A grammar of Pukapukan. Unpublished PhD Thesis, University of Auckland.

Saxena, A. 2004. Pronouns. In Keith Brown (ed.), *Encyclopedia of language and linguistics*. Vol 10. 2nd edn. Oxford: Elsevier: 131–3.

Sinclair, John (ed.), 1987. *Collins COBUILD English language dictionary*. London: HarperCollins.

Smyth, David 2002. *Thai: an essential grammar*. London and New York: Routledge.

Sommerstein, Alan H. 1977. *Modern phonology*. London: Arnold.

Spencer, Andrew 1996. *Phonology*. Oxford and Cambridge, MA: Blackwell.

Steinlen, Anja K. 2005. *The influence of consonants on native and non-native vowel production*. Tübingen: Narr.

Stevens, Kenneth N. 1989. On the quantal nature of speech. *Journal of Phonetics* 17: 3–45.

Strawson, P.F. 1950. On referring. *Mind* 59: 320–44.

Strawson, P.F. 1964. Intention and convention in speech acts. *Philosophical Review* 73: 439–60.

Sweet, Henry 1877. *A handbook of phonetics*. Oxford: Clarendon Press.

Taylor, F.W. 1959. *A practical Hausa grammar*. 2nd edn. Oxford: Clarendon.

Thomson, Colin D. 1987. *Íslensk beygingafræði*. Hamburg: Buske.

Urbanczyk, Suzanne 2000. The bases of double reduplication. In Roger Billerey and Brook Danielle Lillehaugen (eds), *WCCFL19*. Somerville MA: Cascadilla Press: 518–31.

Villoing, Florence 2009. Les mots composés VN. In Bernard Fradin, Françoise Kerleroux & Marc Plénat (eds), *Aperçus de morphologie du français*. Paris: Presses Universitaires de Vincennes: 175–197.

Walters, Minette 2007. *The Chameleon's Shadow*. London: Macmillan.

Watkins, Lauren 1984. *A grammar of Kiowa*. Lincoln and London: University of Nebraska Press.

Watters, David E. 2002. *A grammar of Kham*. Cambridge: Cambridge University Press.

Wells, J.C. 1982. *Accents of English*. Cambridge: Cambridge University Press.

Wells, J.C. 1990. Syllabification and allophony. In Susan Ramsaran (ed.), *Studies in the pronunciation of English*. London: Routledge: 76–86.

Westermann, D. & Ida C. Ward 1933. *Practical phonetics for students of African languages*. London: Oxford University Press.

Wheatley, Julian K. 1987. Burmese. In Bernard Comrie (ed.), *The major languages of East and South-East Asia*. London and New York: Routledge: 106–26.

Wood, Sidney 1979. A radiographic analysis of constriction locations for vowels. *Journal of Phonetics* 7: 25–43.

Wray, Alison & John J. Staczek 2005. One word or two? Psycholinguistic and sociolinguistic interpretations of meaning in a civil court case. *Speech, Language and the Law* 12: 1–18.

Wu, Chaolu 1996. *Daur*. München and Newcastle: Lincom Europa.

Yip, Moira 2002. *Tone*. Cambridge: Cambridge University Press.

Zee, Eric 1999. Chinese: (Hong Kong Cantonese). In *Handbook of the International Phonetic Association*. Cambridge: Cambridge University Press: 58–60.

Zemlin, Willard R. 1968. *Speech and hearing science; anatomy and physiology*. Englewood Cliffs, NJ: Prentice-Hall.

General index

Language index

Afrikaans 159, 281
Alabama 77, 281
Amahuaca 77, 281
Amuesha 77, 281
Arabic 44, 123, 281
Aranda 75, 281
Armenian 76, 281

Bakwiri (Bakwpe) 124, 281
Bandjalang 77, 281
Bardi 76, 281
Basque 108, 206, 226, 282
Beembe 76, 282
Bella Coola 111, 112, 282
Burmese 106, 282

Caddo 125, 282
Campa 77, 282
Cantonese 61, 75, 282
Cayapa 77, 282
Chiquito 241, 282
Chukchee 206, 282
Comox 137, 164, 282
Cree 75, 282, 302
Creek 160, 161, 282
Croatian 3, 282

Dan 78, 283
Dani 25
Danish 20, 78, 105, 108, 151, 208, 209, 228,
   283
Daur 91, 283
Diyari 163, 164, 202, 283, 308
Dutch 75, 78, 80, 228, 283
Dyirbal 160, 203, 204, 205, 206, 283, 306

Efik 80, 126, 283
English 258, 312, *et passim*
   American 52, 93, 96, 97, 98, 99, 101, 105,
      154, 236, 251, 296, 300
   Australasian 97, 98
   Australian 52, 97, 101, 105
   British 93, 98
   Canadian 39
   case 180
   compounds 153
   deixis 235
   derivation 141

Durham 97
features for 103, 107
Glasgow 97
inflection 148
Irish 96, 97
Middle 99
morphophonemics 138, 150
New Zealand 52, 69, 78, 88, 93, 97, 98, 105,
   296, 300
non-standard 251
Northern 101, 154, 251, 300
Northumbrian 251
of England 88, 96, 97
official language 283
Old 71, 287
phonetics of 47, 49, 51, 60, 63, 121
phonology of 95-100, 106, 113, 118, 123
RP 97, 98, 100, 101, 106, 107, 121, 275, 300
Scottish 96, 97, 98, 101, 251, 300
South African 96
spelling of 40
Standard 105
syntax of 20
terms of address 226-7
Welsh 97
Yorkshire 300
Even 62, 283
Ewe 76, 283

Finnish 62, 75, 99, 134, 135, 149, 164, 177,
   179, 212, 283, 303, 305
French 18, 20, 31, 114, 122, 258, 283, 302
   deixis 236
   determiners 188
   language games 124
   Louisiana 131, 285
   morphology 253, 254
   pronouns 227, 228
   pronunciation of 47, 65, 72, 85, 86, 105,
      108, 111, 112
   vocabulary 131, 151, 152, 153

German 20, 227, 228, 283, 292, 312
German, compounds 151
   deixis 236
   pronunciation 47, 85, 108, 123
   sentence structure 4-5, 19, 209
   Swiss 3

333